10.50

Cultural Anthropology

Peter Beard

Cultural Anthropology

John Friedl
THE OHIO STATE UNIVERSITY

A Robert Carola Book

Harper's College Press
A Department of Harper & Row, Publishers
NEW YORK HAGERSTOWN SAN FRANCISCO LONDON

Library of Congress Cataloging in Publication Data

Friedl, John.
Cultural anthropology.

Includes bibliographies and index.
1. Ethnology. I. Title.
GN316.F74 301.2 75-28142
ISBN 0-06-167405-2

A Robert Carola Book

Copyeditor Claire Thompson
Picture editor Myra Schachne
Designer Robert Carola
Compositor Computer Typesetting Services, Inc.
Printer and binder The Book Press, Inc.

The illustrations on pages 6–7 were drawn by Gregory Downer.
All other illustrations by Vantage Art, Inc.

Cover photo: *Yap children playing* (Jack Fields. Photo Researchers)

Acknowledgments

I could not have written this book alone, nor would I want to. Much of the enjoyment is in the interaction and the intellectual tug-of-war that comes from collaboration and criticism. I was very fortunate to work with many talented and sincere people, and I learned a great deal from them.

My main debt of gratitude goes to Bob Carola, who nursed me along from the beginning, helping me to develop the original idea and urging me on when I needed it. The final product is due in large part to Bob's collaboration, and to his continuing input throughout the various stages of writing and production.

A good editor is hard to come by, and it was my good fortune to work with three of them. Caroline Eastman and Raleigh Wilson at Harper's College Press offered me much encouragement and support, and I am especially grateful to them for having enough faith in me to give me a free rein to produce the kind of book I had envisioned. Claire Thompson did the copy editing, too often a thankless job, but one which contributed much to the clarity of the book.

Comments and criticisms from reviewers helped eliminate some of the more glaring errors and inconsistencies, and brought out some basic questions that I had overlooked. I wish to thank Laurie DeCourcy, Monro S. Edmonson, Carol Morris, Dennis E. Shaw, and several anonymous reviewers for their generous assistance. Of course, any errors in the final work are my responsibility alone.

My intellectual debts will be obvious to some readers, but I would like to point them out more specifically. Many of my ideas about cultural anthropology, and particularly my thoughts in Chapter 11, are a result of my first experience in the field, in a course with Gerald Berreman. My interest in culture change has grown from my work with Jack Potter, and a great deal of Chapter 9 reflects his influence upon my thinking. George Foster impressed upon me the value of applied anthropology, and taught me always to think of anthropology in terms of solving problems, not just working with abstract ideas. Imitation is indeed a sincere form of flattery, as is evident in my treatment of applied anthropology in Chapter 10.

There is always a lot of tedious work that accompanies the more pleasant task of writing. My thanks go to Cathey Jenkins and Janet Nickerson for their help in typing the manuscript. Sandy Siegel offered many helpful suggestions along the way, and I am particularly grateful to him for the excellent job he did on the Instructor's Manual. I would also like to offer my sincere thanks to my colleagues in the Department of Anthropology at Ohio State for their support and encouragement of my work; I hope I have produced something that will be useful to them.

Finally, I wish to thank the most important people of all—my students. This book is, more than anything else, the result of feedback from students, and hopefully it reflects their concerns about the way anthropology is taught. If there is a spark of enthusiasm evident in the pages that follow, it is because teaching anthropology has been such a rewarding experience.

JOHN FRIEDL

Preface

If the Marquis de Sade could have invented education as it is now, he would probably have given up beating women.

ARTHUR PEARL *Schools versus Kids*

The lesson of cultural anthropology is not a collection of trivia such as one might be examined on in a TV quiz program. It is the fact that we as Americans are both similar to and different from each other and the various peoples around the world. Anthropology teaches tolerance and understanding, pointing out that we are strange not only to others, but among ourselves. Yet we are all basically the same, and share not only a common physical heritage, but, within a certain range, a common patterning of our behavior. To bring some sense of reality to this lesson is the goal of this book.

In the pages that follow, you will be introduced to the field of anthropology—first the scope and method of the discipline, then some of the basic areas of study within it, and finally some of the ways in which it can be meaningful to us in understanding and solving the problems of living in the twentieth century. In writing this book, I have departed from the usual style and format of anthropology textbooks in that I have tried to relate each topic to modern American life. The anthropologist James Spradley has pointed out that as kids brought up in middle-class America we learn the myth of the melting pot—that groups with cultural differences come together and work out their differences, becoming truly "American," in a way of life best for everyone. This myth leads us to the goal of *preserving* our institutions to restore bygone days, with a sense of commitment to old values. What we learn in anthropology should lead us to question this goal as we expose the myth of *one* American culture shared by all Americans. We should be aware of differences and seek to change institutions or create new ones to deal with differences. And we must work hard to do so quickly and peacefully before it happens spontaneously and violently.[1]

1. James P. Spradley, *You Owe Yourself a Drunk*. Boston: Little, Brown, 1968, pp. 2–3.

This does not mean that no societies other than the American will be used to illustrate points, but rather that the emphasis is placed heavily upon our own culture. Further, it is *not* taken as understood that we all share the same culture; in fact we might assume the opposite: that no two Americans share exactly the same culture, and any examples given will thus have different impacts upon readers with various backgrounds.

A second major departure of this book is that I have tried to avoid the use of jargon. Sometimes new terms are unavoidable, and where they are necessary I have tried to define them in context. Of course, not all jargon is bad, or necessarily unintelligible. We have all learned, for example, to follow the news reports by wading through official government language which frequently bears no relation to reality. We are familiar with phrases like "winning the peace," which at least to some observers clearly means "losing the war." When we hear of "differential affluence" we immediately think "poverty." "Famine" becomes "distribution of hunger," while our polluted environment is spoken of in terms of "ecological variability." (We had ecology before we had pollution, but few people knew what the term meant in those days.) Many other social problems are likewise masked in official jargon which does not really cover them up, but somehow seems to make them more palatable. Unemployment, formerly a problem, now becomes "involuntary leisure," a non-problem. And so on.

Social scientists, including anthropologists, are as guilty as anyone of the gamesmanship involved in the use of jargon. Sociologists have all but defined away the problems of drug addiction, prostitution, gambling, etc., by calling them "victimless crimes." Anthropologists, in an attempt to describe the life of the slum dweller in terms that do not convey middle-class values and judge by middle-class standards, have invented the term "culture of poverty." We can thus set out to describe this life style in purely objective terms, immune from criticism for taking slum dwellers to task for not living like suburban middle-class businessmen, but we never really solve the problem we are describing. We simply make a word game out of it.

A few terms are obviously necessary, because anthropologists deal with concepts that are not commonly used by others. All too often, however, the use of specialized language is carried to extremes. In a notable controversy, the sociologist C. Wright Mills criticized his colleague Talcott Parsons for writing in such an unintelligible style that it was never really clear what he had to say. Mills was able to take passages several pages in length from Parsons' work and "translate" them in a paragraph, a few lines, or even a single sentence. At one point he concludes that

> grand theory, as represented in [Parsons' book] *The Social System*, . . . is only about 50 per cent verbiage; 40 per cent is well-known textbook sociology. The other 10 per cent, as Parsons might say, I am willing to leave open for your own empirical investigations. My own investigations suggest that the remaining 10 per cent is of possible—although rather vague—ideological use.[2]

Finally, one other device will be used in this book, although I take no credit for originating it. At the end of each chapter I have added an article to serve as an illustration of the material in the chapter. I have selected the articles because they are short, well-written, interesting, in some cases even humorous, and in general related to American culture. These articles are not necessarily the best anthropological papers on each subject, but they are consistent with my purpose: to make anthropology interesting and to make this book readable. I assume that the instructor will assign additional reading that will illustrate material from the text in a different way, perhaps with examples from other cultures. Also, at the end of each chapter I have listed a number of references to other anthropological works that bear upon the material discussed, so that the reader can follow up on any topic that may have stimulated his or her interest.

The idea for this book arose out of my experience in teaching introductory cultural anthropology. It is my attempt to solve some of the problems I have encountered in that experience, and it is based to a great extent upon my students' comments concerning the reading I have assigned and the material I have covered in lectures. I do not for a moment think that it is a perfect solution, and I hope that as a result of this first attempt, I will be able to get additional feedback so that I can improve the book in subsequent editions. Therefore, I would be most grateful for any comments from students or instructors who use this book, and who feel strongly enough about its strengths and/or weaknesses to take the time to drop me a note. I am presently on the faculty in the Department of Anthropology at The Ohio State University, Columbus, Ohio 43210.

2. C. Wright Mills, *The Sociological Imagination*. New York: Grove Press, 1961, p. 49.

Contents

Cultural Anthropology

Introduction: What is Anthropology?

Chapter One

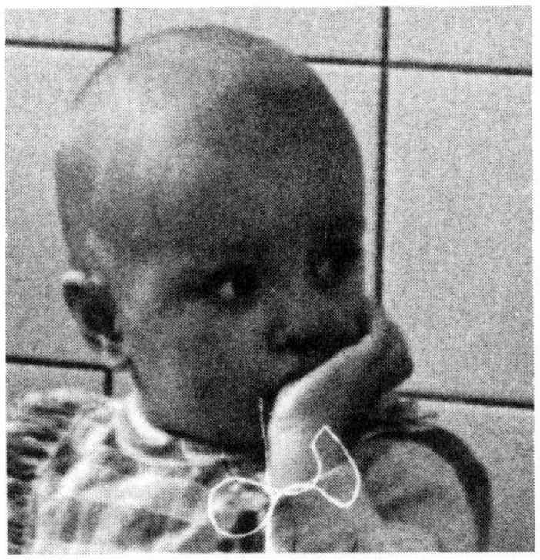

Most people have never heard of anthropology, or if they have it was in the context of an exotic foreign tribe or the "missing link" between monkeys and humans. So I will begin by defining the subject of this book.

We used to say that anthropology was simply the study of man. Then women's liberation came along and quite rightly pointed out that we studied women as well, and so now we might say, tongue in cheek, that anthropology is the study of man—embracing woman.[1] But that leaves us with much too broad a range for a single discipline. After all, don't all of the social sciences, including sociology, psychology, economics, political science, and even some aspects of geography, study people? Yet anthropology is different from these other approaches to the study of the human species. In this chapter we will see exactly what the differences are, and how anthropology fits in with the total picture of social science. We will also look at the various sub-disciplines within the field of anthropology, to see what different kinds of anthropologists are interested in, and how these interests fit together and build upon one another to give us an overall perspective for understanding all of human behavior.

1. Unfortunately, the English language does not provide a distinct word to designate the human species, but instead uses the same word that also refers to the male gender of the species. Many people have correctly argued that this places undue emphasis upon males and is indicative of a male-dominated society. The word "mankind" is little better, and while "people" avoids the sexual bias, it is awkward and cumbersome in current English usage. Where possible we will avoid using the word "man" to mean "people" or "the human species" in the hope that the awkwardness of the transition to other terms will be worth the effort.

Anthropology is the most
scientific of the humanities,
the most humanist of the sciences.
ERIC WOLF *Anthropology*

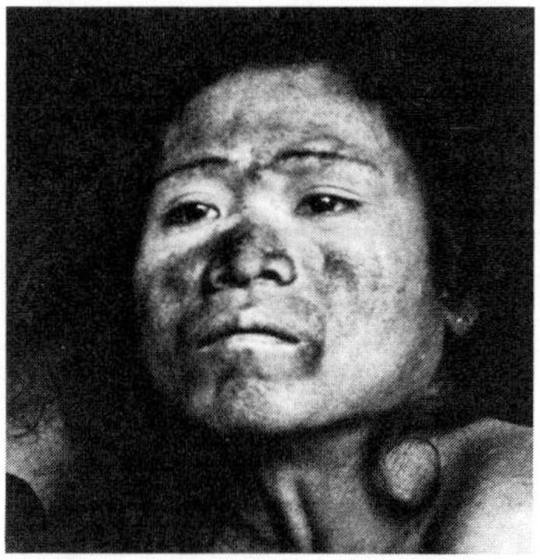

The actual word "anthropology" is derived from two Greek words, *anthropos* (man) and *logos* (study or science). Anthropologists are interested in all aspects of the human species and human behavior, in all places and at all times, from the origin and evolution of the species through its prehistoric civilizations, down to the present. And remember too that understanding behavior is the ultimate aim of anthropology—not just economic behavior, the focus for the economist, or political behavior, the central concern of the political scientist—but all behavior.

Anthropology is as old as humanity. The term might be a relatively recent innovation, and the acceptance of anthropology as a discipline worthy of a separate department within the university hierarchy is less than a century old. But people have always been curious about themselves, and have always asked anthropological kinds of questions and sought the answers to them in the spirit in which anthropologists conduct research today. Of course, we have no written records to take us back to the dawn of the human species, but for as far back as we do have records they indicate that people had an interest in human nature and the diversity of people in the world around them. Herodotus, the Greek historian who is sometimes referred to as the Father of History, might also be called an anthropologist. In writing of the events of his time, he raised a number of questions concerning the differences between the Greeks and other peoples in surrounding areas. He theorized that the peoples encountered in the Persian Wars must represent an earlier stage of Greek society. Later, Thucydides, in his accounts of the Peloponnesian War, made an even stronger statement of the evolutionary notion that these barbarians represented a stage through which Athenian culture had already passed in its rise to civilization. Thus he was not only comparing different groups, but also actually engaging in analysis of the differences, trying to understand what caused them and what could explain the current state of his own society.

In Western Europe the age of exploration and discovery that followed the decline of the Middle Ages saw an increased interest in the varieties of peoples and customs around the world. As Europe broke out of its isolationist shell, explorers, adventurers, missionaries and travelers came into contact with curious societies. These people lived in ways the Europeans found so strange that they felt compelled to describe these practices in utmost detail. The more contact they had with different cultures around the world, the more information was collected and published, creating greater and greater interest in the study of such people. Although some of the early attempts at scientific analysis of foreign customs and peoples of radically different appearance were quite unsophisticated—almost comical in retrospect—still they represented the beginning of a movement that was to lead to the development of anthropology as a science. Are these strange peoples in the far corners of the earth related to each other, and to us? How do their customs compare to ours? And how can we explain such a wide range of behavior? These were the kinds of questions for which early anthropologists sought answers. Never mind that today such questions seem a bit simplistic. If they hadn't been posed and their answers sought, we wouldn't be any farther along today than our fifteenth-century forerunners were.

It wasn't until the nineteenth century that anthropology really began to gel as a separate discipline. The roots of anthropology as a science can be found in the natural sciences of that period, including biology, botany, and zoology. There had been a long tradition in these fields of recording all of the diverse species of animals and plants discovered in different parts of the world and trying to figure out the relationship between them, as well as how they had grown apart and changed in different directions—in other words, their evolution. Charles Darwin's early research is typical of this era. During his five-year voyage around the world in 1831–1836, he gathered the information about animal and plant varieties that ultimately enabled him to put together his ideas about evolution. But Darwin was only one of many naturalists who were piecing together the story of evolution, and while he was concentrating upon plants and animals, others were concerned specifically with the human species. Anthropologists were

Culver Pictures, Inc.

Charles Darwin (1809–1882) *is the man most often linked with the discovery of evolution. Actually, his major contribution to evolutionary theory was the concept of natural selection. He saw organisms in competition against the forces of nature, and those best able to cope with the pressures survived at the highest rate and passed on their advantageous characteristics. Although Darwin did not mean for his theory of evolution to be applied to human social and cultural change, it was proposed by many social scientists that cultures evolved in a struggle for survival, just as animals did. This doctrine, inappropriately called "Social Darwinism," was ultimately used to justify white supremacist policies of western nations in their domination of Third World peoples.*

Amahuaca Indian (Peru) with boa constrictor. Early European encounters with foreign peoples produced bizarre descriptions of so-called "savages" and their way of life. (Cornell Capa, Magnum)

asking the same kinds of questions about similarities and differences in human behavior that biologists and zoologists were posing about animals. Thus the early scientific interest in different cultures paralleled the natural sciences, and might even be seen as an extension of them.

Today anthropology has become a broad-based study, much more than any other scientific discipline. This is perhaps its greatest value, for it provides insights into a wider variety of problems than any other field. Anthropology includes a broad range of approaches derived from both the natural sciences (biology, zoology, anatomy and physiology) and the social sciences (sociology, psychology, human geography, economics, political science and history). Anthropology is able to relate all of these disciplines to its quest for an understanding of human behavior, and draws upon all of them to interpret the way in which biological and social factors enter into the picture.

Proconsul　　Ramapithecus　　Australopithecus　　*Homo erectus*

The Branches of Anthropology

In the sense that anthropology is interested in human behavior, it is no different from any other social science. The main distinctions are found in the method by which anthropology pursues that interest, and in the number of different perspectives—corresponding to the different branches of anthropology—that contribute to the overall understanding. Each branch of anthropology studies one special aspect of behavior, and although each works separately with its own methods and its own subject matter, together they form a whole that is distinct from all other social sciences.

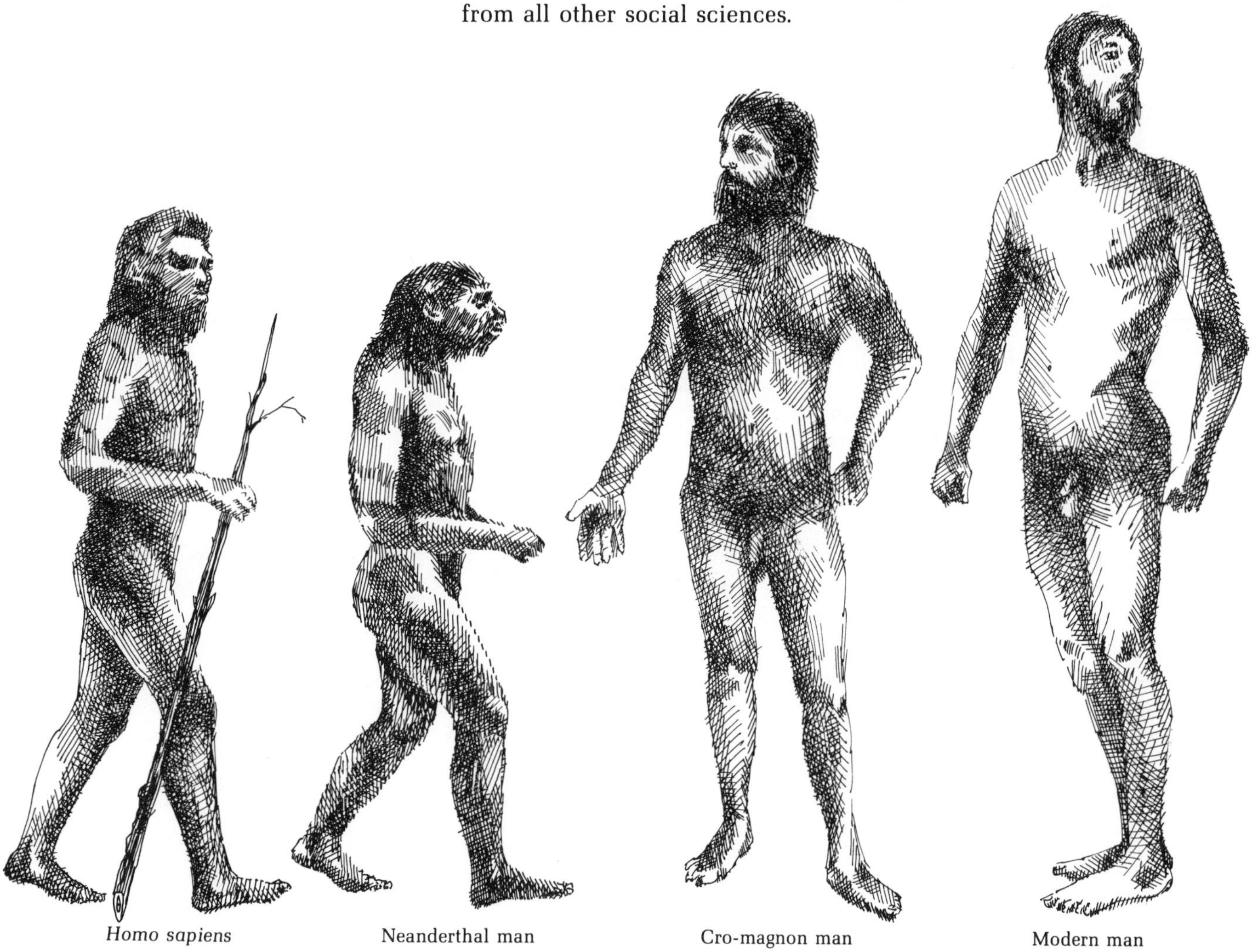

Homo sapiens Neanderthal man Cro-magnon man Modern man

Physical Anthropology

Physical anthropology is that branch concerned with our relationship to other animals, our derivation and evolution, and our special physical characteristics such as mental capacity, shape of the hand, and erect posture. In other words, *physical anthropology studies human evolution and human variation.* It is closely related to several of the natural sciences: zoology, in terms of the relationship to other animals and the overall place of the human species in the process of evolution; biology, in terms of the evolution of humans from early pre-human forms; anatomy and physiology, in its concern with the structure of the human body, the relationship of the various parts, and the operation or function of these different parts; genetics, in its concern with human variation in the world today; and even psychology, in the investigation of our mental makeup and its relationship to behavior.

Physical anthropology considers the human species as a biological entity, as well as a social animal. Some physical anthropologists are concerned primarily with the past forms of pre-human and early human species, an area of study known as *fossil man*. Others concentrate on the similarities and differences between the various primate species, which include not only humans, but apes and monkeys as well. This area of study is called *primatology*. A third area, known as the study of human variation, or *anthropological genetics*, deals with contemporary as well as historical variations among populations of humans. It is concerned with questions such as the adaptation of a group of people to a specific climate, the natural immunity of some peoples to certain diseases, and the all-important question of racial difference.

A Case for Physical Anthropology: Sickle Cell Anemia A current issue of great importance in the United States is the battle against a hereditary disease known as sickle cell anemia. This has become a topic of concern because the disease is found primarily among blacks in this country, although it is not unique to any one racial or ethnic group. The disease is so named because of the shape of the red blood cells in its bearer. They appear curved in the shape of a crescent, or a sickle, rather than in the disc or oval shape of normal red blood cells. A person afflicted with this disease becomes weak and frequently disabled, primarily because these sickle-shaped red blood cells cannot carry enough oxygen through the body to sustain activity.

Physical anthropology gives us an important insight into the nature of this disease, as well as an understanding of how it came to exist in a relatively high proportion of certain groups of people and why is has persisted. Sickle cell anemia originated in areas of the world where there was a high incidence of malaria, itself a serious and often fatal disease. In these areas the sickle-shaped cell could under certain circumstances actually be advantageous, rather than harmful! The reason for this advantage is that the malaria parasite attacks the bloodstream, and the sickle-shaped cell does not offer enough nutrient to support it. But not everyone with sickle cells receives these benefits, for obviously if all of an individual's red blood

A sickle-cell testing center in Berkeley, California. (Sam Falk, Monkmeyer)

cells are abnormal, then whether or not that person is resistant to malaria is unimportant, since he or she will be completely disabled by another disease, sickle cell anemia. Instead, only those people who have some sickle cells and some normal blood cells will benefit from it, since they will be resistant to malaria but will still have normal blood cells to supply enough oxygen to maintain normal bodily activity. This half-and-half condition is called sickle cell *trait*, not anemia, and does not disable the carrier in any way. The problem is that nature does not arrange for everyone in the population to receive some sickle cells and some normal ones. Instead, nature "arranges" to remove from the population those who have all normal cells (through the agent malaria) and those who have all sickle cells (through another agent, anemia).

Thus we can understand how sickle cell anemia persisted in those environments where malaria was prevalent, such as some areas of Africa and the eastern Mediterranean. It just happens that in malaria-ridden areas of Africa, the population is composed primarily of blacks, and thus in the United States this disease is found almost exclusively among that group. The problem is that in a country such as the United States, where malaria has been eliminated, the sickle-shaped blood cell does not confer an advantage upon anyone, whereas in the population of a malarial region the loss of those individuals with all sickle-shaped cells was offset (insofar as the loss of any person can be offset) by the advantage for a greater number of people who had some sickle cells and some normal ones.

The physical anthropologist is able to look at the question of sickle cell anemia among blacks in the United States with scientific objectivity. It is a question of adaptation to a particular environment, with the subsequent change of the environment rendering the adaptation no longer useful. This does not mean that we ignore the whole social question of a disease found almost exclusively among one ethnic group in this country. It means only that if we are to understand the disease and do something about it, we must not look at its racial implications but rather at the scientific facts. Remember, physical anthropologists contribute only one of many perspectives to the study of the human species. Working with their contribution to this problem, the *holistic* anthropologist (one who derives an understanding from all areas of anthropology) can deal better not only with the medical problem of sickle cell anemia, but with its social ramifications as well.

A Case for Physical Anthropology: Lactase Deficiency The case of sickle cell anemia, which as we have seen is not just a medical problem, is a good illustration of the importance of physical anthropology. Here is an interesting example of the interaction between physical anthropology and cultural anthropology (the comparative study of existing peoples). In much of the world, a physiological condition renders a large proportion of the adult population unable to digest milk properly. An enzyme called *lactase* is necessary for the successful assimilation of milk by the body; without it milk causes the bowels to become distended, and cramps, gas and diarrhea ensue. All infants have the capacity to produce this enzyme, but in only two population groups do most adults have it. If this seems odd to us, it is because the United States contains one of these two populations: white Euro-Americans. (The other is comprised of the Nilotic Negroes of East Africa.) Significantly enough, these populations are the two main groups who practice dairying in which raw milk is consumed. Of course, other groups also raise cattle. Typically, however, they

A nomadic cattle-raising tribe bleeding a calf. (George Rodger, Magnum)

do not drink milk as such, but rather consume it in other forms that can be digested more readily. The Chinese, for example, engage in dairying, but adult Chinese generally do not consume raw milk. It is interesting to note that even though inability to produce lactase is not universal among Chinese people, cultural values and taste preferences in China lead even those who can digest raw milk to shun its use.

The conclusion we can draw from this study is that there has been a parallel development in cultural and biological evolution. Cultural values in the form of a taste preference for milk changed, and were associated with genetic change leading to the lack of ability to drink milk. Which came first is not clear, although it seems probable that the taste for milk did not change until the capacity to assimilate it was lost genetically. At any rate, the study leads us to an understanding of the interplay between genetic change and cultural change, and between biology and culture. It also teaches us the interesting lesson that our American habit of drinking milk throughout our adult lives is not only shown to be unnecessary by the experience of other peoples, but also it is undesirable in most cultures. The common advertising slogan "you never outgrow your need for milk" would certainly not be effective in most of the rest of the world!

By studying human nature, the variety of peoples in the world today and in the past, and the relationship of the human species to others, we are better able to understand why we behave the way we do. The physical anthropologist gives us valuable information about the uniqueness and limitations of our physical structure. Why are we different from apes, for example? It is important to know the ramifications of being able to walk with erect posture on two feet, rather than having to use our hands to steady ourselves. It means that we have our hands free to use for other things, such as making tools. Having a thumb opposite the fingers rather than in line with them means that we can grasp and manipulate tools and use them to our advantage, as weapons or as precision instruments. The physical anthropologist has also contributed to our understanding of another factor of crucial importance in the process of becoming human, namely, the origin of language. We know that only humans have the capacity for speech, not only because of our vocal apparatus, but also because of the size and structure of our brains. By providing answers to the question of what makes human beings unique among animals, physical anthropology gives us the first clues in understanding human behavior.

It tells us what the basis for that behavior is, and what the limitations upon it are. It tells us why we should expect others to behave within those limitations, and what variations are possible. In other words, physical anthropology spells out the limits of human behavior. Perhaps most important of all, physical anthropology teaches us that no matter how much diversity we might find in the world around us, the most remarkable fact is not how different people are but how similar they are, and this is a crucial lesson in getting along in the world today.

Archeology

A second branch of anthropology is *archeology*, sometimes called *prehistory* because it is concerned primarily with the period of human existence prior to written records or historical accounts. The aim of this branch is to reconstruct the origin, spread and evolution of culture. It does this by examining the remains that we are fortunate enough to find of past societies.

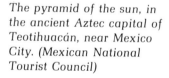

The pyramid of the sun, in the ancient Aztec capital of Teotihuacán, near Mexico City. (Mexican National Tourist Council)

Archeology is obviously related to history, in that both attempt to reconstruct as much of the past as possible. The main difference is that history deals primarily with the written records of literate civilizations, while archeology goes back beyond where history begins, reconstructing the past prior to the invention of writing. Moreover, because early written records were kept by a very small elite group of people at the top of their society, they tend to describe the lives of the leaders rather than those of the common people. Literacy was until very recently restricted to only a few scholars and priests, and it was natural that those who could write would be more interested in the events and activities surrounding themselves and others in the elite class—the kings and generals, the great heroes of the day. They paid little attention to the peasant. In contrast, archeology finds its information wherever it may lie. The archeologist is just as likely

Archeologists at work at the ruins of Pergamum, an ancient Greek site located in what is now western Turkey. (Mahoney, Monkmeyer)

to dig up a peasant house or a merchant's workshop as a king's castle (except that the castle is likely to have been larger and built of sturdier and longer-lasting material). In uncovering an entire city or fortified settlement, the archeologist will find remains of the life styles of all the inhabitants, even though a literate historian, had their been one, might have ignored a large proportion of the population because he considered it unimportant. The result is that while history deals primarily with great people, and is in a sense a succession of biographies, archeology deals with entire societies, and is the study of the anonymous man or woman as well as the king.

The archeologist assumes the same task as other kinds of anthropologists, in that he also is concerned with understanding as much as possible about human behavior. The difference is that his materials are the unwritten records of past societies, and he does not have the opportunity to sit down with living members of those societies and go over the various interpretations of what he finds. He cannot observe living people, but must abstract from the remains of the past whatever he can about how they once lived. The result is that he tries to understand behavior from physical remains, rather than from actual observation. He must assume much about behavior from what remains in the way of tools, weapons, clothing, buildings and whatever else he can find. Any ideas he obtains about the intangibles of past cultures, such as patterns of marriage, child rearing and so on—the major interests of cultural anthropologists today—can be supported only partially from what the archeologist has to go on, and can be presented only in a tentative manner in the absence of written records.

Archeology differs from physical anthropology in that physical anthropology is concerned with the origin and evolution of the human species, while archeology focuses primarily upon the origin and evolution of culture. The physical anthropologist can tell us roughly when humans first began to use tools, and what major contributions of evolution enabled this to come about. Archeologists, on the other hand, can tell us when people first began to use agriculture, and what were the major stages in its development. They can tell us, at least partially, when men and women first began to live in cities, and what the earliest necessities of urban life might have been. In other words, the archeologist takes up where the physical anthropologist leaves off in the reconstruction of human history. The physical anthropologist takes us to the evolution of the *capacity* for culture, and then the archeologist begins to tell us what happened once we obtained that capacity.

Limitations of Archeology Archeological reconstructions are severely limited by the nature of the evidence. For one thing, we cannot examine the conscious activity of prehistoric people. We have no way of knowing what they believed, what they valued, or even how they organized their society, beyond a very minimal outline. We can guess a few things—for example, that early human beings believed in a form of magic created by imitating the image of a natural object. At least, one interpretation of the famous cave paintings is that they were meant to ensure success in a hunting expedition by depicting a successful hunting scene in advance. But we are not sure about even that much. Recently an expert on the subject has suggested that these paintings are simply a form of erotic art, filled with sexual symbolism, and have nothing to do with magic.

Artifacts such as this stone axe are the most durable elements of a culture, and provide the archeologist with more information about technology than any other aspect of culture. (John Nance, Panamin/Magnum)

Another limitation upon archeological reconstruction is that what remains is only the accidentally durable material of a past culture. This can give us a lopsided picture, leaving out more than it includes. Furthermore, what remains is not necessarily what the people might have left had they wanted to give us a clear picture of what was important to them. Prehistoric people did not have the historians of the future in mind when they emptied their garbage or buried their dead; they did not provide us with a time capsule containing records of their total life. Thus we must not only interpret the materials left behind within the limited context in which we find them, such as a burial site or a refuse pit, but we must attempt to paint a picture of an entire way of life without hope of ever recovering physical evidence for much of it. We can make an inventory of the kinds of tools or weapons early humans used at a particular site, and we can note which ones are found most frequently, how they are made, and so forth. But we can never know what a tool meant to the individual who used it. We can only make guesses based upon our own personal involvement with the items of our own material culture.

Archeological Inference What, then, can archeology contribute specifically to our understanding of human culture and social behavior? First, we can learn much about the technology of early civilizations through the discoveries of material remains such as tools and their uses, as well as through the analysis of such aspects of their life style as what they ate, and perhaps even how much of it. We can tell, for example, whether a particular group lived primarily from hunting or fishing, or whether they practiced agriculture. We can infer much about their technological level from the kinds of buildings they used and the techniques involved in constructing them. The pyramids offer a good example of this. And each case, when we put the whole picture together, contributes to a broader picture of human evolution and the advance of culture through time.

A second aspect of the life of early people that is revealed to us through archeology has to do with the economic practices they engaged in. For example, occasionally we find pottery or jewelry made from materials known to be available only in distant places. This usually indicates that these items were not manufactured on the scene, but were obtained through some other means—either by traveling to the place where they were available, or more likely through trading with other groups, exchanging local products for them. If we put together a wide distribution of such items over a period of time, we

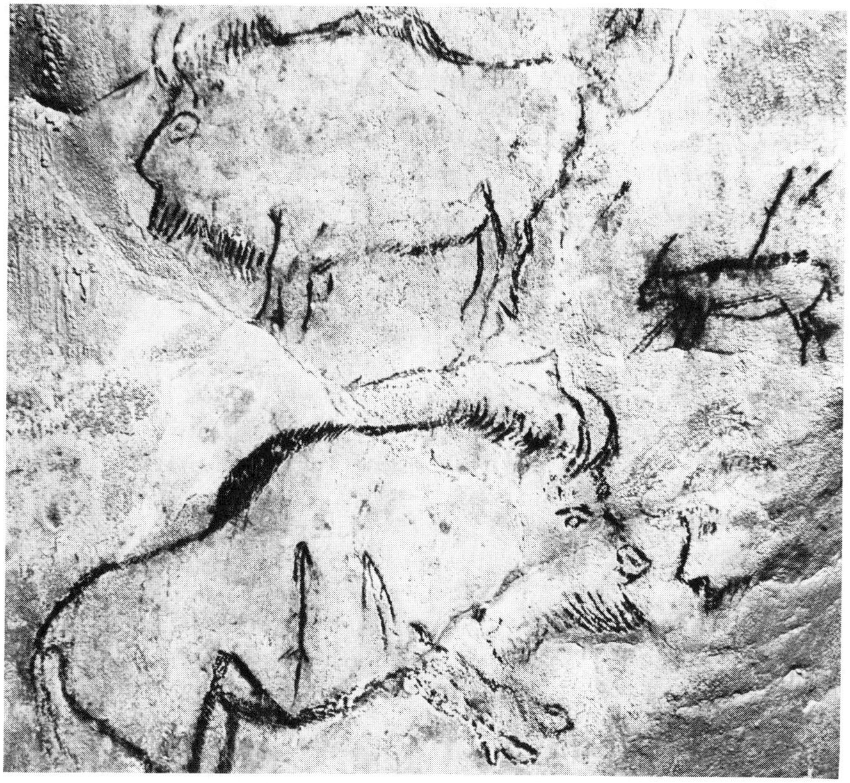

Cave paintings at Dordogne, France—hunting magic or sexual symbolism? (Monkmeyer Press Photo Service)

Stonehenge, in southwestern England. Although we know little about the way of life of its builders, we do know enough about their technology to explain how they constructed this huge monument. (Ray Graham, DPI)

get a good picture of the interaction among neighboring groups, and this in turn gives us clues about other aspects of culture that might have been borrowed or traded as well. We might assume that if pottery was being traded between two groups, they also influenced each other in other ways, such as exchanging wives or agricultural techniques or ideas about their gods.

Less evident than economics or technology, but still recognizable in some archeological reconstructions, is the political and social structure of past cultures. We can assume a great deal about the organization of a city from the layout of the buildings and the types of housing found in it. For example, if we find a large temple in the center of an ancient city and it is surrounded by fairly substantial dwelling sites, and then on the outskirts of the settlement there are smaller and less substantial buildings, we know already that there were at least two classes of people and that the temple formed the center of the city not only in a physical sense, but socially as well. By investigating burial sites or cemeteries we can also tell something about the different classes of people within the society. Perhaps some people were buried near the temple with a great deal of material wealth in their graves, while others were buried farther from the temple in mass graves with nothing else included. We might also learn something about kinship structure by looking at burial sites. Is a male skeleton found in the same grave with (or near) a female skeleton, or several females? Obviously a lot of this type of reconstruction is guesswork, but usually it is an educated guess that is based upon much more than just a hunch about the way things were.

Finally, archeological evidence can reveal a great deal about certain aspects of the religious and spiritual life of ancient societies. We can recognize sacred objects by their location in known centers of religious activity, or in burial sites. When we are fortunate enough to find temples or other religious structures, we can determine their relative importance and influence upon the society as a whole. But in other areas, it is extremely difficult to interpret the evidence. Thus we know little about people's belief systems, or their values and morals, their feelings about spirits, and so forth. Even when we find material objects that might suggest such beliefs, we cannot ask anyone for an explanation of their meaning, but must simply go on what we know about other aspects of the society, and later societies that seem to have certain parallels.

In sum, archeology offers an opportunity to look into the distant past of the human species and try to reconstruct the picture. But it is like doing a jigsaw puzzle with most of the pieces missing, and without the picture of the finished puzzle on the box to work from. We have a few things that fit together, we can guess about many others, but we really don't have enough to put it all together with complete confidence. Every new piece we find fits somewhere, though, and we never know when the next piece will give us the key to interpreting a whole new section of the puzzle of life in prehistoric times. That is the challenge and the excitement of archeology.

Anthropological Linguistics

The study of language from an anthropological perspective forms a third branch of the discipline. Of course, linguistics also exists as a separate discipline, but the anthropologist who specializes in this area is particularly concerned with the relationship between language and cultural behavior. He asks questions about language from the point of view of the human species, rather than trying to describe the language or its structure. His central focus is still people, and he regards language as a part of our social world.

One area of interest in anthropological linguistics deals with the origin of language. This could just as well be a question for the physical anthropologist. There is presently an important controversy over what form of fossil person was the first to have the capacity for speech. Another area of concentration deals with the role of language in the context of social behavior. This is a relatively new field known as *sociolinguistics,* and it is concerned with the way we use the language we speak (or the different forms of it, for we all know different variations of the English language that we use in different contexts).

Language and Perception One of the most interesting aspects of anthropological linguistics from the perspective of cultural anthropology is the study of how our language determines the way we order our universe. This does not mean that people who speak different languages perceive things differently, but rather that they tend to arrange the things they perceive in different ways according to the language they speak. This is something that varies from one culture to another. For example, we all recognize that there is an extremely wide range of colors in nature. In fact, if you have ever tried to decide what color to paint your house, and have pondered over dozens of color charts at the paint store, you know just how many variations of the same color there can be. We can look at ten different shades of green, and even though we recognize that they are different, we will still call them all "green," thus lumping them into the same category. An interesting experiment is to take finely graded colored samples (such as come on a custom-mixed paint color chart) ranging from green to blue, containing perhaps thirty different shades. If you look at both extremes, you will say with ease that one is green, and the other blue. The hard part comes in drawing the line somewhere in the middle between one shade and another, saying that one belongs to the category "green" and the other to the category "blue." In fact, sometimes we get around this problem by inventing another category, "blue-green."

In our language we know that this category "blue-green" is really not a separate category but merely a convenient designation for the transition between two categories. We know this because we do not have a separate word for it. This indicates to us that while blue and green are significant, the transition from one to the other is less significant. But in another language, spoken by people of another culture, there could easily be a word which designates "blue-green" as a separate category. Certainly there is no reason why this could not be done—after all, isn't green a transition between blue and yellow?

Here we begin to see how language can affect the way we order the universe, by establishing artificial categories into which we plug all of our perceptions. The point is that they *are* artificial; our culture, through our language, determines the way we order our perceptions. Now if one language can set up more categories for color than we have, certainly another can set up fewer such categories. In fact, some Indian languages have words for only two or three colors, and everything with color that the individual sees is placed in one of these two or three categories—for example, gray, blue, or red. What about yellow, orange, green, etc.? Are these people color blind? Of course not, only the distinction between, say, green and blue is not significant. It doesn't mean that they can't tell the difference between a cardinal and a robin. It simply means that they don't classify them as different in terms of color, although they certainly perceive color differences. Where we divide the spectrum and establish arbitrary boundaries around colors is a purely subjective cultural factor, and it is important to know that it can vary from one culture to another. The expression of such differences is found in the language spoken by each group.

Perhaps another example, using specific words and languages, will help illustrate this concept. In English we have several words to describe a cluster of trees. We can say that they are merely "trees," which suggests that there are only a few of them, perhaps scattered about, and that they do not extend very far in any direction. Or we can use the word "woods," which denotes more trees (e.g. a thicket), covering a larger area, and perhaps clustered together more tightly. Or we can use the word "forest," which suggests that there are countless trees covering a very large area. If a large group of people were asked to look at pictures of trees and use one of these three words to describe them, there would probably be a great deal of agreement on which word applies in each case.

Now let us turn to some other languages to see how they cover the same question. In German there are also three similar words to describe trees. The word *Baum* means tree, and its plural *Bäume* describes almost exactly the same phenomenon as our English word "trees." Another word, *Holz,* corresponds to our word "woods" except that it does not extend as far—that is, it is not used to describe quite as many trees as our word "woods" does. Instead, where we would say a large "woods," German would substitute a small *Wald*, or forest. Thus if we were to plot on a chart the number of trees described by each word in these two languages, we would not have an exact parallel.

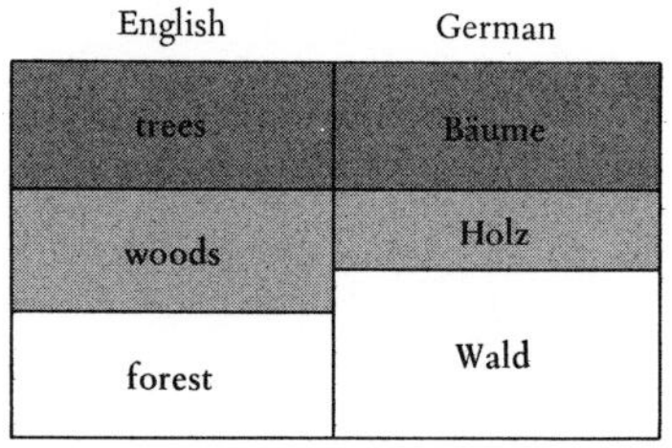

This does not mean that trees grow differently in Germany than they do in the United States, but it does mean that German speakers tend to organize what they see into categories different from those used by English speakers.

Looking at another language, Danish, we find an even greater difference. In Danish there are only two words that cover the same range of trees as our three English words. The Danish word *trae* includes not only what we would call "trees," but also the lower limits of what we would call "woods." Then the upper portion of what we refer to as "woods," plus "forest," is all included in the word *skov*. Comparing the two languages in this regard we find the situation shown below.

The idea that the structure of one's language affects one's thought processes is a fascinating concept. If you have ever studied a foreign language, you have found that there are some words that simply cannot be translated into an English equivalent. This is an illustration of the importance of language in patterning the way we look at the world. Each language has certain words that describe experiences or feelings peculiar to the group of people who share that language and that culture. To translate such a word literally into English is often impossible, for there is no way to capture the essence of it in one English word. Instead, we usually end up with several words in a rather awkward phrase that perhaps captures some of the meaning but is never really satisfactory. Learning a foreign language is thus not merely an exercise in memorization, but a lesson in cultural anthropology, for by learning the language we learn something about the way other people think, about the ways in which they are different from us. Language gives us an insight into culture, and as such it is a valuable tool for studying and understanding people.

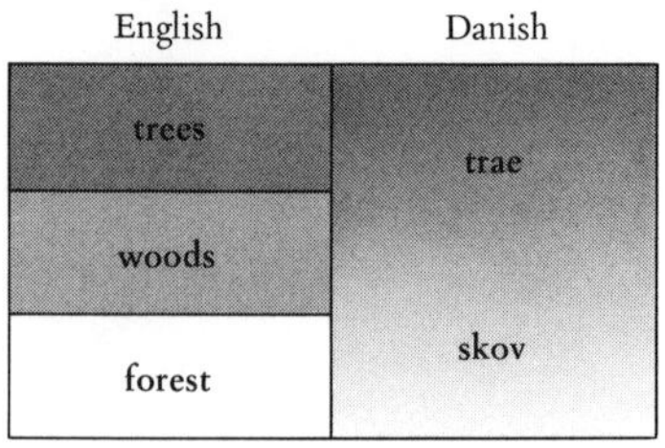

Language and Culture Language can tell us a lot about what is important in a particular culture. For example, if we look just at the vocabulary of a language we will find a great deal of elaboration in words describing certain phenomena, while in other areas there will not be any elaboration at all. The Eskimo languages, for example, have a vocabulary rich in words describing details of the Arctic environment that those of us living in temperate climates would tend to disregard. In one Eskimo language there are 12 separate and unrelated words for wind and 22 words for snow. That is, 22 different kinds of snow are recognized and given names that are not simply different forms of the same root word, but different words altogether. It is apparently not significant to us who speak English that there are minute variations in snow types, and so we use adjectives to describe these variations—wet snow, powder snow, etc. Occasionally we use different words, such as sleet or hail, but that is about all the elaboration we have in our language. On the other hand, we have an extremely large vocabulary to deal with complex technological aspects of our culture, which are more significant to us. Let's look at the automobile, for example: we have sedans, convertibles, coupes, fastbacks, wagons, buses, vans, trucks, and so on down the line. Obviously we would not expect a member of a society where automobiles are not found to understand our distinctions—to him, a car is a car, period. But then to us, snow is snow, period.

To these Eskimo children, variations in the texture of snow are extremely important, a fact reflected in their language. (Ward W. Wells, DPI)

Finally, another interesting aspect of the study of language by the anthropologist deals with the way people learn their language. Since language conveys so much of the content of the culture, it is important to know how new members of a group are taught language, and thereby to understand how they are "socialized"—that is, how they are trained to be members of that group. A Japanese baby becomes a Japanese adult, adept in the ways of Japanese culture, not because they are programmed into him at birth, but because he is taught Japanese culture in his childhood. The Japanese language is the medium for that learning process. And the same is true for a member of any other cultural group. Understanding the process by which the training takes place, and the medium in which it is transmitted, is a major goal of the anthropological linguist.

Cultural Anthropology

We come now to the main area of this book, cultural anthropology. Actually, in a strict sense, we could also include archeology and anthropological linguistics under this heading, for they are both concerned with culture—the archeologist with the cultures of prehistoric peoples, and the linguist with a specific aspect of culture in both the past and the present. But since these sub-disciplines are generally acknowledged to be separate from the major focus of cultural anthropology, it is better to accept this distinction.

Cultural anthropology, as the term is commonly used today, generally refers to the study of existing peoples. Further, it is based upon a comparative approach, that is, its aim is to understand and appreciate the diversity in human behavior, and ultimately to develop a science of human behavior, through the comparison of different peoples throughout the world. In the United States we frequently make a distinction between two areas of cultural anthropology: *ethnology* and *ethnography*. Ethnology is the comparative study of culture and the investigation of theoretical problems using information about different groups. Ethnography is simply the description of one culture, and is not a comparative study. In other words, an ethnological study is based on two or more ethnographies; the latter form the raw material for the former. To avoid confusion we will use the term *cultural anthropology* to cover both of these, but you should know what the terms mean since you will certainly come across them in other anthropological readings.

Thus there are two main tasks involved in the work of the cultural anthropologist, to describe the cultures of other peoples and to compare them. As we saw in the example of a foreign language, such description is not an easy task, since putting something from another cultural context into the concepts and words available in the English language is not always possible. In fact, we might consider an anthropologist's description of a foreign culture somewhat of a cultural translation—the aim of the description is to make it clear to the reader just what it is like to live as an individual of the other culture lives. Aside from the problems of language, the anthropologist also encounters difficulties in trying to relate that elusive "flavor" of life, what we might refer to as the untranslatable "essence" behind many words in a foreign language. Also, since language is so essential to understanding another

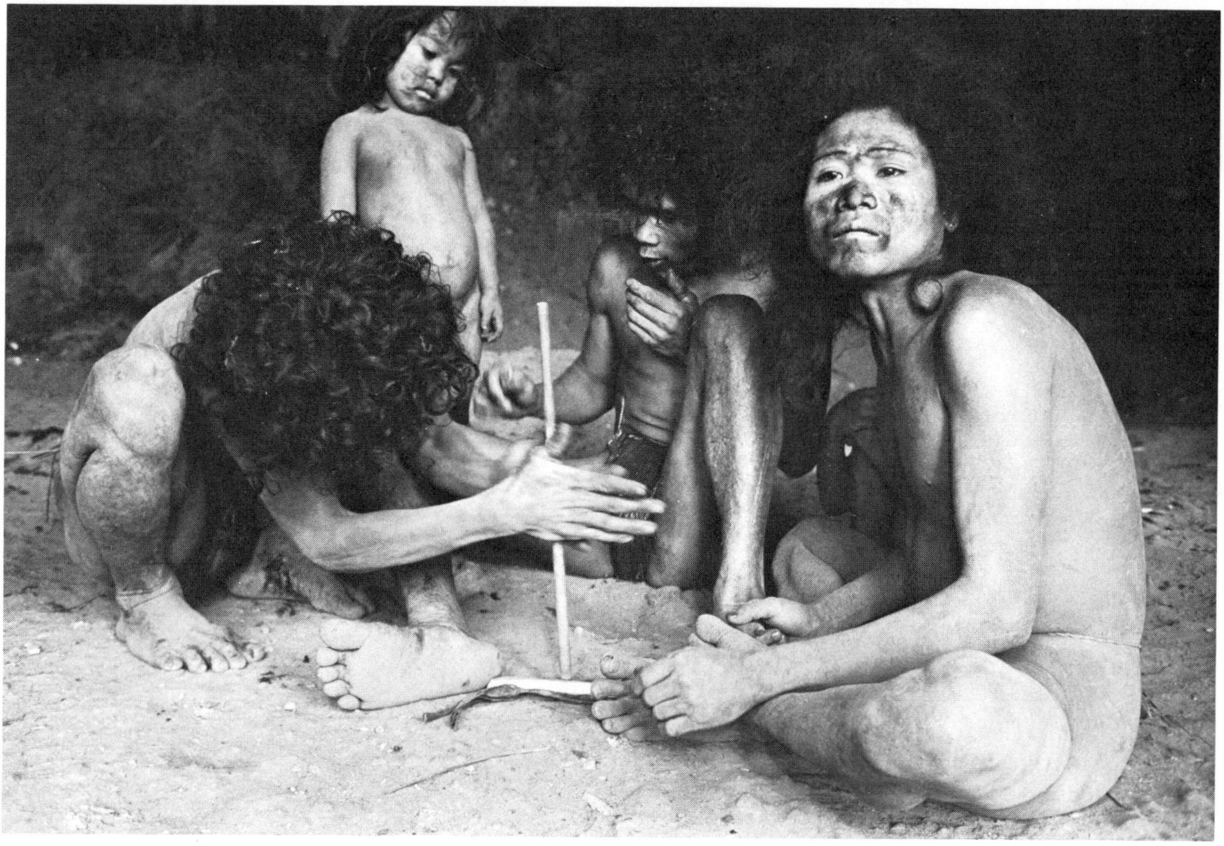

Members of the Tasaday tribe making a fire by friction of the fire drill. (John Nance, Panamin/Magnum)

culture, there is another barrier built into this translation, for the anthropologist who has lived among another group has had the time and opportunity to learn their language, while the reader, whose only contact with them is through a book, has no such opportunity. As you study further in anthropology, you will arrive at a better understanding of some of the barriers involved in trying to gain a feeling for a way of life different from your own. It is difficult to explain just what the problem is. There is no substitute for actual experience in a foreign culture to make one aware of the perspective necessary for a cultural anthropologist. But it is essential to understand the importance of accurate descriptive work as the basis for comparative studies, which after all are crucial to understanding human behavior.

Cultural anthropology includes a broad range of work covering a number of different approaches. Many of these will be discussed in the pages that follow, and therefore we will not dwell upon them here. But it is necessary to emphasize, in concluding this section on the integration of the branches of anthropology, the relevance of all of them to each other. Without an accurate understanding of the physical nature of the human organism—how it came to be the way it is, what its unique capabilities and limitations are, what the past history of the human species has been and the importance of symbolic communication through language to the ongoing patterns of behavior—we cannot hope to understand the present or predict the future. Indeed, although this is a textbook specifically dealing with cultural anthropology, it is only proper to mention at the outset that the different areas of anthropology cannot legitimately be separated. To be an anthropologist one must undertake studies in all four branches, for each is vital to the others, and the subject matters of all ultimately contribute to the same goal.

The Relationship of Cultural Anthropology to Other Social Sciences

Since, as we have admitted above, other social sciences have the same goal as anthropology, what makes cultural anthropology different? Perhaps the most obvious difference is that the scope of anthropology is much broader than that of any other social science. Economics deals only with economic behavior, political science only with political behavior, and so on. Cultural anthropology, on the other hand, is concerned with all of those areas, from a comparative perspective, and especially with the interrelationships between these areas of behavior in any particular society. It overlaps with every other social science in at least some areas of interest, yet it still retains its individuality.

Geography

Studies in human geography can be seen as fundamental to the origin of cultural anthropology. Long before anyone ever thought of comparative cultural studies, geographers were busy describing not only far and distant lands, but the people who inhabited them. The early work in human geography was very much akin to the descriptive studies of the cultural anthropologist, although the methods used were not as refined and the perspective of the anthropologist was lacking. Geographers tended to focus on the exotic aspects of the people they encountered, stressing the most bizarre differences, and either ignoring or failing to notice the strong similarities that existed between all people throughout the world.

In comparing cultural anthropology to present-day studies in human geography, the main difference is one of emphasis. The geographer tends to relate the study of people to the study of the land, stressing ecological factors such as terrain and climate and their relationship to cultural patterns. Anthropology also stresses such relationships, but is not limited to them. Geography does not delve as deeply into areas of primary interest to the cultural anthropologist, such as values, beliefs, and culturally patterned attitudes and responses. Anthropology studies human behavior not only with regard to the land and the physical surroundings, but also in the context of the social surroundings, which are considered at least as important.

History

For many years there was a debate among anthropologists as to whether there was a valid distinction between history and anthropology: Is anthropology, after all, merely the study of human history in all its various forms? Although this debate has subsided, one cannot truthfully say that it has been completely resolved. No anthropologist can work without an awareness of the past, of what the particular sequence of events was that led to the situation under study. In describing another culture, or in comparing aspects of two cultures, the anthropologist dares not ignore the historical background. If, for example, we are describing a community in rural Mexico in 1976, we cannot simply list our observations at one point in time and expect to be able to explain what we observe. Rather, we must go back to the history of that community, back even further to the Spanish Conquest, to understand the events that brought Spanish and Mexican Indian culture together to form the unique blend that today we call Mexican. Not to do this would be unforgivable.

Yet there is no doubt that history and anthropology are distinct disciplines. For one thing, historians focus on past events, and their investigation of values, motivations, and behavior is directed toward the explanation of why things occurred the way they did in one particular sequence of events. Anthropology seeks to generalize from such historical explanations. It is not enough to say that history is more of an art, while anthropology is more of a science, or that anthropologists use history more than historians use anthropology. Indeed it is difficult to distinguish history from anthropology in many respects, except to point out the historian's retrospective approach to past events, in contrast to the cultural anthropologist's emphasis upon understanding contemporary events as they are happening.

Alfred Louis Kroeber
(1876–1960)
was for many years considered the dean of American anthropology. His early work centered on the study of American Indians. Kroeber was also interested in the process of culture change, and relied heavily upon history to support his studies of the growth of civilization. In Configurations of Culture Growth *(1944) he compared six major civilizations of the world through historical records in an attempt to find a regular pattern of change. He was inclined to see history and anthropology as much more closely related disciplines than many of his colleagues, as reflected in* An Anthropologist Looks at History, *published after his death.*

Psychology

A major difference between a psychological approach to the study of human behavior and an anthropological approach is that the psychologist tends to take his own culture as a starting point, whereas ideally the anthropologist does not. Psychology, moreover, is generally limited to the study of the mind, and thus a psychological approach does not produce a complete case study comparable to the ethnography produced by the cultural anthropologist. Anthropology seeks to document the entire range of human behavior, and that is the first step in attempting to understand it on a cross-cultural level, rather than on the level of a single culture.

Marston Bates, the noted biologist, describes this well in his book *Gluttons and Libertines:*

> It is a commonplace comment on Freudian psychology that its emphasis on sex comes from its basis in western culture where sex is scarce—or at least strictly controlled—while food is reasonably abundant and generally available. The British anthropologist Audrey Richards, in rebellion against this preoccupation, set out some years ago to study human relations in an African tribe where sex was abundant and food restricted. In these circumstances she found, as expected, that food dominated the subconscious as well as the conscious life of the people.[2]

Let me illustrate this difference between psychology and anthropology further with an example from my own experience. Recently I was asked to serve as a consultant to the child psychology division of the medical school at the university where I teach. A case had been referred to them, and the director of this particular program thought it would be of interest to see whether there were other cultures in which the behavior under question was acceptable. The case concerned a foster mother who was discovered to be practicing strict toilet training upon an infant placed in her care. The infant was only a few weeks old, and training at such an early age is certainly an unacceptable practice in American culture. As the story unfolded, it became apparent that the woman took good care of the child, showed it warmth and affection, and in all other ways was an ideal foster parent. However, the fact that she had trained the infant to defecate while she held it over newspaper alarmed the officials assigned to the case.

I was asked, as consulting anthropologist, to cite references to early toilet training in other cultures. Apparently the medical personnel in charge of the program thought that if an anthropologist could show that such a pattern was practiced elsewhere, it would make it more acceptable to the local officials. I was able to cite a few examples of early training, although none so early as the case under consideration. But the main thrust of my presentation to the group called together to hear the case was that in order to understand the practices of the mother, we had to know something about her own culture and her background. If in fact this was a common practice within the subculture of American society in which she was raised, and if it

2. Marston Bates, *Gluttons and Libertines.* New York: Vintage Books, 1967, pp. 20–21.

Toilet-training practices vary greatly from one culture to another, as this scene from a European nursery school indicates. (Fred Mayer, Woodfin Camp)

was successful (that is, if people raised this way turned out to be healthy, normal individuals in American society), then we should not question its validity. I was even able to get the case worker to admit that the mother herself had been trained this way, and that several other members of her family had also been raised with similar practices.

The difference between psychology and anthropology comes through strongly in this example. My approach as a cultural anthropologist was to see if what was considered deviant in our own middle-class American culture was in fact acceptable in another cultural setting. However, I am sorry to say that I was overruled by the psychologists (and Freudian psychiatrists). Their main concern was whether the child was being raised according to the norm in American society, and they took that norm to be the way they, as white, middle-class Americans, were raised. Deviation from that norm was strictly forbidden, no matter whether it might be perfectly acceptable and common practice in another culture, or in another American subculture. They spoke of the "harm" that would come to the child, as if the absence of a strict middle-class upbringing were the kiss of death. There was discussion among the Freudians in the room about the problem of the child mixing up his sexual identity, and the failure of the mother to relate to anything but an "empty" baby. But no sense of relativity was evidenced; no mention was made of other deviant practices in other cultures, which ultimately produced healthy, normal adults.

Sociology

Perhaps the most difficult distinction to make between disciplines in the social sciences is between cultural anthropology and sociology. One important difference is that sociology is concerned more with the study of our own society, while anthropology is a comparative discipline which focuses on all societies at all times. Sociology is primarily interested in the present; anthropology deals just as much with the past. These distinctions, however, are growing less valid every day, as anthropologists begin to adopt sociological methods and sociologists adopt the comparative approach of anthropology.

Another way of looking at the difference between the two disciplines is to note that sociology tends to be more quantitative, while anthropology tends to be more qualitative. What this means is that sociology generalizes from broad surveys of large numbers of people. The anthropologist relies upon a close and intimate knowledge of just a few members of the total group to form his impressions, and while they might not be valid for the society as a whole (i.e., quantitative), they are certainly valid in greater depth for the small sample studied (i.e., qualitative). The anthropologist will spend weeks tracing a lead to the answer to a particular question, mainly because of his intense personal involvement in his study. The sociologist, on the other hand, cannot afford to become so deeply involved if he is to survey a larger sample of the society. This is not to condemn either discipline, but rather to point out a basic difference between them. Perhaps it is best illustrated by the comment of one anthropologist, who, in poking fun at the expensive studies of inner-city social problems conducted at a great social distance, described a sociologist as someone who spends $50,000 to find a whorehouse. (One wonders if after all this expense, the sociologist might not be led into the parlor only to find an anthropologist playing the piano.)

Thus probably the major difference between anthropology and sociology lies in the methods used in each discipline. Anthropology uses the intensive method of study, while sociology is more inclined to employ a survey approach, less intensive but more inclusive. Since the method of cultural anthropology is the subject of a later chapter, we will not discuss it here, except to illustrate this difference. Each approach has its limitations. An anthropologist using the intensive method obviously cannot study an entire city of 100,000 people in a single year, or even in a lifetime. A sociologist using house-to-house surveys, questionnaires, and random sampling techniques, and summarizing the results in statistical tables, can indeed study an entire city in a relatively short period of time, but the information he collects will not be nearly as deep as that of the anthropologist.

The late sociologist Howard Becker, who by the way was a champion of the intensive method of anthropology (and somewhat of a maverick in the field of sociology), used to tell a story about a discussion he had with a colleague on the sociology faculty who was dead set against anthropology and its intensive approach to community studies. Becker's colleague was berating him for having spent a year living in a small community, studying it in depth. The colleague pointed out that he, using the sociological approach, could have sent in a team of investigators armed with questionnaires and covered the entire village in but a few weeks, saving Becker valuable time, energy and money. "But how would you know what questions to ask?" Becker inquired. "That's easy," answered the colleague, "we'd simply ask an anthropologist."

Holism: The Trademark of Anthropology

We conclude this chapter on the definition and scope of anthropology by pointing out again that anthropology, as distinct from all other social sciences, is an integrated approach including the study of the physical nature of the human species, our past, our unique capabilities as well as our limitations, and the tremendous variety as well as the startling similarities across cultural boundaries. The anthropological approach is sometimes called *holistic,* because it integrates so many different areas of concern. It is not just the study of economic behavior, or the structural relations between social groups. It is the attempt to understand all of human behavior in all contexts, in all places, and at all times. And it does this by drawing from many different disciplines. The anthropologist is a person who brings to his study a wide background from many different fields. Biology and physiology are frequently required for graduate students in physical anthropology; geology, geography, ancient history, and sometimes even architecture are necessities for the archeologist; and cultural anthropologists have come from all walks of life. To study peasant society cross-culturally we have to know something about agriculture; to study personality cross-culturally we must have a background in psychology; and so on for every possible area of concentration within cultural anthropology.

Let me point this up by using an example. Suppose we want to make a comparison of the way in which children learn their culture in two different groups. Because the primary topic of concern is culture, we would logically assume that cultural anthropology would be the place to start. But when we look deeper, we find that the cultural anthropologist must rely upon training in any one of a number of different fields to insure the success of such a study. For example, he must know something about psychology, to understand the processes of the formation of personality and character in the early years of infancy. He must have expertise in at least some areas of elementary education to comprehend the process of training in the early years. It would help if he had some knowledge about the physical nature of the infant, which he could obtain through studies in physical anthropology, to enable him to tell what the physical process of child training was all about. Linguistics could give him a better understanding of the ways in which a child learns a language and the kinds of patterns that are instilled upon the infant's brain at that early age. And in addition to all of these outside factors, he must be knowledgable in the culture of each group, to understand the attitudes of parents toward children in the societies (e.g., do they favor males over females? do they expect males to accept different roles than females at an early age? do parents treat their children with much care and personal attention or do they leave them relatively unattended?)

As this example illustrates, holism in anthropology is the attempt to get the whole picture, to put it all together and to apply knowledge from many different spheres to the understanding of any aspect of behavior. It is this holistic approach, more than anything else, that distinguishes anthropology from other social sciences. And it is this holistic approach that makes an anthropological study so difficult to carry out and at the same time so rewarding when it all fits together.

Summary

Cultural anthropology is one of four branches of the discipline. *Physical anthropology* deals with the evolution of the human species, the relationship between humans and other primate species, and the variety of human forms in the world today. From the physical anthropologist we learn of the capabilities for bearing culture that distinguish humans from all other animals. *Archeology* is the branch that takes up where physical anthropology leaves off, reconstructing the evolution of culture (rather than the evolution of the capacity for culture). The archeologist is necessarily limited by the kinds of information that remain thousands of years after the people have lived, and much of what archeology can tell us about the past is based upon inference from societies we can observe in the present. *Anthropological linguistics* is a third field within anthropology that treats the relationship between language and culture, and the functions of language and communication for human social behavior. *Cultural anthropology,* the subject of this book, is the study of human societies, both present and past. It seeks to describe the wide variety of cultural forms throughout the world, and to compare and analyze them, with the ultimate goal of understanding human behavior.

Anthropology is related to other social sciences in that all share a common interest in understanding human behavior. It differs, however, in that it is a broader approach, whereas geography concentrates primarily upon the relationship of people to the land, economics focuses upon economic behavior, political science upon political behavior, etc. This multifaceted approach, called *holism,* is the trademark of anthropology. Holism is the ability to consider a wide variety of viewpoints in understanding human behavior—for example, the physical anthropologist's knowledge of the human capacity for culture, the archeologist's information about past examples of human behavior, the anthropological linguist's assumptions about the role of language and communication in social relations, and the cultural anthropologist's understanding about the variety of culturally accepted behavior in the world today. All of these approaches contribute to the breadth of anthropology as a discipline.

Glossary

adaptation The result of a group of animals or plants being molded by the environmental forces or pressures (climate, altitude, etc.) in a specific region.

anthropological genetics The area of physical anthropology that studies the contemporary and historical variations among human populations. The investigation of human variation focuses upon the way groups are related to the environmental pressures (climate, altitude, etc.) in specific regions.

anthropological linguistics The sub-discipline of anthropology that is concerned with the relationship between language and cultural behavior. This perspective focuses upon language as a part of our social world.

anthropology The discipline that utilizes the holistic approach to investigate all aspects of human behavior, in all places and at all times.

archeological site Any location that demonstrates disturbance from human activity or that provides material and physical evidence of human activity.

archeology The sub-discipline of anthropology whose aim is the reconstruction of the origin, spread and evolution of culture. This sub-discipline is sometimes called *prehistory* because it is concerned primarily with the period of human existence prior to written records or historical accounts.

cultural anthropology The sub-discipline of anthropology that is based upon a comparative approach to the study of existing peoples. Its aim is to understand the diversity of human behavior, and ultimately to develop a science of human behavior, through the comparison of different peoples throughout the world.

ethnography A branch of cultural anthropology that is concerned with the description of a single culture.

ethnology A branch of cultural anthropology that is concerned with the comparative study of culture and the investigation of theoretical problems using information about different groups.

evolution The natural process in which forces from the environment (climate, altitude, etc.) mold the characteristics of groups of plants and animals.

fossil man The area of physical anthropology that studies the past forms of pre-human and early human species.

holistic approach The approach utilized in anthropology that integrates a wide variety of disciplines in the study of human behavior.

lactase deficiency A physiological condition found in much of the world in which a large proportion of the adult population is unable to digest milk properly. The inability to produce the enzyme lactase is associated with the cultural preference to abstain from the consumption of raw milk.

physical anthropology The sub-discipline of anthropology concerned with the study of human evolution and human variation.

primate The order in the Linnaean taxonomy that includes monkeys, apes and humans.

primatology The area of physical anthropology that investigates the physiological and behavioral similarities and differences among the various primate species—monkeys, apes and humans.

sickle cell anemia The hereditary disease that affects the red blood cells, and which originated in areas of the world where there is a high incidence of malaria.

sickle cell trait A hereditary condition in which an individual possesses half normal red blood cells and half sickle-shaped red blood cells. Such an individual is usually resistant to the disease malaria.

sociolinguistics A branch of anthropological linguistics that studies the way that people use language or communicate in different situations (e.g. lecturing to a class, speaking to one's parents, talking to friends).

Questions for Discussion

1 Medical science is now able to keep people alive who suffer from sickle cell anemia. Their children will definitely have sickle cell *trait*, and will have a greater chance of being born with sickle cell *anemia* themselves. What are the implications of this for future generations? Is a program of genetic counseling prior to marriage or reproduction desirable in such cases?

2 Suppose your town were suddenly struck by a major catastrophe that wiped out the entire population and left only the physical remains, such as buildings, monuments and cars. What inferences would future archeologists be likely to draw from these remains a thousand years from now? What aspects of your life would go undiscovered because no lasting records survived? What does this tell us about today's archeological reconstruction of the past?

3 If language is inextricably connected with culture, can we ever achieve an international language (such as Esperanto) as long as there are cultural differences in the world? What would be the limitations upon communicating in such a language? What benefits would it have?

Suggestions for Additional Reading

Physical anthropology

Pfeiffer, John E.
1972 The Emergence of Man. Second Edition. New York: Harper & Row.

An up-to-date and authoritative exposition of human evolution as shown by the fossil record and studies of living primates and contemporary human populations.

Poirier, Frank E.
1974 In Search of Ourselves. An Introduction to Physical Anthropology. Minneapolis: Burgess Publishing Company.

A more complete basic introduction to contemporary physical anthropology.

Archeology

Deetz, James
1967 Invitation to Archeology. Garden City, N.Y.: The Natural History Press.

A brief and very readable book covering archeology in much less detail than a more complete textbook such as the one mentioned below. Recommended more for the curious reader than the serious student of archeology.

Hole, Frank, and Robert F. Heizer
1973 An Introduction to Prehistoric Archeology. Third Edition. New York: Holt, Rinehart and Winston.

A thorough textbook surveying the field of prehistory, including the types of data archeologists depend upon, the methods of acquiring data, and the use of data in reconstructing the past.

Anthropological linguistics

Carroll, John B.
1964 Language and Thought. Englewood Cliffs, N.J.: Prentice-Hall.

A short analysis of language as it functions in a cultural context. Although it leans toward a psychological approach to the study of language, this book is useful in understanding some of the basic questions of anthropological linguistics as well.

Hymes, Dell (editor)
1964 Language in Culture and Society. New York: Harper & Row.

A collection of articles on various topics in anthropological linguistics, including a thorough survey of both the classical approach to the study of language, and more modern methods and research problems.

Cultural anthropology

Downs, James F.
1971 Cultures in Crisis. Beverly Hills: Glencoe Press.

A short, entertaining and extremely well-written book, although necessarily superficial because of its short length. Especially valuable is the author's illustration of how the basic principles of cultural anthropology can help us in solving some of the major "crisis areas" of our society in modern times.

Keesing, Roger M., and Felix M. Keesing
1971 New Perspectives in Cultural Anthropology. New York: Holt, Rinehart and Winston.

One of many cultural anthropology textbooks, this volume is thorough and well-written, and benefits from the use of lengthy ethnographic examples to illustrate the major points raised in the text.

General anthropology

Hoebel, E. Adamson
1972 Anthropology: The Study of Man. Fourth Edition. New York: McGraw-Hill.

Long a standard text in anthropology, this book covers all of the subdisciplines of the field.

Wolf, Eric R.
1974 Anthropology. New York: W. W. Norton

Now available in a reprinted paperback edition, this is a short but insightful look into the growth of anthropology as a discipline and as a concept.

Practical information on anthropology as a career

Bernard, H. Russell, and Willis E. Sibley
1975 Anthropology and Jobs: A Guide for Undergraduates. Washington, D.C.: American Anthropological Association.

A survey of career opportunities outside college teaching open to those with degrees in anthropology.

Frantz, Charles
1972 The Student Anthropologist's Handbook. Cambridge, Mass.: Schenkman Publishing Co.

Fried, Morton H.
1972 The Study of Anthropology. New York: T. Y. Crowell.

Two practical guides to some of the most common questions concerning the study and practice of anthropology.

The Concept of Culture

Chapter Two

Since the subject of this book is cultural anthropology, we ought to have a clear idea of what we mean by "culture" at the outset. It is a term everyone uses quite freely, but with only a vague sense of agreement on its meaning. Even social scientists don't always agree on the definition of culture; two anthropologists once collected more than 160 meanings of the term! Sometimes we think of culture as referring to the life style of the upper class. In order to "have culture," one must attend the opera, art museums, and other such events. Other times we might call a person "uncultured," meaning uncouth or rude, although technically, as anthropologists use the word, there is no such thing as an uncultured person since every individual participates in some cultural tradition. And the list of definitions goes on and on. Yet obviously there must be some commonly accepted meaning if cultural anthropologists are to be able to work together and compare their knowledge and understanding of human behavior.

Definition of Culture

Culture is that aspect of our existence that makes us similar to some other people, yet different from the majority of the people in the world. We are all basically the same physically, in that we are members of the same species. And we are all different in that each of us has an individual personality that cannot be duplicated. It is culture that binds us together into a group sharing a certain degree of similarity, overcoming the individual differences among us yet setting us apart from other groups. Thus when we speak of culture we mean a way

The true test of civilization is
not the census, nor the size of cities,
nor the crops,—no, but the kind of man
the country turns out.
RALPH WALDO EMERSON *Civilization*

of life common to a group of people, a collection of beliefs and attitudes, shared understandings and patterns of behavior that allow those people to live together in relative harmony, but set them apart from other peoples. Culture is what makes us "Americans" rather than Germans, Chinese or Bantu.

Perhaps the best definition of culture, as it is used in anthropology, is still the one proposed by Edward B. Tylor more than 100 years ago in his book *Primitive Culture.* Tylor was a major figure in anthropology in the nineteenth century, and his genius and contribution to the field are evident in the fact that his definition of the main subject of anthropology has withstood the test of time. Tylor defined culture as *"that complex whole which includes knowledge, belief, art, morals, law, customs, and any other capabilities and habits acquired by man as a member of society."*

That complex whole . . .

Let us take a closer look at this definition to see what some of its implications are. First of all, culture is "that complex whole." It is not just a series of unrelated things that happen to have been picked up and thrown together by a group of people as they wandered around the earth. It is a whole, an integrated unit. The parts of any culture fit together—not just the physical aspects such as tools, houses and clothing, but the nonmaterial aspects of culture such as the patterns of behavior followed by the members of the group. As Tylor's definition indicates, culture includes those intangibles such as knowledge, belief, art, morals, law, customs and other capabilities and habits. They form a context for each other. Law and morals and customs must be based upon knowledge and belief, and must be reflected in the way people act toward one another.

. . . acquired by man . . .

Secondly, Tylor's definition tells us that culture is "acquired by man." This has several implications, among them that culture is not inherited or instinctive, and also that culture is unique to the human species. Many anthropologists no longer believe that culture is a uniquely human characteristic, and we will discuss this problem in more detail in the following section. But the fact that culture is *acquired* is important for understanding why people behave the way they do. A person learns a culture from the members of his or her group. If you had been born and raised in Japan, you would speak fluent Japanese and feel perfectly comfortable following Japanese customs and traditions. There is no biological basis for one culture as opposed to another, just as there is no relationship between a person's racial characteristics and his or her culture.

Alfred Kroeber provided an interesting example to illustrate this distinction between the inborn character of most nonhuman behavior and the learned cultural behavior of human beings. Suppose we hatch some ant eggs on a deserted island. The resulting ant colony will be an exact reproduction of the previous generation of ants, including their social behavior. Ants have a set of rules they follow in acting together as a group, but these rules are not learned as a result of interaction with other ants of the previous generation. They are instinctive and part of the heredity of the ants in each new generation. That is why we can be sure that the newly hatched ants will be and act exactly like their parents' generation, even though they will never see any members of that generation.

Suppose we do the same with a group of infants from our own society (pretending for the sake of argument that it were possible). Certainly we would not expect the same results—a generation of people just like their parents. Rather, the result would be a horde of people essentially without culture. If they were somehow able to survive (which would also be impossible), they might develop their own culture, different from any other way of life on earth. They would not speak a language that was intelligible to anyone else, nor would they dress or eat or do anything else in a way that reflected their parents' culture. Although born of American parents, there is no way that

Edward Burnett Tylor
(1832–1917)
is frequently called the father of modern anthropology. In 1865 he published Researches into the Early History of Mankind, *establishing himself as a major figure in the field of anthropology and a proponent of the theory of cultural evolution. Tylor was particularly concerned with refuting the ideas of a group of biblical scholars known as the "degenerationists," who argued that humans were created in God's image—the most perfect form—and that contemporary "savages" must have degenerated from an earlier higher level. He countered this belief with the argument that humans were continually improving and progressing, and that contemporary nonwestern peoples simply had not changed as rapidly nor in the same direction.*

such individuals could acquire American culture without being taught. Only in science fiction can test-tube babies be programmed for a specific way of life before they are born.

. . . as a member of society.

A third implication of Tylor's definition is that culture is shared and that learning takes place within the confines of a group. Culture is a group phenomenon, not an individual one; it pertains to societies, or people who share a way of life. Of course, ants and bees are organized into what we call societies, as are some higher primates, including baboons and chimpanzees. But we distinguish between the social life of insects, which is instinctive, and the social life of human beings, which is learned or acquired. In the case of nonhuman primates the distinction is less clear, as we shall see in the following section.

Social behavior such as this communal dining scene among the Ancas tribesmen indicates how an individual acquires culture as a member of a group. (Cornell Capa, Magnum)

Do Other Species Have Culture?

Recently anthropologists have begun to question whether culture is a uniquely human phenomenon, or whether some nonhuman behavior might also be considered cultural. We know that culture has a biological basis. The *opposable thumb,* found in other primates as well as in the human species, enables us to make and use tools and gives us an advantage in grasping and manipulating many objects. *Bipedal locomotion*—walking on two feet instead of four—and *erect posture* have freed the arms and hands for other uses. In the course of human evolution, we have become more dependent upon our *sense of sight,* at the expense of other senses, particularly hearing and smell. The human species is characterized by *fewer offspring* and a *prolonged childhood,* leaving the infant relatively defenseless. Compare a five-year-old child to a five-year-old horse, for example, which is fully mature and able to take care of itself. These factors and many other results of evolution have led to culture taking over our adaptation to the environment, making up for our physical weakness. We make up for having lost our strength, claws, long teeth and other defenses by using tools, communicating with language, and cooperating with one another. But these aspects of human life can also be found in nonhuman primate behavior.

We used to think that tool using was the dividing line between human beings and other animals. Lately, however, we have discovered that this is not the case. Chimpanzees are capable not only of using tools, but of actually manufacturing tools themselves, a significant advance over simply picking up a convenient object and using it. For example, chimps have been observed stripping the leaves and twigs off a branch, then inserting it into a termite nest. When the termites bite at the stick, the chimp removes it and eats them off the end—not unlike our use of a fork!

The standard yawn-threat gesture of a baboon. (Toni Angermayer, Photo Researchers)

For some time we assumed that while human beings learned their culture, other animals could not be taught such behavior, or even if they could learn, they would not teach one another in the way that people do. This too has proven to be untrue. A group of Japanese macaques (a type of monkey) being studied at the Kyoto University Monkey Center in Japan were given sweet potatoes by scientists who wanted to attract them to the shore of an island. One day a young female began to wash her sweet potato to get rid of the sand. This

The famous chimpanzee, Washoe, has been trained to use sign language to communicate. Here Washoe and her trainer give the sign for "drink." (Courtesy of R. A. and B. T. Gardner)

practice soon spread throughout the group, that is, it became *learned* behavior, not from human beings but from other monkeys. Now almost all members of that monkey group wash their sweet potatoes, but other macaques who have not come into contact with this group do not; thus we have a "cultural" difference on a nonhuman level.

Having discarded tool use and invention and the learning and sharing of behavior as ways of distinguishing primate behavior from human behavior, we still held onto the last distinguishing feature—language. But even the use of language can no longer separate human cultural behavior from nonhuman primate behavior. Attempts to teach apes to *speak* have failed because they are not equipped with the proper vocal apparatus. But teaching them *language* has been highly successful, if we are willing to accept a broader context than simply the spoken word, and consider symbolic forms of communication as language. Two psychologists, R. Allen Gardner and Beatrice T. Gardner, trained a chimpanzee named Washoe to use Standard American Sign Language, the same language used by deaf people. In this language communication is made by using symbolic gestures, and not by spelling out words with individual letters. By the time she was five years old, Washoe had a vocabulary of 130 signs. Moreover, she could put them together in new ways that had not been taught her originally, that is, she could *create* language and not just mimic it. She creates her own sentences that have real meaning, and this has enabled significant two-way communication, not just a single-direction command and response.

Of course, there are limitations to the culture of nonhuman primates. As far as we know, no ape has developed social institutions such as religion, law, ethics, or economics. While some chimps may be able to learn sign language, this form of language is limited in its ability to communicate abstraction, while with a spoken language we can communicate our entire culture to anyone else who shares an understanding of that language. Perhaps the most important thing we have learned from studies of nonhuman primates is that the line dividing us from them is not as clear as we used to think. As Ralph Linton noted almost four decades ago in his classic book *The Study of Man,*

> The ability of human beings to learn, to communicate with each other, and to transmit learned behavior from generation to generation . . . and their possession of a social as well as a biological heredity . . . are features which link man to the other mammals instead of distinguishing him from them. The differences between men and animals in all these respects are enormous, but they seem to be differences in quantity rather than in quality. . . . In each of these things, the human condition is such as might logically be expected to result from the orderly working-out of tendencies already present at the sub-human level.[1]

Cultural Universals

So far we have been dealing with qualitative differences between human beings and other primates, showing how human social behavior is really different. Another way of comprehending the fundamental difference between people and apes is in the quantitative separation between them—the sheer amount of cultural behavior practiced by human beings as opposed to the relatively small proportion found among other primates. Anthropologist George Peter Murdock has compiled a list of what he calls *cultural universals,* basic solutions to the problems of living that are found in one form or another in all cultures. This list gives us an intuitive feeling for the humanness of our species by pointing out how many different kinds of behavior

1. Ralph Linton, *The Study of Man.* New York: Appleton-Century-Crofts, 1936, pp. 78–79.

are shared by all human beings no matter where they come from. We may be able to define some nonhuman behavior as "cultural," but this does not mean that other animals have a culture in the same sense that we do, as this list illustrates. In reading over some of these universals, presented below, think about their form in your own culture, and then try to imagine them in any form among chimps or baboons or other nonhuman species.[2]

age grading
athletics
bodily adornment
calendar
cleanliness training
community organization
cooking
cooperative labor
cosmology
courtship
dancing
decorative art
divination
division of labor
dream interpretation
education
eschatology
ethics
ethnobotany
etiquette
faith healing
family
feasting
fire making
folklore
food taboos
funeral rites
games
gestures
gift giving
government
greetings
hair styles
hospitality
housing
hygiene
incest taboos
inheritance rules
joking
kin groups
kin terminology
language
law
luck superstitions
magic
marriage
mealtimes
medicine
modesty
mourning
music
mythology
numerals
obstetrics
penal sanctions
personal names
population policy
postnatal care
pregnancy usages
property rights
propitiation of supernatural beings
puberty customs
religious ritual
residence rules
sexual restrictions
soul concepts
status differentiation
surgery
tool making
trade
visiting
weaning
weather control

Some of these cultural universals can also be found among nonhuman primates. Baboons, for example, have a form of age grading, community organization, courtship (in a technical sense), division of labor, education (if the term is interpreted loosely), games, gestures, sexual restrictions correlated with status differentiation, tool making to a limited degree, and so forth. Chimps have even been taught a form of language. But the sheer quantity and elaboration of human culture outweighs all of these similarities. It is hard to imagine a baboon troop in a state of mourning over a deceased member. It is even harder to imagine talking to a chimp (in sign language, of course) about his philosophy of death or immortality. Apes do not have a

2. George Peter Murdock, "The Common Denominator of Cultures." In Ralph Linton (ed.), *The Science of Man in the World of Crisis.* New York: Columbia University Press, 1945, p. 123.

mythology or a folklore, they do not recognize a system of law other than the natural "law of the jungle," and it would be impossible to convey to them the meaning of an institution like marriage.

Cultural Variation

Although the basic types of cultural behavior are universal, in most cases they differ in form from one culture to another. It is much the same as with language, which we discussed in the first chapter—the potential for variation in culture is enormous, and the only limitations are that a particular way of doing things get the job done relatively efficiently and that it fit in with the rest of culture. Take bodily adornment, for example. In the United States we have many ways of altering the natural appearance of the human body. On a relatively simple level, some people do things such as comb their hair, pierce their ears, or polish their nails. Others have parts of their body designed with tattoos, a permanent mutilation of the body following a prescribed pattern of adornment unique to our culture. (Tattoos in

Though the actual designs are unique, the practice of bodily adornment is a cultural universal. (Leo Vjals, Frederic Lewis; Marc and Evelyne Bernheim, Woodfin Camp)

What is attractive in one culture may be abhorrent to another. Here a native of the New Hebrides Islands in the South Pacific displays various forms of adornment. (Kal Muller, Woodfin Camp)

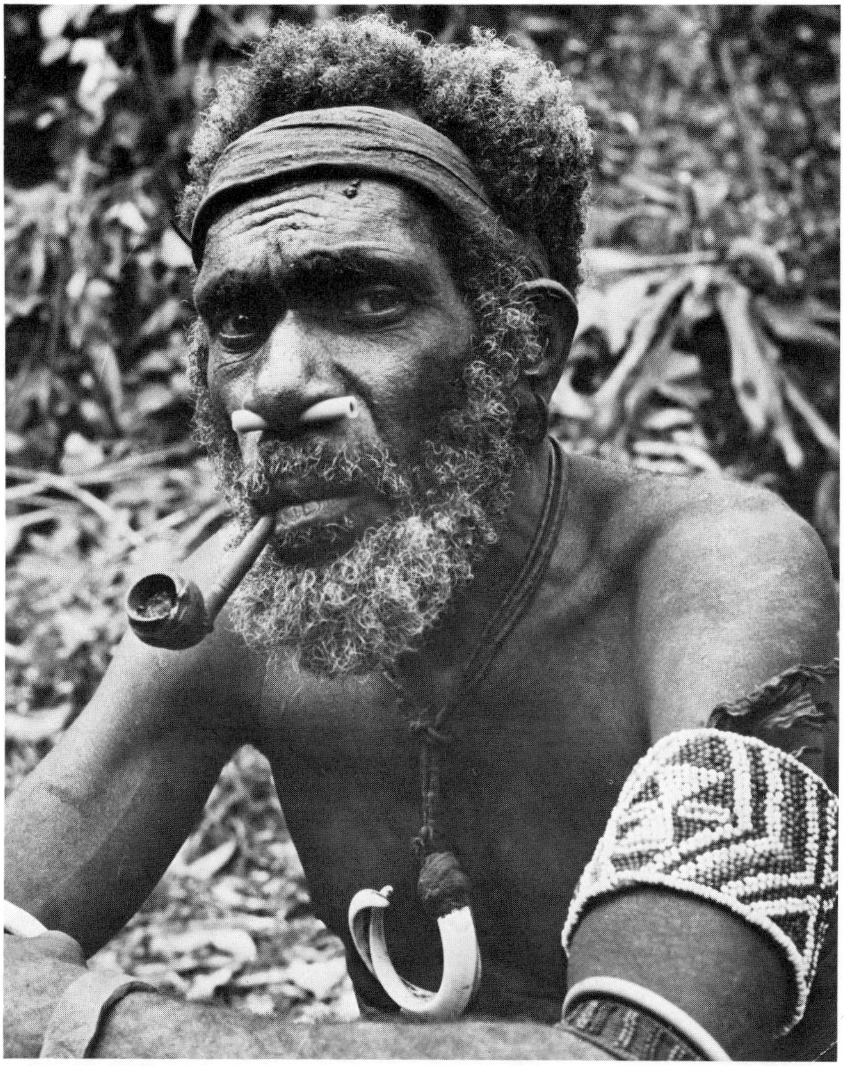

other cultures are quite different from ours.) Still others have cosmetic surgery such as nose jobs, hair transplants, and silicone injections to alter their natural appearance. Young people frequently strive to look older, men growing facial hair or women styling their hair in a particular fashion, while older people strive to look younger, by having a face lift, wearing trendy clothes or altering the color of their hair.

In other cultures, the ways in which bodily adornment is practiced are quite different from our own. Some of the better known examples, such as the large extended lower lip of the Ubangi women, or a bone inserted in a pierced nose, are perhaps bizarre instances of this practice among human societies. But in every culture we do find some kind of bodily adornment. Among some South American Indian tribes the shape of the head is altered artificially by tying boards firmly against the head of an infant to exert pressure while the skull is still quite malleable. Among the Dugum Dani, a highland New Guinea tribe in the western Pacific, women and particularly young girls will have a finger amputated as a part of the funeral service for a close relative, in order that they may be reminded of that person for the rest of their lives. This form of bodily alteration is not necessarily decorative, but serves another purpose in the religious and family life of the people. It is not likely that a woman will forget the individual for whom she sacrificed a finger!

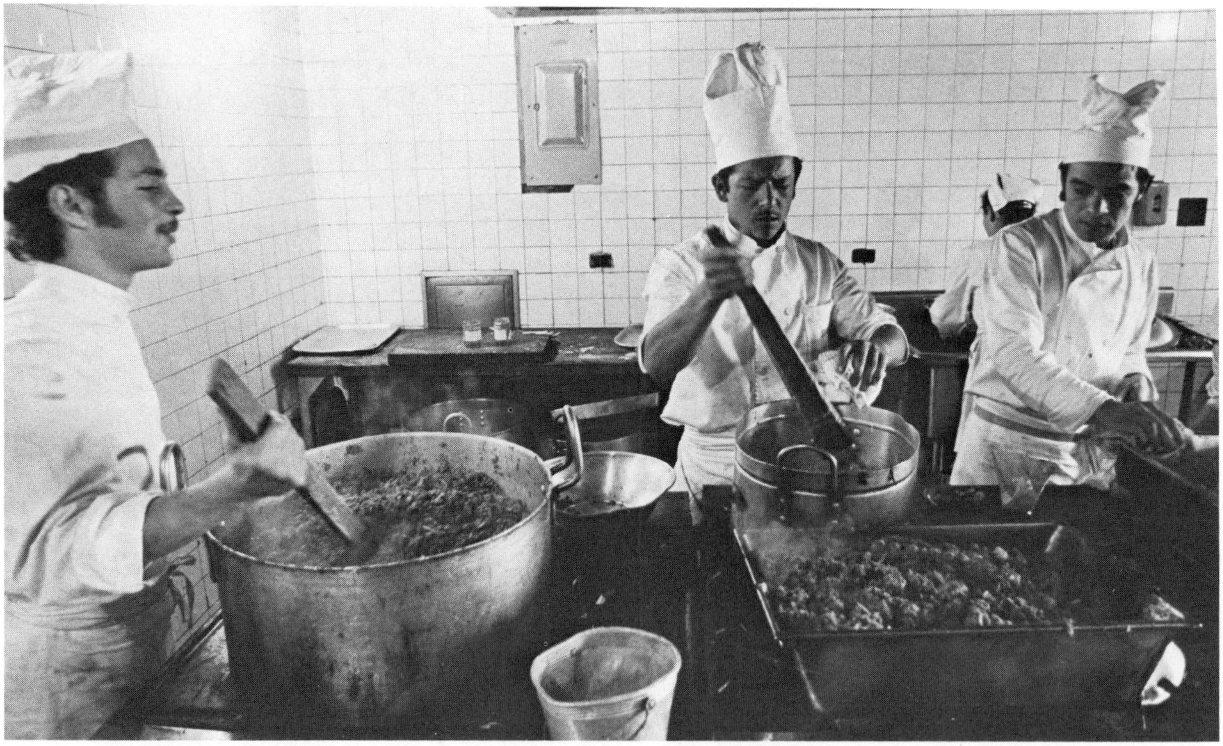

Another obvious example of cultural variety can be found in cooking practices. Different cultures not only have tastes for different foods, but they have different methods of preparing those foods. Many Japanese eat raw fish, as do Eskimos, but relatively few Americans indulge in this practice. A typical curry dish from India can burn the mouth of an American who is not used to this kind of spicy food so that he won't be able to taste another meal for weeks afterward. Mexican chili peppers likewise can send an uninformed diner scurrying for the ice water. England, on the other hand, is noted for its bland cuisine, Germany for its heavy foods and reliance upon potatoes and sausages, France for its delicate tastes and sauces. The difference in cooking practices is only partly a question of the food products used; it also centers on the inherent differences in behavior within the universal category of cooking. We can see a similar variety in almost every one of the items on the list of universals, each case indicating the wide range of behavior acceptable under different circumstances

Food preferences are one of the most variable aspects of culture. (United Nations; Jerry Frank, DPI)

in one culture or another. If we avoid looking upon some of the more bizarre practices with abhorrence and disgust, then the study of cultural variation throughout the world can be a fascinating and exciting activity.

The Paradoxes of Culture

The study of variation brings out one of several paradoxes built into the concept of culture: *although culture is universal, each local or regional manifestation is unique.* Every group of people has a culture and shares a way of life, yet in each region of the world different sets of experiences and particular ecological and historical factors impinge upon the culture, resulting in regional variation. The universals of culture provide a framework within which this variety occurs.

A second paradox of culture is that while it is stable and predictable for the people who share it and use it as a basis for organizing their lives, it is at the same time undergoing constant and continuous change. If we look at the process by which children are taught the culture of their parents, we can see this paradox at work. As children learn their culture, they provide stability and continuity over time, and they are able to carry on the traditions of previous generations. This presents us with a static view of culture. However, the process of training a child is never complete, so that no one generation is a mirror image of the previous one. If each succeeding generation is different from the preceding one, the result will obviously be change in the culture over time. This presents an apparent contradiction in the concept of culture, for it is at the same time both static and dynamic, preserving tradition while having a built-in mechanism for continuous change. We can see this in our own lives, as stability and change operate together, sometimes creating problems as they come into conflict. For example, in terms of technology our culture is extremely dynamic. Technological change is not only common in America today, it is expected. We are urged to buy certain products because they are "new," "improved," and different from what they were in the past. Our culture places heavy emphasis upon change in the technological realm. But other aspects of our culture have not kept pace with our technology, and this has led to disastrous results. Our inability to limit our use of energy and to foresee the possible crisis of pollution and depletion of resources has led to the present situation where our cities are being smothered and our waterways are unable to support life. This is an example of how we are relatively static in terms of the changes in our values and attitudes about our way of life, and as a result we fall behind the rapid advances in our technology.

A third paradox is found in the fact that we are to a large extent unconscious of our culture, and unaware of many aspects of it. This is in part due to the way in which we learn our culture. We internalize our way of life to the point where it becomes so "natural" that we do not pay attention to what we do. We become unconscious of the rules that govern our behavior because we are so used to following the patterns prescribed for us. No individual ever knows his entire culture, for each is acquainted with only a portion, depending upon his position in society. There are many social positions that are mutually exclusive; that is, if we occupy one position we are automatically excluded from another. For example, if a person occupies the role of father he is automatically excluded from the role of mother. A person in the upper class cannot share in the culture of the lower class, and vice versa. Even though the upper and lower classes are both a part of American culture, they have separate cultural contents of their own, and no one can know what it is like to be in both at the same time. This same kind of cultural isolation is true for all kinds of specialized knowledge, such as occupational specialization. Clergy, politicians, police officers, students and farmers all share in American culture, yet all have their own unique aspects of it. The more complex the social organization—the more different kinds of people there are in a society—the smaller proportion of the total culture any one individual can possibly know. Thus both because of the way we learn our culture and because of the nature of culture itself, we are both unconscious of and excluded from much of it.

Socialization: Learning the Culture

Social behavior is based upon mutual expectation. We are able to operate in our normal daily routine because we have complete confidence that other people will behave in a predictable and orderly fashion, responding to the same cues in much the same way that we do. If this were not so, we could not have the kind of society that we do. Cultural anthropologists are interested in how people learn the proper behavior in each social setting, and the appropriate cues to trigger that behavior. We want to know how people learn the values that they share as members of the same group. And we try to show how all of what we learn and how we learn it fits together into a pattern, or what we call a configuration.

Socialization is the term we use to describe the process of learning to be a member of a society, a process that is slightly different in every society. Obviously groups of people vary in terms of how they teach their new members to act in acceptable ways. It is these differences and similarities in the process of teaching and learning the culture that are of interest to the anthropologist. Socialization includes the teaching and learning of all aspects of culture. It is not limited to physical considerations such as table manners or driving a car, but includes values, morals, attitudes, suspicions, literally everything, mental as well as physical. Furthermore, socialization is never really complete, because no individual is an exact social replica of his or her parents, any more than an individual can be an exact physical replica of his or her parents. Each succeeding generation differs

Left: an American mother with her three-week-old infant (front) and two-year-old boy (back). Right: A Cree Indian mother with her child tied to her back. (Annan Photo Features)

slightly from the preceding one, indicating that the socialization process is imperfect at best.

The primary interest of anthropologists is in the aspects of personality shared with all other members of a society, rather than in the deviant nature that makes every person a unique individual. This assumes that there is some pattern or regularity in the way children of a culture are brought up, and in the things they learn. The process of learning the culture begins in infancy and continues throughout life, as a person forms a general outlook toward life and then continues to adapt that outlook to changing social and material conditions. The basic focus of anthropology, in dealing with the subjects of culture and personality and how they are related, is upon the relationship between the way a culture molds its youths' personalities and their psychological makeup in later life. In other words, we look for regularities both in the way children are raised and in the way adults behave, assuming that early childhood experiences have a lot to do with the formation of adult personalities. We study the actual childrearing techniques practiced by parents and other socializing institutions such as schools, peer groups in which the children interact, and a variety of experiences that most children share. In each case, we try to see how these experiences affect behavior in the adult population, assuming that values learned in infancy have a way of showing up in many adults. If children are encouraged to behave in a certain way, and are positively rewarded for such behavior, they are likely to associate a positive value with that behavior that will carry on throughout their lives.

We can see how the anthropological approach can help us understand personality patterns in our own culture. Adult behavior considered appropriate in American society is reinforced through the way we train our children. Positive values such as individual achievement, competition, and freedom of choice are a strong part of almost every parent's approach to childrearing. Negative feelings are transmitted just as strongly to children through parents, teachers, peers, and even impersonal media such as television. We cannot underestimate the role of television in the transmission of American culture to the youth of today, particularly its effects on homogenizing the members of the impressionable young age group that is growing up in a TV culture. In our present-day society, experiencing an increasing wave of crime and violence and an apparent loss of realism concerning war and the death and destruction it brings, we are beginning to look at this relationship between television programming and cultural values more closely. In a recent study of television programs aired on Saturday mornings—prime time for young children—the following results were discovered: 89 percent of the time was devoted to entertainment programs, including 70 percent comedy drama, primarily cartoons; 62

Children are taught appropriate behavior as part of the socialization process. Top: Bushmen children cracking roasted Mungongo nuts. (Irven DeVore, Anthro-Photo) Bottom: Young Navajo students learn the traditional techniques of sand painting to illustrate modern concepts in ecology. (Dennis Stock, Magnum)

percent of all programs were animated; 3 out of 10 dramatic segments were saturated with violence, and 71 percent had at least one instance of human violence with or without the use of weapons. Another interesting conclusion was that although in 52 percent of the segments the violence was directed at humans, in only 4 percent did this result in death or injury. Is it any wonder that our children are growing up with the idea that violence is entertaining, and relatively harmless?

Television has also brought war to our living rooms, a sort of adult version of Saturday television for the kiddies. The close network coverage of the Vietnam War, and more recently the Arab-Israeli Conflict, has created an aura of artificiality around warfare for those Americans who did not actually participate in them, and who were not veterans of earlier wars and have not had similar experiences. Vietnam made millions of Americans even more oblivious to the outside world by illustrating how far they were actually removed from it. Hundreds of people—not just soldiers, but civilian men, women and children—could die in a single day's fighting, but life rolled on for us just as it always had, with none of the hardships or insecurities of a country engaged in a battle for its own survival. Indeed, television is becoming increasingly important as an institution for socializing the young members of American culture, and its role in molding their minds and instilling in them the American values and the American way of life is growing at a startling rate. We can no longer speak

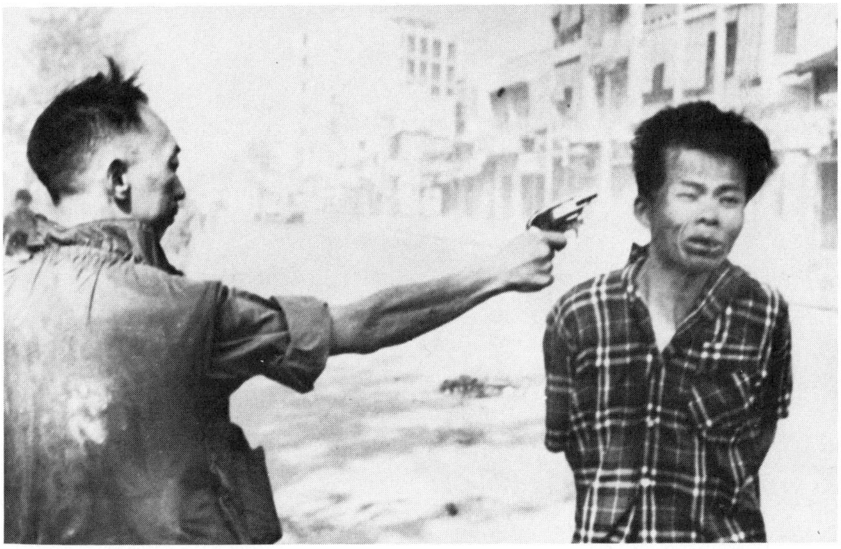

This assassination of a Viet Cong terrorist by a South Vietnamese police chief was shown on network television news broadcasts. (Wide World)

of the family as the primary institution for child-training. It must now share the spotlight with "the tube."

We must qualify the anthropological approach to the study of culture and personality by noting that there is always a tremendous range of personalities within a given society. When we speak of similarities, we do not mean any kind of unanimous personality trait found in all members of the society, but rather are referring to a personality type that is found most frequently. We may speak of a society as characterized by an aggressive type of individual, or by a cooperativeness or a strong feeling of anxiety. This implies that this characteristic will be dominant in most people, but by no means does it exclude other personality types from existing with it at the same time. In every passive society there will be aggressive individuals. We must also recognize that these dominant personality types can change rapidly within a culture. For example, during the era when Hitler was in power in Europe, the Jews as a group offered relatively little armed resistance. There were minor uprisings, but the Jewish population of Europe did not band together and stand against Hitler

Twentieth-century version of an armed warrior dressed for battle. Is violence becoming a pattern of American culture?

in armed conflict. Yet their descendants who make up a large part of the population of Israel today have developed exactly the opposite personality type. Partly as a result of the Jews' experiences in Europe a generation ago, the Israelis of today defend themselves and their small country in a way that has enabled them to survive in what can only be described as most hostile surroundings.

Basic Personality and World View

The study of socialization and how it molds personality types was developed in the late 1930s by the anthropologist Ralph Linton and the psychiatrist Abram Kardiner. They used the term *basic personality type* to refer to the personality configuration shared by the bulk of society's members as a result of the early childhood experiences they have in common. In the concept of basic personality the emphasis is placed upon what are called "primary institutions," that is, those that are fundamental in the process of child rearing, such as the family, peer groups and early schooling.

According to this concept of basic personality, when anthropologists study foreign cultures one of the things they are frequently interested in documenting is the way children are raised within the context of the family. When anthropologists go to another culture, they are often treated as children, because despite their age in years they have not yet learned the language or the proper rules of behavior, and often speak and act much as a child in that culture. Much of the anthropologist's work in a new culture involves learning what the appropriate patterns of behavior are, but it is difficult to find someone to teach you those rules as an adult. It is often extremely frustrating for an anthropologist with children in the field to find that at the end of the field experience their young children not only speak the language better than they do, but also have learned more about the rules of behavior. People don't think twice about correcting a child's behavior, but to do so with an adult seems most inappropriate.

The result of the anthropologist's investigations into the personality type of another culture, whether it be through the study of primary institutions or an actual observation and analysis of adult behavior (usually it is a combination of both), is a general sketch of what we call a culture's *world view.* This includes the values and morals, attitudes and beliefs, and everything about the outlook on life, from how a person relates to his fellow human beings to how he relates to the universe. The anthropologist Edward Banfield described the world view of the Italian peasants in the village he studied in southern Italy. Banfield said that their personality, their interaction with other villagers, and in fact their whole way of life was characterized by what he called *amoral familism.* It was as if they were following a rule that stated: "maximize the advantage of your immediate family at the expense of the rest of the community." This led to patterns of suspicion and envy, mistrust and lack of cooperation, for everyone was out to gain as much as possible for himself, and to do as little as possible for others. Banfield suggested that this personality type made it almost impossible for the village as a whole to experience any progress, because people could not be brought together to work in the common interest. When they went to the polls they voted for the man who promised them the greatest immediate reward, with little concern for the future. They avoided such things as public works projects, because they required an investment of their labor for the benefit of others. Most important of all, they maintained this personality pattern through their treatment of children, insuring that it would continue in future generations. Children were punished in an irregular, almost whimsical fashion. Sometimes an action would bring praise, other times a spanking. Since there was no regular pattern of rewards or punishments, children quickly learned that there was no authority that could be trusted. Politicians and government officials were similarly characterized, and as such were not to be trusted either. Cooperation with anyone implied that one would be exploited.

A world view in many ways similar to amoral familism is described by the anthropologist George Foster in what he calls the *image of limited good.* According to Foster, the behavior of the Mexican villagers he studied can be predicted and explained by assuming that the desired things in life exist in a finite quantity and are always in short supply. It is as if the good things in life were like a pie, cut up into slices. If a person takes a larger slice than his allotted portion, the difference has to be made up by someone else's receiving a slightly smaller portion. There is no way to increase the existing supply, and therefore the advantage obtained by one person necessarily rests upon the disadvantage of others. As a result, villagers are envious and suspicious of each other, and it is difficult to get them to cooperate.

People hide their wealth, and are wary of letting others too close to their private lives, lest someone grow envious and do them harm. Everyone tries to present the image that he is poorer than the others in his community. The only way an individual can get ahead is to bring in wealth from outside the community, which is not recognized as a threat because it does not take anything from the "pie" of good available within the village. A man who goes to the city to work, or a *bracero* who works in the United States as a migrant laborer, can return to the village proud of his newfound wealth. Of course, others will still envy his success, but he will not be in danger because he has not lowered their standard of living or their possession of "good" by his own achievements.

Such personality types as are characterized by amoral familism or the image of limited good are not necessarily incompatible with reality as it is perceived and as it affects the people. World view is different from basic personality, for it is a product not only of early experiences in learning the culture, but also of adjusting to environmental conditions, both physical and social. Thus if in fact the desired things in life are limited and there is only so much that can be derived from the land, then the viewpoint of limited good makes sense as far as the everyday life of the people is concerned. It may not get to the real source of the problem, but at least it allows them to cope with it.

Measuring Personality

As any political election will illustrate, evaluating an individual's personality is a very subjective act, and one which few people will agree upon. If as anthropologists we hope to be scientific about the study of personality in various cultural settings around the world, how can we do this without injecting our own personal bias into our analysis? When we read about the residents of a village being uncooperative and suspicious, how do we know whether it is because they really are that way, or just because the anthropologist is looking for that kind of behavior and thus tends to find it even where it might not exist? One possible answer lies in the use by anthropologists of the same kinds of projective tests that are used by psychologists in personality studies in our own culture. The major difference is that while psychologists use such tests to determine whether an individual is "normal" according to our standards, the anthropologist uses projective tests to determine what "normal" means in another culture.

One type of projective test familiar to most Americans is the *Rorschach test,* more commonly known as the "ink-blot" test. The idea behind the Rorschach is that when an individual is shown a design such as can be created by spilling ink on a piece of paper and folding the paper to make a symmetrical shape, the viewer will describe it according to his own particular perceptions. The psychologist evaluates the responses of the person being tested in terms of how they compare to the responses of "normal" Americans. Does the individual tend to see scenes that represent violence or aggressiveness, or does he describe designs of the opposite nature? The trained psychologist can evaluate the responses of the informant in terms of what they reveal about that individual's personality, and the accompanying behavioral tendencies.

The anthropologist who uses Rorschach tests does not have a norm against which he can measure a single informant's reponse. In fact, the use of such tests is meaningless unless a relatively large sample is gathered. What good would it do to test a single individual from a foreign culture if we could not determine whether he was normal or not? We might be testing what that culture would define as a marginal individual, one who did not fit into the personality pattern at all, and if we did not check his responses against others in that culture we would have a completely false picture of the personality type. Instead, the anthropologist must collect as many responses as possible, and look for patterns in them. It should be stressed that not everyone can administer or evaluate these tests, and there is more to them than just spilling ink and making designs. A standard set of designs must be administered in a prescribed manner if the test is to be done properly.

Another type of test designed to determine personality characteristics and used by anthropologists in cross-cultural personality studies is the *Thematic Apperception Test,* or TAT. In this test, the informant views a series of pictures, and in each case is asked to invent a story around the scene in the picture. The pictures are designed so that they do not conflict with existing cultural patterns. Dress, housing, and other variable aspects of culture are all carefully controlled so that each picture presents a typical scene. The story is recorded and then analyzed for the meaning of its content. Again,

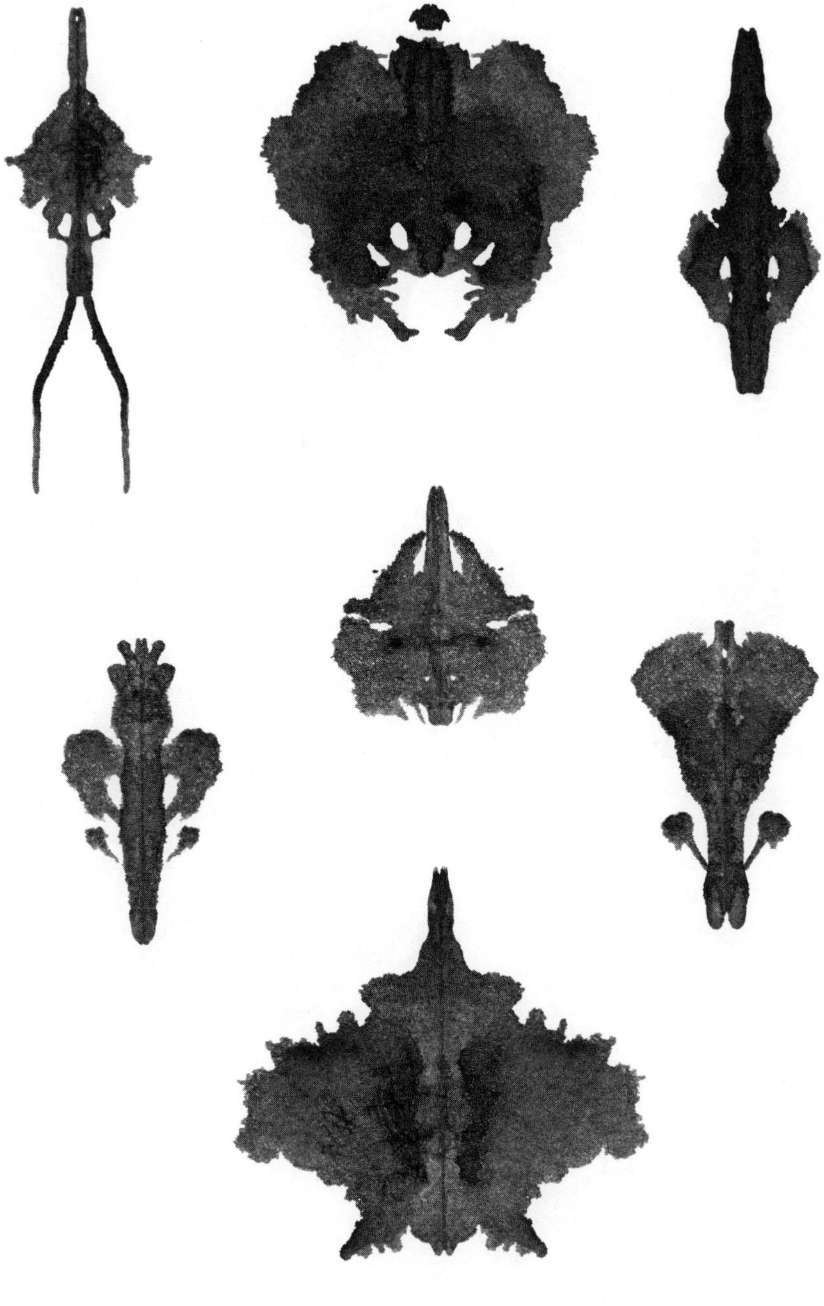

Inkblots similar to those used in the Rorschach test.

A picture used in administering TAT tests. The informant is asked to make up a story about the scene. (H. A. Murrary, Harvard University Press)

while the analysis of a single TAT test can indicate something about the personality of the individual respondent for the psychologist, the anthropologist is concerned with collecting a number of responses so that he can put together a picture of the "normal" personality for the culture as a whole. Since the pictures include a variety of scenes and poses by individuals, much can be learned about the values of the respondents based upon how they interpret the pictures. For example, we might show a picture of a boy standing next to a table upon which there is a violin. The boy has a sad look on his face. A typical American response might be something like the following: the boy wants to go outside and play baseball, but his mother has told him that before he can do this he must practice his violin lessons. This answer tells us something about the nature of American culture in general, and if we were to obtain a large number of similar responses from American informants we could confirm our inferences about their meaning.

On the other hand, suppose we asked an Italian informant to tell us about the same picture. The story might go something like this: the boy's grandfather has died and left him the violin, but his family is too poor for him to take violin lessons, and he is sad because he cannot play the instrument well. Suppose for the sake of argument that we were to obtain a number of responses similar to the fictitious ones I have suggested. By evaluating them we could learn a great deal about Italian culture, as well as about the differences between Italian and American boys and their attitudes toward certain kinds of behavior. Remember, though, that for the anthropologist these tests are valuable only when used in large numbers, and they are not designed to get at a single individual's personality characteristics.

Other types of projective tests are designed to uncover the same elements of personality configurations on a cross-cultural basis. For example, we can ask informants to complete sentences, giving them the first few words, or we can ask them to answer open-ended questions such as "What would you do if . . . ?" Some anthropologists have experimented with having informants draw pictures (this is especially valuable for working with children). In short, there are a variety of ways of measuring personality. The goal is to make this type of study less subjective and to achieve a great degree of certainty that our observations are not based upon working with a single informant who might not be "normal" in the eyes of the rest of his culture. In all, there are over 500 different personality tests. Most are difficult to use and even more difficult to interpret, and they are not used by all anthropologists. But the tests can be extremely helpful in certain kinds of investigations that have to do with cross-cultural comparisons of personality.

Cultural Patterns

The study of the basic personality of a society and the use of projective tests such as the Rorschach and the TAT enable us to perceive patterns in a culture. By looking at a number of individual personalities we can arrive at an abstraction about the typical individual in a culture and what his or her personality will tend to be like, in a very general sense. But if we carry that study further, we can see how the personality and almost all other aspects of the culture fit together and form a specific pattern.

One of the first anthropologists to investigate personality and cultural patterning was Margaret Mead. In the 1920s Mead conducted research on Samoa, during which she became interested in comparing the period of adolescence for Samoan girls and American girls. She concluded that the patterns of stress that characterize the American adolescence are absent from Samoan culture, with the result that the adult personality is different in the two cultures. But even beyond the question of personality, the period of adolescence in the two cultures is typical of an overall pattern that emerges for each. Samoan culture does not emphasize the drastic and abrupt change in status during adolescence that American culture does. In general, Mead found that Americans experience a number of abrupt status changes, and as a result there is more stress involved in the American life style than in the Samoan. There is a correlation not only between child rearing and adult personality, but with the majority of the rest of cultural institutions and values as well. They all form a pattern that can be expressed through the personalities of the members of that culture, through the form that each institution takes.

The kinds of status changes that Mead was describing are commonly called "life crisis rites." Every culture includes a number of these ceremonies, but the particular content of each ceremony and the degree to which they are emphasized are factors that vary considerably from one culture to another. We are all familiar with a large

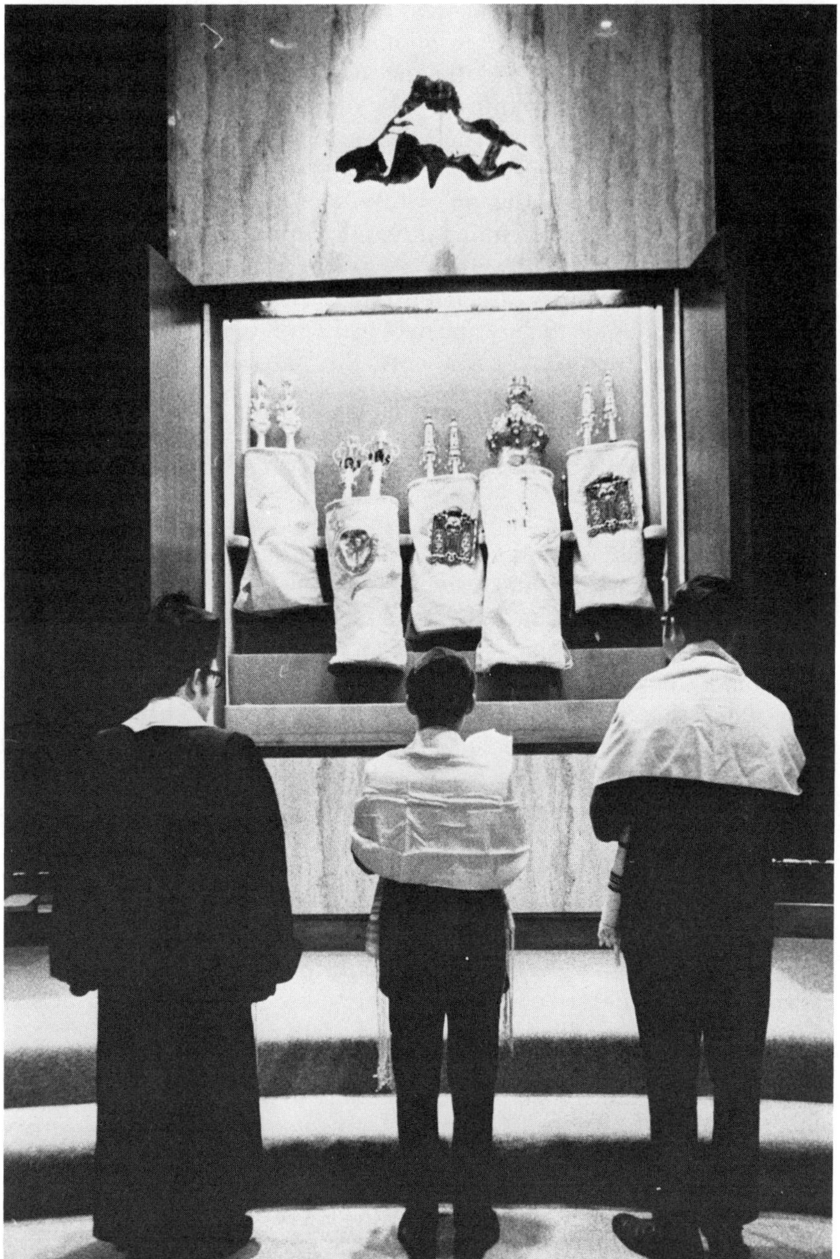

The Bar Mitzvah is an example of a life crisis rite in the Jewish tradition. (Jan Lukas, Rapho/Photo Researchers)

number of life crisis rites, each of which signifies the passage out of one period or stage and into another. For example, the baptism ceremony for Christians and the circumcision ceremony for male Jewish infants signify entry into the religious community, and are major religious ceremonies. Other such religious ceremonies include first communion, confirmation, bar mitzvah, and so forth. Then there are secular life crisis ceremonies, most of which do not carry with them the important ceremonial value, although they are in many ways no less important for the participant. A girl's sixteenth birthday and a boy's eighteenth birthday are important secular life crisis rites. At eighteen, for example, a boy must register for the draft. He is also legally responsible in some social contexts; he is old enough to drink in some states, to drive in others, to file suit or be sued, and to be tried as an adult for any crime that he commits. Recently the voting age has been reduced to 18, which assigns yet another new status to the 18-year-old.

Marriage is another important life crisis ceremony. In American culture it is usually celebrated as both a religious and a secular event. New responsibilities and new privileges are bestowed upon an individual at marriage, reflecting much more of American values and the general pattern of American culture than is first evident. Other secular ceremonies include such events as graduation from high school or college and the first experience of parenthood. Minor life crisis rites continue with each new social position one achieves, until the final rite occurs at death.

Every culture emphasizes different points in an individual's life, or emphasizes the same ones in different ways. Different rights and obligations go with different stages in the individual development of the members of the culture. Some cultures make a big thing of a particular rite, while others seem to exhibit a pattern of gradual change over time, with little or no stress at any one particular time—such as the situation described by Margaret Mead for adolescent girls in Samoa. It is admittedly a rather abrupt distinction between being 17 years and 364 days old and not being allowed to drink, vote, or be legally responsible for oneself, and being 18 years old. Surely one day cannot make much of a difference, but the American youth is brought up with the belief that there is something magical about the 18th birthday (and again about the 21st), and as a result the American boy or girl somehow actually *feels* different on the 18th birthday. It is part of a pattern of abrupt life crisis rites that is found throughout American life.

It is interesting to note how this American pattern fits in with so many other aspects of American culture. Schooling, for example, begins not when a group of impartial observers decide that a child has reached the point where he or she can handle the classroom situation; it begins when the child reaches a certain age. No one would argue that every child is equally ready for school at that age, but that does not mean that all will not attend. Likewise, no one would suggest for a moment that all Americans who are over 18 are capable of acting in a mature and responsible manner, that all can accept their responsibilities of voting or drinking with equal success. Some young people under 18 are far more mature, or are capable of much more rational thought, than adults well over that age. Yet in the eyes of the law a person becomes legally responsible upon reaching the age of 18. These are but a few examples of the abruptness in the changes through which most Americans must pass. Such a pattern is found throughout American culture. In politics, there is not a gradual transition of power from the hands of one leader to another, but a total change at election time. In religion and law, as noted in the example above, the situation is similar. Margaret Mead's observations about the "crisis-oriented" American adolescents, compared to Samoan girls who did not share this cultural pattern, certainly illustrate the uniformity of our cultural experience.

Cultural Configurations

Life crisis rites are only one of several ways in which patterns of culture emerge and are reflected in the behavior of members of a group. All of the basic institutions that are a part of the culture tend to mirror the overall pattern for that culture. This point was made quite succinctly by the anthropologist Ruth Benedict, whose book *Patterns of Culture* is a classic work in anthropology. Benedict emphasized that cultures must be taken as wholes, each one integrated on its own principles, each with its own *configuration*. She stressed that a culture is organized around a basic theme, and that all of the various elements of that culture fit together.

In applying this approach to cross-cultural studies in her book, Benedict looked at several different societies and described them in terms of their basic personality configurations, pointing out how these personality types fit in with the overall configuration. Among the societies she studied were two North American Indian groups, the Zuni Indians of the southwestern United States, and the Kwakiutl Indians of the northwest coast. She described the basic configuration of Zuni culture as "Apollonian." According to this configuration, the Zuni were very cooperative, were never excessive in any aspect of their life, and did not seek to express their individuality. The typical Zuni was a person who sought to blend into the group, and who did not wish to stand out as superior or as being above the other members of the tribe. Benedict then went on to point out how this basic personality type was reinforced in other elements of Zuni culture, thus forming the overall cultural configuration. Child-training patterns were designed to suppress individuality. Initiation ceremonies were characterized by a lack of ordeal (the Apollonian type is never excessive), and the youths were initiated in a group setting. Marriage was relatively casual. Leadership among the Zuni was declined whenever possible, and was accepted only with great reluctance. People tended to shun positions of authority. Ceremonial and religious associations likewise reinforced this configuration. Priests were low-key individuals, and special positions of power were delegated on a group basis, so that there was a medicine *society* rather than a single powerful medicine *man*. Death was an occasion for little fuss or mourning.

The Kwakiutl Indians presented a cultural configuration much different from that of the Zuni. Benedict termed this configuration "Dionysian." According to this pattern, the Kwakiutl were characterized by a frenzied outlook, excess being the rule rather than the exception. They were ambitious and striving, and individuality was emphasized in every aspect of their life. The ideal man among the Kwakiutl was one who had a will to power and always attempted to prove his superiority. Child-training practices reinforced this pattern, emphasizing the achievement of the individual over cooperation with the group. In the initiation ceremonies, a boy was expected to go out by himself and experience a personal relationship with the supernatural. Marriage entailed a tremendous celebration and was not the casual kind of ceremony between two people that it was among the Zuni. Leadership among the Kwakiutl was sought by any possible means, and Kwakiutl society was characterized by a constant struggle for power. Religious positions included that of the shaman, a priest who wielded enormous personal power. Even the death ritual among the Kwakiutl reinforced this overall configuration. A death was a major

Culver Pictures, Inc.

Ruth Fulton Benedict
(1887–1948)
conducted research in various American Indian cultures, and in 1934 she published Patterns of Culture, *a major contribution to the anthropological literature of the period. She had studied under Franz Boas, who was noted as the leading opponent to cultural evolutionism of the nineteenth century, because it implied racist attitudes of white and Western superiority. Benedict's writings showed the influence of Boas, and in* Patterns of Culture *she offered a strong justification for the doctrine of cultural relativism. She argued that one could not judge a culture or rank it against another, for all cultures are unique entities, each with its own separate identity, history, and intrinsic value.*

event, an occasion for much mourning, and was not accepted calmly and peacefully as among the Zuni.

Benedict's study of cultural configurations illustrates how numerous aspects of life in a culture reinforce the basic pattern of culture, whatever it might be. This is not to say that everyone is just like this—there are frenzied Zunis just as there are passive Kwakiutls—but rather that it is a pattern that describes the typical member of the society, and to which all members conform to some extent. Benedict's approach suggests that, based upon the configuration of the culture, the personality is *more likely* to conform to one type than to another. Her main point is that we have to recognize cultural differences as valid and not impose our own morals and values on all people—whether they be foreigners or simply members of our own culture who are not as "American" as we are.

Kwakiutl masked dancers exhibit some of the characteristics described by Ruth Benedict as part of the "Dionysian" pattern of culture. (American Museum of Natural History)

In 1959 John Howard Griffin, a white writer, decided to find out first-hand what it is to be a black man in the South. With the help of a doctor he took medication and sun lamp treatments in order to darken his skin in only five days. Griffin shaved his head to remove the final outward trace of his whiteness, and set out through Mississippi, Alabama, New Orleans, and Atlanta. His excursion lasted more than a month as he traveled as a black man by foot, hitchhiking, or by bus. Throughout his experiment, Griffin lived in cheap hotels and rooming houses in the black sections of town and found out what it was like to be denied a glass of water, or access to a rest room.

Although *Black Like Me,* the complete book of Griffin's experiences as a black man, was published 15 years ago, it remains a vivid chronicle of the differences between cultures, even within any given state in this country. One of the most vivid impressions in the book is contained in the following excerpt, which demonstrates the white man's fascination with (and misconceptions about) the sex life among blacks.

Black Like Me

John Howard Griffin

November 19

I arrived by bus in Biloxi too late to find any Negroes about, so I walked inland and slept, half-freezing, in a tin-roofed shed with an open south front. In the morning I found breakfast in a little Negro café—coffee and toast—and then walked down to the highway to begin hitching. The highway ran for miles along some of the most magnificent beaches I have ever seen—white sands, a beautiful ocean; and opposite the beach, splendid homes. The sun warmed me through, and I took my time, stopping to study the historic markers placed along the route.

For lunch, I bought a pint of milk and a ready-wrapped bologna sandwich in a roadside store. I carried them to the walk that runs along the shallow sea wall and ate. A local Negro stopped to talk. I asked him if the swimming were good there, since the beaches were so splendid. He told me the beaches were "man-made," the sand dredged in; but that unless a Negro sneaked off to some isolated spot, he'd never know how the water was, since Negroes weren't permitted to enjoy the beaches. He pointed out the injustice of this policy, since the upkeep of the beaches comes from a gasoline tax. "In other words, every time we buy a gallon of gas, we pay a penny to keep the beach up so the whites can use it," he said. He added that some of the local Negro citizens were considering a project to keep an account of the gasoline they purchased throughout the year and at the end of that time demand from the town fathers either a refund on their gasoline tax or the privilege of using the beaches for which they had paid their fair part.

After a time I walked again on legs that grew weak with weariness. A car pulled up beside me and a young, redheaded white man told me to "hop in." His glance was friendly, courteous, and he spoke with no condescension. I began to hope that I had underestimated the people of Mississippi. With what eagerness I grasped at every straw of kindness, wanting to give a good report.

"Beautiful country isn't it?" he said.

"Marvelous."

"You just passing through?"

"Yes sir . . . I'm on my way to Mobile."

"Where you from?"

"Texas."

"I'm from Massachusetts," he said, as though he were eager for me to know he was not a Mississippian. I felt the keenest disappointment, and mentally erased the passages I had mentally composed about the kindness of the Mississippian who gave the Negro a ride. He told me he had

Reprinted from John Howard Griffin, *Black Like Me*. Boston: Houghton Mifflin Company; Cambridge: The Riverside Press, 1960, 1961. Abridged with permission.

no sympathy for the "Southern attitude."

"That shows," I said.

"But you know," he added, "these are some of the finest people in the world about everything else."

"I'm sure they are."

"I know you won't believe it—but it's really the truth. I just don't ever talk to them about the race question."

"With your attitude, I can understand that," I laughed.

"They can't discuss it," he said. "It's a shame but all they do is get mad whenever you bring it up. I'll never understand it. They're blocked on that one subject. I've lived here over five years now—and they're good neighbors; but if I mention race with any sympathy for the Negro, they just tell me I'm an 'outsider' and don't understand about the Negroes. What's there to understand?"

I walked what—ten, fifteen miles? I walked because one does not just simply sit down in the middle of a highway, because there was nothing to do but walk.

Late in the afternoon, my mind hazed with fatigue. I concentrated all my energy in putting one foot in front of the other. Sweat poured down into my eyes and soaked my clothes and the heat of the pavement came through my shoes. I remember I stopped at a little custard stand and bought a dish of ice cream merely to have the excuse to sit at one of the tables under the trees—none of which were occupied. But before I could take my ice cream and walk to one of them some white teen-agers appeared and took seats. I dared not sit down even at a distant table. Wretched with disappointment I leaned against a tree and ate the ice cream.

Behind the custard stand stood an old unpainted privy leaning badly to one side. I returned to the dispensing window of the stand.

"Yes sir," the white man said congenially. "You want something else?"

"Where's the nearest rest room I could use?" I asked.

He brushed his white, brimless cook's cap back and rubbed his forefinger against his sweaty forehead. "Let's see. You can go on up there to the bridge and then cut down the road to the left . . . and just follow that road. You'll come to a little settlement—there's some stores and gas stations there."

"How far is it?" I asked, pretending to be in greater discomfort than I actually was.

"Not far—thirteen, maybe fourteen blocks."

A locust's lazy rasping sawed the air from the nearby oak trees.

"Isn't there any place closer?" I said, determined to see if he would not offer me the use of the dilapidated outhouse, which certainly no human could degrade any more than time and the elements had.

His seamed face showed the concern and sympathy of one human for another in a predicament every man understands. "I can't think of any . . ." he said slowly.

I glanced around the side toward the outhouse. "Any chance of me running in there for a minute?"

"Nope," he said—clipped, final, soft, as though he regretted it but could never permit such a thing. "I'm sorry." He turned away.

"Thank you just the same," I said.

By dark I was away from the beach area and out in the country. Strangely, I began getting rides. Men would pass you in daylight but pick you up after dark.

I must have had a dozen rides that evening. They blear into a nightmare, the one scarcely distinguishable from the other.

It quickly became obvious why they picked me up. All but two picked me up the way they would pick up a pornographic photograph or book—except that this was verbal pornography. With a Negro, they assumed they need give no semblance of self-respect or respectability. The visual element entered into it. In a car at night visibility is reduced. A man will reveal himself in the dark, which gives an illusion of anonymity, more than he will in the bright light. Some were shamelessly open, some shamelessly subtle. All showed morbid curiosity about the sexual life of the Negro, and all had, at base, the same stereotyped image of the Negro as an inexhaustible sex-machine with oversized genitals and a vast store of experiences, immensely varied. They appeared to think that the Negro has done all of those "special" things they themselves have never dared to do. They carried the conversation into the depths of depravity. I note these things because it is harrowing to see decent-looking men and boys assume that because a man is black they need show him none of the reticences they would, out of respect, show the most derelict white man. I note them, too, because they differed completely from the "bull sessions" men customarily have among themselves. These latter, no matter how frank, have generally a robust tone that says: "We are men, this is an enjoyable thing to do and to discuss, but it will never impugn the basic respect we give one another; it will never distort our humanity." In this, the atmosphere, no matter how coarse, has a verve and an essential joviality that casts out morbidity. It implies respect for the persons involved. But all that I could see here were men shorn of respect either for themselves or their companion.

In my grogginess and exhaustion, these conversations became ghoulish. Each time one of them let me out of his car, I hoped the next would spare me his pantings. I remained mute and pleaded my exhaustion and lack of sleep.

"I'm so tired, I just can't think," I would say.

Like men who had promised themselves pleasure, they would not be denied. It became a strange sort of hounding as they nudged my skull for my sexual reminiscences.

"Well, did you ever do such-and-such?"

"I don't know . . ." I moaned.

"What's the matter—haven't you got any manhood? My old man told me you wasn't really a man till you'd done such-and-such."

Or the older ones, hardened, cynical in their lechery. "Now, don't try to kid me. I wasn't born yesterday. You know you've done such-and-such, just like I have. Hell, it's good that way. Tell me, did you ever get a white woman?"

"Do you think I'm crazy?" I tacitly denied the racist's contention, for he would not hesitate to use it against the Negroes in his conversations around town: "Why, I had one of them admit to me just last night that he craves white women."

"I didn't ask if you was crazy," he said. "I asked if you ever had one—or ever really wanted one." Then, conniving, sweet-toned, "There's plenty white women would like to have a good buck Negro."

"A Negro'd be asking for the rope to get himself mixed up with white women."

"You're just telling me that, but I'll bet inside you think differently . . ."

"This is sure beautiful country through here. What's the main crop?"

"Don't you? You can tell me. Hell, I don't care."

"No sir," I sighed.

"You're lying in your teeth and you know it."

Silence. Soon after, almost abruptly he halted the car and said, "Okay, this is as far as I go." He spoke as though he resented my uncooperative attitude, my refusal to give him this strange verbal sexual pleasure.

I thanked him for the ride and stepped down onto the highway. He drove on in the same direction.

Soon another picked me up, a young man in his late twenties who spoke with an educated flair. His questions had the spurious elevation of a scholar seeking information, but the information he sought was entirely sexual, and presupposed that in the ghetto the Negro's life is one of marathon sex with many different partners, open to the view of all; in a word, that marital fidelity and sex as love's goal of union with the beloved object were exclusively the white man's property. Though he pretended to be above such ideas as racial superiority and spoke with genuine warmth, the entire context of his talk reeked of preconceived ideas to the contrary.

"I understand Negroes are much more broad-minded about such things," he said warmly.

"I don't know."

"I understand you make more of an art—or maybe *hobby* out of your sex than we do."

"I doubt it."

"Well, you people don't seem to have the inhibitions we have. We're all basically puritans. understand Negroes do a lot more things—different kinds of sex—than we do. Oh, don't get me wrong. I admire your attitude, think it's basically healthier than ours. You don't get so damned many *conflicts*. Negroes don't have much neuroses, do they? I mean you people have a more realistic tradition about sex—you're not so sheltered from it as we are."

I knew that what he really meant was that Negroes grew up seeing it from infancy. He had read the same stories, the same reports of social workers about parents sharing a room with children, the father coming home drunk and forcing the mother onto the bed in full view of the young ones. I felt like laughing in his face when I thought of the Negro families I had known already as a Negro: the men on the streets, in the ghettos, the housewives and their great concern that their children "grow up right."

"You people regard sex as a *total* experience—and that's how it should be. Anything that makes you feel good is morally all right for you. Isn't that the main difference?"

"I don't think there's any difference," I said cautiously, not wanting to test the possibility of his wrath at having a Negro disagree with him.

"You *don't?*" His voice betrayed excitement and eagerness; gave no hint of offense.

"Our ministers preach sin and hell just as much as yours," I said. "We've got the same puritanical background as you. We worry just as much as white people about our children losing their virginity or being perverted. We've got the same miserable little worries and problems over our sexual effectiveness, the same guilts that you have."

He appeared astonished and delighted, not at what I said but at the fact that I could say it. His whole attitude of enthusiasm practically shouted, "Why you talk *intelligently!*" He was so obtuse he did not realize the implied insult in his astonishment that a black man could do anything but say "yes sir" and mumble four-letter words.

Again, he asked questions scarcely different from those that white men would ask themselves; especially scholars who would discuss cultural differences on a detached plane. Yet here the tone was subtly conniving. He went through the motions of courteous research, but he could not hide his real preoccupation. He asked about the size of Negro genitalia and the details of Negro sex life. Only the language differed from the previous inquirers—the substance was the same. The difference was that here I could disagree with him without risking a flood of abuse or petulance. He quoted Kinsey and others. It became apparent he was one of those young men who possess an impressive store of facts, but no truths. This again would have no significance and would be unworthy of note except for one thing: I have talked with such men many times as a white and they never show the glow of prurience he revealed. The significance lay in the fact that my blackness and his concepts of what my blackness implied allowed him to expose himself in this manner. He saw the Negro as a different species. He saw me as something akin to an animal in that he felt no need to maintain his sense of human dignity, though certainly he would have denied this.

I told myself that I was tired, that I must not judge these men who picked me up and for the price of a ride submitted me to the swamps of their fantasy lives. They showed me something that all men have but seldom bring to the surface, since most men seek health. The boy ended up wanting me to expose myself to him, saying he had never seen a Negro naked. I turned mute, indrawn, giving no answer. The silence rattled between us and I felt sorry for the reprimand that grew from me to him in the silence. I did not want this cruelty to him, since I knew that he showed me a side of his nature that was special to the night and the situation, a side rarely brought to light in his everyday living. I stared at the dimly lighted car dashboard and saw him attending an aunt's funeral, having Sunday dinner with his parents, doing some kindness for a friend—for he was kind. How could I let him see that I understood and that I still respected him, and that I formed no judgment against him for this momentary slip? For instead of seeing it as a manifestation of some poor human charity, he might view it as confirmation that Negroes are insensitive to sexual aberration, that they think nothing of it—and this would carry on the legend that has so handicapped the Negro.

"I wasn't going to do anything to you," he said in a voice lifeless with humiliation. "I'm not a queer or anything."

"Of course not," I said. "It's nothing."

"It's just that I don't get a chance to talk to educated Negroes—people that can answer questions."

"You make it more complicated than it is," I said. "If you want to know about the sexual morals of the Negro—his practices and ideals—it's no mystery. These are human matters, and the Negro is the same human as the white man. Just ask yourself how it is for a white man and you'll know all the answers. Negro trash is the same as white trash. Negro decency is about the same, too."

"But there are differences. The social studies I've read . . ."

"They don't deal with any basic difference in human nature between black and white," I said. "They only study the effects of environment on human nature. You place the white man in the ghetto, deprive him of educational advantages, arrange it so he has to struggle hard to fulfill his instinct for self-respect, give him little physical privacy and less leisure, and he would after a time assume the same characteristics you attach to the Negro. These characteristics don't spring from whiteness or blackness, but from a man's conditioning."

"Yes, but Negroes have more illegitimate children, earlier loss of virginity and more crime—these are established facts," he insisted without unkindness.

"The fact that the white race has the same problems proves these are not Negro characteristics, but the product of our condition as men," I said. "When you force humans into a subhuman mode of existence, this always happens. Deprive a man of any contact with the pleasures of the spirit and he'll fall completely into those of the flesh."

"But we don't deprive you people of the 'pleasures of the spirit,' " he said.

"In most places we can't go to the concerts, the theater, the museums, public lectures . . . or even to the library. Our schools in the South don't compare to the white schools, poor as they are. You deprive a man of educational opportunities and he'll have no knowledge of the great civilizing influences of art, history, literature and philosophy. Many Negroes don't even know these things exist. With practically nothing to exalt the mind or exercise the spirit, any man is going to sink to his lowest depths. It becomes vicious—and tragic."

"I can't imagine how it must be," he said. "I don't think it's fair. But just the same, plenty of whites don't have access to these things—to art, history, literature and philosophy. Some of the finest people I know live in the country where they never get to museums, concerts."

"Living in the country, they are surrounded by natural museums and concerts," I said. "Besides, those doors are always open to them.

The Negro, too, fares better in the country. But most are deprived of education. Ignorance keeps them poor, and when a town-dwelling Negro is poor, he lives in the ghetto. His wife has to work usually, and this leaves the children without parental companionship. In such places, where all of man's time is spent just surviving, he rarely knows what it means to read a great book. He has grown up and now sees his children grow up in squalor. His wife usually earns more than he. He is thwarted in his need to be father-of-the-household. When he looks at his children and his home, he feels the guilt of not having given them something better. His only salvation is not to give a damn finally, or else he will fall into despair. In despair a man's sense of virtue is dulled. He no longer cares. He will do anything to escape it—steal or commit acts of violence—or perhaps try to lose himself in sensuality. Most often the sex-king is just a poor devil trying to prove the manhood that his whole existence denies. This is what the whites call the 'sorry nigger.' Soon he will either desert his home or become so unbearable he is kicked out. This leaves the mother to support the children alone. To keep food in their bellies, she has to spend most of her time away from them, working. This leaves the children to the streets, prey to any sight, any conversation, any sexual experiment that comes along to make their lives more interesting or pleasurable. To a young girl who has nothing, has never known anything, the baubles she can get—both in a kind of crude affection and in gifts or money—by granting sex to a man or boy appeal to her as toys to a child. She gets pregnant sometimes and then the vicious circle is given impetus. In some instances the mother cannot make enough to support her children, so she sells her sex for what she can get. This gets easier and easier until she comes up with still another child to abort or support. But none of this is 'Negro-ness.' "

"I don't know . . ." he sighed. "It looks like a man could do better."

"It looks that way to you, because you can see what would be better. The Negro knows something is terribly wrong, but with things the way they are, he can't know that something better actually exists on the other side of work and study. We are all born blank. It's the same for blacks or whites or any other shade of man. Your blanks have been filled in far differently from those of a child grown up in the filth and poverty of the ghetto."

He drove without speaking through a thundershower that crinkled the windshield and raised the hum of his tires an octave.

"But the situation is changing," I said after a time. "The Negro may not understand exactly *how,* but he knows one thing—the only way out of this tragedy is through education, training. Thousands of them sacrifice everything to get the education, to prove once and for all that the Negro's capacity for learning, for accomplishment, is equal to that of any other man—that the pigment has nothing to do with degrees of intelligence, talent or virtue. This isn't just wishful thinking. It's been proved conclusively in every field."

"We don't hear about those things," he said.

"I know. Southern newspapers print every rape, attempted rape, suspected rape and 'maybe rape,' but outstanding accomplishment is not considered newsworthy. Even the Southern Negro has little chance to know this, since he reads the same slanted reports in the newspapers."

The young man slowed to a halt in a little settlement to let me out.

"I'm sorry about a while ago—I don't know what got into me," he said.

"I've already forgotten it."

"No offense?"

"No offense."

"Okay. Good luck to you."

I thanked him and stepped out onto the wet neon reflections of the road. The air, cool and mist-filled, surrounded me with its freshness. I watched the red taillight of his car fog into the distance.

Summary

As anthropologists use the term, *culture* is the way of life shared by a group of people. It is what makes people similar to one another and unites them as a group, overcoming individual differences in personality. Culture is *acquired* behavior; it is learned rather than inherited genetically.

Not too long ago, anthropologists believed that culture was a uniquely human phenomenon, but as more was learned about the behavior of other primates, this notion has been discarded. First we found that some primates use tools in their natural setting. Then it was discovered that they even manufacture the tools that they use. More recently, we have witnessed primates inventing new patterns of behavior (such as washing sweet potatoes in sea water) and then transmitting that behavior to one another. Attempts to teach chimpanzees sign language have shown us that human beings are not the only animals capable of language, or even conceptual thought. In other words, we have recognized that culture as a dividing line between the human species and other animals is not as clear-cut as we used to believe.

One way of comprehending the distinction that sets us apart from other animals is to look at the sheer quantity of cultural behavior in human beings, as opposed to other animals. Also, if we look at the kinds of behavior that are found in all societies, or what we refer to as *cultural universals,* we recognize many things that are not found in the behavior of any other species.

Culture is transmitted from one generation to the next through the process known as *socialization.* Although the methods of teaching children the appropriate behavior patterns may vary from one society to another, all societies engage in some form of child training. We assume that early childhood experiences will have a lasting effect upon an individual, and insofar as the same basic experiences are shared by most children in a society, a general personality pattern will be shared among most adults in that society. Anthropologists sometimes describe such a pattern in terms of the *world view* of a culture. Examples are the *amoral familism* described by Banfield in a southern Italian peasant community, or the *image of limited good* analyzed by Foster in a Mexican peasant village. In some cases personality patterns can be described by using psychological tests administered to a large number of people. The most familiar tests used by anthropologists are the *Rorschach*, or ink-blot test, and the *Thematic Apperception Test*, or TAT. The aim of such personality tests is not to determine whether a particular individual is "normal" according to *our* standards, but to find an overall pattern for another culture. Studies of Samoan culture by Margaret Mead and studies by Ruth Benedict comparing several different cultural configurations are early examples of the approach in anthropology known as *culture and personality*.

Glossary

age grading The organization of groups in some societies based upon the association of individuals of similar age.

amoral familism The personality pattern, interaction with other villagers and the whole way of life (described by anthropologist Edward Banfield) characterized by maximizing the short-term advantage of one's immediate family at the expense of the rest of the community.

basic personality type The features of personality that are shared by most of a society's members and that result from the early childhood experiences the group's members have in common.

bipedal locomotion The ability to walk upright on two feet. Other nonhuman primates can also stand on two feet, but they cannot do this for long periods of time, nor can they extend their legs to straighten their knees.

erect posture The ability to stand upright, so that the arms and hands are free for other activities, such as making and using tools.

fewer offspring Many animals have numerous offspring per birth to increase the chances that some of them will survive. Our species has fewer offspring, but care for them better, thus increasing the chance for survival.

opposable thumb The ability to cross the thumb over the other fingers in a position similar to that used in holding a pencil. This grip allows the manufacture and use of tools, and also the manipulation of other objects in the environment.

prolonged childhood Human children are born defenseless and depend upon the care and attention provided by mothers. This provides a long period in which children can learn the culture shared by the members of the group.

sense of sight The reliance upon the sense of sight and the capacity for three-dimensional or binocular vision. This ability evolved at the expense of the senses of hearing and smelling.

configuration The integration of the different traits of a culture into a dominant pattern or central theme. The different institutions of the culture are organized around this central theme.

cultural universals The basic solutions to the problems of living that are found in one form or another in all cultures.

culture The shared way of life, common to a group of people and acquired as a member of society. This way of life is learned through interaction with other people, and includes both material aspects and intangible knowledge (beliefs, attitudes, values, rules of behavior, etc.).

culture and personality The branch of cultural anthropology that studies the relationship between the way the culture molds children's personalities and the psychological makeup of the adult personalities. This assumes that early childhood experiences play an important part in the formation of adult personalities, and the anthropologist investigates the childrearing practices of a group to discover their relationship to personalities in later years.

eschatology The philosophy that each culture has concerning the nature of death.

image of limited good The way of life (described by anthropologist George Foster) found in many peasant societies in which desired things are viewed as existing in a finite quantity and always in short supply. The advantages gained by one person are seen as losses to others.

instinct The inborn traits that characterize most nonhuman animal behavior.

life crisis rite (also called **rite of passage**) A ceremony marking the change from one period or stage of life into another (e.g., baptism, bar mitzvah, marriage, funeral).

nonhuman primates New World monkeys, Old World monkeys, and apes.

primary institutions The groups and individuals that play a fundamental role in the process of child rearing (e.g., peers, family, early schooling).

primates The order in the Linnaean taxonomy that includes monkeys, apes and humans.

Rorschach test A technique to measure personality that is based upon an informant's description of an "ink-blot" design. It is assumed that the description is given according to the informant's perceptions, and thus reveals the individual's personality.

socialization The process of learning to be a member of a society. A child learns the appropriate rules of behavior by interacting with people in the society.

society An organized group of individuals engaging in social interaction and forming a unit bound together by their shared way of life or culture.

Thematic Apperception Test (TAT) A technique to measure personality based upon a series of pictures designed according to the cultural context. For each scene the informant invents a story, which can be analyzed to reveal personality characteristics.

world view The basic outlook (relationship to nature, the native's point of view, values, attitudes, morals, beliefs) held in common by most members of a society.

Questions for Discussion

1 In American society there are many smaller groups, which we refer to as *subcultures* (e.g., black subculture, student subculture, drug subculture, etc.). What subcultures are present in your community? Which of these do you belong to? What types of values, attitudes and beliefs are shared by the members of these groups, and how are they different from the general pattern in American society?

2 Looking at Murdock's list of cultural universals, in what form is each of these found in American culture? Which of these might also be present in other animals?

3 Thinking in terms of Benedict's configurationist approach, what themes are present in American culture? What institutions and behavior support these themes and how are they integrated (e.g., individualism, Protestant ethic, capitalism, etc.)?

4 What are some common child-rearing practices found in American culture? How might you perceive their relationship to the adult personality type?

5 What are the secular and religious rites of passage in American society? What sort of transition or change in the stage of life is marked by each, and what type of ceremony is associated with each?

6 What are the primary or basic socializing institutions in American society (e.g., family, school, peer groups, etc.)? What influence does each

have upon the child's early experiences? How would you explain the "generation gap" in American society on the basis of the incompleteness of the socialization process?

Suggestions for Additional Reading

Definitions of culture

Bohannan, Paul
1963 Social Anthropology. New York: Holt, Rinehart and Winston.

An excellent textbook in social anthropology, although somewhat outdated. Contains a detailed discussion of the paradoxical nature of the concept of culture, as discussed in this chapter.

Kroeber, Alfred L., and Clyde Kluckhohn
1952 Culture: A Critical Review of Concepts and Definitions. Papers of the Peabody Museum of American Archaeology and Ethnology, Harvard University, volume 47.

A collection of definitions of culture, with comments on their utility for anthropology.

Linton, Ralph
1936 The Study of Man. New York: Appleton-Century-Crofts.

One of the earliest attempts at a synthesis of anthropological theory, this book still stands as one of the outstanding reference works in the field.

White, Leslie A., with Beth Dillingham
1973 The Concept of Culture. Minneapolis: Burgess Publishing Company.

A short discussion of the anthropological view of the culture concept by the leading cultural evolutionist in modern anthropology.

Culture among primates

Gardner, R. Allen, and Beatrice T. Gardner
1969 Teaching Sign Language to a Chimpanzee. Science 165: 664–672.

Premack, Ann J., and David Premack
1972 Teaching Language to an Ape. Scientific American October 92–99.

Two influential studies of language use among higher primates.

Socialization and child-rearing

Mead, Margaret
1928 Coming of Age in Samoa. New York: William Morrow & Company.

A comparison of the process of growing up among Samoan and American adolescent girls.

Whiting, Beatrice B. (editor)
1963 Six Cultures: Studies of Child Rearing. New York: John Wiley & Sons.

Comparative studies of child-rearing practices in the Far East, India, Africa and North America.

Personality and culture

LeVine, Robert A.
1973 Culture, Behavior and Personality. Chicago: Aldine.

A review and criticism of previous theories of personality and a discussion of a Darwinian model as the framework for the author's own approach to the study of personality.

LeVine, Robert A. (editor)
1974 Culture and Personality: Contemporary Readings. Chicago: Aldine.

An up-to-date collection of significant articles on the study of personality and culture.

World view and cultural configurations

Banfield, Edward C.
1958 The Moral Basis of a Backward Society. New York: The Free Press.

A study of southern Italian peasant world view, which the author describes as "amoral familism."

Benedict, Ruth
1959 (orig. 1934) Patterns of Culture. Preface by Margaret Mead. Boston: Houghton Mifflin Co.

The classic study of three societies—the Zuni, Kwakiutl and Dobu—and the patterns of culture in each.

Dundes, Alan
1968 The Number Three in American Culture. In: Alan Dundes, editor, Every Man His Way. Englewood Cliffs, N.J.: Prentice-Hall.

A fascinating analysis of one of the most common patterns in American culture.

Foster, George M.
1967 Tzintzuntzan: Mexican Peasants in a Changing World. Boston: Little, Brown.

A study of a Mexican peasant community, in which the author describes the world view of "the image of limited good."

Values, Ethnocentrism, and Cultural Relativism

Chapter Three

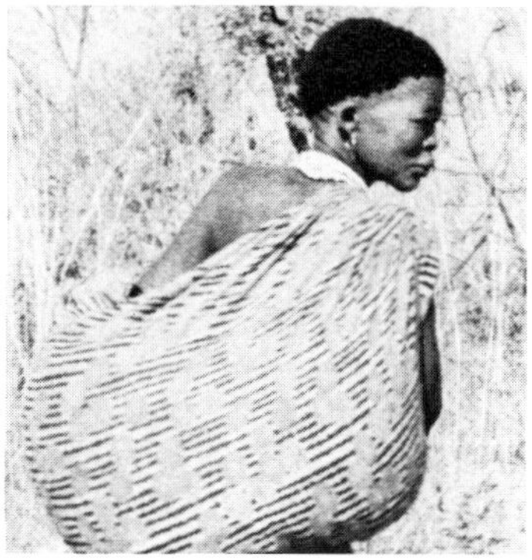

Culture is the way of life shared by a group of people, setting them off from others. Anthropologists who go to live in a foreign culture necessarily leave the familiarity of their own culture and enter a situation in which they do not know all the rules of proper behavior. Eventually they learn a new culture, and are then able to describe it and analyze it. This is the way cultural anthropologists conduct research. As you can see, it can be very exciting, but it can also cause many problems.

Culture Shock

An anthropologist's experience in living and working in a foreign culture can be lonely and frustrating; we must disregard much of our own cultural background in order to get along in the new world in which we find ourselves. In the process of shedding our cultural preferences, we frequently experience what we call *culture shock*. This is not something limited to anthropologists, for if you have ever spent much time outside your own country, or even in a vastly different subculture within the country, you have probably had a taste of it yourself. Culture shock is a feeling of depression and utter frustration that overcomes a person when he first begins to comprehend the tremendous difference between the way of life he is used to and the way of life in his new setting.

Why does culture shock occur? In the process of being brought up in a society, every individual is trained to accept the values of the group, and to follow the unwritten code of behavior. But it does not stop there, for the acceptance of a particular way of life is not

The best reason for exposing oneself
to foreign ways is to generate
a sense of vitality and awareness—
an interest in life which can come only
when one lives through the shock of
contrast and difference.

EDWARD T. HALL *The Silent Language*

simply based upon fear of punishment or social isolation. As part of the process of learning a culture, we are taught to believe in that culture, to believe that it is the right way, the best way to live. The values are not only seen as the ones that fit in with that particular way of life, they are considered the best ones for all people to follow. Any other way of doing things that does not follow the same value system is wrong, and often even repugnant.

Thus when a person leaves his own culture and enters another, his old values come into conflict with the new ones he finds. The solutions to the problems that we face daily are not the same from one culture to another, and the patterns of behavior, the norms and the morals differ as well. The experience in a new culture leads to intense frustration. For one thing, in working in a new language, it is always frustrating not to be able to express yourself completely, both in fieldwork and in terms of your private feelings and emotions. I can recall many such occasions when I was forced to skip over what I thought was an important question simply because I could not think of the proper word or could not make my request understood. Not being able to keep up with a conversation, or to eavesdrop on what others are saying, can be difficult to cope with, especially when the anthropologist is trying to get the message across to the people he is working with that he, too, is human, that he is very much like them, and that he has something to contribute to their conversations and to their lives. This lack of communication is something we have all experienced in our own society, when we try to cross barriers in order to make ourselves understood, or to understand others. There are gaps between generations, between sexes, between occupational groups, between any two different groups, and we all know how upsetting it can be not to be able to bridge them.

While working in a village in the Swiss Alps, I was curious about what aspects of their traditional culture the villagers accepted and what they rejected, and why. To understand the effects of modernization in a formerly agricultural village, I asked all kinds of questions about personal identity, morality, self-evaluation, attitudes toward family and friends, goals and ambitions, and so forth. At the same time, I wanted them to get to know me better, and I tried to engage them in conversation which would enable me to reciprocate. But somehow, whenever we started talking about my personal experiences, the topic always shifted to what were currently the key issues in their picture of America. They could not have cared less about my own values, attitudes, goals, etc. What they wanted to know was why Jackie Kennedy married Aristotle Onassis. Did she really need the money? And did Lyndon Johnson really have John Kennedy killed, and how did he get away with it? Did they still wear guns in the wild West, and ride horses, and shoot each other in the streets? Did gangsters in Chicago still carry sub-machine guns and rub each other out in gang wars? The more vehemently I protested against this image of my culture that they had apparently picked up from TV, movies and popular magazines, the less they wanted to talk to me about America. I was ruining their fun by telling them things they did not want to hear, and so they avoided me. In all the time I was there I was never able to portray myself to them, and despite my attempts to alter my image I remained a mystery to adults and young people alike in the village.

Ethnocentrism

Culture shock can be an excellent lesson in relative values and in the general understanding of human differences. The reason that culture shock occurs is that we are unprepared for these differences. By the very nature of the way we are taught our culture, we are all what is called *ethnocentric*. The term comes from the Greek root *ethnos*, meaning a people or group. Thus ethnocentric refers to the fact that our outlook or world view is centered around our own way of life to the exclusion of others. Ethnocentrism is the belief that one's own patterns of behavior are the best, most natural, beautiful, right, or important. A corollary to this is the belief that everyone else, to

Young Kau-Nyaro girls in the Sudan have been "beautified." (George Rodger, Magnum)

the extent that he lives differently, lives by inhuman, irrational, unnatural or wrong standards.

Ethnocentrism is the point of view that one's own culture is preferred to all others, and as such it is characteristic of how all people feel about themselves as compared to outsiders. There is no one in our society who is not ethnocentric to some degree, no matter how liberal and open-minded he might claim to be. There will always be something he will find repugnant in another culture, whether it be a pattern of sexual practices that conflicts with his own moral code, a way of treating friends or relatives, or simply a favorite food that he somehow cannot manage to get down with a smile. It is not something we should be ashamed of, because it is a natural outcome of growing up in our society, or in any society. However, as anthropologists who study other cultures, it is something we should constantly be aware of, so that when we are tempted to make value judgments

Although we might find these Masai styles of bodily adornment unattractive, each culture defines beauty in its own way. (Marc and Evelyne Bernheim, Woodfin Camp)

about another way of life, we are able to hold back and look at the situation objectively, recognizing our bias.

Ethnocentrism can be seen in many aspects of the culture—in myths, folk tales, proverbs, and even the language of most peoples. For example, in many languages, particularly among non-Western societies, the word used to refer to one's own tribe or ethnic group literally means "man" or "human." The implication of course is that those who are members of other groups are somewhat less than human. For example, the term "Eskimo," used to designate those Indian groups that inhabit the arctic and sub-arctic regions, is an Indian word used by neighbors of the Eskimos who observed their strange way of life, but did not share it. The term means literally "eaters of raw flesh," and as such is an ethnocentric observation about cultural peculiarities that were normal to one group and thoroughly repulsive to another. On the other hand, if we look at one term by which a subgroup among the Eskimos called itself (they obviously did not perceive their eating of raw flesh as a significant way of differentiating themselves), we find the term *Inuit,* which literally means "real people." Here, then, is a contrast between one's own group, which is real, and the rest of the world, which is not so "real." Both terms, Eskimo and Inupik, are equally ethnocentric—one as an observation about differences, the other as a self-evaluation.

Another example of ethnocentrism in language can be found in the origin of the English term "barbarian." Originally a Greek word, the term was used to refer to the tribes that lived around the periphery of ancient Greek society. The Greeks referred to these people as "barbars," because they could not understand their speech. Bar-bar was the word in Greek for the sound that a dog makes, a cognate to our English word bow-wow. The Greeks, in a classic example of ethnocentrism, considered those whose speech was unintelligible to be on the level of dogs, which were likewise unintelligible. They did not accord such people the status of human being, in much the same way that the word "Eskimo" relegates those people to a lower than human status.

Shifting from language to myths and folk tales, we can see an excellent example of ethnocentrism in the creation myth of the Cherokee Indians. According to this story, the Creator made three clay images of man and baked them in an oven. In his haste to admire his handiwork, he took the first image out of the oven before it was fully baked, and found it was too pale. He waited a while, then removed the second image, and it was just right, a full golden, reddish-brown hue. He was so pleased with his work that he sat there and admired it, completely forgetting about the third image. Finally he smelled it burning, but by the time he could rescue it from the oven it had already been burnt, and it came out completely black.

Food is perhaps the most common manifestation of ethnocentrism. Every culture has developed special preferences for certain kinds of food and drink, and equally strong negative attitudes toward others. It is interesting to note that much of this ethnocentrism is in our heads, and not in our tongues, for something may taste perfectly delicious until we are told what it is. We have all heard stories about someone being fed a meal of snake or horse meat or something equally objectionable in American culture, and commenting on how tasty it was—until, that is, he was told what he had just eaten, upon which he turned green and hurriedly asked to be excused from the table.

Certain food preferences seem perfectly natural to us. We usually do not recognize that they are natural only because we have grown up with them; they are quite likely unnatural to someone from a different culture. In southeast Asia, for example, the majority of adults do not drink milk, a result of lactase deficiency in the population, as discussed in the first chapter. To many Americans it would be positively inconceivable that people in other parts of the world do not drink milk, for it is a "natural" food for us. Likewise, it seems to many of us to be entirely irrational that in India people do not eat beef because of their religious belief that the cow is a sacred animal. Beef is the mainstay of the middle-class American diet, and any culture in which cattle are available but are not eaten seems very strange indeed. In some parts of Africa, where cattle are raised, there is a similar practice of not killing them for their meat. In these societies, cattle are primarily a form of wealth, and they are only eaten after they die a natural death, a practice that would certainly dull the appetites of most Americans.

One of the favorite delicacies in China is dog meat; the thought of eating a dog is enough to make most Americans sick to their stomachs. Yet we can see how this is part of a cultural pattern. Americans keep dogs as pets, and develop close relationships with them. Thus we tend to think of a dog as almost human, and would not dream of eating its meat. Horses, too, sometimes become close pets, and horse meat is likewise rejected by most Americans, although certainly not because of its taste. You may have eaten it without even knowing it, and probably you would not recognize it if someone didn't tell you what you were eating. On the other hand, we generally do not develop close relationships with cows or pigs, animals that we eat without any twinge of conscience. In India a cow is treated with the kind of personal care that a horse or even a dog receives in our country, and the thought of eating beef is similar to our feeling about eating dog meat. On the other hand, in China dogs are not treated as kindly as they are in the United States. In the absence of a personal relationship with a dog as a pet, it becomes quite similar to a cow in our culture, and can be eaten easily.

We learn to be ethnocentric as part of growing up in our society. By chance I happened upon an old geography textbook used in grammar schools in the United States around 1920, entitled *Our Wonder World,* Volume 1: The World and Its Peoples. It begins with a discus-

Food tastes are culturally prescribed. Balinese men prepare a routine meal to be roasted over coals. (George Rodger, Magnum)

sion of the heavens, the place of the earth in the heavens, the origin of the earth, the nature of the earth's surface, and the animals that live and have lived here. It then goes into the story of human evolution and the evolution of culture.

Of particular interest to me, as a cultural anthropologist, were the two chapters on human variation and cultural diversity, entitled "The Queer People of the World," and "Other Peoples of the World." In "The Queer People of the World," subtitled "The Black, Brown, Red, and Yellow Races and Their Ways," the reader is taken on a tour of some of the more bizarre customs of other cultures, described in the most ethnocentric terms conceivable. The chapter begins with a rather sophisticated statement of the awareness of cultural differences:

> To be queer is to be different from what is ordinary and normal. Each one of us decides from his own experience and surroundings what is natural and reasonable. Then we feel that everybody who departs from these ways of ours is a bit queer.
>
> So "queer peoples" are no more strange and odd to us than we are to them. If you visited some of the places and tribes about which you are going to read, you would find yourself such an odd sight that children and grown persons would turn and follow you in the streets, just as you might turn and follow a circus parade if you met one. In the great human family there are many peoples whose ways and habits are unlike ours, and our interest is in these very differences. Some are uncivilized, and so take us back to a kind of life more like that of our ancestors than anything we are acquainted with; others are highly civilized, but their civilization is on another plane from ours.[1]

Despite this disclaimer, the chapter goes on to make some incredible claims, totally unscientific and unacceptable in light of today's knowledge about other cultures. In the subsection "Peoples of the Negro or Black Division," we read the following:

> First, let us take some of the black peoples, who live mostly in the Sudan, South Africa, and Australasia, but have migrated to many other parts of the world. Some of the most interesting of these black-skinned peoples live still in Africa. The true black people are the Negroes, whose home is in the middle part of Africa. They are the people with the black skins, the woolly heads, the thick lips, the flat noses, and the beautiful white teeth. The home of the Bantu race is the great southern

1. *Our Wonder World*, Vol. 1. Chicago: Geo. L. Shuman & Co., 1918, p. 308.

> section of Africa. They are not so black as the Negroes. Both peoples are brave, intelligent, and able to adapt themselves to new conditions and take on civilization. Smaller tribes are the Pygmies, the Hottentots, and the Bushmen, all far below the Negroes and Bantus in intelligence.[2]

The scene shifts to "The Wild Bushmen," described in some detail. It is interesting particularly to note how the evaluation of these people according to white middle-class American standards of the time continually creeps into the description. Is it any wonder that a school child of 1920 who read the following textbook description of a non-Western society would come away with a feeling of superiority?

> Almost every people has passed through a hunting stage in its development. The Bushmen stayed at that stage. They represent the typical hunters of the world. Free of all property, never settled in one place, never held by any industries or agricultural ties, they range the hunting grounds of Africa. Their arrows are tipped with wood, bone or stone. They need no home, for they can make one in a few hours out of brushwood. Their usual garb is a robe of sheepskin thrown over the body and fastened with a sharp thong. The Bushman needs no fireplace or cooking utensils, for his only way of preparing food is to throw the raw flesh on the fire or on hot stones for roasting.[3]

Compare this description of Bushmen society with that of the anthropologist Richard B. Lee.[4] After a lengthy study of the way Bushmen relate to and blend into their environment, Lee concluded that they were the original "leisure class." He estimated that based upon the way they exploited their environment to obtain food, they could survive quite well with a balanced diet and high caloric intake, on only a few hours of work each day. The rest of their time they could devote to leisure, without fear of starvation. Given the harshness of their desert surroundings, it is improbable that the extra labor to acquire and maintain the trappings of civilization such as industry and agriculture would be worth the effort. Yet as we read this account of Bushmen culture, we come away with an altogether different feeling. The reason is clear: It is a description full of ethnocentric statements, with values injected into every line, comparisons made on a purely

2. *Ibid.*, p. 308.
3. *Ibid.*, p. 309.
4. Richard B. Lee and Irven DeVore, *Man the Hunter.* Chicago: Aldine, 1968.

subjective basis. Strange practices are portrayed not as different, but as inferior. But the story does not end here, for a few pages later we read of the "Fuzzy-Haired Papuans:"

> You have all heard of cannibals, that is, savages who eat human beings. You will be surprised to hear that these Papuans, who can be so polite to one another, were, until within recent years, given to this dreadful habit of cannibalism. The idea of eating others was that when a man ate another man he acquired the victim's qualities, physical strength, courage, cleverness, or cunning. Since the coming of the missionaries to the islands the Fijians have largely become Christians, and have given up cannibalism and almost all their other barbaric customs.[5]

There is no attempt to describe other ways of life in a total cultural context, but only to show how inferior they are when compared to our civilized customs. The other side of the coin is never presented, so that the young, impressionable minds of the readers of this textbook could learn that values are a relative thing. There is a description of the Bushmen, who "eat every creeping, running, and flying thing they can lay their hands on, including snakes and slugs." But nowhere is it mentioned how utterly repulsive it might seem to a Bushman, who shares all of his food with his relatives and friends and everyone in his society, if he were to see a rich fat-cat in our industrial society who gorged himself on food and was 50 pounds overweight, while others in his society went to bed hungry. We are ethnocentric because we are not taught to question our own way of life, but only to evaluate other practices against ours as a standard.

It is necessary to stop right here for a moment, to make a very important point. I have been describing anthropology in such a way that the reader might come to the conclusion that by studying it he or she can avoid being ethnocentric. This is not true. Modern anthropology as a discipline is moving away from ethnocentrism, and is advocating a perspective that allows for the acceptance of all diverse cultural practices without culture-bound evaluations. However, anthropologists, as human beings raised in a cultural setting, are and always will be ethnocentric. We can produce lofty treatises on how one must accept other ways as valid, but that does not mean that we can accept them in our own lives and practice them. Anthro-

5. *Our Wonder World*, p. 315.

Bushwomen of the Kalahari Desert in Botswana, southern Africa, gathering nuts for an evening meal. (Shostak, Anthro-Photo)

pologists, through long hours of training and personal discipline in their fieldwork, can learn to be more tolerant, but they will always be culture-bound to some extent. We can never completely get inside someone else's skin and live our lives according to the rules of another culture. Thus I cannot guarantee that by the time you finish this book you will no longer be ethnocentric, any more than I could say that I have shed myself of all the narrowmindedness that was a part of my upbringing. Ethnocentrism is not something we can will away—it creeps back constantly, as the following story illustrates.

A woman anthropologist was conducting field research in Colombia, and in the course of her work she learned that a particular Indian group there practiced the custom known as bride-price. According to this tradition, when a man took a woman as his wife, he or his family was obliged to offer a payment (in cattle, other goods, or money, or a combination of them all) to the bride's family. Although this is a fairly common practice in many non-Western societies (and elements of it can be seen in our own marriage customs, if you look closely), the anthropologist became upset at it, for she felt that it challenged the dignity of a woman to be bought and sold like any other possession. It never occurred to her that while it might rob a woman of her dignity in Western society, it could have exactly the opposite effect in the culture she was studying. Allowing her own values to come through, she asked one recent bride if it didn't bother her to be purchased like a cow. The woman replied by asking the anthropologist how much her husband had paid for her when they were married. Of course, the anthropologist explained that her husband had not paid anything, that we did not do such things in our society. "Oh, what a horrible thing" replied the Indian woman. "Your husband didn't even give a single cow for you? You must not be worth anything."[6]

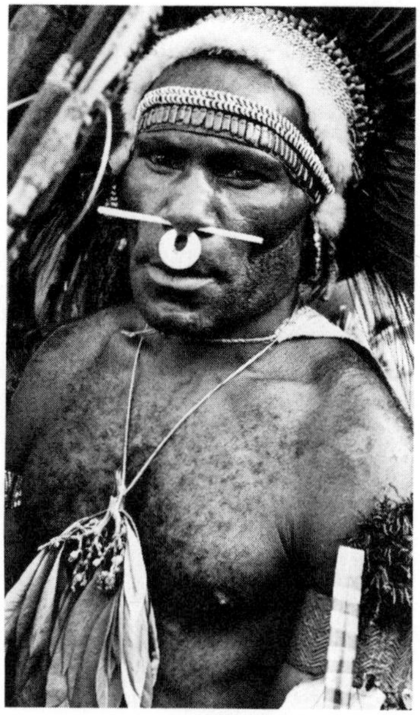

A Sepik River tribesman of New Guinea. (Elliott Erwitt, Magnum)

Cultural Relativism

The widespread reaction against ethnocentrism in anthropology is a relatively recent occurrence. The leading figure in the battle against the beliefs espoused in nineteenth-century anthropology was a man named Franz Boas, a dominant figure in the field of anthropology in the United States from the beginning of this century until his death in 1942. Not only did he influence anthropology through his many writings on all aspects of the field, but he taught a generation of anthropologists his methods and his beliefs, and his legacy has had a profound impact upon the discipline long after his death.

Anthropology in the nineteenth century was riddled with ethnocentrism, as were other social sciences. The theory of Charles Darwin, innocuous enough when applied to the natural world of plants and animals, became a dangerous tool in the hands of social scientists who applied it to cultural differences among human populations. Of course, Darwin himself never meant his theory of evolution to be applied to social change—on this point he is very clear—but others took some of the principles on which he based his theory and used them to explain the course of social evolution, usually in the absence of hard facts to support their claims. It was this "Social Darwinism," which really was not Darwin's theory at all, but a misapplication of it by others, that Franz Boas reacted against so strongly.

6. George M. Foster, *Traditional Societies and Technological Change*, Second Edition. New York: Harper and Row, 1973, p. 87.

Darwin's evolutionary scheme rests upon three main points: (1) There is variation among individuals of a given species—just look around the room and you will see it in the human species. (2) Sooner or later, either through population growth or a change in the environment or both, the resources necessary for survival will grow scarce (e.g., the food supply for a species of birds). In addition, when this happens, there will be a struggle for survival, and those that are better adapted to the environment because of their minor variations will tend to survive at a higher rate. (This is the famous notion of "survival of the fittest," although Darwin did not mean an actual physical battle; fittest among a bird population could mean having a different-shaped beak that enabled the bird to dig deeper into the tree bark for its food, but not to defeat other birds in battle.) (3) The survivors pass on the advantageous characteristics to their offspring, so that the next generation reflects their makeup to a greater extent. In this way evolution proceeds slowly over many generations, reflecting minor variations in a population that become more adaptive to the changing environment.

When this scheme was transferred to social evolution, the result was a number of ethnocentric doctrines, all of which were based upon a very superior attitude toward Western society, and a condescending attitude toward the so-called "primitives" who were the subject of investigation by anthropologists and some sociologists. This view of evolution prompted a racist theory that placed non-Western, nonwhite societies on a lower scale of cultural and physical development, simply because they did not have the technological and military capabilities that were found in the Western countries. It was felt that if we, as Westerners, could conquer and subdue other societies through our military superiority, then the rest of our culture—our political system, our religious convictions, our moral code—must also be superior. This in turn led to the belief that if we compared all of the societies around the world to our own, we could set up a scale on which we could rank them; those most like us were higher up the ladder, while those least like us were placed at the bottom.

This view of social evolution tended to justify the policy of colonialism and domination of the non-Western countries. It was felt, for example, that if the forces of evolution were operating on societies, eliminating those that were unfit, then the best thing to do was to let nature take its course. Colonizing a group of people was a way of helping them to survive in the face of impending extinction. Of course, the fact that they would have to be made more like Westerners (in dress, language, religion, and the like) was a necessity that was never questioned. Until Boas, no one ever challenged the logical fallacies in such a theory—the fact that there is a clear difference between societies and organisms, and that the mechanisms of change in one are not the same as in the other. No one mentioned that societies struggled for survival in a completely different context than organisms did (it was a physical battle, rather than a question of adaptation). No one pointed out that Social Darwinism was a conservative philosophy designed to maintain the status quo, which happened to be the domination of the world by the Western nations. Also, and perhaps most importantly to Boas, no one questioned the racist implications of this theory.

Nineteenth-century theories of social evolution were inherently racist because they were based upon the assumed superiority of the Western world, which meant the white world; non-Western, nonwhite societies occupied the lower levels of the evolutionary sequence. Anthropology, as a newly developing science in the nineteenth century, had inherited the problem of classifying the different peoples of the world, and had to devise a way to document the obvious racial differences in a more scientific manner. Of course the political and economic situation in America had a strong impact upon the directions that anthropologists took in their research and reporting. Despite the fact that the slaves had been emancipated and attained equal rights in law after the Civil War (or perhaps because of that fact), many Americans sought more scientific verifications of their prejudices, a more acceptable proof of the inferiority of the nonwhite races. Thus anthropology, along with all other branches of science in the nineteenth century, became a way to soothe the troubled conscience of the American middle class.[7]

It was against this background that Boas entered the scene. Perhaps he had an advantage in his opposition to the previous half-century of American anthropology, in that he was German by birth, trained in German universities, without the heritage of American culture and American history to influence his ideas and penetrate his values. He rejected the attempts that had been made to show a correlation between race and level of cultural evolution—that is, the superiority of Western,

The New York Public Library

Franz Boas (1858–1942) *received his early training in mathematics and physics, but became interested in anthropology after a trip to Baffinland, in the Northwest Territories of Canada. In 1899 Boas became Professor of Anthropology at Columbia University, where he remained throughout his career. Boas was a leading figure in the attack against the theory of cultural evolution prominent in the nineteenth century. Most evolutionary scales ranked non-Western societies lower than Europeans because they did not have a pattern of monogamous marriage or a fully developed concept of private property or a complex bureaucratic system. Instead, Boas argued strongly for a position of cultural relativism, in which one culture may not be judged or ranked according to the standards of another.*

7. For more detailed analysis, see the excellent summary of nineteenth-century scientific attitudes on the question of race in John S. Haller, *Outcasts from Evolution*, Urbana: University of Illinois Press, 1971.

white cultures. He was particularly vexed by the assumption that nonwhites were less intelligent, as the following passage indicates:

> It has often been claimed that the very primitiveness of human handiwork of early times proves organic mental inferiority. This argument is certainly not tenable, for we find in modern times isolated tribes living in a way that may very well be paralleled with early conditions. A comparison of the psychic life of these groups does not justify the belief that their industrial backwardness is due to a difference in the types of organism, for we find numbers of closely related races on the most diverse levels of cultural status. . . . It is safe to say that the results of the extensive materials amassed during the last fifty years do not justify the assumption of any close relation between biological types and form of culture.[8]

In his opposition to the ethnocentrism of nineteenth-century anthropology, Boas arrived at a position best described as *cultural relativism*. By this he meant that the anthropologist must maintain strict neutrality in describing and comparing other cultures, and make no judgments concerning the merits of one culture over another. Cultural relativism for Boas was an ethical position, by which all cultures were taken as equal, each as a separate unit with its own integrity, none of which should be compared to our own culture in terms of how they measure up to our standards. This position dominated anthropology in the early 1900s, and has been an important part of the field ever since.

Cultural relativism was a logical outcome of Boas' work in showing that the history of each group was distinct. Thus, whatever a culture is like today, it became that way as a result of its own development, and therefore cannot be ranked against another culture with a different history. Each culture has changed over time, some more than others in particular areas, and some as a response to certain pressures that others did not face. The point for Boas was that because each culture had its own independent history, all groups could not be compared on a scale of excellence that conformed to any one particular group. There could be no assumption that there was a model toward which all change had been directed in the past, for change had proceeded in many different directions at the same time.

Boas' position, which he passed on to his students as perhaps

8. Franz Boas, *Race, Language, and Culture*. New York: The Free Press, 1966, pp. 249–250.

his greatest gift to anthropology, involves both an attempt to maintain neutrality in analyzing cultural differences, and at the same time an awareness of one's own cultural biases, which inevitably creep in. If we are to make judgments about another culture, they should not be based upon our own background, but on the basis of our experience in that other culture—and only on that basis. In short, the anthropologist should put everything else out of mind when describing another people. One of Boas' students, Margaret Mead, tells how she came to this conclusion in her first field trip to Samoa in the 1920s. Her autobiography, *Blackberry Winter,* from which the following passage was taken, offers the reader a myriad of insights into the nature of perhaps the most famous anthropologist of our time.

> . . . field work is a very difficult thing to do. To do it well, one has to sweep one's mind clear of every presupposition, even those about other cultures in the same part of the world in which one is working. Ideally, even the appearance of a house should come to one as a surprise that there are houses and that they are square or round or oval, that they do or do not have walls, that they let in the sun or keep out the wind or rain, that people do or do not cook or eat in a dwelling house. In the field one can take nothing for granted. For as soon as one does, one cannot see what is before one's eyes as fresh and distinctive, and when one treats what is new merely as a variant of something already known, this may lead one far astray. Seeing a house as bigger or smaller, grander or meaner, more or less watertight than some other kind of house one already knows about cuts one off from discovering what *this* house is in the minds of those who live in it. Later, when one has come to know the new culture, everything has to be reassimilated into what is already known about other peoples living in that area, into our knowledge about primitive peoples, and into our knowledge about all human beings, so *far*. But the point of going to the field at all is to extend further what is already known, and so there is little value merely in identifying new versions of the familiar when we might, instead, find something wholly new. But to clear one's mind of presuppositions is a very hard thing to do . . .[9]

Every culture proposes solutions to the problems people face. If the anthropologist is to look at these solutions—for example, looking at a house as a solution to the problem of shelter—then he must consider it from the point of view of those people, in the context of their culture.

9. Margaret Mead, *Blackberry Winter, My Earlier Years*. New York: Simon and Schuster, 1972, pp. 143-144.

If a solution seems to him impractical based upon his background and his knowledge of a different way of doing it, he must not overlook the fact that within its own context it may be very practical indeed. For example, Americans tend to be critical of people in other societies who have high birth rates, yet who suffer from periodic famine and a high death rate through starvation or malnutrition. It seems "irrational" to us to have more children when there is not enough food to feed the people already alive. We make a value judgment based upon

Margaret Mead and a Samoan girl, during one of Mead's early field trips. (Margaret Mead, Blackberry Winter*)*

our calculation of the situation. We do not attempt to see the context in which the people themselves make decisions. In fact, if we do look deeper, we will find that it is for them a very rational decision. They know that the chances of an infant's surviving to adulthood are not very good—not just because of the dangers of starvation, but because

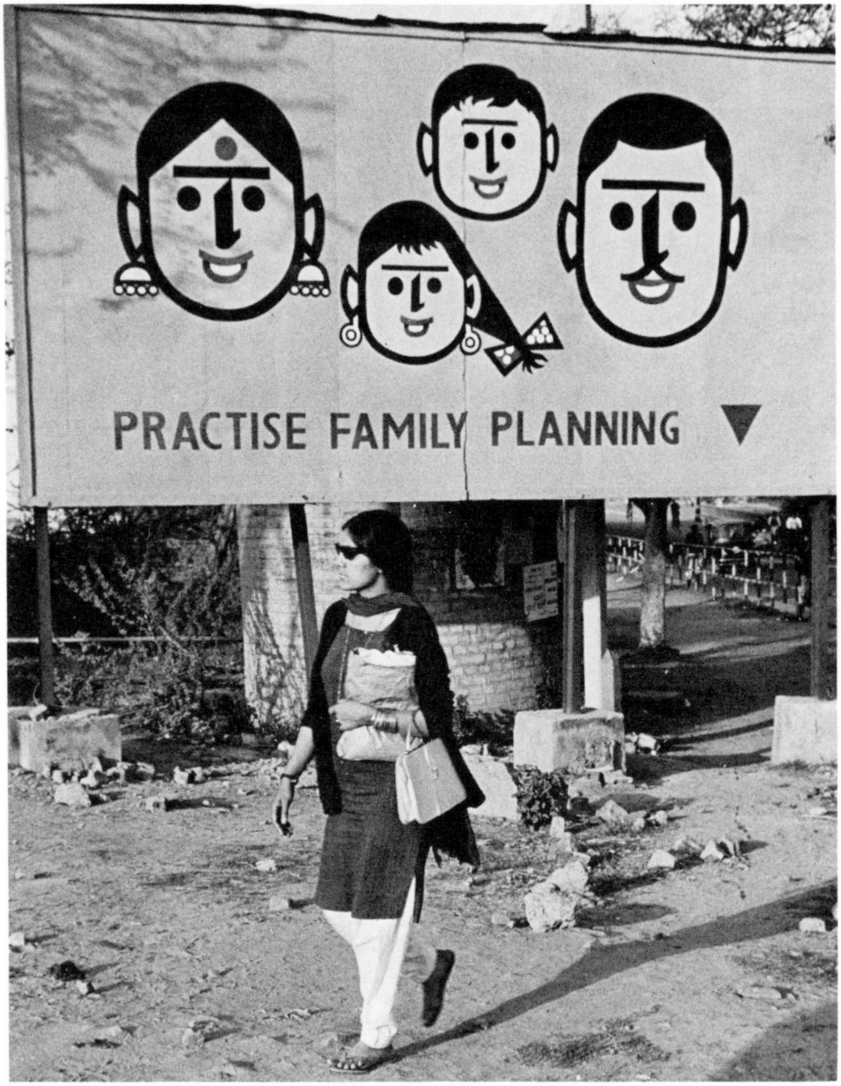
PRACTISE FAMILY PLANNING

If Western ideas of birth control are to be effective in India and in other non-Western cultures, they must conform to existing cultural patterns. (Hubertus Kanus, Rapho/Photo Researchers)

of the high rate of disease and the poor medical facilities available to them. Therefore, they calculate that if they wish to have a certain number of children survive to adulthood (perhaps a number sufficient to insure them support in their old age), then it is necessary for them to have more than that number of infants. How much more "rational" can you get?

Or let us take the example of a young man who works as a day laborer. He does not work every day, but only a few days a month, and only earns as much as he has to in order to support his family at a minimal level of survival. We might be inclined to think that he is lazy, that he has no ambition, and that he will never get ahead. Within our cultural context that might be an accurate assessment of the situation. Let us look more closely, however, at the context in which the man makes his decisions. Indeed, we may find that in his society it is customary for a man to open up his house to his relatives, and never to refuse them his hospitality. If he lives at a bare subsistence level, he has nothing left over to offer his relatives, and they will probably leave him alone. However, if he earns more than is necessary for him to survive and to feed his immediate family, he is likely to be invaded by all kinds of relatives who have a legitimate claim to his hospitality. He knows this, and his decision to work only as much as is necessary is very rational. He realizes he would not be working for himself, and that he would not be able to get ahead, and therefore values his leisure time according to what he knows about his own culture. For us to suggest that he is lazy would be for us not to put out of our minds what is the case in our own society—to judge others by our own standards.

Even one's perception of the physical world is affected by relative cultural interpretations. In the first chapter of this book, it was noted that not every language contains the same number of basic words for colors. We might find a language in which blue and green and red were all called by one term. It is hard for us to comprehend, but that does not make it any less valid a solution to the problem of describing the physical world. To turn the tables slightly, in many societies there are distinct words used to refer to relatives that we lump together under one term in the English language. We use the word "uncle" to describe several different kinds of relatives: father's brother, mother's brother, father's sister's husband, and mother's sister's husband, as well as occasionally people who are great-uncles, and sometimes even people who are not uncles in any biological relationship, but who are close to us in a social sense. Yet in many societies there are distinct terms for each of these different types of uncle. If we find these societies strange because they call red and green and blue by the same term, think of how strange we must seem to them, when we can't even tell the difference between our mother's brother and our father's brother, or between an uncle by birth and an uncle by marriage. How ignorant we must be of the entire biological process of reproduction!

Relative Values

One of the most fruitful discussions of cultural relativism concerns values and morals. It is a particularly interesting topic because it is the strongest factor in culture shock, yet so easily identifiable as the most ethnocentric area of our behavior. We tend to be much more defensive about our moral behavior than most other aspects of our culture, perhaps because it is so strongly ingrained in us from our early childhood throughout our lives. A system of morals and values is based upon the entire cultural and physical environment in which we grow up, and cannot be separated from it. Yet when the anthropologist goes into the field, he is confronted with a totally new value system that most likely conflicts with his own in many ways. He may find many values totally unacceptable to him personally—a perfectly valid conclusion to come to—yet if he is true to his discipline he will not let this enter into his work. Rather, he must describe and analyze them as they fit into the entire culture of which they are a part. He may not approve, and he most certainly will reject the opportunity to participate, but if he is to translate the total culture he is studying, then he must present the practices he disapproves of in a completely objective fashion, so that the reader can understand what they mean to the people of that culture, without any outside evaluation by the anthropologist.

We may be studying a society where infanticide—the killing of young children—is practiced in order to maintain control over the population, a sort of retroactive birth control. The anthropologist might strongly disapprove. But if he is to present the culture objectively, he must explain this custom as it is perceived by the people who practice it. Among some traditional Eskimo groups, a similar practice existed. When a person became too old to contribute his share of the workload, he or she was left out on the ice to die. This may seem like an uncivilized way of dealing with one's parents, who raised one and gave one their love and care. Yet to describe it as that, and not to go into how it fits in with the rest of Eskimo culture, would not be acceptable according to anthropological standards. It is important to know, for example, that this is not done against the will of the old person. It is also necessary to recognize that this is an accepted practice for which people are adequately prepared throughout their lives, and not some kind of treachery sprung upon an individual as a result of a criminal conspiracy. Finally, it should be considered in light of the ecological situation in which the Eskimos live. Making

Our attitudes toward the elderly are based upon our economic capacity to support them. In a society where the major activity is producing food, we would expect different attitudes to develop. (Wide World)

a living in the Arctic is difficult at best, and the necessity of feeding an extra mouth, especially when there is little hope that the individual will again become productive in the food-procurement process, would mean that the whole group would suffer. It is not a question of Eskimos not liking old people, but rather a question of what is best for the entire group. We would not expect—and indeed we do not find—this practice to exist where there was adequate food to support those who were not able to contribute to the hunting efforts.

Sexual practices that do not conform to our moral standard have frequently been the basis upon which non-Western societies have been condemned as "primitive," or "barbaric." In the nineteenth century, the American anthropologist Lewis Henry Morgan claimed that all of human history pointed to the development of monogamy as the most perfect form of marriage. The closer to monogamy the marriage pattern of a society, the higher up the ladder of evolution it was. Conversely, the farther removed from monogamy a society's customs were, the more primitive it was. This view failed to take into account that marriage practices and sexual behavior are tied in with the rest of the culture, and what may make sense in one context might not make sense somewhere else. Let us look at the example of a society where there is no advanced medical science, and where the theory of how a child is conceived differs somewhat from our own scientific understanding. Whereas in our society monogamy is perhaps necessary if we are to determine the paternity of a child, in other societies this might not be the case. If it is thought that the sperm continue to contribute to the makeup of the child throughout pregnancy, rather than simply at the moment of conception (not a completely illogical conclusion, even though scientifically incorrect), then it might be considered proper for the mother to have intercourse with as many different men as possible during her pregnancy. In this way, she could insure that her child would have the best traits of all of her lovers. In fact, not to do so might be considered immoral, in that she would deprive a helpless child of its rightful opportunity.

Suppose, instead, it is believed that only the mother contributes to the makeup of the child. After all, the baby comes from the mother, and not at all from the father, when it is born. In this case, there would be a closer link between the mother and the infant than between the father and his child. To carry this argument further, because the father is unrelated to either the mother or the infant by birth, he would be even more distant from the child than the mother's brother, who is a blood relative to the mother, having been born of the same woman. Such a kinship system contradicts all of our Western notions about the role of the father in the family, yet in a different setting it makes perfect sense.

As you can tell from these examples, morality is not always as clear-cut as it might seem. While we can be firmly convinced of the validity of our own moral standards, we must recognize that they fit only one way of life. The lesson of cultural relativism is that we must always be on guard against applying our values and our moral standards to other ways of doing things. There can be no absolute standards. Anything that is possible is potentially acceptable in a particular cultural context. Every society has a system of morals and values, even if they vary tremendously from one to another. We may make judgments about whether that system is effective in any one society, but we may not make judgments about the specific content of such a system. For example, we might ask whether cultural relativism can be used to justify any sort of practice, such as cannibalism. We can explain it on the basis of conditions affecting the group. We can analyze it and determine whether it is effective, and how it fits in with other related practices. We can compare it to other practices in other societies as long as we maintain the distinctness of each. As an anthropologist it is my place to explain why certain cultural practices occur among a given group and others do not. Any justification I offer is based on my own private opinions, which are determined by my own cultural background. This does not mean that if I feel something is wrong, I do not have the obligation to say so. I cannot sit back in my chair and explain the extermination of the Jews in Hitler's Germany or the racism in the United States, and claim that my responsibility is over. I must speak out against injustice whenever and wherever I find it. But I must make a distinction between my obligation as an objective observer of other cultures, and my responsibilities as a human being. Cultural relativism is a way of attaining objectivity. It is not a stopping point, but a starting point.

The short article by Ralph Linton that follows, "One Hundred Percent American," is an appropriate way to bring this discussion of ethnocentrism and cultural relativism to a close. Most of us feel some degree of patriotism as a result of being brought up in America. We feel superior about our way of life, and we compare other practices and products of other cultures to our own in a rather unfavorable light. American cars are better, American athletes are better, American food is better—and better for you, too—and even the American political system is the best. We tend to argue over where something comes from, especially when the Russians claim to have invented it before we did. Linton's article takes this notion of "all-Americanism" and pokes a little good-natured fun at it.

One Hundred Percent American

Ralph Linton

There can be no question about the average American's Americanism or his desire to preserve this precious heritage at all costs. Nevertheless, some insidious foreign ideas have already wormed their way into his civilization without his realizing what was going on. Thus dawn finds the unsuspecting patriot garbed in pajamas, a garment of East Indian origin; and lying in a bed built on a pattern which originated in either Persia or Asia Minor. He is muffled to the ears in un-American materials: cotton, first domesticated in India; linen, domesticated in the Near East; wool from an animal native to Asia Minor; or silk whose uses were first discovered by the Chinese. All these substances have been transformed into cloth by methods invented in Southwestern Asia. If the weather is cold enough he may even be sleeping under an eiderdown quilt invented in Scandinavia.

On awakening he glances at the clock, a medieval European invention, uses one potent Latin word in abbreviated form, rises in haste, and goes to the bathroom. Here, if he stops to think about it, he must feel himself in the presence of a great American institution; he will have heard stories of both the quality and frequency of foreign plumbing and will know that in no other country does the average man perform his ablutions in the midst of such splendor. But the insidious foreign influence pursues him even here. Glass was invented by the ancient Egyptians, the use of glazed tiles for floors and walls in the Near East, porcelain in China, and the art of enameling on metal by Mediterranean artisans of the Bronze Age. Even his bathtub and toilet are but slightly modified copies of Roman originals. The only purely American contribution to the ensemble is the steam radiator, against which our patriot very briefly and unintentionally places his posterior.

In this bathroom the American washes with soap invented by the ancient Gauls. Next he cleans his teeth, a subversive European practice which did not invade America until the latter part of the eighteenth century. He then shaves, a masochistic rite first developed by the heathen priests of ancient Egypt and Sumer. The process is made less of a penance by the fact that his razor is of steel, an iron-carbon alloy discovered in either India or Turkestan. Lastly, he dries himself on a Turkish towel.

Returning to the bedroom, the unconscious victim of un-American practices removes his clothes from a chair, invented in the Near East, and proceeds to dress. He puts on close-fitting tailored garments whose form derives from the skin clothing of the ancient nomads of the Asiatic steppes and fastens them with buttons whose prototypes appeared in Europe at the close of the Stone Age. This costume is appropriate enough for

Reprinted from *The American Mercury,* 40, (1937), pages 427–429. Reprinted by permission of *The American Mercury,* P.O. Box 1306, Torrance, Calif., 90505.

outdoor exercise in a cold climate, but is quite unsuited to American summers, steam-heated houses, and Pullmans. Nevertheless, foreign ideas and habits hold the unfortunate man in thrall even when common sense tells him that the authentically American costume of gee string and moccasins would be far more comfortable. He puts on his feet stiff coverings made from hide prepared by a process invented in ancient Egypt and cut to a pattern which can be traced back to ancient Greece, and makes sure that they are properly polished, also a Greek idea. Lastly, he ties about his neck a strip of bright-colored cloth which is a vestigial survival of the shoulder shawls worn by seventeenth-century Greeks. He gives himself a final appraisal in the mirror, an old Mediterranean invention, and goes downstairs to breakfast.

Here a whole new series of foreign things confronts him. His food and drink are placed before him in pottery vessels, the popular name of which—china—is sufficient evidence of their origin. His fork is a medieval Italian invention and his spoon a copy of a Roman original. He will usually begin the meal with coffee, an Abyssinian plant first discovered by the Arabs. The American is quite likely to need it to dispel the morning-after effects of over-indulgence in fermented drinks, invented in the Near East; or distilled ones, invented by the alchemists of medieval Europe. Whereas the Arabs took their coffee straight, he will probably sweeten it with sugar, discovered in India; and dilute it with cream, both the domestication of cattle and the technique of milking having originated in Asia Minor.

If our patriot is old-fashioned enough to adhere to the so-called American breakfast, his coffee will be accompanied by an orange, domesticated in the Mediterranean region, a cantaloupe domesticated in Persia, or grapes domesticated in Asia Minor. He will follow this with a bowl of cereal made from grain domesticated in the Near East and prepared by methods also invented there. From this he will go on to waffles, a Scandinavian invention, with plenty of butter, originally a Near-Eastern cosmetic. As a side dish he may have the egg of a bird domesticated in Southeastern Asia or strips of the flesh of an animal domesticated in the same region, which have been salted and smoked by a process invented in Northern Europe.

Breakfast over, he places upon his head a molded piece of felt, invented by the nomads of Eastern Asia, and, if it looks like rain, puts on outer shoes of rubber, discovered by the ancient Mexicans, and takes an umbrella, invented in India. He then sprints for his train—the train, not the sprinting, being an English invention. At the station he pauses for moment to buy a newspaper, paying for it with coins invented in ancient Lydia. Once on board he settles back to inhale the fumes of a cigarette invented in Mexico, or a cigar invented in Brazil. Meanwhile, he reads the news of the day, imprinted in characters invented by the ancient Semites by a process invented in Germany upon a material invented in China. As he scans the latest editorial pointing out the dire results to our institutions of accepting foreign ideas, he will not fail to thank a Hebrew God in an Indo-European language that he is a one hundred per cent (decimal system invented by the Greeks) American (from Americus Vespucci, Italian geographer).

Summary

Our culture establishes a pattern of life for us that is very difficult to live without. When we travel to a foreign country and take on another way of life, we become very uncomfortable. Our values no longer fit the situation, our expectations usually prove to be wrong, and it is difficult for us to fit in with other people and behave as they do. This creates a feeling known as *culture shock,* something that is not limited to anthropologists who conduct fieldwork in another culture, but can be experienced by anyone.

In the process of learning our culture, we also are taught to believe that our way of life is correct, that it is good, indeed the best possible way to live. This attitude is known as *ethnocentrism,* and is a feeling of cultural superiority. It is found in our reactions to foreign customs, in our myths and proverbs, even in our dietary preferences. And ethnocentrism is perpetuated (not always consciously) through our educational system, which tends to put down other people's ways of doing things as bizarre or inferior.

Through our training in anthropology and the study of other customs, we attempt to overcome as much of our ethnocentrism as possible. We try to become more objective about cultural differences, to be tolerant of other people. This attitude is known as *cultural relativism,* and is based on the proposition that all values are relative and that there are no absolute standards that are valid in all cultural settings. Before an anthropologist can be objective about another people's way of life, it is essential that he or she attain a degree of cultural relativism and learn to accept foreign customs for their own sake, rather than comparing them to their Western counterparts.

Glossary

creation myth An account of the origins of the first member or members of a group. In nonliterate societies, these elaborate "stories" are passed from one generation to the next through an oral tradition.

cultural relativism A doctrine (developed by Franz Boas in opposition to nineteenth-century ethnocentrism) that states that every anthropologist must maintain strict neutrality in describing and comparing other cultures. Judgments should not be made concerning the merits of one culture over another; rather, each culture has its own integrity.

culture shock The trauma experienced by people who enter a new cultural setting. The depression and frustration result from the confrontation of a way of life very different from their own culture.

ethnocentrism The belief that one's own patterns of behavior are preferable to those of all other cultures. When employed as a standard to judge outsiders, it becomes an attitude that one's own cultural patterns are correct and natural, while different patterns are wrong and unnatural.

infanticide The killing of infants, usually practiced in order to maintain control over the population.

Social Darwinism A theoretical orientation prevalent in the nineteenth century. The theory is based upon the erroneous application of Darwinian principles to social and cultural evolution, and from the ethnocentric standpoint that Western culture is more advanced or superior to the world's "primitive" cultures.

Questions for Discussion

1 How does the United States government utilize ethnocentrism in its propaganda concerning other countries? How do these attitudes change according to official policy (e.g., Germany and Japan in the 1940s as compared to today)? What changes have you seen in recent years regarding countries such as China, Russia and Cuba?

2 Culture shock is not limited to the experience of the anthropologist. What types of experiences have you had in a different society or a subculture in the United States that created culture shock for you? What values and beliefs have you encountered that were most unlike your own, and what was your reaction?

3 There are changes in the values and attitudes in every culture from one generation to the next. How have our prejudices changed in recent years, and how can you measure this change in American society (e.g., the acceptance of long hair and beards on Congressmen and movie stars)? Why do you think these values have changed? What other changes can you predict in the future?

4 Have you ever dined with a family from a different culture or ethnic group? What sorts of foods were offered to you that you had never

had before? What was your reaction to their offering? Were there any cultural rules associated with your accepting or refusing the food?

5 What types of slang words or expressions are used in American ethnic groups or subcultures that demonstrate ethnocentrism and divide the group from others (such as "soul brother" or "hillbilly")? Can you think of any myths or stories which support these differences?

6 What is it about culture that makes us convinced that our way of life is right? How can we learn to be more tolerant through the study of other cultures? What have you learned about other cultures that has led you to accept cultural relativism?

7 How does the debate concerning abortion reflect the existence of ethnocentrism and relative values in our society? While the ideal is for the anthropologist to become neutral in observing another culture, do you think it is possible to be objective in your own culture? How can cultural relativism help one attain this objectivity?

Suggestions for Additional Reading

Bates, Marston
1967 Gluttons and Libertines: Human Problems of Being Natural. New York: Vintage Books.

A humorous study of eating and sexual practices in cross-cultural perspective. Particularly valuable in light of the preceding discussion of relative values and ethnocentrism regarding foods and morals.

Boas, Franz
1940 Race, Language and Culture. New York: The Free Press.

A collection of essays by the leading figure in the movement toward cultural relativism. The author argues that there is no causal relationship between race, language and culture, that is, that nonwhite cultures are not inferior or inherently different.

Bowen, Elenore Smith (Laura Bohannan)
1954 Return to Laughter. New York: Harcourt, Brace & World.

The author, who is better known as the anthropologist Laura Bohannan, describes her experiences among the Tiv of Nigeria in this delightful novel. Her accounts of the frustrations of fieldwork and her initial difficulties in relating to the Tiv are an excellent documentation of culture shock. The selected reading for Chapter 6 is also by the same author.

Brown, Dee
1970 Bury My Heart at Wounded Knee. New York: Bantam Books.

The story of the white settlement of the American West, from the Indian's point of view. This book is a strong testimony to the role that ethnocentrism continues to play in American society.

Eiseley, Loren
1958 Darwin's Century. Garden City, N.Y.: Anchor Books.

A classic book on the theory of evolution and the men whose ideas played an important role in its formulation. Valuable for its discussion of the views of Europeans on strange cultural practices around the world, and how these views affected the arguments for and against evolution.

Griffin, John Howard
1961 Black Like Me. Boston: Houghton Mifflin.

The author, a white man, altered his appearance and passed as a black man in the South. His account of his life as a black, after seeing the world from the point of view of a white, is a perfect example of culture shock, and a lesson in cultural relativism. The selected reading for the previous chapter was taken from this book.

Haller, John S., Jr.
1971 Outcasts from Evolution. Urbana: University of Illinois Press.

A history of anthropological views on race in the nineteenth century.

Kosinski, Jerzy N.
1972 The Painted Bird. New York: Bantam Books.

An excellent novel depicting the prejudices toward Gypsies and Jews on the part of Eastern European peasants. A valuable illustration of ethnocentrism.

LeVine, Robert A., and Donald T. Campbell
1972 Ethnocentrism: Theories of Conflict, Ethnic Attitudes and Group Behavior. New York: John Wiley & Sons.

A study of the causes and problems of ethnocentrism.

Levi-Strauss, Claude
1966 The Savage Mind. Chicago: University of Chicago Press.

One of the leading figures in modern anthropology, the author demonstrates that there is no qualitative difference between the mentality of the so-called "primitive" and ourselves. Suggested primarily for the more advanced student.

Post, Emily
1969 Etiquette. 12th Edition. New York: Funk & Wagnalls.

One of the standard books on what is "proper" in American society. This can be read as an illustration of the narrow-mindedness that any culture creates for people, in defining a particular set of behaviors as the best or the only ones.

Turnbull, Colin
1972 The Mountain People. New York: Simon and Schuster.

A fascinating, if somewhat grim, account of the Ik, a tribe in Kenya, East Africa, who were displaced and in the process of starving to death when the author made his study. The unbelievable lengths to which people would go to get food, and the seeming breakdown of all sense of value and common decency, make this book an outstanding contribution to the study of cultural relativism.

Aims and Methods of Cultural Anthropology

Chapter Four

If, as we said in Chapter 1, one of the major distinctions between cultural anthropology and sociology is found in the methods of research and analysis practiced by each, then just what is the method used by anthropologists? In this chapter we will look at the way in which a cultural anthropologist seeks to understand the cultures he studies, and kinds of comparisons he makes between them. We will also focus upon some of the more difficult problems of doing fieldwork in a foreign culture, and try to relate these problems to the study of our own culture as well.

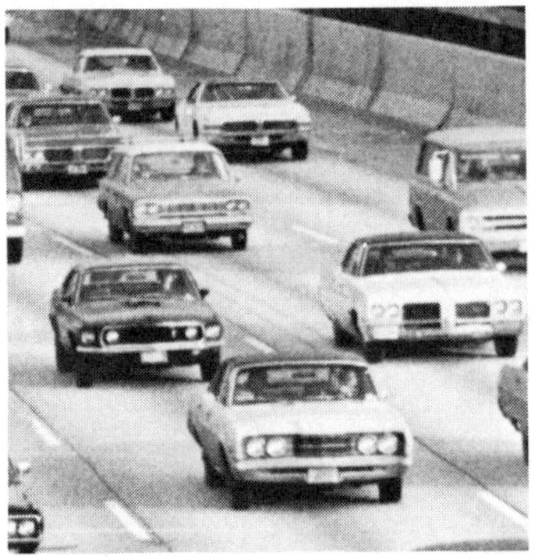

Revolutionizing Field Work

Throughout the nineteenth century anthropology was frequently taken up as the hobby of well-to-do scholars who had the means and the opportunity to travel to out of the way places and study exotic peoples. A number of anthropologists also engaged in the analysis of the peoples of the world through written accounts put together by others, especially if they could not afford the time and expense of a field expedition on their own. This type of "armchair" anthropology, based upon travel diaries and missionary accounts rather than on intensive field research, led to a particular style of analysis that could not hope to capture the true nature of traditional societies. Even among those who were fortunate enough to engage in field research, there was still no systematic attempt to adhere to a rigorous control of research techniques.

It was not until the twentieth century that anthropologists grew

In science as in sex,
too much concentration on technique
renders one impotent.
PETER BERGER

really concerned with the quality of their research, and began to develop a set of standards for the field worker. One of the most important figures in leading the way toward a controlled method for cultural anthropology was Bronislaw Malinowski. Born in Poland, Malinowski was first trained in mathematics, but early in life he became interested in anthropology. He studied in London, then went to the Pacific, where he was carrying out research when World War I broke out. He ended up in Australia, where, as a citizen of the German nation with whom Australia was at war, he was subject to internment for the duration of the conflict. He was, however, able to persuade the officials to allow him the alternative of internment not in Australia itself, but on a small group of islands just to the north, called the Trobriands. Here, he argued, he could do no harm, yet would be able to continue his research. Malinowski lived in the islands for several years, sharing the way of life of the natives. Isolated from civilization, he was forced to live in native villages, learn their language, and participate completely in their way of life.

As a result of his lengthy field experience, Malinowski published a series of books and articles on the culture of the Trobriand Islanders, dealing successively with their economics, their forms of social control, kinship and marriage patterns, and religion and magic. In the course of his work he also laid out in great detail his experiences in the field, emphasizing many ways in which they were different from the more traditional anthropological fieldwork, and pointing out the necessity of some of his novel approaches to his research. In *Argonauts of the Western Pacific,* published in 1922, Malinowski offers one of the earliest statements of the problems and requirements of anthropological fieldwork.

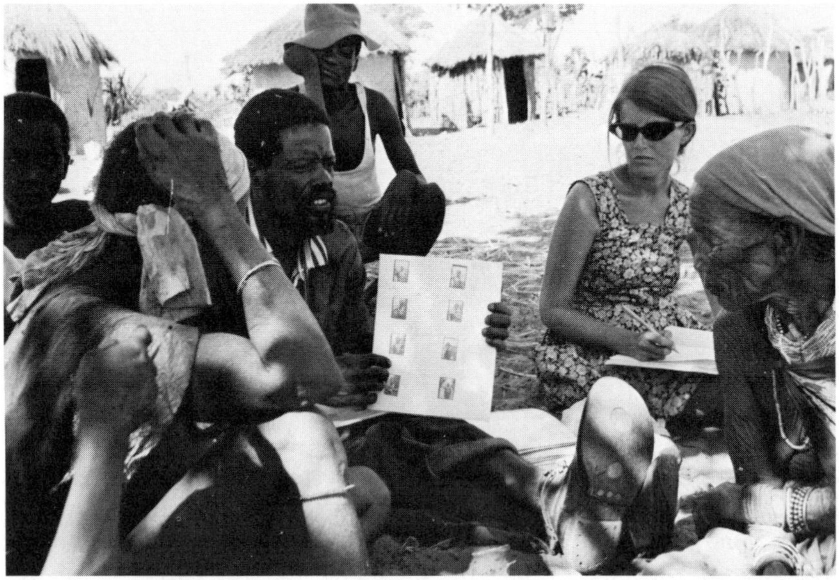

Nancy Howell studying acquaintance networks among the Bushmen of the Kalahari Desert. (Lee, Anthro-Photo)

First, he said that to be effective and to produce valid results, the anthropologist must *live in the native community.* Until his time researchers had indeed conducted field studies out among the natives, but rarely so intensively. A typical research design would have the anthropologist working out of a mission outpost or a colonial office, perhaps making short trips into the field for more thorough investigations, but never really penetrating the day-to-day life of the natives. Frequently interpreters would be used, adding another filter through which information about native customs must pass, removing the anthropologist yet another step away from the object of his study. Malinowski's experience on the Trobriand Islands convinced him that only by becoming a part of the daily life of the community could the anthropologist hope to be able to put together a valid picture of what the culture means to the members of the group.

Secondly, Malinowski insisted that the anthropologist must *learn the native language.* If, as we noted in Chapter 1, the goal of the anthropologist in a descriptive ethnography is to translate one culture into another without losing accuracy, then first he must be able to comprehend it on its own terms. This requires learning to think in the language of the natives, not just learning to understand their utterances. Only when we are able to see the world as a native does can

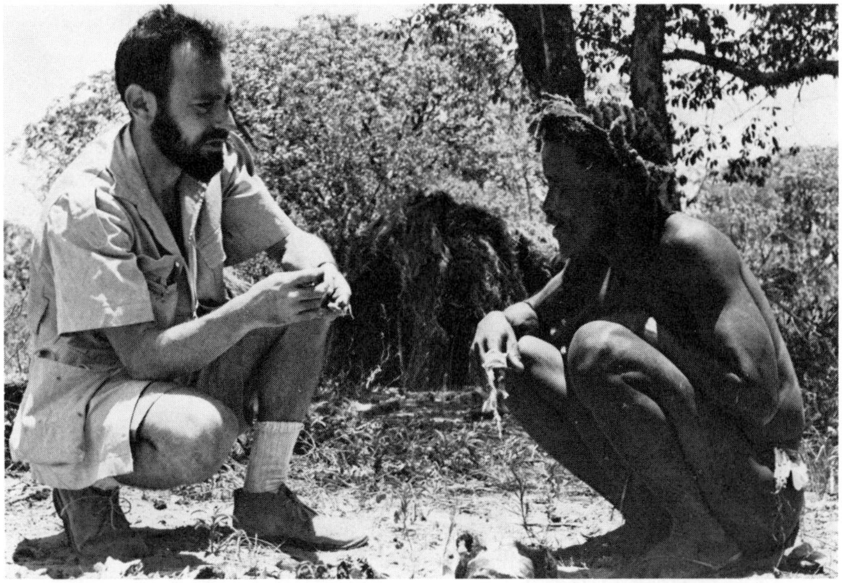

Richard Lee interviewing a Bushman hunter about a recent kill. (Irven DeVore, Anthro-Photo)

we begin to translate his culture, and if language determines the way we order our observations, then thinking in another language is essential to sharing another culture. Again, this was a revelation for the anthropological method when Malinowski first suggested it, for most anthropologists had become accustomed to working with interpreters, especially in areas where the native language was not widely known or was not a part of a literary tradition that could have been incorporated into the anthropologist's formal education.

We must stress the need to be able to evaluate not only the literal meaning of the native's language, but the idiomatic meaning as well, and this usually entails learning the language so well that we become fluent in it. If we simply take the literal meaning of an informant's statement we can arrive at some very bad conclusions. For example, for many years anthropologists were puzzled by the fact that in some societies a child refers to many different male adults by the same term, which translates roughly as "father." They assumed this meant that actual paternity could not be established, and that there was a kind of group marriage, or "primitive promiscuity." But such an assumption was based upon an incomplete understanding of the meaning of the term, derived from the fact that the analogous term in our language refers to a biological relationship. In some societies this is not the case, and the term which was translated as "father" really meant "male of the generation of my father."

You can see how important an accurate command of the language can be, for without it the anthropologist is in danger of attributing a literal meaning to an informant's statement that contradicts the meaning intended by the speaker. But certainly the speaker will not provide this information. He will not qualify every idiomatic phrase he uses with a scientific explanation. It is up to the anthropologist to avoid such problems of interpretation.

Finally, Malinowski advocated that the anthropologist adopt the method known as *participant observation.* Observation alone is not enough, he argued, for an observer cannot know the true meaning of the actions of others until he himself has an opportunity to participate in them. Conversely, participation alone is insufficient, for without the ability to step back and observe objectively, we are unable to grasp the meaning of our actions. This is clearly the case in our own culture, where we are frequently unaware of the meaning of many of our daily activities or the interrelationships between them, as the rest of this book will point out. Therefore the anthropologist must

Close relationships can develop as a result of fieldwork. Here an anthropologist poses with a native of New Hebrides, a Pacific island. (Kal Muller, Woodfin Camp)

both participate in and observe the daily routine of life in the native community in order to learn the culture. In addition, he must include in his participant observation the special irregular occurrences which, although not part of the daily routine, are equally important to the overall picture of the culture. Deaths, ceremonials, quarrels and the like are just as important a topic for research as the routine activities of raising a family, making a living, maintaining social relationships and so forth.

Initially it may seem that anthropological field research is a romantic escapade into the exotic life of a far-off tribe; however, a closer look at Malinowski's experiences reveals much about the effects of this forced life style upon the individual. Although clearly a master of objective research, an innovative and multi-talented investigator, Malinowski's life in the Trobriands was filled with anxiety and frustration. Many years after his death his diary of the fieldwork in the Trobriands was published, revealing an altogether different picture of the man and his work. If we tend to look at such an experience as an escape, in which the anthropologist can "go native" for a short time and then return to civilization relaxed and refreshed, such a view is patently false. It ignores the utter frustration of working with a foreign culture, of not being able to share all of the values and comfortable habits that one has grown up with. It does not take into consideration the personal satisfaction of communication with others about topics of mutual interest. It overlooks the needs of the individual that arise out of growing up in one particular cultural setting, and cannot be fulfilled in another. It forgets that we have expectations about the way others will act, and that these expectations no longer are valid for members of another culture. In Malinowski's diary we read of a man who was constantly frustrated by his inability to overcome his cultural background. No matter how well he could intellectualize his experiences, there simply was no substitute for the familiar and reassuring culture that had until then been a part of his life. We read of a man who was transplanted into another world, and of the trauma—we call it "culture shock"—that he endured throughout his entire period of field research. Yet as revealing as Malinowski's diary is about the weaknesses of the man, it reaffirms even more his greatness, for not everyone could have put up with the problems he faced daily and yet retain the objectivity evidenced in his later writing.

If you are still not convinced that fieldwork isn't always the romantic adventure it is cracked up to be, then perhaps the following passage describing Napoleon Chagnon's first encounter with the Yąnomamö, an Indian society in Venezuela, will cause you to reconsider:

> The excitement of meeting my first Indians was almost unbearable as I duck-waddled through the low passage into the village clearing. I looked up and gasped when I saw a dozen burly, naked, filthy, hideous men staring at us down the shafts of their drawn arrows! Immense wads of green tobacco were stuck between their lower teeth and lips making them look even more hideous, and strands of dark-green slime dripped or hung from their noses. We arrived at the village while the men were blowing a hallucinogenic drug up their noses. One of the side effects of the drug is a runny nose. The mucus is always saturated with the green powder and the Indians usually let it run freely from their nostrils. My next discovery was that there were a dozen or so vicious, underfed dogs snapping at my legs, circling me as if I were going to be their next meal. I just stood there holding my notebook, helpless and pathetic. Then the stench of the decaying vegetation and filth struck me and I almost got sick. I was horrified. What sort of a welcome was this for the person who came here to live with you and learn your way of life, to become friends with you?[1]

Maintaining Objectivity

In the midst of all the distractions, pressures and problems of personal adjustment, the anthropologist must always remember that the basic necessity in fieldwork is the exercise of scientific detachment. It is hard to imagine how one could remain detached when faced with a scene such as Chagnon first encountered among the Yąnomamö, but without removing himself from a position of judging another culture, the anthropologist's work is worthless. In Chagnon's case, after overcoming his initial shock, he was able to describe and analyze Yąnomamö culture objectively and thoroughly, leaving us with the impression that even if he did not enjoy every waking hour in the field, and even if he did have some rather unpleasant and frightening experiences, he was still able to remain detached and avoid evaluating Yąnomamö culture by comparing it to his own or to any other standard.

1. Napoleon A. Chagnon, *Yąnomamö, The Fierce People*. New York: Holt, Rinehart and Winston, 1968, p. 5.

A typical Yąnomamö Indian, with green slime running from his nose. As Chagnon describes, this tribesman appears to be drugged. (Napoleon A. Chagnon)

Of course, complete detachment is impossible. No one can escape his past, nor is it necessary to do so in order to become an anthropologist. Rather, the best solution is to remind oneself constantly that there are two cultures working at the same time—the culture of the observer, which lurks in the back of his mind, and the culture of the observed, which lies before him. The anthropologist must always make a conscious effort to keep these two worlds separate, and to take any cultural bias he might have into account when writing about others. The main point is to devote oneself to an understanding, and not a judgment, of the culture under study. And this is not always as easy as it sounds, for deeply ingrained values and preferences cannot be overcome by sheer willpower. It takes long hours of training and experience in the field, for which no amount of lectures, readings, and classroom discussions can substitute.

In addition, the anthropologist must avoid going into the field with preconceived ideas of what he will find; there is no surer way to determine the outcome of a research project than to make up one's mind at the outset what the results will likely be. It takes an open mind and a willingness to alter the research design on the basis of the situation at hand to yield a truly valid result. Fieldwork is the anthropologist's laboratory, much as in any other science. Just as a scientist in a chemistry lab must be willing to accept results of an experiment, even if they disprove the law he is testing, so the anthropologist must be willing to accept what he finds at face value, whether it fits into the pattern or not. Despite the fact that in high school chemistry most of us wrote up the results of the experiment before we ever performed it because we knew what they *should* be according to the textbook, the scientist may not legitimately reach conclusions before he has finished the experiment. The anthropologist is no different.

The lesson of this scientific detachment and objectivity can be seen in an important controversy between two famous anthropologists who studied the same community. In the 1920s Robert Redfield went to the Mexican village of Tepoztlán, where he conducted field research.[2] Seventeen years later another anthropologist, Oscar Lewis, also went to Tepoztlán to do a restudy of the same community.[3] Lewis had read Redfield's work and was puzzled by it, finding many inconsistencies with what he found to be the case. Redfield's description of life in Tepoztlán is one of an idyllic rural setting where people were happy, healthy, and well-integrated. When Oscar Lewis studied the same community he found exactly the opposite: Tepoztlán was characterized by constant suspicion and tension, there was no cooperation among the villagers, and social relations were typically weak and strife-ridden.

The first question that comes to mind is: How can the village have changed so much in such a short period of time? But a deeper look at the situation reveals that it was not the village that changed, but the outlook of the two different observers. Redfield's personal outlook was one which favored the rural life style over that of the city. He considered the city to be the source of cultural decay, a center of disorganization where the "pure" character of the countryman breaks down under the pressures of the fast-paced urban routine. Thus,

The University of Chicago Press

Robert Redfield (1897–1957) *first studied the Mexican village of Tepoztlán in 1926. He concluded that there are basic similarities among peasant societies throughout the world, and led cultural anthropology out of its narrow concentration upon isolated, so-called "primitive" tribal societies. Redfield also developed what has come to be called the "folk-urban continuum," contrasting the way of life of the city with that of the isolated tribal or "folk" community.*

2. Robert Redfield, *Tepoztlán, A Mexican Village*. Chicago: University of Chicago Press, 1930.

3. Oscar Lewis, *Life in a Mexican Village: Tepoztlán Restudied*. Urbana: University of Illinois Press, 1951.

Arnold Katz

Oscar Lewis (1914–1970) *engaged in a restudy of the village of Tepoztlán in 1943, where Robert Redfield had conducted his research 17 years earlier. Lewis centered upon conflict in the village, and was concerned with the causes of suffering and discomfort for the villagers, whereas Redfield had centered upon harmonious interaction and the source of enjoyment for people. The result, of course, was a completely different picture of life in Tepoztlán, calling into question the objectivity of anthropological research.*

Redfield had a predetermined preference for rural life, and when he lived and worked in Tepoztlán he was not able to overcome this bias. He saw everything good in the life there, and overlooked much of what was bad. Lewis, on the other hand, approached his research from the opposite point of view. He felt that peasant life was one of suffering, that poor people were disadvantaged, and that Redfield's notion about the relative values of country versus city life was backwards. Thus in his work in Tepoztlán he looked for—and found—suspicion and distrust where Redfield had described harmony and cooperation. We can derive a lesson from the errors of both men. We must be aware not only of our culture and its impact upon our evaluation of another way of life, but also of our own personality and the preferences we hold for certain parts of our culture as opposed to others. We do not have to change in order to be good anthropologists, but we do have to suppress some of our stronger feelings for the duration of our research in order to insure that our observations will be objective.

Methods of Research

So far we have concentrated on the prerequisites for anthropological fieldwork. But once these have been met, how does the anthropologist do his research? What does he look for when he goes to work in a foreign culture? What kinds of questions does he ask, and how does he know whom he should ask? Obviously the anthropologist must structure his research in some way; he cannot simply move into a village and expect the people to flock to his doorstep, presenting a description to him in tightly organized pieces corresponding to the chapters of a book.

Unwritten Rules

One way in which anthropologists seek to understand another culture is to uncover the rules that govern behavior for members of that group. This is not restricted to the written laws covering transgressions of acceptable behavior in a legal sense, but includes the unwritten codes of conduct for all kinds of actions. Every society has these rules, and they are shared by almost all members to an extremely high degree. We are able to interact with other members of our society because we expect that in certain situations they will respond in a limited number of ways. Without such an expectation all social interaction would be chaotic. Thus, if you meet someone for the first time and extend your hand, you do so with the understanding that he will do likewise and the two of you will shake hands. You do not expect that he will pour hot coffee on your hand, or grab it and give you a judo flip. Indeed, if something like that did happen, you would be justifiably shocked. Thus we have a basic rule that governs behavior in this kind of situation, and when we put together a collection of this kind of rules for all situations we are able to behave as a native in American culture.

The anthropologist going into a foreign culture is at a distinct disadvantage in that he does not know all of these rules. Furthermore, it is not easy to uncover them. He cannot simply sit down and ask a native to recite all the rules of behavior in his society. Rather, he must learn these rules by observing how other people react in certain situations, and by piecing together what information he has at hand.

Social behavior is predictable because people share understandings of what is proper in a given situation. (Rene Burri, Magnum)

The trouble is that at the same time he is trying to be a part of this group, to participate as well as to observe, and in his participation he is likely to break many of the rules of conduct unknowingly, making it all the more difficult for the adult members of the society to accept him as one of them and treat him as an equal.

Let us look at another example from our own culture, to point out how difficult it can be for an outsider to learn these rules. Suppose a foreigner, in the United States for the first time, comes from a culture where it is customary for a person to bargain with the seller over the price of an item he wishes to buy, a practice found in many societies. Our visitor no sooner arrives in the country than he realizes he has forgotten his toothpaste. So he walks into a drug store, picks up a tube of toothpaste marked 69¢, and takes it to the counter, where he offers the pharmacist 50¢ for it. The pharmacist would probably look at this kook in disbelief and think about calling the men in the white coats to come and get him. No doubt the strong reaction would lead our foreigner to conclude rather hurriedly that bargaining over the price of something is simply not done—he has broken an unwritten rule of behavior in American society, and the reaction over a paltry 19¢ was so strong that he would not likely do it again. But let's put him in a different situation, where instead of buying a tube of toothpaste he is shopping for a used car. He walks onto Honest John's Used Car Lot, where he sets his eyes upon a 1948 Plymouth, priced at only $995. Remembering his escapade in the drug store, and wanting very much to fit in with American culture, he doesn't even think twice, but simply forks over the money. Bargaining, he has concluded, is un-American. Imagine the look on Honest John's face!

Right away you can see the problem. Picture yourself in a foreign country not knowing the rules, and you can imagine how difficult it would be for you. I remember my first trip to Europe, not knowing how much to tip for which services, being afraid to ride the bus or use the telephone, dreading the look of disapproval that inevitably followed upon even the slightest little mistake. The more intimate our interaction becomes, the more likely we are to make these mistakes, and until people get to know us well enough to overlook them, we are in for a lot of disapproving glances. One of the problems is that we are adults, and as such we are expected to know what the rules are. Children don't know what is proper behavior in all situations, but that is expected of them as a part of growing up. But for adults

Tourists in an unfamiliar setting can look pretty silly. (Thomas Höpker, Woodfin Camp)

to act like children, to be ignorant of what is expected of them, is an altogether different story. Perhaps this explains why in more than a few cases the anthropologist has a much easier time getting to know the children of the community than the adults—and ultimately this can make it even more difficult to break into the adult world.

Once the fieldworker begins to uncover the rules of behavior, he must put them together into a related system or code. The problem is that they are nowhere consciously formulated or recorded; in contrast to the written legal restrictions on what may not be done, there is no written handbook on the minute details of how one should behave in everyday interactions. Sometimes only a minor variation in style can have a major effect on meaning, changing an ordinary action into the most serious insult, yet nowhere will you find these variations described and accessible to an outsider. I am reminded of an experience in a department store in Switzerland, in which I was quite embarrassed over a completely innocent mistake. We are all aware of the symbolic meaning of various hand gestures. In our country, for example, holding up the middle finger of the hand conveys a certain meaning to the observer, a meaning sufficiently strong in some cases to prompt arrest, or to invite physical confrontation. In some parts of Europe this gesture is replaced by one in which you hold up both the index and the middle fingers, with the back of the hand facing the observer (and not the front of the hand, as in the noted "V for Victory" sign made famous by Winston Churchill during World War II). Anyway, there I was in a department store in Geneva, asking the saleslady for two pairs of socks. "How many?" she asked. "Two," I replied, holding up two fingers to emphasize my request.

In trying to uncover these rules of behavior, the anthropologist is limited in the questions he can ask. It is much easier, for example, to construct a hypothetical situation and ask an informant to describe proper behavior than it is to ask about what is correct in the abstract. For example, we might want to know about the philosophy of crime and punishment in a society; we could be interested in what crimes were taken most seriously, and for what reasons. This is not as simple as it sounds, for even if there is a written legal code that defines punishments for various crimes, it does not capture the variation in everyday occurrences of these crimes, the kinds of things that influence a jury but do not become part of the formal legal code. Thus, in doing research on crime and social control in a village, we might sit down with an informant and ask specific questions in the abstract, such as what he thinks is the most serious crime. The answer will probably parallel the formal legal answer for the society as a whole, but it will not necessarily enable us to understand how that legal code would be carried out in a specific case. We might then supplement our question by asking what would happen if A stole from B, using specific members of the community as examples. We could gain further insight by asking the same question about two other individuals, noting whether the reaction would be the same. Then we could change the circumstances somewhat. Suppose A's family needed food and he stole from B, who was wealthy? As you can see, the question becomes rather involved, and only by collecting a variety of examples and observing behavior in many different contexts can we begin to understand the complexity of social life in a foreign culture. It is

Sir Winston Churchill and his famous "V for Victory" sign—or was he flipping Hitler the bird? (Wide World)

much like the example of bargaining over the purchase price in our country: We cannot set a hard and fast rule for an outsider to follow, because so many different factors can affect whether we bargain or whether we accept the price as given.

Real vs. Ideal, Back Region, and Impression Management

There are always many aspects of their way of life that informants cannot accurately describe. Most of an individual's daily routine is so much a part of him that he cannot stop to analyze it, but simply acts it out without thinking. Thus to ask a question about it might not bring any response, because the individual does not perceive it either as important or as fitting in with a set of rules governing his behavior. In other words, we are unaware of much of the meaning of our behavior to an objective observer. This raises the distinction between what we call the "real" and the "ideal" behavior in culture. Everyone sees himself as conforming to the ideals, and frequently there is substantial agreement on what those ideals are. But when we observe a group of people in the same activities, we find that there is not as much conformity with those ideals as people would lead us to believe. It is here that the anthropologist must supplement his questions with observations; asking yields the ideal, while observing yields the real. Both are essential to understanding behavior in any society.

For example, if we were to inquire about driving an automobile in the United States, we would most likely be told the basic rules upon which all Americans agree: Stop for stop signs and red lights, do not exceed the speed limit, do not double park, etc. This yields the "ideal." But if we were to observe American driving practices, we would have a picture of the "real" behavior involved in driving a car. The next time you're out in traffic, watch and see how many people roll through a stop sign without coming to a complete halt. Or better still, drive 55 miles per hour on the freeway and count the number of cars that pass you, compared to the number you pass. You'll soon see why participation must go hand in hand with inquiries about a people's way of life.

In addition to the discrepancy between real and ideal behavior, there is always an area which people conceal from some observers, so that their actions appear to correspond to the ideal, even when they themselves know that other times this is not the case. This is

Driving on American highways requires an understanding of unwritten rules as well as the formal code of traffic laws. (Wide World)

what the anthropologist Gerald Berreman has called the "back region."[4] By this term he means an area of behavior concealed by a group of people in order to control the impression an outsider obtains about them. Berreman was referring specifically to the situation in a village he studied in India, where members of the lower caste, or social group, tried to give the outsider (in this case the anthropologist) the impression that their behavior was more in line with what was expected of members of the higher castes, even though when the observer was not around this was not the case. But the concept of a back region applies also to the individual as well as the group, and we all have aspects of our behavior which we hide from some observers (but not from all) in order to give them the impression we would like them to have about us. For example, if you are away at school and you go home over Christmas, your parents will probably ask you how much you study. You will most likely exaggerate somewhat, concealing some of your activities that detract from your study time. Students definitely have a back region which they keep hidden from parents (and frequently from their professors as well).

4. Gerald D. Berreman, *Behind Many Masks*. Monograph Number 4 of the Society for Applied Anthropology, 1962.

The back region is thus the conscious effort to conceal deviations from the ideal behavior. This feature of social interaction is called *impression management*, for it involves the attempt of the individual to manage the impression that others have of him. If you stop and think for a minute about the different kinds of clothes you wear on different occasions, you can see this as a form of impression management. You probably don't wear a coat and tie or an expensive suit to anthropology class, but if you were going to a bank to ask for a loan, you certainly wouldn't want to go in wearing torn Levi's and a sweatshirt. You would want to create the impression that you were stable and employed, and that you could be counted on to repay the money, and grubby clothes just do not convey that impression. So you "manage" your impression by dressing up, concealing the back region of your life from the bank official. There is nothing dishonest about this, and we really don't feel guilty about doing it. It is just that we all have many facets to our social life, we all fit into society in many different ways, and we control which ways we fit in at any particular time according to the impression we wish to create.

The importance to the anthropologist of the concepts of back region and impression management is obvious. The people we observe, if they are aware of our presence, are managing their impression. While we want to get to know their "normal" behavior, they want to conceal certain aspects of it from us.

Impression management also creates problems for us when we read accounts of foreign cultures written by people who are not trained in the techniques of analysis in anthropology. Many such early accounts of foreign peoples were written by missionaries who had been sent by their church to convert people to Christianity. Of course, the missionaries set themselves up in the society in a particular role, demanding certain kinds of behavior from the people, and rewarding them when their standards were met. But they were content to describe what they saw on the surface, and did not look deeper into the native life. Thus, they might have described how successful they had been at getting the native women to wear halters, and at teaching them modesty as a Christian virtue. But they might never have been aware of the fact that the women only wore the halters when they came to church services at the mission outpost, and that when they went back to their village the first thing they did was to take them off. Or the missionaries might have written accounts of how they had persuaded the natives to give up practicing magic, and to accept the

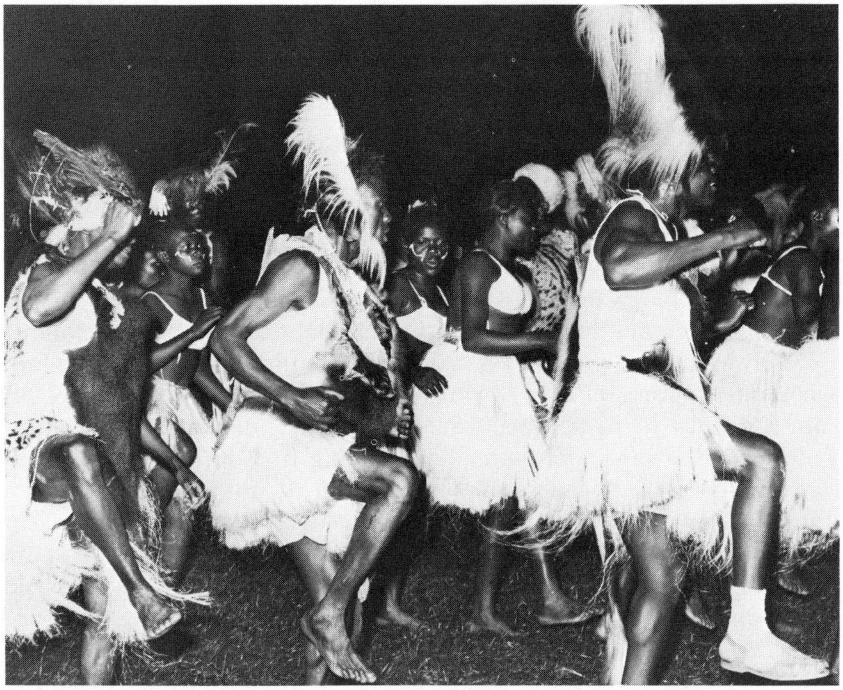

Women from the Jaluo tribe of Kenya showing a mixture of native and western dress. (R. S. Virdee, Frederic Lewis)

church's doctrines and the belief in the power of the Christian God, while the natives went on practicing their magic but simply didn't tell the missionaries because they knew it would upset them. Thus if we read descriptions of other cultures, we must always look closely at who is writing them and what his training has been, for not everyone is so careful about getting past the barrier of impression management and portraying an accurate and objective picture of the total life style of the people.

This leads us to the question of how we can evaluate the information we receive in the process of doing fieldwork. How do we know when we ask an informant a question that he will tell us the truth? How can we evaluate his version of the truth as opposed to someone else's? One way to get around this problem is to obtain as much information about a particular question from as many different people as possible. In this way, we can put together a composite picture that will be more accurate, in much the same way as a jury weighs the conflicting evidence in a trial and tries to come up with a more accurate picture of what happened.

Structuring Behavior

Another important distinction that anthropologists make in doing their research contrasts the structure they assign to behavior they observe, with the way it is perceived to be ordered by the people themselves. There is usually a discrepancy between what we call the "folk image" in the minds of the natives of another culture, and the "analytical image" in the mind of the anthropologist. Of course, neither one is right or wrong; both can be completely accurate in entirely different ways.

People perceive their behavior as fitting into a pattern according to what they have learned about their culture. The anthropologist is an outsider who brings with him a knowledge of many different ways of life, not just his own. He may view the behavior in a completely different light, seeing different meanings in it or a different structure to it than the people themselves. For example, as a result of the way you were brought up in American culture, you treat your brothers and sisters in a certain way (your folk image of what is proper within the family), but the anthropologist might see your interaction with your siblings as an example of family structure and patterns of authority, tied in with patterns of inheritance, the relative importance of age and sex, the prescribed roles for various family members, and so on (his analytical image of the American family in the abstract sense). This does not mean that the anthropologist ignores the folk image, for it is his job to understand behavior not just as it would be explained to an outsider, but as it has meaning to a member of the culture. But he does tend to look beyond specific events and try to form an overall pattern. People are not always conscious of the implications of what they do. They act in a certain way because it is "natural," or because it is "the right thing to do." By using an analytical image, the anthropologist can obtain a better understanding of these implications, even if the people themselves cannot substantiate his claims. This distinction is explained very well by the anthropologist John Middleton in the following passage from his book about the Lugbara, a society in Uganda, East Africa:

> The reader may well wonder why it is necessary for the anthropologist to use these special terms to describe a society whose members do not themselves find it necessary to do so. The anthropologist is sometimes accused of building up a needlessly complex structural model, while the people he is studying seem to manage very well without it. In the

> case of a people like the Lugbara the reason is simple, but I think it is important to state it. The Lugbara "live" their society; they do not have to describe it or analyze it so as to make sense of it to outsiders. For a Lugbara, the range of everyday social relations, the context of his everyday life, is narrow. He is concerned with at the most about a score of small local groups and lineages . . . . But the anthropologist is in a different position. He is, in a sense, outside and above the society. . . . To describe this pattern, which is found throughout Lugbara, the anthropologist requires special terms which are not needed by the people themselves.[5]

We can see how discrepancies of folk and analytical images can arise. Suppose we take the example of a funeral in American society. We might observe the rituals accompanying the funeral, in which the family and friends of the deceased get together and perform certain acts intended to aid the dead person's spirit in the afterlife. Prayers will be said, holy water may be sprinkled on the coffin, and a variety of similar acts will be carried out for the benefit of the deceased. This is the folk image—that the behavior in this ritual aids the spirit. The analytical image of the anthropologist offers another perspective. The outside observer sees the actions of people together at the funeral not only in terms of the spirit of the deceased, but in the overall social context of the group. Thus the analytical image is based upon the observation of a number of people gathered together united in a common cause. The funeral thus not only has religious significance, but is also a way of promoting the solidarity of the group, and it can be seen in a social, nonreligious sense as well.

Margaret Mead (1901–) *undertook her doctoral research in Samoa, designed to study the relationship between patterns of child-rearing and adult personalities. She was particularly interested in the experiences of adolescent girls in Samoa as they compared to American cultural experiences, and the differences in general personality types that resulted.*
Along with Ruth Benedict, Margaret Mead was an important early link between psychology and anthropology. She conducted a pioneer study of women and children in foreign cultures—until then, male field researchers had been relatively unsuccessful at gathering confidential information on females in other cultures.

Studying World View

So far we have discussed the way in which the anthropologist studies the structure of society and the rules that govern everyday behavior, both from the perspective of the participant in the culture, and from the objective, analytical viewpoint of an outsider. There is a third area of study that can only be approached from the insider's perspective, something we call world view. The world view of a culture refers

5. John Middleton, *The Lugbara of Uganda*. New York: Holt, Rinehart and Winston, 1965, p. 36.

to the basic outlook held in common by most members of a society. It is not something that we can ask about directly in questioning informants; rather we must learn about it through inference, through compiling the various clues about what is in the minds of the people we are observing. Furthermore, we cannot be content to get inside one individual's head, but have to focus on the general attitudes of the entire society. We may be able to ask a person how he feels about

A member of the Nutuyama tribe making arrows. Such a person still maintains a basic relationship with the land. (Cornell Capa, Magnum)

a particular question, but we are interested in the thoughts of an individual as he typifies the outlook of the entire society, not as a single person or a unique case.

If we recall the controversy mentioned earlier between Robert Redfield and Oscar Lewis concerning their interpretations of life in the Mexican village of Tepoztlán, it was a basic disparity in the picture of world view painted by each that caused their disagreement. That is, Redfield's own world view, including his attitudes toward rural life and his preference for it over city life, led him to seek a compatible world view in the people he studied. The same might be said for Lewis. Obviously a problem in studying world view is to avoid imposing our own cultural or even personal preferences upon another culture. At the same time, we must try to portray the outlook of people within another culture, to present the world as they see it. This is perhaps the most difficult part of the cultural translation that the anthropologist is responsible for, because those who read his description already have a world view different from the one he is writing about.

A common aspect of the world view of people who in a sense live closer to nature than we do in industrial society is that they perceive themselves to be a part of the natural system on earth, whereas we see ourselves as being outside that system. We in industrial society have learned to control the environment, and we see ourselves as dominant over nature. People who live off the land, through hunting and gathering or cultivation or both, do not participate in this technological mastery over the earth. They have a different world view, in that they feel a closer affinity to nature. When a Bushman of the Kalahari Desert in South Africa kills a giraffe, he feels a loss, for he recognizes that a living spirit has departed from the world. When a Plains Indian killed a buffalo, it was not a part of his plan to dominate nature and exploit it, but it was a part of his interaction with nature.

Perhaps the anthropological approach to the study of world view is best summed up by Malinowski:

> . . . the final goal, of which an Ethnographer should never lose sight . . . is, briefly, to grasp the native's point of view, his relation to life, to realise *his* vision of *his* world. We have to study man, and we must study what concerns him most intimately, that is, the hold which life has on him. In each culture, the values are slightly different; people aspire after different aims, follow different impulses, yearn after a different form of happiness. In each culture, we find different institutions in which man pursues his life-interest, different customs by which he

> satisfies his aspirations, different codes of law and morality which reward his virtues or punish his defections. To study the institutions, customs, and codes or to study the behaviour and mentality without realising the substance of their happiness—is, in my opinion, to miss the greatest reward which we can hope to obtain from the study of man.[6]

Conclusion

To conclude our discussion of the method of anthropology, it is important to note just how difficult it is for the anthropologist to fit into the society he is studying. He is coming into a community as a perfect stranger, not knowing the cues and rules for behavior, yet wanting people to accept him and take him into their homes and their private lives and reveal to him the most intimate details of their behavior. Is it any wonder that they reject him, or that they think he is crazy? Colby Hatfield has made an interesting analysis of the role of the anthropologist in the field, separating it into three parts corresponding to the impression the fieldworker frequently makes upon the people he is studying.[7] First of all, he says the anthropologist is seen as a child. He speaks the language poorly and makes many mistakes, both serious and silly. He does not know the rules of behavior, and is often discourteous or insulting. He is incompetent at even the simplest of tasks, because he has not had the opportunity to learn the techniques prevalent in that culture. All of these characteristics are true of children, whose experience in the culture is equally limited (although they master the language at a much earlier age and much more rapidly, a torturous thing for an anthropologist to watch as he is being teased by little children).

A second role the anthropologist slips into in a community, especially if it is a poor rural village such as anthropologists have traditionally sought out, is what Hatfield calls the "Fort Knox" syndrome. The Western anthropologist on even the skimpiest of research grants

6. Bronislaw Malinowski, *Argonauts of the Western Pacific*. New York: E.P. Dutton, 1922, p. 25.

7. Colby R. Hatfield, Jr., "Fieldwork: Toward a Model of Mutual Exploitation." *Anthropological Quarterly* 46:1:15–29, 1973.

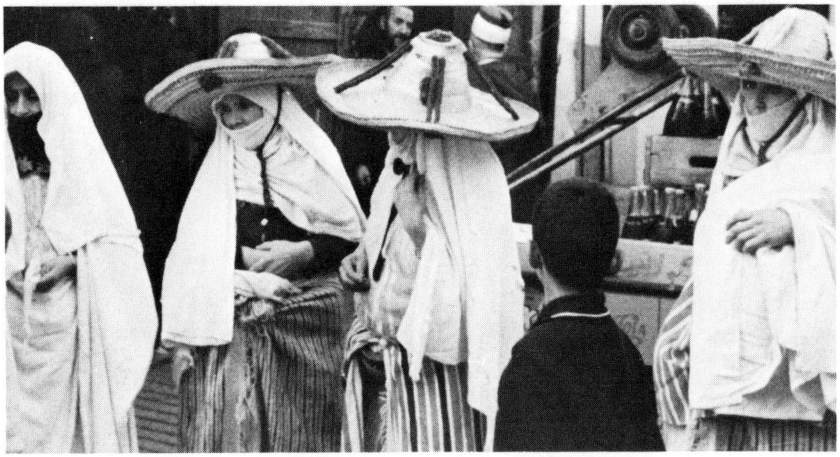

Women of the Riff Mountains of Morocco. A male anthropologist would find it very difficult to get a rounded picture of life in a society where women are isolated and must keep their faces covered. (Eugene Gordon, Taurus)

generally has much more capital at his disposal than the average villager. Thus they view him as a storehouse of wealth. He is willing to pay for the services the villagers render, and to their mind it seems as if he never runs out of money. At the same time, he obviously does not have to work for a living, because all he does is walk around the village all day asking questions. His money miraculously appears in the mail every month, but it is not clear who is paying him for what, nor is it clear that the source of this interminable wealth is not a money tree that never dries up. So the anthropologist is constantly battling against this image in the eyes of the people he is studying, although frequently it is a losing battle.

Third, the anthropologist is often assigned the role of "Sahib," as Hatfield calls it, the expert in all things, the exalted foreigner who possesses power that the community members could not hope to acquire. After all, the anthropologist is literate, whereas the people anthropologists have traditionally studied have not been. The anthropologist is able to deal with government bureaucracies, which in itself is a kind of power. He knows about people and places in the four corners of the world, and can tell stories that challenge the imagination of even the most cosmopolitan villager. Despite the fact that he comes on like a child in their own culture, there is obviously something there, and so the anthropologist is given the artificial status of village expert.

Try as I might during my fieldwork in the Swiss Alps, I could not get the farmers to let me help them with their tasks. They felt that a city fellow like me shouldn't get his hands dirty working in the fields. When I pointed out to them that I had put on my work clothes, and actually wanted to help, they would respond by saying something like "Oh, what do you have work clothes for?" They would laugh at the silly questions I asked about their farming and livestock raising practices, much as if I were a naive young boy. And they were amazed at the fact that I bought all my food, and did not even grow my own potatoes. On the other hand, they did respect my ability to deal with aspects of the outside world with which they had had little experience. I was asked to translate for them, to type letters and reports, and to interpret the meaning of various happenings. Perhaps most important of all in their minds was the fact that I could explain American television programs that appeared on their TV screens, appropriately dubbed in German. Hatfield's description of the fieldworker as child–Fort-Knox–Sahib certainly rings true from my own experience, and points out some of the problems the anthropologist faces.

I have said much about these problems, and about the kinds of situations the anthropologist encounters, but little about actual techniques of fieldwork. I have not, for example, gone into great detail describing the proper way to phrase a question or to write up an interview, or the best way to use a tape recorder or a camera. This is perhaps due to the fact that I firmly believe in the individuality of each fieldworker and the need for flexibility according to the situation. The graduate student trained in anthropology generally does not receive this kind of instruction in the narrow detail of the methods he is to use. It is assumed he will adjust to the demands of the community he lives in, and any attempt to arrive at a hard-and-fast rule of how to do research would not be valid. Besides, doing anthropological research calls for a lot of personal qualities that simply cannot be acquired through training—the perseverence to stick it out, the control over one's temper when people laugh at you and kids throw snowballs at you, the ability to eat whatever you are given with a smile and compliment the chef even if you don't like fried lizard, and perhaps above all the ability to cope with the loneliness when you are so far away from home for so long. There is no technique to these aspects of fieldwork, and there is no way to train for them. Not everyone who starts out to become an anthropologist finishes the task, but those who do usually develop their own personal way of doing research that fits both their personal idiosyncracies and the unique demands of the research setting.

In the following article, John C. Messenger describes one result of his experiences in doing field work in Inis Beag, an island off the coast of Ireland. He tells of a problem not discussed in the preceding chapter—namely that even after the anthropologist's fieldwork is finished, he is never really free from it. The memories of a year or more of living in a foreign culture invariably linger on, and in Professor Messenger's case, it was more than a memory that remained, as you will discover in reading his amusing account.

A Critical Reexamination of the Concept of Spirits: with Special Reference to Traditional Irish Folklore and Contemporary Irish Folk Culture

John Messenger

We named him "Brendan" for a literary figure who occasionally visits Inis Beag and is renowned among the islanders for his love of "spirits" and his practical jokes. Our friends thought it strange for us to name a *leipreachán,* since it is not an Irish custom to do so. The folk peoples of the west country avoid the fairies, seldom talk about them publicly, and refer to them respectfully as the "gentry" or the "good people" if the need arises. But during our stay on the island, we came to feel the immaterial presence of this creature so intensely and to anticipate his pranks with such enthusiasm that we eventually came to view him as a third member of our family, well deserving an affectionate and suitable name.

Initially, Brendan's particular mode of expression was to open our door or one of our windows during the night when we were asleep, a practice that continued intermittently month after month, no matter how carefully we checked bolted door and locked windows before retiring. At first we suspected an actual or potential thief, but nothing was ever stolen; besides, crime of any nature is virtually unknown on the island. Then we considered a practical joker, but no one ever admitted "codding" us in this manner, and local pranksters eventually call attention to their deeds. Finally, after examining and discarding in turn other possible explanations, we were forced to conclude that a leipreachán had taken up residence in our apartment and was calling attention to his presence in this way.

Our neighbor, an elderly, unmarried nurse who lived in the adjoining apartment of our ancient building, complained of hearing violin music emanating from beneath the eaves outside her bedroom window late at night. Her door and windows were never opened, and we never heard violin music, but Brendan may have been responsible for both. We don't know if the music continues, but we suspect not, for it has become obvious that Brendan returned home with us.

My wife and I spent last year on Inis Beag, off the west coast of Éire, as anthropologists documenting recent history and the contemporary way of life of the people living there. Because of an interest arising out of a previous research experience, when we studied the effects of Christianity on a Nigerian tribe, we spent a good deal of time describing the religious beliefs of the islanders. These consist of both Roman Catholic elements and pagan Celtic survivals which coexist or are syncretized, much to the dismay of the more sophisticated curates who have lived on Inis Beag. The pagan array of spiritual beings includes shades, changelings, mermaids, *púca,* witches, *bean sidhe,* water spirits, workers of good and evil magic, those with the evil eye, and, of course, Brendan and his ilk. The youth overtly disallow the existence of other than Church approved

Reprinted from *American Anthropologist,* **64** (1962).

supernatural entities, but the elders cling to traditional pagan beliefs, about which they are extremely secretive for fear of being ridiculed. After we were well known and accepted by the islanders, we talked with many old people who admitted having seen shades, mermaids, púca, and the like in corporeal form, but try as we might we met only Brendan, and then indirectly through his nocturnal escapades rather than face to face.

The fairies of Ireland are divided into two camps: the trooping fairies and the solitary ones. Of the latter, the most notorious is the leipreachán, who is noted for his shoe-making and treasure-burying proclivities, although his versatility extends beyond mere cobbling and hoarding. Hardly two Irish writers are in agreement as to whether the leipreachán, the clúracán, and the *fear dearg* are three different spirits or are one spirit, the leipreachán, in different moods and shapes. The islanders prefer the former interpretation, but we prefer the latter in light of Brendan's singular behavior. The *clúracán* is best known for making himself drunk in cellars, while the fear dearg limits his activities to practical joking of a bizarre nature. Since joining our present household, Brendan has displayed both tendencies, as well as others I will describe presently. So we have decided that, contrary to island opinion, he is a leipreachán of rather remarkable talents. I must admit, however, that to the best of our knowledge he has thus far produced neither shoes nor shillings. This fact led us to suspect he was a *sprid i dteach* after we had become accustomed to his presence in our domicile on Inis Beag; but this spirit, although inhabiting many cottages in nearby Clare and Connemara, appears never to have ventured out to the Western Isles. Perhaps he is less of a seaman than the leipreachán, or thinks Inis Beag is Tir na nÓg and, being more of a recluse than his solitary mates, does not wish to mingle with the good people who are said to abide there.

W. B. Yeats describes Brendan's multifarious companions as ". . . withered, old, and solitary, in every way unlike the sociable [trooping fairies]. . . . They dress with all unfairy homeliness, and are, indeed, most sluttish, slouching, jeering, mischievous phantoms." We heartily dislike the thought of Brendan possessing such unwholesome qualities, but who are we to challenge ancient tradition? It may be that since we have departed from island standards in classifying him as a leipreachán, it is also permissible for us to deviate in portraying his character and be much kinder than Yeats. We cannot vouch for Brendan's appearance and thus will have to depend upon the eye witness accounts of our island informants and those fortunate individuals who advised Yeats. Leipreachán will not reveal themselves in any manner to most human beings, will make their presence known to some by various deeds, and will appear to only a very few whom they especially favor. By firmness of belief in their existence, services rendered, and disservices shunned does one win their favor. Evidently our conviction of belief left something to be desired, for we offered Brendan every material comfort the island had to offer, including access to our Tullamore Dew, and were very cautious so as not to offend him in word or deed. All to no avail. Even today he refuses to materialize despite every inducement.

Our last few days on Inis Beag were hectic ones, filled as they were with packing, finishing a written report to our sponsors, and bidding farewell to dear friends. Realizing that we were experiencing severe emotional stress, Brendan quite obligingly chose not to distract us during the last week. This revealed a strength of character that I am sure would have surprised Yeats. As soon as we boarded the ship in Galway, all thoughts of Brendan disappeared from mind until a morning early in September, only two weeks after we had settled again in a duplex near the university campus. The first indication of the fact that we had been followed across the Atlantic and half way across the continent came with my discovery of an open front door, when I made my initial sally downstairs at dawn to bring in the newspaper and put on the water to boil. I thought little of the incident at the time and may not even have mentioned it to my wife, because I remembered that I had failed to try the doors before going to bed. It was an oversight which has prompted me to check them conscientiously each night since that fateful event. But the front door continued from time to time to gape open, in spite of all precautionary measures, and was soon joined by the back door. After three such episodes, the truth at last dawned upon us; Brendan was here. We were very pleased, for his presence, insubstantial though it was, served as a link between ourselves and Ireland, whose people and beauty we missed so much during those first weeks at home. With the passing of time and the increase in Brendan's versatility, we have come to accept his presence with deep satisfaction and more than a touch of pride. Let me tell you of his ever growing repertoire of pranks, which reveal those typically Irish traits of resourcefulness, humor, and imagination.

Brendan has always shown a predilection for opening doors and windows, but after settling down here he soon took to switching on the basement lights and manipulating the thermostat. When the weather first became uncomfortably cold in late October, we turned on the furnace and kept the thermostat at 68 degrees during the day and six degrees cooler at night. The outdoor temperature suddenly rose one night, and we were awakened by the discomfort of being bathed in perspiration. Our warm room was being fed even warmer air from the vent. I hurried downstairs to find the thermostat set at 74 degrees. My immediate reaction was to sit down then and there in the living room and check through in my memory my final movements before retiring; they most certainly did not include pushing *up* the thermostat control! Conversely, a week later, when the thermometer plunged to the lower regions for the first time, we were once again aroused from sleep, but rather from the discomfort of an icy bed. The cause of this condition was an upper window opened wide in the front bedroom, which had been locked since late August. Brendan's great strength was attested by the fact that locking and relocking the window almost proved too much of an effort for me.

As well as possessing heroic thews for one so diminutive, Brendan is telepathic. One evening I went to bed suffering from a severe headache and, once comfortably settled under the covers, recalled that I had neglected to take an aspirin. So I swung out of bed muffling curses, but as my feet touched the floor I heard the sound of running water from the bathroom. Both my wife and I were startled into a quick exchange of baffled exclamations, following which I stumbled into the bathroom to find the cold water faucet fully opened. Brendan had anticipated my desire. It took us more than an hour to recover from this experience and compose ourselves for sleep. Had the aspirin bottle with cover removed been standing on the ledge above the cooperative tap, we would never have slept that night. However, Brendan is seldom too obvious. Another example of his psychic powers is his ability to awaken one of us a few minutes before the alarm clock is due to sound, so that we can discover that he has depressed the alarm button sometime during the night. Pulling out the button marks the final stage of an almost compulsive retirement ritual we follow.

Early on election day, while standing in a cold schoolroom at the end of a long, slow moving line that led to two polling booths, my wife and I had occasion to chat for several minutes with our landlady. She introduced the subject of cold weather and storm windows, which gave rise to a train of thoughts in my mind leading, as you might guess, to Brendan. I very cautiously broached the subject of self-opening doors and windows in her half of the duplex, but found that her doors and windows opened only at her own bidding. Soon her curiosity was aroused by my further, rather clumsy probing into the allied matter of self-regulating basement light switches and thermostat controls, and I was at last put into the position of revealing all. Rather than describing the uncommon happenings either in a light manner, punctuating my conversation with gay laughter, or in a serious mode consonant with my genuine sentiments, I unfortunately tried to do both. This left her bewildered, to say the least, not knowing whether or not to believe me and possibly a little uncertain as to the wisdom of renting to us. I have not mentioned the matter again in her presence, nor has she in mine. This is an unfortunate state of affairs, for I forgot to ask her about hearing violin music. The Inis Beag nurse refuses to answer our questions concerning her island virtuoso, and we are curious to know if Brendan has a penchant for entertaining elderly widows and spinsters with lively jigs.

In Éire we could never induce Brendan to drink our whiskey; thus we were forced to conclude that he was either a deviant or a member of the Pioneer Total Abstinence Society. Early in December, surprisingly, he began to imbibe. I became aware of it when twice the cork was pushed only part way into the neck of the bottle, a practice that my wife and I assiduously try to avoid. So we began to mark the liquid level by pencilling a line on the label each time that we put the bottle away. Frequent inspections of the fifth revealed that at least once each week the level dropped an eighth of an inch. Does such pilfering reflect Brendan's size, or is he an inexperienced drinker, polite, or of the opinion that he is outwitting us? More important, however, is the question: why did he choose to reveal his clúracán tendencies here rather than on Inis Beag? Possibly he disliked the Tullamore Dew that we ordered monthly from a shop on the mainland, as did some of the islanders, but finds the Powers that we brought back with us (duty free) more to his taste. On the other hand, he may be reading our magazines and has been taken in by those clever Whiskey Distillers of Ireland advertisements.

None of Brendan's doings are malicious, you must understand. The fairies most often harm those who have maltreated them, and many fairy pranks are gestures of amicability. A careful examination of the circumstances surrounding Brendan's many deeds reveals that each is committed shortly before our attention is drawn to it, as in the case of the impotent alarm clock. The purloined whiskey is, of course, another story, but Brendan knows that we can well afford a thimbleful of Irish each week. We do wish, however, that he would switch his allegiance to the cheap Scotch or bourbon we keep on hand to serve guests who insist upon mixed drinks. Irish whiskey is never cheap in this state.

Brendan has affected our lives beyond merely furnishing us with unexpected and amusing diversions and a sense of Gaelic camaraderie. He has, for instance, provided a stable marriage with even greater stability; for when either of us is forgetful so as to irk the other, Brendan serves as a convenient scapegoat. If appointments are missed, letters are mailed unstamped, or the car is left unlocked overnight, and it is obvious that Brendan cannot be blamed, Brendan is blamed. Doing so channels discharged emotions in a most effective way and restores an atmosphere of affability within minutes.

I have made a point of giving my students at the university a weekly rundown on Brendan's doings ever since delivering a well received lecture on comparative religions some weeks ago. I have found that these reports work quite as effectively as a boisterous joke, mention of "Charlie Brown," or questioning a football player in drawing them away from their school newspapers, opening their sleepy lids early on a Monday morning, or revitalizing lectures that tend to be boring because of my mood or the topic under discussion. I suspect that I have converted several students to a belief in fairies by sheer enthusiasm and by the obvious honesty of my own convictions. If only Brendan could observe me in the classroom, he would surely become convinced of my sincerity and appear.

The proselytizing efforts of my wife, on the other hand, have met with far less success among small school children. They are disbelievers one and all and brand as "tall tale tellers" the folklorists whose stories about the Irish fairies they have heard. To these youngsters Brendan represents nothing more than coincidence coupled with forgetfulness, naive enthusiasm, and possibly even deception on my wife's part. This has been a bitter pill for us to swallow, we who were nurtured on Andersen and the Grimms and who looked for ghosts beneath our beds before the lights were turned out.

Needless to say, my colleagues have been even more reluctant to accept the reality of Brendan. Anthropologists are a tough-minded lot who espouse cultural relativism, naturalism, and the other "isms" that humanists and theologians find so repugnant. The customary attitude of the fieldworker toward what his subjects interpret as supernatural events is one of extreme scepticism or active disbelief. There are some anthropologists, however, who at least maintain an open mind where these phenomena are concerned. I am reminded of a friend and his wife, both members of the secret society of anthropologists, who are the parents of several obstreperous children and, as a result, take great care to prevent an African fertility figurine from crossing the threshold of their bedroom. My wife and I have witnessed events, both in Nigeria and in Éire, whose causes could be explained by recourse to either the sacred or the profane. Having been unable to determine to our own satisfaction the naturalistic causes of these occurrences, we have always been willing to consider the reality of the supernatural, but with something less than open minds. This tender-minded attitude is regarded as poison oak in the more scientific groves of academe.

Twice tongue in cheek colleagues have suggested that my wife and I take steps to rid our apartment of Brendan. I have both times met the suggestion by reaffirming our strong devotion to Brendan and his ways, but the exchanges have set me to thinking of what we might do were he to become unruly. We have a friend in Nigeria, a particularly competent worker of magic, who would be able to compel Brendan to return to Inis Beag if the need arose, but utilizing his services would be out of the question. We brought back with us from Africa several indigenous icons that once would have accomplished the desired end, but I am afraid that lack of use and storage in damp basements for several years have reduced their potency. I am sure that local Catholic priests, unlike their Irish brethren, would regard exorcism as out of the question, even though we were of their faith. Quite frankly, we are at a loss as to how we might cope with a leipreachán Jekyll turned Hyde.

Which brings me to the present. At Christmas we visited relatives in a nearby city and there had occasion one evening to show colored slides and talk about the island with seldom seen friends. One of them, of obvious Irish descent, was considerably stimulated by the pictures and the conversation, and he questioned us at great length about the varieties of fairies and their activities and about our experiences with Brendan. It seems that as a youth, at his grandfather's knee, he had heard tales of the good people in the old country and had retained a vivid impression of their reality. If today he entertains doubts as to their existence, he at least has the will to believe, which he expressed with fervor as the evening wore on. Early the next morning we were awakened by the insistent ringing of the telephone to find that it was our Irish friend, who excitedly told us of discovering his front door wide open just 10 minutes earlier and of being unable to draw water from any faucet in the house. It was apparent from his almost inarticulate utterances that he hoped it might be Brendan's handiwork, and we were crestfallen to think it might. Had Brendan followed us once again; was he attracted to this charming and sympathetic

Gael; and would he choose to remain behind?

For a week after returning home we were restless and impatient, awaiting some sign of Brendan's continuing presence. At last we were rewarded by finding the turntable and preamplifier of our phonograph system turned on several hours after it had been dusted and nothing found amiss. Then the following morning the level of spirits in the Powers' bottle had lowered perceptibly, and we were jubilant! Manipulation of the phonograph was a new achievement for Brendan, one he had mastered during our absence, no doubt to demonstrate his joy at our return. There may be another motive underlying the accomplishment, however, for we discovered upon our arrival home several misplaced records, of unaccompanied Irish fiddling, in one of the album racks; the implications of this are intriguing to contemplate. We have no idea what the future will bring, but we will welcome each new manifestation of Brendan's virtuosity and hope that he will remain a member of our household, at least until we return once again to the Western Isles.

Some will think that I have written this piece to arouse consternation or envy in my fellow professors. Nothing could be further from the truth. When it is published, I will sign a copy with our favorite island toast—"Seo dhuit; gob fliuch, sláinte an bhradáin, grásta Dé, agus bás i nÉirinn." ("May you always have a wet mouth, the health of a salmon, the grace of God, and die in Éire.")—and stand it against a newly opened fifth of Powers. If this doesn't induce Brendan to materialize, nothing will.

Summary

The methods used by anthropologists to conduct their research have been one of the distinguishing features between anthropology and other related disciplines. One of the leading figures in revolutionizing the field techniques of anthropology was Bronislaw Malinowski, who engaged in what is called *participant observation.* Malinowski recommended that all anthropologists live in the native community, learn the native language, and try to understand the culture from the native's point of view.

A major difficulty in conducting research in a foreign culture is maintaining objectivity in the face of massive culture shock. If the anthropologist is reduced to making value judgments about the way of life of the people being studied, then he or she will never be able to describe or analyze that culture without personal prejudices slipping in. An interesting controversy arose over the objectivity of two anthropologists who studied the same community and arrived at contradictory conclusions about the people who lived there. Robert Redfield and Oscar Lewis both conducted field research in the Mexican village of Tepoztlán. Redfield described the village as being harmonious and happy, while many years later Lewis found it to be characterized by suspicion and lack of cooperation. Much of the difference in these two views can be assigned to the different temperaments of the two authors, each of whom was looking for something different and managed to find what he sought.

In doing research in a foreign culture, the anthropologist tries to uncover the unwritten rules that govern people's behavior. Frequently it is difficult to do this simply by asking people why they act in a particular way. Therefore the anthropologist must combine several different methods, including actual participation in the culture, questioning informants who share the culture, and standing back and observing as an outsider. One of the problems the anthropologist must overcome is the universal tendency of all people to create an impression of themselves by concealing certain aspects of their lives and emphasizing others, a process we call *impression management.* In uncovering the hidden behavior of people in another culture, the anthropologist must engage in a bit of impression management himself, proving that it is just as natural for us as for anyone else.

The anthropologist's role in another culture is frequently made difficult by the fact that although we are in many ways similar to children, in that we do not know all the rules of behavior and we do not speak the language perfectly, we are nonetheless adults and cannot be treated as children. In addition, anthropologists are frequently in command of more resources—money, an automobile, books and specialized knowledge, etc.—than the people they are studying. This leads people to place all kinds of demands upon the visitor, and makes it difficult for the anthropologist to be completely accepted as "one of the gang."

Glossary

analytic image The manner in which an anthropologist organizes or structures the behavior of a particular culture.

back region A term referring to an area of behavior concealed by a group of people in order to control the impression an outsider obtains about them. The people may wish the anthropologist to believe that their real behavior conforms more to the ideal than is actually the case.

culture shock The trauma often experienced by an anthropologist conducting field research among a people foreign to his or her own culture. This may happen to any person who enters a new cultural setting. The depression and frustration result from the confrontation of a way of life very different from one's own culture.

folk image The manner in which the natives of a particular culture organize or structure their own behavior.

"going native" The tendency to emphasize participation at the expense of observation in field research. The extreme form of this situation occurs when an anthropologist adopts the cultural behavior patterns of the natives being studied and remains in their community.

ideal behavior Those rules of conduct that are learned and shared by the members of a particular culture. The anthropologist can arrive at these rules by questioning an informant about the nature of any behavior.

impression management The attempt of an individual to control the opinions that others have of him. We all do this, through the clothes we wear, the way we talk and act in a given situation, and in many other ways.

participant observation The method employed by the anthropologist in conducting field research, aimed at an equal balance between actual participation in the community and objective observation of that community.

real behavior The actual behavior patterns participated in by members of a particular culture, which do not necessarily conform to the ideal behaviors expressed by the natives themselves. The anthropologist can arrive at real behavior patterns only through observation of social interaction within the community.

world view The basic outlook (relationship to nature, the native's point of view, values, attitudes, morals, beliefs) held in common by most members of a society.

Questions for Discussion

1 Have you ever found yourself in a situation where you were an outsider with little understanding of the appropriate behavior (such as at a wedding ceremony of a different religious faith)? How did you seek to learn what was appropriate? What mistakes, if any, did you make and how were they corrected? What bias did your own background create in your observations? Can you see a parallel between this type of experience and the fieldwork of an anthropologist?

2 Have you ever been in a foreign country where you didn't speak the language, or have you ever had contact with a foreigner who had trouble speaking English? How did this language problem affect your interaction? What difficulties would this create for an anthropologist, and how could they be overcome?

3 What are some of the unwritten rules in American culture that a foreigner might have trouble learning? How would you, as an anthropologist, go about learning these rules in a foreign culture?

4 What forms of impression management do you practice in your daily life? What are some of the impressions you try to create in various situations, and how do you behave differently (e.g., by varying the clothes you wear, the speech patterns you use, etc.)?

5 Select a subculture within your community and design an anthropological research program to investigate it. What would be the most important methods you would use? What problems do you foresee in doing this research? What kinds of information would be easiest or most difficult to obtain, and why?

Suggestions for Additional Reading

Berreman, Gerald D.
1972 Hindus of the Himalayas. Second Edition. Berkeley: University of California Press.

Included in this new extended edition is an introduction entitled "Behind Many Masks," in which the author describes the process of impression management and how he learned to deal with it during his own research.

Bowen, Elenore Smith (Laura Bohannan)
1954 Return to Laughter. Garden City, N.Y.: Doubleday & Company.

A novel by a woman anthropologist based upon her study of the Tiv, an African society. The author captures many of the problems and emotions involved in fieldwork and communicates them in a delightfully entertaining fashion.

Goffman, Erving
1959 The Presentation of Self in Everyday Life. Garden City, N.Y.: Doubleday & Company.

A detailed analysis of how we manipulate the image we present in various social situations, as a part of our normal pattern of behavior.

Golde, Peggy (editor)
1970 Women in the Field. Chicago: Aldine.

As the title implies, a collection of papers by 12 women dealing with the specific problems of being a woman involved in anthropological research.

Hall, Edward T.
1959 The Silent Language. Greenwich, Conn.: Fawcett Publications.

A fascinating study of the nonverbal communication that accompanies all social interaction. The author points out that patterns of this "silent language" are culturally determined, and are quite different from one society to another, adding to the difficulties in cross-cultural communication.

Lewis, Oscar
1951 Life in a Mexican Village: Tepoztlán Restudied. Urbana: University of Illinois Press.

The restudy of a village first studied by Robert Redfield in the 1920s, in which the author arrived at many conclusions that contradicted Redfield's findings two decades earlier.

Malinowski, Bronislaw

1922 Argonauts of the Western Pacific. London: Routledge & Kegan Paul.

One of the classic ethnographic studies based upon intensive fieldwork. In the introduction the author sets out his requirements for field research, and then proceeds to show how necessary it is to do intensive fieldwork in order to arrive at a complete picture of the native culture.

1967 A Diary in the Strict Sense of the Term. New York: Harcourt Brace Jovanovich.

The private notes taken by Malinowski during his fieldwork in the Trobriands, published after his death. This book is particularly revealing of the stresses and strains of research in a foreign culture and the problems of culture shock.

Naroll, Raoul, and Ronald Cohen (editors)

1970 A Handbook of Method in Cultural Anthropology. Garden City, N.Y.: Natural History Press.

One of the most complete and detailed collections of readings on anthropological methods and approaches to research.

Pelto, Pertti J.

1970 Anthropological Research: The Structure of Inquiry. New York: Harper & Row.

One of the more detailed books treating the various research techniques and approaches used by anthropologists, this book is especially valuable for its blend of the humanistic and scientific elements of fieldwork.

Powdermaker, Hortense

1966 Stranger and Friend: The Way of an Anthropologist. New York: W. W. Norton.

A personal account of the author's research in four societies, and the different approach adopted in each.

Redfield, Robert

1930 Tepoztlán, A Mexican Village. Chicago: University of Chicago Press.

The original study of the Mexican village of Tepoztlán, later restudied by Oscar Lewis, leading to a controversy over the discrepancies between the two anthropologists' descriptions of the way of life in the village.

Spindler, George D. (editor)

1970 Being an Anthropologist: Fieldwork in Eleven Cultures. New York: Holt, Rinehart and Winston.

Eleven anthropologists describe their experiences in conducting research in other cultures.

Social Organization

Chapter Five

In its simplest sense, a *society* is an organized group of individuals who interact with one another and form a cohesive unit. This definition would include not only human groups, but baboons, bees, ants and any other nonhuman "social" animals. There is no implication of culture in the definition of society, for we can talk of baboon "social organization" without recognizing baboon culture. It is only when we speak of human societies that we refer to the concept of culture, for among people we find that the basic principle around which the group is organized is the way of life that its members share—their culture. The society forms a cohesive unit because its members share the same language, values, knowledge, and beliefs. In short, the society is unified by the similarity of its members in the way of life that they follow; they tend to think of themselves as members of the same group. A society can range from a complex civilization such as "American society" all the way down to a small unit such as an army company or a ship's crew. There need not be political boundaries setting it off from others; although we tend to think in terms of nation-states as viable, independent units, a society can exist below the national level or across national boundaries. We might speak of Jewish society or Chinese society as extending into many widely separate political units.

Definition of Society

The term *society* refers to an association of individuals. When we speak of social relations we are dealing with interaction among mem-

All animals are equal,
but some animals are more equal
than others.

GEORGE ORWELL *Animal Farm*

bers of that group. Further, when we speak of social organization, we are referring to the patterns of that interaction. We assume that there is some sort of structure to the personal interaction within a society, and in analyzing that structure we tend to assign behavior to certain categories we have created. In doing this we divide the people of the society into various groups, many of which cross-cut each other, such as families, clans, states, classes, clubs, and so on. Further, we can analyze behavior in terms of its political, economic or religious components, although the people themselves might not make these distinctions in everyday life.

Society, then, is an artificial construct used by anthropologists to see patterns in other people's behavior. As we group these patterns together, the behavior takes on a structure with separate units that we refer to as *institutions.* An institution is simply a pattern of behavior which focuses upon a central theme. We may speak of a market as an economic institution, but there is more to a market than simply a building where people buy and sell. We also mean the activities involved in production, distribution, sales and consumption. We refer to the patterns of behavior involved in exchanging goods, and the values and preferences and other intangibles associated with that exchange. Thus a market as an economic institution is much more than a simple economic consideration of supply and demand, or a compilation of sales figures—it is a total realm of behavior involved with exchange.

The same is true for religion. When we speak of a religious institution, we are referring to much more than the church and what goes on inside it. We include in our scope of religious institutions all kinds of behavior that might be considered religious, such as the

Baboons "grooming" one another, a social act reinforcing the hierarchy and cohesion of the group. (Tierpark Hellabrunn, Photo Researchers)

control that religious beliefs exert over individuals in their daily behavior, or the nature of community integration through shared belief systems. When we put all these patterns of behavior together from all of the different institutions we have analyzed, we can begin to see how they are tied together and how they affect one another. This provides us with the basic framework of the social structure.

Social Solidarity

If a society is a group of people, then there must be something that holds them together, something that provides the group with continuity through time. In part it is a system of values shared by the members of the group which keeps them from splitting off into countless smaller groups. In other words, there is a certain degree of consensus about how people ought to behave, and as long as the members of a society share these beliefs and follow the basic rules, they remain together in a cohesive group. At the same time, it is clear that people cooperat-

A market is much more than just a physical structure—it includes a wide range of patterned behavior. (United Nations)

ing and working together as a group can usually accomplish more than each individual working separately; it is to everyone's advantage to operate as a group, since society can provide more for each individual than he can obtain by himself. Another principle of social cohesion can best be termed "negative" solidarity, in the sense that people are held together by negative rather than positive forces. Although an individual might not think he is receiving positive benefits from the group, there may be no viable alternative—there may be nowhere else to go. The limitations upon moving from one group to another can be geographical, or they can simply be cultural. Language barriers, for example, can be a major stumbling block in moving from one society to another. In some cases people are forced to remain together because no one else wants them. Many minority groups in the United States are held together in part by the fact that there is nowhere else for the members to go in American society. Indians, Blacks, Mexican-Americans, and many other minorities are frequently unwelcome in middle class American society, and thus they are forced to establish a solidary group by negative pressures from the outside, in addition to the positive pressures drawing members to the group from within.

The question of social solidarity was the main focus of the French sociologist Emile Durkheim. In *The Division of Labor in Society,* Durkheim offers us an understanding of one of the fundamental differences between traditional societies that anthropologists have studied in non-Western settings, and our own modern industrial society. He points out that social solidarity is directly linked to the division of labor in society, which is another way of referring to the degree of specialization or the extent to which the tasks that people perform are divided among different groups of specialists, rather than everyone doing basically the same work and repeating the efforts of others in the society.

The New York Public Library

Emile Durkheim (1858–1917) *a noted French sociologist, is also an important figure in the history of anthropology.* The Division of Labor in Society (1893), *his first major book, was an attempt to solve the problem of alienation. He argued that in a complex civilization where specialization occurred, people must be bound together by their dependence upon one another—but they must not become so specialized that they lose sight of their affinity for each other. In a later book,* Suicide (1897), *he put this theory into practice once again, by explaining the higher rate of suicide in some societies as a result of alienation. In his last great work,* The Elementary Forms of the Religious Life (1912), *Durkheim identified many factors in the relation of religion to the rest of society.*

Mechanical Solidarity

Durkheim proposes two contrasting models of society, each with a different kind of social solidarity. The first type he calls *mechanical solidarity,* in which there is very little division of labor—that is, in which everyone does basically the same tasks, and therefore they share the same experiences. It is highly likely that their sharing of culture will go further, then, to incorporate values and beliefs as well. If there is little variety in experience, there will be little variety in attitudes toward how things should be done, and this similarity will be reflected in other aspects of the social structure as well.

This kind of homogeneity exists not only in communities in foreign societies, but within small groups in our own. For example, if we examine a group such as a labor union we find a greater degree of solidarity than if we look at a typical middle class neighborhood made up of many different kinds of people from different walks of life, with various occupations, religions, and levels of education. Within a trade union, the members are all at basically the same income level with the same occupation and to a certain extent the same kinds of experiences. And the same situation will hold not only for trade unions, but for any small group of relatively similar individuals—ethnic groups, religious associations, other professional associations, or whatever. As the group gets larger in size and more varied in its membership base, the tendency toward solidarity based upon uniformity will disappear, and the pressures exerted upon members to conform will have less effect, and will be less successful.

Organic Solidarity

Durkheim then turned to the opposite type of solidarity, which he found in what he called *organic society.* He used the term *organic* to refer to the fact that in such a society the situation was similar to the way the parts of an organism operate. The human body, for example, is composed of a number of different organs—heart, lungs, liver, kidneys, brain, etc. Each contributes something different to the operation of the whole organism. If the heart suddenly stopped pumping blood and started digesting food, the organism would not survive. It depends upon each organ performing its own special task, each contributing something different to the whole.

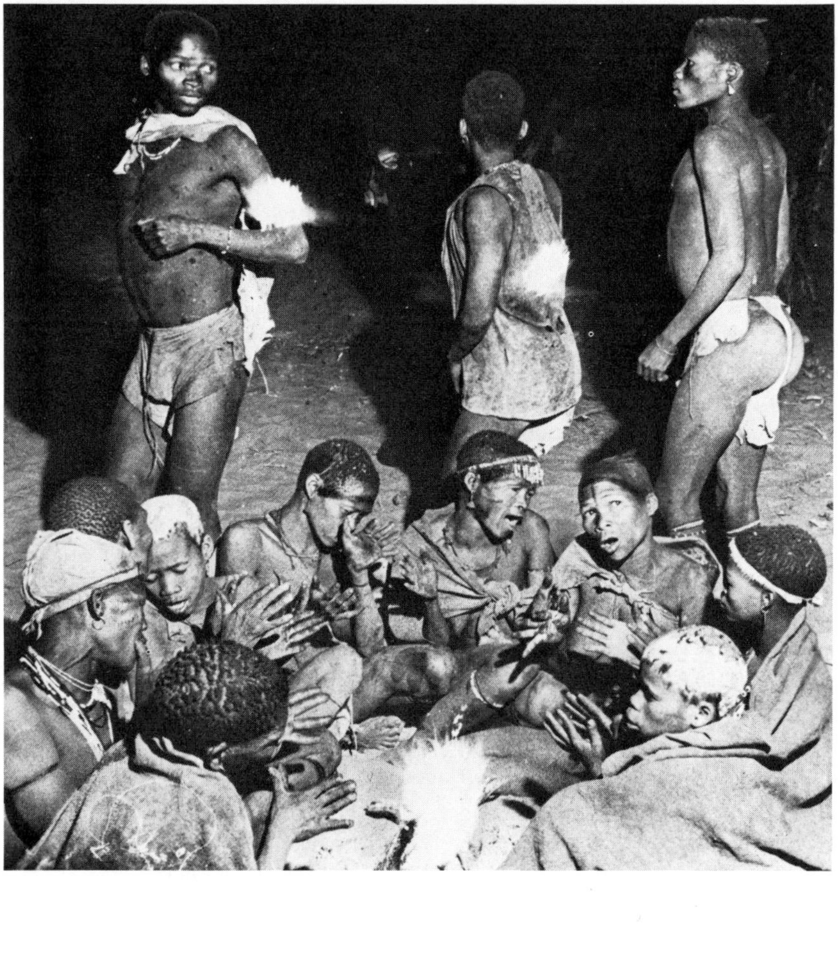

Bushmen dancing and singing around a campfire. Their wide range of shared behavior places the Bushmen relatively closer to the model of mechanical solidarity. (Wide World)

This is how Durkheim viewed organic society, as made up of many different parts, each with a different and specialized contribution to make to the overall operation of society. The farmer would produce food, the manufacturer would produce material goods, the middleman would specialize in the exchange of food and manufactured goods, and others would perform various specialized services. The more specialized people become, the greater the interdependence of the different parts of society.

Durkheim suggested that history has seen a progression from mechanical to organic society, and with it a change in the kind of solidarity that holds people together in societies. We can see how this is directly related to cultural anthropology, for it enables us to understand a basic difference between the nature of the groups that anthropologists have tended to study in the past, and our own society. We are a very specialized country, with a wide variety of people each doing their own thing.

When we examine social structure, we have to take into account that as the society becomes more complex—more like the organic model—the structure becomes more difficult to see clearly. If everyone is a hunter or a cultivator, we have no difficulty figuring out how they relate to each other. But it is not as evident how the various specialized groups are related in our own society. Thus anthropologists have tended to confine their studies to societies with simpler social structures, and when they have gone into complex societies they have zeroed in on a small segment which they can describe as if it were a homogeneous, isolated unit. Anthropologists are more inclined to write about an ethnic neighborhood in a city than about the entire city itself; they write about specialized groups within American society, but not about the totality of American society. It is much easier to see what members of a trade union have in common than to try to figure out what the nature of social solidarity is among 210 million Americans. And it is much more productive to study small groups where our findings can be applied, than to study a group so large and diverse that even if we did come up with some results we could not use them in a practical manner.

Thus Durkheim's distinction between a society in which people are held together through similarity and one in which they are bound together by virtue of their interdependence can give us a starting point from which to overcome some of our ethnocentric bias in looking at other ways of life. We must realize that our values arise out of

A General Motors auto assembly line. The specialization evident here is typical of the model of organic solidarity. (General Motors)

experiences that we share with only a small proportion of our fellow Americans, and even fewer of our fellow world citizens. If we are to rely upon other people for providing us with their specialized products and services, we must also recognize their differences and respect them. Our culture is simply too complex for us to be able to comprehend all aspects of it.

Structure and Function

Durkheim's discussion of social solidarity and its relationship to the division of labor is important not only for its explanation of one of the fundamental differences between Western and non-Western societies, but also for its analysis of how the different elements of a society fit together. Anatomy and physiology detail the structure of the different parts of the human body and how each of them functions to contribute to the working of the overall organism. In the same way, the anthropologist seeks to understand the structure of society—how the different institutions fit together, and how each element in that structure functions to maintain the whole. It was Durkheim who contributed the concept of the functional integration of society by showing how the division of labor (a social institution) is related to the legal and moral codes (two other social institutions) and how each contributes something different to the social solidarity (the maintenance of the whole). The concepts of structure and function are intertwined. Society is an integrated unit made up of many different parts, each related to the others, each contributing something different, functioning in its own different way to keep the system intact. As an institution changes, the others will react to that change and will compensate for it, thus changing themselves in the process. All will remain integrated into a single unit.

We can see how this principle of functional integration operates on a number of different levels in our society. For example, on a rather general level we can discuss the relationship between religion, economics, and politics in American society—three different institutions. The political system is basically democratic, offering a relative degree of freedom to each individual to act as he wishes within certain limits. The economic system is one of free enterprise, so that each individual can engage in whatever economic activities he chooses (again within certain limits) in an attempt to maximize his own advantage. Individual achievement is fostered by the political freedom allowed. Finally, the religious ethic of American Protestantism emphasizes hard work and savings and achievement as positive virtues, so that a religious person is not driven to devote all of his time to worship, but instead is encouraged to work hard to support his family and his community. In the process, he is encouraged to take advantage of the economic and political freedom offered him. In this way the political ideology of democracy, coupled with the economic system of free enterprise, and supported by the religious ideology of the Protestant Ethic, all combine to form an integrated unit centered around a basic theme. We could also assume that if one of these basic institutions were to change, it would affect the others. If Americans all of a sudden adopted a religious outlook that stressed withdrawal and prayer to the exclusion of work, or if political freedom were withdrawn, the free enterprise system would no longer be effective, and would most likely be replaced by something else. But in the long run a new means of integrating the parts of the social structure would be found.

We can also look at functional analysis on a more microscopic level, in that we can search for direct links with certain aspects of the social structure and the immediate results that they produce. Government economists do this all the time when they talk about the relationship between the rate of inflation and unemployment, or the cost of living and the balance of trade. Criminologists make the same kinds of functional links between different elements of the social structure when they relate a major drug bust in Marseille, France, to a rise in street crime in New York City: As the drug supply diminishes, the demand rises, hence the cost rises, hence the crime rate rises because people who need money to support a drug habit must now find a way to get more money.

The anthropologist Walter Goldschmidt once suggested to me, tongue in cheek, that without a large number of old maids, the British could not have won World War II. When I looked at him with astonishment he proceeded to give me a functional explanation, albeit one that stretched the imagination somewhat. It seems that during the war the British soldiers kept alive by eating tins of corned beef. The cows that supplied this beef fed on clover. The clover depended upon bees for cross-fertilization, and the bees could only flourish if rats and mice were kept in check, for they would raid the honeycombs.

The rodent population was controlled by cats, and as everybody knows, cats are dependent upon old maids who put out a saucer of milk for them. It's kind of like a Rube Goldberg machine, but a functional analysis nevertheless.

It is important to point out that we cannot observe social structure any more than we can observe culture. Both are abstractions. What we observe is the behavior of human beings in a social context. As we do so, it becomes obvious that this behavior is predictable and that it is ordered into some sort of pattern. From this point we conclude that there is a structure which guides social relations, even though it is an abstract structure that we apply as observers, rather than as actors. This structure is just as real as the structure we apply to organisms, or to language; it is a generalization about the relationships of the parts. Just as all organisms are unique, all societies are unique, and we can only compare them by making generalizations about the similarities we perceive in their structures. Without concepts such as structure and function, we could not have a science dealing with human behavior, any more than we could have a science of anatomy or physiology.

Manifest and Latent Functions

Another aspect to the concept of function is a distinction made by sociologist Robert Merton between what he calls manifest and latent functions. Merton points out that an activity may have more than one function, and one or more of its functions may be unconscious or at least not obvious to those who practice it. The *manifest function* of a pattern of behavior is the effect or result that is apparent to the members of the society. It is the reason they will tell you why they are doing something, if you inquire. It is the agreed upon value of the action, the ideal as opposed to the real. The *latent function* of the activity is the effect or result that is not apparent to the members of society who are engaging in it.

Let us look at an example to illustrate this distinction. In American society, when a person dies we frequently follow a pattern of behavior collectively designated as a funeral. This can include a religious service, a meeting of family and friends either before or after the service, and the burial service in which the body is interred in a cemetery. If we were to inquire of Americans who engage in this practice what its functions were, we would probably receive some of the following answers, which we could designate functions of a funeral: (1) The funeral serves to dispose of the body of the deceased, an obvious necessity in any case. (2) The gathering of friends and relatives at the funeral functions to console the family of the deceased, to support them and comfort them in their time of sorrow. (3) The religious service, in which prayers are offered for the deceased, is designed to aid the soul or spirit in its journey to whatever lies beyond in the afterlife. (4) In addition, a part of the funeral service can be designed to commemorate the achievements of the deceased, and thus serve as a memorial to that person, which in turn also comforts

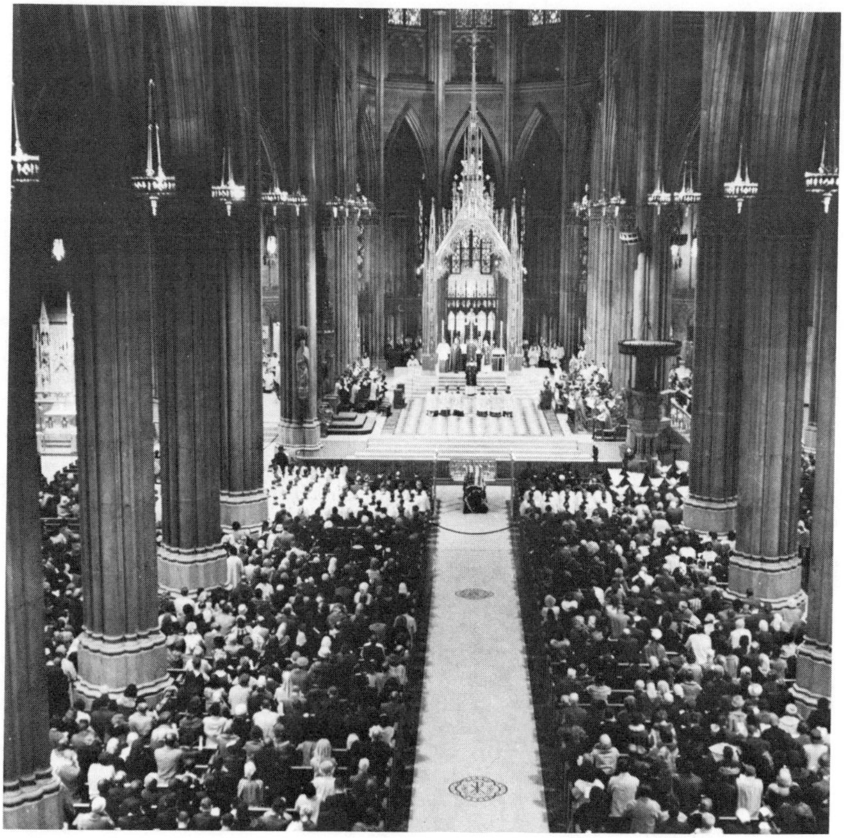

Worshippers at St. Patrick's Cathedral mourn the late President Kennedy. How many functions of a funeral are evident? (Wide World)

the family. All of these are fairly obvious functions of a funeral, functions which Merton would term manifest because they are known to the participants.

But what about some of the less obvious functions of the funeral, which might be apparent to the anthropologist looking at it from the outside but not to the participants? For one thing, the funeral service unwittingly becomes a vehicle for exhibiting wealth. The family may rationalize it in a different way, but their actions are quite clearly part of a pattern commonly called *conspicuous consumption*, which means that the things that we buy (consume) and then openly exhibit (conspicuously) are designed not just for our own enjoyment, but also for the impression they will make upon others who observe us. In the case of a funeral, we can see this pattern of exhibiting wealth in many ways. The size, shape, and material of the casket are important, not because we are concerned about whether the deceased will be comfortable in the grave, and certainly not because we are worried about how long it will last under the ground. Instead, the expense of the casket is important simply because for the few minutes when it will be observed by those who attend the funeral it is a way of indicating wealth and social position. Surely no one would claim that the deceased is more likely to be admitted to heaven in a metal casket than in a pine box!

Other aspects of the funeral also contribute to the pattern of exhibiting wealth and social position for those members of the family left behind. The kind of car used to head the funeral procession is a good example of this. The most common car used is a Cadillac limousine, not because it necessarily rides smoother than a Ford or a Chevy, although it might, but because it is a high-prestige car. In fact, in more expensive funerals there might well be several Cadillac limousines, to carry not only the deceased, but the members of the immediate family as well. Other ways of exhibiting wealth include the type of funeral home used, the way it is decorated, and the number and type of floral arrangements displayed. In addition, there is the cemetery itself, which offers another opportunity for conspicuous consumption. The location of the grave, the neighborhood in which the cemetery is located, even the view from grave site (as if the deceased could enjoy it!). All of these are examples of how the family takes the opportunity of a funeral to exhibit its wealth. Finally, the tombstone will vary depending upon how much the family wishes to spend, and again it is not so much for the deceased as for those

The wide variety of tombstones in this cemetery indicate that they do more than just identify the grave site. (Bill Powers, DPI)

left behind. The size, shape and material of the tombstone can range from a simple metal plate placed in the ground above the grave, to a large marble statue.

Another latent function of a funeral is to provide a break in the routine for those who attend, although most people will certainly exclaim that they would rather have the deceased back among the living than use the funeral as an excuse to have a family reunion. In some societies the funeral actually becomes a party event, as in the case of the Irish wake, where liquor flows freely and people gather together into the night.

In the process of bringing people together, a funeral serves the latent function of reinforcing the solidarity of the group. Members of the typical middle class American family of today are frequently spread throughout the city, state, and even the country, making close contact difficult and family gatherings a relatively rare occurrence. However, the funeral offers the family a chance to get together, bringing close and distant relatives to the same place at the same time; weddings and other similar events also serve the same purpose. At such an occasion the members of the group are able to reaffirm their ties of kinship or friendship, and to pledge their allegiance to the group. In addition, close friends who are not related by blood, but only by a common bond which included the deceased, can once again reestablish contact with each other and maintain their commitment to their friendship through their common interest and concern.

A typically non-Western funeral in New Guinea. (Magnum)

A funeral can also serve the latent function of elevating another person into a higher social position. When someone dies, the position he or she held is vacated, and must be filled by someone else. In the family, if the father or breadwinner dies, then someone else—usually the eldest son or perhaps the brother of the deceased—must step into that role. The funeral ceremony and ritual can thus indicate this elevation of another individual into the vacant position through the tasks assigned in the actual ceremony. A son, for example, might be called upon to take an active role in the funeral, or he might at least be mentioned by the clergyman who performs the ceremony, a subtle instruction in his new duties. The same is true for each of the many different social positions that the deceased held during his or her lifetime, all of which must be filled anew.

Finally, there is the latent function in the funeral ceremony of alleviating the innate human fear of death. Through the religious and social rituals, these fears can be minimized. Those who participate in the ceremony become aware of their concern for the deceased, and in the process they convince themselves that just as they have not forgotten the individual after his death, so too they will not be forgotten by their friends and relatives when they are gone. As they pray for the soul of the deceased, they help to alleviate their fears about the afterlife, for just as they hope to aid the spirit of the deceased and bring him closer to God and to heaven, so they expect that others will do the same for them. In short, while people are openly acting out their concern for the deceased—the manifest function of the funeral—at the same time they are in an unconscious way acting out their concern for themselves, exchanging their time and effort now for the time and effort of others on their behalf in the future.

Of course, it might be difficult to get anyone to admit that they had any of these feelings in mind when they attended a funeral, and this is one reason why anthropologists stress the importance of studying the latent functions of social behavior as well as the manifest functions. It is only through a combination of analyzing what the people think they are doing, as well as what it appears to the objective and impartial observer that they are doing, that we obtain a full and clear picture of how the society works. The functions of various institutions cannot be limited to the conscious interpretations the people themselves attribute to them, for as we have seen in the example of a funeral, there are many more functions that are obvious to us as outside observers and social scientists. To ignore these functions would be to ignore a large portion of the structure of society. If our goal as cultural anthropologists is to understand human behavior, then we must investigate it from all points of view, and not limit ourselves to what the members of a particular group want us to see, or to the functions that they feel are important.

Status

The concept of social structure in general, or specifically the structure of any particular society, really refers to an abstraction of the typical behavior of members of the society. If every individual behaved differently and every situation were completely new and unexpected, there would be no way for us to know what people would do under certain circumstances, or to predict how they would act. Thus in order for us to arrive at this kind of abstraction, social behavior must be consistent. People must act in pretty much the same way in similar situations, even though technically no two sequences of events are exactly the same in all respects. As participants in society, therefore, we must be able to generalize about social interaction—that is, we must be able to say that even though a personal interaction we are now engaging in is unique, it is similar enough to an activity we experienced in the past that we can also expect others to recognize it as such and to act in a predictable manner. In other words, social interaction must be based upon two factors: *expectation* and *reciprocation.*

The fact that we can predict what others will do in a certain situation is essential to the structuring of social behavior. Without this element of expectation society would be disorderly and chaotic. Just imagine what it would be like if you never knew how anyone would act toward you. You feel perfectly comfortable extending your hand to shake hands with someone you meet for the first time, only because you expect them to do the same. If each time you did it you received a different response, ranging from a handshake to a punch in the nose, you would soon grow wary of handshaking. But that doesn't happen, because in our society, as throughout the world, there is a way of defining every situation so that the expected behavior is immediately clear. Behavior becomes structured and orderly because we send out signals which define situations and place them in categories that we and those we interact with can relate to.

The definition of the situation rests in part upon the assignment of *status* to individuals. The term comes from the Latin word for position, and in general it refers to the social position a person holds relative to a particular situation. A status can be either *ascribed* if a person is born into it, or *achieved* if it requires competition or special effort. "Sister," "male," and "King of England" are all ascribed statuses, since you as an individual have nothing to say about occupying such a position. Achieved statuses would include "student," "bricklayer," and "husband." The majority of statuses in all societies are ascribed. Even in our own society, of all the positions we hold, most were determined for us at birth. Besides our age and sex, over which we have no control, we are also restricted by being born into a particular ethnic and social group that largely determines our place in society.

We can arrive at a structure for society by assigning statuses or social positions to all individuals as actors in a social setting. In

Queen Elizabeth being greeted by Sultan Asdul Balin. Status plays an important part in international relations. (Wide World)

the example above, when two individuals meet for the first time and are introduced, they immediately assign the position of "newcomer" to themselves and to the other person. The situation then takes on structure, just as if we could calculate it with a mathematical formula: (newcomer + newcomer) × introduction = handshake. This formula applies to all similar situations governed by the same rules, so that even though we have never seen the particular individual before, we are reasonably certain that he will reciprocate and shake our hand. If he does not, we immediately assign him a new status, something like "different kind of newcomer," and make a mental note of all that we know about him so that we can predict the behavior of others more accurately in the future. For example, in recent years the traditional handshake has been replaced among some members of American society (many blacks, most athletes, and many college students, among others) by a slightly different way of holding the hand, with the fingers extending over the other individual's wrist rather than into the palm of his hand. If you have ever shaken hands with someone like this before, think back to the first time you did it. It probably came as a surprise to you when you extended your hand and someone grasped it differently, so you made a mental note of it. Then you tried to figure out what it was all about, and perhaps after a few more times you were able to predict relatively accurately who would shake hands in this new way, and who would stick to the old way. By now you probably have it pretty well mastered, so that you can operate in the way that others expect of you—you still shake hands in the traditional manner with the older members of your family, but with your classmates or teammates you adopt the new way. The difference between the two groups—although you may not be conscious of it—is that you have assigned a different status to them. You now employ two formulas for similar social situations: (1) (self + newcomer type 1) × introduction = traditional handshake; (2) (self + newcomer type 2) × introduction = new handshake.

We are constantly assigning statuses to those individuals with whom we come in contact in our daily lives. Often we have cues about what status to assign new individuals, and then as we get to know them better we change our evaluation of them, and thus their social position. When we meet a policeman in uniform, for example, we immediately know what that individual's social position is in the situation at hand, because the uniform gives us the cue we need. However, if we meet an off-duty policeman socially and he is not introduced as such, we probably will not be able to place him immediately as a policeman (although some people would disagree), and we would put him in a nebulous category of strangers who are as yet undefined.

A status can be defined as a *collection of rights and duties.* In terms of social interaction, if we are to have structure in our behavior it is essential that we are able to expect certain things of others (rights) and in return they must be able to expect certain things of us (duties). Obviously not every status entails the same collection of rights and duties. In the case of a policeman, the definition of appropriate behavior for all individuals engaged in interaction is quite clear. The policeman, by virtue of the authority invested in him by law, is entitled to strict obedience. In return, as private citizens we are entitled to—and the policeman is obliged to give us—fair and impartial enforcement of the law and protection from violations of the law by others. The fact that this ideal situation is not always achieved, and that there are varying interpretations of what is fair and how far the letter of the law extends, does not negate the fact that the status of policeman (and alternately of private citizen, criminal, etc.) does define a situation in which we can predict behavior with reasonable accuracy. Remember, status is a combination of the ideal situation and the real behavior of people who occupy statuses in social interaction. We are always reevaluating people in the light of their behavior and the behavior of others in similar positions, so that the structure we assign to society changes as the statuses of different groups of people change.

Role

If a status is a position with certain rights and duties, then we can refer to the behavior appropriate to that position as a *role.* A role refers to the *expected behavior in a particular situation.* Thus the position of professor means that it is my role to act as teacher and scholar. The traditional position of father entails the role of breadwinner, disciplinarian, decision maker, and general head of the household (although such roles are rapidly changing, indicating that the concept of social structure is not at all static). In this sense, role and status are inseparable. Just as statuses combine to form the social structure, roles combine to form the behavior patterns that we call institutions.

An indication of the dynamic nature of roles occurs when a large number of people do not follow the ideal pattern of behavior we assign to their status. For example, we all recognize the need for a certain amount of compromise in politics, a certain amount of force in law enforcement, or a certain amount of elitism in the world of entertainment. However, when it appears to us that the majority of people who hold a particular status are exceeding the limits we have in mind, then we either change the behavior of those individuals or else we simply redefine the role of those individuals so that we alter our evaluation of what is appropriate behavior for them. The Knapp Commission's investigations into corruption in New York's police force was an attempt to change the behavior of policemen and restore public confidence in their law enforcement agencies; likewise, the Watergate trials and the forced resignations, first of former Vice-President Agnew, then of former President Nixon, were attempts to change the role assigned by the public to politicians. It is interesting to follow these reevaluations in public opinion polls, where people are asked to rank a number of statuses according to their prestige. Because of the widespread corruption among public officials uncovered in recent years, the status of politicians has fallen lower and lower on this ranking scale, now resting somewhere near the bottom along with used car

When the Watergate hearings showed that politicians were not behaving according to their expected role, the American public assigned them a new lower status. (Wide World)

salesmen, well below many positions requiring far less education and responsibility. What this indicates is that although our ideals concerning the behavior of politicians are still the same, we are recognizing that in reality these ideals are less likely to be met. We therefore expect something different, which affects the prestige of those occupying the position of politician in our society.

The concepts of status and role are meaningful only in relation to other statuses and roles, and therefore they cannot exist in isolation. All individuals occupy a number of different statuses, each with its own appropriate role behavior, and usually these positions operate in harmony so that there are no basic contradictions. An individual might occupy the statuses of bank president, churchgoer, country club member, upper class suburban dweller, husband, father, lodge member, and so on. All of these positions fit together, and we would not be surprised to find an individual who occupied them at the same time. On the other hand, we would be shocked to find a person occupying an unlikely combination of statuses such as bank president, race car driver, ex-convict, ghetto dweller, and suburban country club member. The behavior appropriate to some of these positions would conflict with that appropriate to others, and while it would not be impossible for one person to occupy all of these positions, it certainly would not be very likely.

If this sounds like some obscure, difficult theory concocted to make life confusing, it is not; it is exactly what you yourself do every day, only you do it unconsciously. Every time you interact with other people, you are following the model that you have constructed in your mind for how society is structured, and what your position in that structure is. The reason for pointing this out to you is that while it might not be necessary to know it in order to be a functioning member of American society, it is absolutely essential to understand how any other society works. Just as you learned to speak English long before you studied grammar and learned the formal structure of the language consciously, you have learned the rules of social behavior without being aware of their structure. If, as an anthropologist, you want to learn the rules for another society, it helps to know what their basis is, and how your own society works. Thus anthropology teaches us not only about other people, but most important of all, it teaches us about ourselves.

Change in Status and Role

The concepts of status and role are fairly stable for society as a whole, although they are constantly changing for individuals within the society. The social structure is based upon a certain number of positions filled by various individuals. It is unimportant who fills what positions for the overall structure of the society. Thus although the new army recruit or draftee is likely to spend only a few years in the service, making for a rapid turnover of personnel, nevertheless the army maintains continuity over time. Likewise, although the makeup of Congress changes every two years after each election, with new members replacing old ones, still the present session of Congress is not too different from the last one, nor will the next one be too different from the present.

On the other hand, for the individual member of society the concepts of status and role are dynamic, changing frequently and drastically. A person's statuses and roles change throughout his life. They change with his age, from child to adult to senior citizen; they change with his generation, from child to parent to grandparent; and they change as he learns new skills and achieves new social positions. In addition, one's status and role can change with relation to the social situation, in that an individual can retain the same level of skills and the same income, yet his status will change as all of his contemporaries pass him by, elevating their own positions relative to his.

Just as our statuses change, learning new roles is a continuing process throughout our lifetime. We learn our initial roles through the training we receive as children. We are taught what is appropriate in each situation, not based upon any absolute standard, but relative to our particular ascribed characteristics. Thus we are taught one thing if we are male, another if we are female; we learn different limitations based upon what our "appropriate" social position is perceived to be. Later in life we may reject the appropriateness of that position, and seek a different social position, in which case we will have to learn new patterns of behavior to go with our new status.

A role must be validated if we are to achieve a particular status. Once we have in mind what that status is, we set out to gain the appropriate responses from people, to convince them that we are in fact entitled to the status we seek. If we want to achieve the status of student, we dress accordingly, carry books under our arms, attend classes (sometimes), and go through the whole set of behaviors appropriate to students. On the other hand, if we want to achieve the status of "deviant," we simply act in a way that we think will convince people that we are different and that we do not follow the rules. The degree depends upon just how deviant we want to be considered. Curiously enough, even the path to deviance in our society is predictable. Have you ever noticed how the present generation of college students, who are shaking off the codes of behavior taught them by the previous generation, all look quite similar?

This movement from one status to another is called *social mobility*. We usually speak of mobility from a lower to a higher position, such as from the lower to the middle class, or from a working-class blue-collar job to a middle-class white-collar job. As we move from one status to another we again seek to have our new position validated by society. For example, we usually think of membership in the middle class as being mainly a function of income. Yet in recent years many members of the working class, particularly those who belong to strong

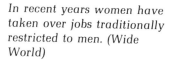

In recent years women have taken over jobs traditionally restricted to men. (Wide World)

unions, have experienced a rise in income that places them in the middle class if we stick to that criterion alone. However, if you were to place two individuals on a scale of social standing—one a school teacher earning $10,000 per year, the other a truck driver earning $15,000 per year—you would probably make a distinction between the two based on factors other than income. You might consider, for example, that the teacher has had five years of college, or that he wears a suit and tie to work, while the teamster probably has not attended college and might not have finished high school, and he does not wear dress clothes when working. In fact, the teamster himself most likely would recognize these differences, and would have aspirations for his children which included the kind of college education that the teacher experienced.

In such a case, social mobility is obviously based upon more than just income. For the teamster to move into the middle class entails many elements of change. Some of these changes can be made simply based upon a rise in income, such as moving into a different neighborhood, buying a more expensive car, or wearing better clothes. Other changes can be made only with great difficulty, and frequently take another generation. Thus the teamster sends his children to better schools, not because education is important to him in making a living, but because in his quest to validate his role as a member of the middle class he finds that education is an important criterion. While he may not be able to return to school himself, he wants at the very least to insure that his children will have their middle-class membership validated. Likewise, the speech patterns that identify one as less educated—the frequent use of double negatives, or words such as "ain't"—cannot always be dropped in a single generation, but at least they can be eliminated in future generations. Again, this is not because the teamster needs to speak "textbook English" in order to communicate effectively in American society, but because he recognizes that his middle-class status will more likely be validated if he speaks in a particular way.

Role Conflict

Sometimes we occupy several different positions in our society, and the behavior appropriate to one is not in harmony with what is appropriate to another. This creates a situation called *role conflict,* when two roles clash with each other in a given situation. This is the kind of theme that makes for great soap operas, where the plot centers on a person torn between two duties, and no matter which one he or she chooses, someone will be hurt or some obligation will be violated. One of the basic problems with role conflict is that others hold conflicting expectations of you and your behavior, and no matter how you act in a given situation, you cannot meet the expectations of all. This problem is described quite well by the anthropologist Lloyd Fallers, who discusses the problems of the chief in Africa after the British colonized the area.[1]

The setting of this study is among the Basoga, a tribal group located in East Africa. Prior to the British colonization of Basoga society, the chief had a clearly defined set of obligations and duties in his interaction with members of his society. The Basoga chiefdom was not a secure position, and constant warfare and threat of revolt checked the ruler's power. Thus if the chief was to remain in office he had to balance the opposing factions in his society, and the lack of a stable leadership attested to the fact that such a balance was difficult to maintain for long periods of time.

When the British took over, they wanted to set up a stable system through which they could operate their colonial administration more efficiently. In order to do this, they made the position of chief more secure, giving him both economic and military support. The chief received a fixed salary from the native administration treasury, and he was granted civil service status complete with a pension. All of these developments strengthened the chief's ties to the British, but at the same time they weakened his ties to his own people. The salary he received lowered his prestige in the eyes of his fellow tribesmen, for it created a dependency upon someone else. The chiefdom became an achieved status based upon education, rather than an ascribed status based upon royal birth, and the entry of non-royal blood into the chiefdom somehow cheapened the office as far as the natives were concerned. Thus the men who held the position of chief were torn between two worlds, as their ties with the British strengthened and they moved farther away from the role of traditional Basoga leader.

Also, the obligations of the two roles of chief came into conflict. As a member of the British civil service system, the chief had to take

1. Lloyd A. Fallers, "The Predicament of the Modern African Chief: An Instance from Uganda." *American Anthropologist* 57:2:290–297, 1955.

on a new set of values, which frequently conflicted with the old values he had held as a Basoga tribesman. As a Basoga, the chief owes loyalty to members of his own family or tribe, and must respond to the requests of his subjects according to how closely they are related, and how obligated he feels to them. However, as a civil servant he must remain impartial and not grant favors to anyone for any reason. The result is that at different times, and depending upon the individual and the situation, both systems of values function. If the chief maintains his impartiality he will alienate his friends and relatives, and go against his own values which he has learned throughout his life. On the other hand, if he gives in to his tribesmen's demands, he will not be faithfully exercising his authority as a civil servant, and stands a good chance of losing his job. One consequence of this role conflict is a high casualty rate among chiefs, and a rapid turnover. Either the chief is caught breaking civil service rules, or else he applies them strictly and is framed by his own family and friends, who resent the violation of traditional obligations.

Social Stratification

In addition to holding a particular status within many different social circles, we all have a more generalized position in our society based upon the sum total of all of our statuses. Every society ranks its members according to their overall position. In larger groups, such as the population of the United States, this ranking is relatively inexact, but in small groups where all people know and interact with each other as individuals, the entire population can be ranked, with each individual occupying a separate rung on the social ladder. This ranking of the members of a group according to status is called *social stratification*. It occurs on the basis of both ascribed and achieved statuses: people are ranked according to ascribed characteristics such as age, sex, and family affiliation, and according to achieved characteristics such as occupation, wealth, or special talents.

Every society makes a social distinction based upon sex, and almost universally women are accorded a lower status than men. Age is also used as a frequent basis for determining relative position on the social ladder, and when combined with sex it forms a concrete set of criteria by which people are ranked. In China, for example,

There is nothing unusual about this picture. But what if the dentist were a woman and the assistant a man? (Paolo Koch, Rapho/Photo Researchers)

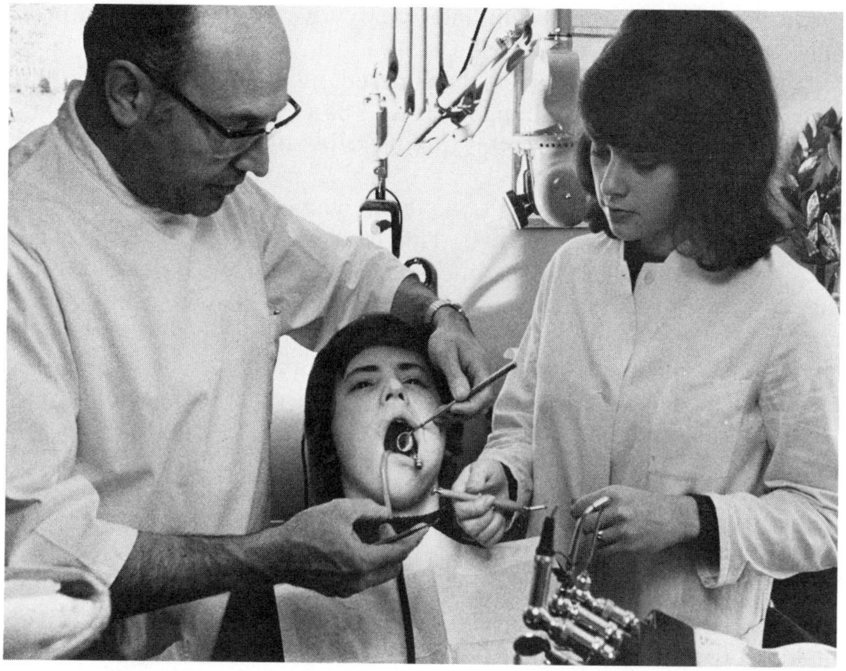

two principles operate in determining on the most general level what a person's rank is: maleness is above femaleness, and age is a positive value. Thus the oldest man in the village is usually the highest ranking member of his lineage, even though he might not be recognized for specific skills or for his wisdom and experience. This is not to suggest that in traditional China only age and sex mattered—obviously people were respected for their accomplishments as well. However, in any social setting, age and sex were always taken into account.

The universal distinction between the sexes is usually backed up by a myth to substantiate the social order as somehow divine, correct, or in accord with the order of the universe. It is also a fact that women work as hard or harder than men in most societies, and there is invariably a division of labor by sex in which the women have little authority or control. Each culture has developed its own ideas about the nature of women, independently of one another, and often these ideas are quite different. For example, we traditionally have seen women as ministering angels, the "Florence Nightingale" image. This is certainly nothing like the traditional idea of woman's nature held by the Iroquois Indians, who, when they captured a prisoner in a battle with another tribe, would turn him over for the women to torture, since women were considered much more sadistic than men. Only the exceptional opponent who had exhibited extraordinary bravery would be granted mercy and be killed by the men as a reward for his courage.

Because of the image we have of women, we ascribe certain occupations to them as "fitting." This is an important element in the social stratification that exists in our culture, and one against which the women's liberation movement has reacted so strongly. But notice that in reacting against the stratification itself, women have had to change the idealized image that men had about them, which has included, at least among some of the more militant advocates of woman's liberation, an actual change in women's behavior. Thus we traditionally viewed women as suited for various kinds of jobs that required "feminine skills," including things which did not require physical strength, ability to make decisions, or other intrusions upon accepted male roles. Ask any old-line executive how important his (female) secretary is to him, and he will tell you that he could not get along without her. But ask him why there are no woman executives in his corporation and he will tell you that women simply are not suited for such jobs. Women should be librarians, secretaries, and waitresses, but not construction workers, bank presidents, or professors, according to the traditional American cultural values. Fortunately these views are changing, and with the change comes a realization of the fact that we, like everyone else in the world, are culture-bound and must work hard to shake off some of the preconceived notions we have about social stratification which have no basis in fact.

In other cultures, occupations are similarly ascribed to different sexes based upon the commonly accepted view of what is considered appropriate. Among the Arapesh of New Guinea, for example, women are expected to carry heavier loads than men because their heads, upon which they balance their baskets, are so much harder and stronger. In Tasmania, seal hunting is woman's work. They swim out to the seal rocks, stalk the animals and kill them. They also hunt possums, which requires them to climb large trees. Men would not think of performing these tasks, because it is agreed that they are "woman's work." In Madagascar, when the peasants cultivate rice, men make the seed beds and terraces for planting, and women do the back-breaking work of transplanting the rice. Such division of tasks is typical of most societies, and equally typical is the fact that there is no apparent logic to the way in which jobs are assigned which can explain the practice cross-culturally.

Also, the division of labor by sex can change over time, as the demands upon one or both sexes change. In my study of a Swiss peasant village, I found that in traditional times men and women shared the agricultural tasks according to a fairly clear division of labor. There were certain jobs considered appropriate only for men because they required more physical strength, while other tasks were reserved mainly for women. Agricultural duties were shared but were clearly divided. After World War II, however, men began to take jobs in factories which kept them from participating in the agricultural operation. At the same time, they wanted to keep their farms going so that they would have something to fall back on in case their new industrial jobs did not prove stable. As the men spent more of their time at work, the women began to take over the agricultural labor, including what were formerly defined as strictly male jobs, such as harvesting and carrying the hay to the barns. The men did help out after work

A typical board of directors meeting–no women! (Maxwell Coplan, DPI)

and on weekends, but inevitably women had to bear the brunt of the agricultural labor if the farm operation were to be maintained. As it stands now, the cultural views about what is appropriate for each of the sexes have changed to meet the new economic situation—factory jobs are for men, and household tasks (including agriculture) are for women. Even this pattern is changing, however, as young girls are finding jobs in light industry on assembly lines, working side by side with men.

Stratification by sex is typical of almost all societies. There may be an exception, but I cannot think of one. Scenes such as women wearing veils in public indicate values associated with male superiority that are held almost universally. In a typical peasant society, for example, one rarely sees a woman in a bar or coffee house; these

Left: A man making a pair of shoes. (Eugene Gordon, Taurus) Right: A woman carrying wheat. (Fujihira, Monkmeyer) All cultures assign tasks based on a division of labor by sex.

places are reserved for male gatherings. Women congregate in places associated with female tasks, or in the home, itself the domain of the woman much of the time. The point is that most, if not all, societies attach all sex-derived status distinctions to the fundamental biological difference between men and women. We should recognize, however, that just because this biological difference is invoked to justify sex discrimination does not mean that it is a valid basis. In fact, stratification by sex is a cultural practice based upon culturally determined values, not biological factors.

Stratification on the basis of age is another question. There is no denying the validity of at least some of the biological and cultural arguments about inequality in different age groups. There is no substitute for experience as far as certain skills or capabilities are concerned.

This does not mean that there is a biological justification for extending all of the privileges of high status to the older members of the population. We would not want *all* 80-year-old Americans to be allowed to drive simply because of the supposed maturity and good judgment they possess, any more than we would want 12-year-olds to drive because their reflexes are quick. We compromise by requiring a minimal attainment of both maturity and quick reflexes, in that we consider both an age limit and the successful completion of a performance test as necessary prerequisites to obtaining a driver's license. Again, not all societies would treat stratification on the basis of age in the same way that we do, indicating that stratification based upon any criterion is primarily a cultural question, not a biological one.

Caste

One of the most extreme forms of social stratification is the organization of society into sharply differentiated groups known as *castes*. A caste can be defined as a group of people jointly assigned a position in the social hierarchy. Furthermore, a person is born into a caste and cannot change his affiliation throughout his life. Caste membership is based upon ascribed characteristics acquired at birth, such as the caste membership of one's parents, which is passed down from one generation to the next. It can also be based upon physical features such as skin color, again an ascribed characteristic that is inherited. The boundaries of a caste are maintained socially through the practice of *endogamy* (marriage within a group—derived from the Greek *endo* = within, and *gamy* = marriage), by which a person may only marry someone from his or her own caste. Thus, if there are genetic factors that identify an individual's caste membership, such as skin color, these tend to be maintained through the proscription against marrying outside the group.

The most commonly recognized caste system is found in traditional India. Vestiges of the system still remain there, especially in rural areas, although it has been formally outlawed since India became independent from Great Britain. In this system, caste affiliation carries with it a total social ranking. Every aspect of an individual's life is limited by his caste. Because of the ascribed nature of caste membership, each local caste group is made up of related individuals, usually a series of families within the same village. In India, caste is linked with occupation, at least ideally. A person has a particular occupation based upon the caste into which he was born. A carpenter's son becomes a carpenter, just as a farmer's son becomes a farmer. Of course, in a small village there will not be a representative of every caste to fill every conceivable occupation, and so where a position is not filled by a member of the appropriate caste someone else will take it up. This will not enable him to change his caste, however, and if he is a member of the carpenter caste he will remain so, even though his duties might now include weaving rather than carpentry.

In India the caste system operates according to the customs established by the Hindu religion. Each caste is ranked in a hierarchy according to the principles of Hindu tradition which place positive values on certain kinds of behavior, especially the avoidance of what are considered to be ritually polluting acts. For example, according

Tasks in an Indian village are divided not only on the basis of age and sex, but also according to caste. (Harriet Arnold, DPI)

to Hindu teachings, it is polluting to eat meat, to come into contact with dead animals, and to engage in occupations that deal with death either literally or symbolically (such as a barber or a leather worker). Members of the various castes are expected to follow them to a lesser degree accordingly as they fall lower on the social hierarchy. The lowest rank, commonly called the outcastes or untouchables, are those people who eat meat and engage in polluting occupations such as sweepers or butchers. They are untouchable because they are considered to be so polluted that mere contact with them would defile a member of a higher caste.

Thus, in traditional India a village consists of a number of castes, each with many members. Each caste fulfills a certain function; occupations are linked to castes and limited to their members. With each caste performing a special function all are able to survive, but they become dependent upon one another. The ranking system that places castes in a social hierarchy insures that this system will operate in a stable manner by forcing some individuals into occupations they might not otherwise choose for themselves. And the entire system is supported by the Hindu teachings, which emphasize the fact that different behavior is appropriate for each social level, and that to avoid doing what is prescribed for one's particular station in life is wrong.

Caste in India and the United States

The term *caste* is not limited to India, and can be applied to any similarly stratified group within a social hierarchy, in which membership is hereditary and permanent. For example, consider the racial situation in the southern United States. The relationship between the higher castes and the untouchables in India is similar to that between blacks and whites in the South, since they form separate social groups that are arranged in a hierarchy, maintained through endogamy or in-marriage, and membership in either group is both hereditary and permanent. Furthermore, in India caste also includes an occupational specialization to some degree, or at least the prohibition from engaging in certain occupations. The same situation applies in the South, where certain occupations are restricted to blacks and others are considered suitable only for whites.

In both India and the American South, there are rigid rules of avoidance between castes, and certain types of contact are considered contaminating. These taboos against inter-caste contact are symbolically rather than literally injurious, as evidenced by the inconsistency with which they are applied. For example, sexual contact is supposedly injurious, but in the traditional South the double standard applied, just as it did in India. Upper-caste men were permitted to have contact with lower-caste women (either high caste Indians or white slave masters), while contact of the opposite sort (low-caste men with high-caste women, or black men with white women) was prohibited. In both cases, the high and low castes are economically interdependent,

Until recently, laws preventing interracial contact in public places in the American South reflected a situation similar to the caste system in traditional India. (Wide World)

and the restrictions governing contact between them do not cut into the upper caste's need for lower caste products and services. In other words, the distinction between the two social levels in the South, and between the higher castes and lower castes in India, was made strong enough to maintain clear social boundaries, but not so strong as to impose total isolation and thus negate the economic and social advantages to be gained by the higher castes from the exploitation of the lower. The high caste stood to gain not only in economic terms, through the exploitation of low-caste labor, but in social terms, such as the acquisition of prestige and a higher position in the social hierarchy.

In pointing out the parallels between India and some aspects of our own society, we can see one of the most positive values of cross-cultural studies in anthropology. Most Americans who have had little experience in the study of a foreign culture are limited in the perspectives they can have on their own way of life. For middle-class Americans who have grown up in suburban areas of the United States, the tendency is to look at all aspects of American culture as a variation upon the theme of middle class culture with which they are familiar. It is by bringing in outside models such as the caste system of India—models which present us with a more clear-cut illustration of a social situation than we can find in our own society—that anthropology can contribute this added perspective. The study of other cultures enables us to look for similarities in our own society, rather than viewing everything as purely "American." Indeed, the parallels between caste in India and the racial situation in the South are striking, whether we accept them or not.

Class

Another form of social stratification is the division of society into groups that we call *classes*. A person is a member of a class based upon a number of factors such as wealth, education, and occupation. Unlike a caste system, a class system of stratification is a ranking of different kinds of people based upon their achieved as well as their ascribed characteristics. Class membership is a subjective evaluation. Almost everyone in the lower classes tends to place himself slightly higher, while those in the higher classes tend to look down upon those below them and rank them lower than they would rank themselves.

Outsiders' evaluations are equally subjective, based as they are upon specified criteria which seem important to the outsider but that might not be important to the people themselves. There is no absolute way of defining a person's class, because it is a combination of factors, any one of which can take on greater or lesser importance in light of the others. For example, the "upper crust" in American society might be considerably less wealthy than some of the *nouveau riche*, those business tycoons who have made a fortune in recent years, but who still lack the grace and sophistication of the older, more established wealthy families.

Classes tend to be endogamous, but the restrictions against marrying outside one's class are by no means rigid. We tend to seek out partners from the same class, not because there are overt rules that guide us in that direction, but because the factors of income, education, and general similarity in life style create similar tastes and preferences among members of the same class. In fact, in our own society there are many pressures, some of them not very subtle, that dictate whom we may choose as potential mates, and these pressures are mainly based upon a combination of class and caste characteristics—race and general social position. Of course, the system is not entirely rigid, as evidenced by the occasional rise of a young man or woman out of the lower class and into the limelight, whereby he or she eventually is able to move into a higher class and seek out its members as friends

The only hunting permitted in Ohio on Sundays is fox hunting, typically an upper-class activity. This offers a good illustration of how the law reinforces the inequities of the class system. (Leonard Lee Rue III, Monkmeyer)

and associates, even as potential mates. But the fact that these kinds of stories are considered newsworthy illustrates that they are exceptional, and that they happen in spite of the obstacles they must overcome. We are far less surprised—indeed we are not surprised at all—when we read of Richard Nixon's daughter marrying Dwight Eisenhower's grandson, because it conforms to our expectations of class endogamy.

Comparison of Caste and Class

Although a caste system is a more rigid system of social stratification, it is no more completely closed than a class system is completely open. Although ideally in a caste system there is no mobility, the rules governing the interaction of members of different castes are frequently bent. At the same time, ideally in a class system mobility is freely possible from a lower to a higher class, but in reality class mobility frequently does not exist, and there are often unwritten rules that keep people from advancing out of a lower class ranking and into a higher one. The businessman who rose from the ghetto to become a millionaire can send his children to exclusive schools, drive a fancy car and live in an expensive house, but that will not get him an invitation to join the upper-class elite, who reject him because of his social background.

In contrast to a caste, a class is not joined together in an organized manner. People are not fully conscious of their class affiliation, and are therefore not held together by a mutual feeling of membership in a group. In a caste system, the members of a particular caste are united in a corporate group, with distinct boundaries and close personal ties. Considering the relationship between caste affiliation and occupation as it exists in India, it is difficult for a person *not* to be aware of his caste as he performs his daily tasks and adheres to the ritual behavior demanded of him in his station in life. Likewise, a black in America must constantly live with the fact that he is a different color, just as a sweeper in an Indian village is continually reminded of his untouchable status.

Another contrast between caste and class is the fact that a caste is based upon kinship, whereas a class is a collection of people who are similar in many ways, but are not assumed to be related biologically. Strict caste endogamy maintains the kinship basis for caste membership, while looser marriage restrictions in a class system and the possibility of mobility prevent classes from developing a kinship base. If in fact classes seem to be basically endogamous, it is for different reasons than those used to enforce and justify caste endogamy.

Finally, caste is often viewed as if it were acceptable to all in the system, in the sense that they accept the justification of the system through religious or other doctrines. However, both in India and the United States this is not the case, especially among the lower castes who must bear the brunt of the "dirty work" while receiving only a small share of the social and economic rewards. Neither lower-caste people nor lower-class people accept the justification for their being where they are. In a society such as our own, the social philosophy explains a person's being in the lower social levels through personal inadequacy. The argument goes that if there is unlimited mobility and anyone who has the ability and ambition can get ahead (the Great American Myth), the only explanation for those who are at the bottom is that they either don't have the talent or else they lack the ambition. As we have seen, however, the Great American Myth must be exposed as false. Unlimited mobility does not exist, and our open class system is superimposed upon a closed caste system that keeps people at the bottom of the social hierarchy by virtue of their ascribed characteristics despite their personal abilities. To suggest that all people accept the social or religious philosophy used to justify this situation, either in American society or in Indian society, is a naive attempt on the part of those in the higher social levels to avoid feeling guilty for their disproportionate share of society's economic wealth and social rewards.

Gloria Steinem is the founder and editor of *Ms.* magazine, and has been a leader in the women's liberation movement since its inception. In the following article, which first appeared in *Time* magazine, Ms. Steinem describes "What It Would Be Like If Women Win." She talks about a utopian society, where discrimination based on sex has disappeared, and where equality in general becomes a reality.

The utopian world as Steinem perceives it presents a fascinating situation. Picture it. Women senators, and eventually women presidents; a less aggressive and violent society; equal privileges and responsibilities (including the draft, but apparently not alimony); revised roles in sex, marriage, child rearing, and business; fewer stress diseases among men; more sensible fashions and manners; and who knows what. What would our society produce when sex roles were suddenly equalized? Would women like it after all? Would such a society work?

Steinem points out that when anthropologist Geoffrey Gorer studied the few peaceful human tribes he discovered that "sex roles were not polarized. Differences of dress and occupation were at a minimum."

Toward the end of her article Steinem states that "the most radical goal of the movement is egalitarianism." Egalitarianism has become a fashionable word; it simply means a society where people are not judged on the basis of color, age, sex, etc. Decide for yourself what its consequences would be.

What it Would Be Like If Women Win

Gloria Steinem

Any change is fearful, especially one affecting both politics and sex roles, so let me begin these utopian speculations with a fact. To break the ice.

Women don't want to exchange places with men. Male chauvinists, science-fiction writers and comedians may favor that idea for its shock value, but psychologists say it is a fantasy based on ruling-class ego and guilt. Men assume that women want to imitate them, which is just what white people assumed about blacks. An assumption so strong that it may convince the second-class group of the need to imitate, but for both women and blacks that stage has passed. Guilt produces the question: What if they could treat us as we have treated them?

That is not our goal. But we do want to change the economic system to one more based on merit. In Women's Lib Utopia, there will be free access to good jobs—and decent pay for the bad ones women have been performing all along, including housework. Increased skilled labor might lead to a four-hour workday, and higher wages would encourage further mechanization of repetitive jobs now kept alive by cheap labor.

With women as half the country's elected representatives, and a woman President once in a while, the country's *machismo* problems would be greatly reduced. The old-fashioned idea that manhood depends on violence and victory is, after all, an important part of our troubles in the streets, and in Viet Nam. I'm not saying that women leaders would eliminate violence. We are not more moral than men; we are only uncorrupted by power so far. When we do acquire power, we might turn out to have an equal impulse toward aggression. Even now, Margaret Mead believes that women fight less often but more fiercely than men, because women are not taught the rules of the war game and fight only when cornered. But for the next 50 years or so, women in politics will be very valuable by tempering the idea of manhood into something less aggressive and better suited to this crowded, post-atomic planet. Consumer protection and children's rights, for instance, might get more legislative attention.

Men will have to give up ruling-class privileges, but in return they will no longer be the only ones to support the family, get drafted, bear the strain of power and responsibility. Freud to the contrary, anatomy is not destiny, at least not for more than nine months at a time. In Israel, women are drafted, and some have gone to war. In England, more men type and run switchboards. In India and Israel, a woman rules. In Sweden, both parents take care of the children. In this country, come Utopia, men and women won't reverse roles: they will be free to choose according to individual talents and preferences.

Reprinted from *Time*, August 31, 1970, with permission from the author.

If role reform sounds sexually unsettling, think how it will change the sexual hypocrisy we have now. No more sex arranged on the barter system, with women pretending interest, and men never sure whether they are loved for themselves or for the security few women can get any other way. (Married or not, for sexual reasons or social ones, most women still find it second nature to Uncle-Tom.) No more men who are encouraged to spend a lifetime living with inferiors: with housekeepers, or dependent creatures who are still children. No more domineering wives, emasculating women, and "Jewish mothers," all of whom are simply human beings with all their normal ambition and drive confined to the home. No more unequal partnerships that eventually doom love and sex.

In order to produce that kind of confidence and individuality, child rearing will train according to talent. Little girls will no longer be surrounded by air-tight, self-fulfilling prophecies of natural passivity, lack of ambition and objectivity, inability to exercise power, and dexterity (so long as special aptitude for jobs requiring patience and dexterity is confined to poorly paid jobs: brain surgery is for males).

Schools and universities will help to break down traditional sex roles, even when parents will not. Half the teachers will be men, a rarity now at preschool and elementary levels: girls will not necessarily serve cookies or boys hoist up the flag. Athletic teams will be picked only by strength and skill. Sexually segregated courses like auto mechanics and home economics will be taken by boys and girls together. New courses in sexual politics will explore female subjugation as the model for political oppression, and women's history will be an academic staple, along with black history, at least until the white-male-oriented textbooks are integrated and rewritten.

As for the American child's classic problem—too much mother, too little father—that would be cured by an equalization of parental responsibility. Free nurseries, school lunches, family cafeterias built into every housing complex, service companies that will do household cleaning chores in a regular, businesslike way, and more responsibility by the entire community for the children: all these will make it possible for both mother and father to work, and to have equal leisure time with the children at home. For parents of very young children, however, a special job category, created by Government and unions, would allow such parents a shorter work day.

The revolution would not take away the option of being a housewife. A woman who prefers to be her husband's housekeeper and/or hostess would receive a percentage of his pay determined by the domestic relations courts. If divorced, she might be eligible for a pension fund, and for a job-training allowance. Or a divorce could be treated the same way that the dissolution of a business partnership is now.

If these proposals seem farfetched, consider Sweden, where most of them are already in effect. Sweden is not yet a working Women's Lib model; most of the role-reform programs began less than a decade ago, and are just beginning to take hold. But that country is so far ahead of us in recognizing the problem that Swedish statements on sex and equality sound like bulletins from the moon.

Our marriage laws, for instance, are so reactionary that Women's Lib groups want couples to take a compulsory written exam on the law, as for a driver's license, before going through with the wedding. A man has alimony and wifely debts to worry about, but a woman may lose so many of her civil rights that in the U.S. now, in important legal ways, she becomes a child again. In some states, she cannot sign credit agreements, use her maiden name, incorporate a business, or establish a legal residence of her own. Being a wife, according to most social and legal definitions, is still a 19th century thing.

Assuming, however, that these blatantly sexist laws are abolished or reformed, that job discrimination is forbidden, that parents share financial responsibility for each other and the children, and that sexual relationships become partnerships of equal adults (some pretty big assumptions), then marriage will probably go right on. Men and women are, after all, physically complementary. When society stops encouraging men to be exploiters and women to be parasites, they may turn out to be more complementary in emotion as well. Women's Lib is not trying to destroy the American family. A look at the statistics on divorce—plus the way in which old people are farmed out with strangers and young people flee the home—shows the destruction that has already been done. Liberated women are just trying to point out the disaster, and build compassionate and practical alternatives from the ruins.

What will exist is a variety of alternative life-styles. Since the population explosion dictates that childbearing be kept to a minimum, parents-and-children will be only one of many "families": couples, age groups, working groups, mixed communes, blood-related clans, class groups, creative groups. Single women will have the right to stay single without ridicule, without the attitudes now betrayed by "spinster" and "bachelor." Lesbians or homosexuals will no longer be denied legally binding marriages, complete with mutual-support agreements and inheritance rights. Paradoxically, the number of homosexuals may get smaller. With fewer overpossessive mothers and fewer fathers who hold up an impossibly cruel or perfectionist idea of manhood, boys will be less likely to be denied or reject their identity as males.

Changes that now seem small may get bigger:

Men's Lib. Men now suffer from more diseases due to stress, heart attacks, ulcers, a higher suicide rate, greater difficulty living alone, less adaptability to change and, in general, a shorter life span than women. There is some scientific evidence that what produces physical problems is not work itself, but the inability to choose which work, and how much. With women bearing half the financial responsibility, and with the idea of "masculine" jobs gone, men might well feel freer and live longer.

Religion. Protestant women are already becoming ordained ministers: radical nuns are carrying out liturgical functions that were once the exclusive property of priests: Jewish women are rewriting prayers—particularly those that Orthodox Jews recite every morning thanking God they are not female. In the future, the church will become an area of equal participation by women. This means, of course, that organized religion will have to give up one of its great historical weapons: sexual repression. In most structured faiths, from Hinduism through Roman Catholicism, the status of women went down as the position of priests ascended. Male clergy implied, if they did not teach, that women were unclean, unworthy and sources of ungodly temptation, in order to remove them as rivals for the emotional forces of men. Full participation of women in ecclesiastical life might involve certain changes in theology, such as, for instance, a radical redefinition of sin.

Literary Problems. Revised sex roles will outdate more children's books than civil rights ever did. Only a few children had the problem of a *Little Black Sambo,* but most have the male-female stereotypes of "Dick and Jane." A boomlet of children's books about mothers who work has already begun, and liberated parents and editors are beginning to pressure for change in the textbook industry. Fiction writing will change more gradually, but romantic novels with wilting heroines and swashbuckling heroes will be reduced to historical value. Or perhaps to the sado-masochist trade. (*Marjorie Morningstar,* a romantic novel that took the '50s by storm, has already begun to seem as unreal as its '20s predecessor, *The Sheik.*) As for the literary plots that turn on forced marriages or horrific abortions, they will seem as dated as Prohibition stories. Free legal abortions and free birth control will force writers to give up pregnancy as the *deus ex machina*.

Manners and Fashion. Dress will be more androgynous, with class symbols becoming more important than sexual ones. Pro- or anti-Establishment styles may already be more vital than who is wearing them. Hardhats are just as likely to rough up antiwar girls as antiwar men in the street, and police understand that women are just as likely to be pushers or bombers. Dances haven't required that one partner lead the other for years, anyway. Chivalry will transfer itself to those who need it, or deserve respect: old people, admired people, anyone with an armload of packages. Women with normal work identities will be less likely to attach their whole sense of self to youth and appearance; thus there will be fewer nervous breakdowns when the first wrinkles appear. Lighting cigarettes and other treasured niceties will become gestures of mutual affection. "I like to be helped on with my coat," says one Women's Lib worker, "but not if it costs me $2,000 a year in salary."

For those with nostalgia for a simpler past, here is a word of comfort. Anthropologist Geoffrey Gorer studied the few peaceful human tribes and discovered one common characteristic: sex roles were not polarized. Differences of dress and occupation were at a minimum. Society, in other words, was not using sexual blackmail as a way of getting women to do cheap labor, or men to be aggressive.

Thus Women's Lib may achieve a more peaceful society on the way toward its other goals. That is why the Swedish government considers reform to bring about greater equality in the sex roles one of its most important concerns. As Prime Minister Olof Palme explained in a widely ignored speech delivered in Washington this spring: "It is *human beings* we shall emancipate. In Sweden today, if a politician should declare that the woman ought to have a different role from man's, he would be regarded as something from the Stone Age." In other words, the most radical goal of the movement is egalitarianism.

If Women's Lib wins, perhaps we all do.

Summary

A *society* is an organized group of people who interact with one another and share a common way of life or a culture. We think of the interaction between members of a society as being structured, and we can organize it into categories, or what we call *institutions*. For example, we may speak of economic institutions such as a marketplace, or legal institutions such as a courtroom, or political institutions such as a political party.

People in a society are held together by virtue of the shared values and the way of life common to them. Emile Durkheim, the French sociologist, summarized two types of solidarity found in different societies. One he called *mechanical solidarity,* because everyone was pretty much like everyone else, there was little specialization and people shared the same values, thus behaving almost "mechanically." The other he called *organic solidarity,* because, like an organism, it was made up of different parts that performed different functions. Just as the human body is made up of different organs, such as the heart, lungs, liver and brain, so is an organic society made up of many different specialized groups, each of which makes a different contribution to the overall society.

The kinds of solidarity found in these two types of society are different. In mechanical societies, solidarity is based upon the similarity of the members, and the fact that people tend to agree upon things. In organic societies, it is derived from the dependence that people feel toward one another because of their differences. If you specialize in only one activity, it means you must rely all the more upon other people who have different specialties, and this is what holds the society together.

Because behavior follows predictable patterns, we may speak of a *social structure,* or the relationship between these different patterns. For example, we may consider the relationship between religion and law in American society, noting the basis for our laws in our religious teachings. We may then speak of the *function* that an institution has in relation to this structure, such as the function of religion in providing the basis for our legal system.

Not all functions of our behavior are evident to us. Those aspects that are obvious to us are called *manifest* functions, while those that are not so obvious are called *latent* functions. For example, in a typical

American funeral, manifest functions would include getting rid of the body, consoling the family, offering prayers for the deceased, and commemorating the achievements of the deceased. All of these are carried out consciously by the participants. But many other functions are also carried out, even though the people themselves might not be aware of them. These latent functions might include exhibiting wealth and social standing, providing a break in the routine, reinforcing the solidarity of the group, elevating a person to a higher social status, and coping with the fear of death.

We can get along with other people because we know what to expect from them in certain social situations, and likewise they can rely upon us to act in a predictable manner. In other words, social interaction is based upon *expectation* and *reciprocation.* Part of the way we decide how to behave is determined by the *status* we assign people in a given situation. A status can be *ascribed,* based on characteristics that a person is born with or has no control over, such as age or sex or race, or it can be *achieved,* based upon personal actions or abilities. For each status there is an appropriate pattern of behavior, which we call a *role.*

In the course of a lifetime an individual's social position may change, through the process known as *social mobility.* Movement from a lower to a higher social position may be associated with such changes as an increase in income or education, advance in age, development of new skills, or any other aspect of a person's life that causes others to reassess their evaluation of that person.

Every individual occupies a number of different statuses, each with its own appropriate form of behavior. Occasionally a situation arises where the different expectations are incompatible, a situation known as *role conflict.*

Every society ranks its members according to their overall position, or what we call *social stratification.* This can occur on the basis of both ascribed and achieved characteristics, including such factors as age, sex, occupation, wealth, or special abilities or talents. All societies recognize a social distinction based upon sex, the women usually being accorded a lower status. Age is also a universal factor in social stratification, although not always in the same way. The justification for using age and sex as the basis for stratification is usually culturally derived, and although people might claim a biological reason for assigning different positions to women or to old or young people, cross-cultural research indicates that such justifications are generally incorrect.

Some societies have a system of stratification known as *caste.* A caste is a group of people jointly assigned a position in the social hierarchy, and it is usually a permanent grouping which an individual cannot change. Caste membership is based upon ascribed characteristics: You inherit membership in a caste based upon the caste affiliation of one or both parents. Caste boundaries are maintained through restricted marriage patterns, or *endogamy.* The most common form of the caste system is found in India, and although it has been officially outlawed, some aspects of it still persist in many areas of that country.

In contrast to the caste system is a type of stratification known as *class.* A class is a more open grouping, less clearly defined than a caste. It is often based upon such factors as wealth, education and occupation. People can move in and out of a class, unlike a caste. Although marriage tends to occur within the limits of a class, there is no absolute rule that it must. Although a person's class affiliation is initially based upon that of his or her parents, it ultimately becomes more of an achieved position. Aspects of both caste and class can be found in American society.

Glossary

achieved status A social position that a person holds by virtue of individual effort or competition (e.g., school teacher, wife, football player).

ascribed status A social position that a person holds by virtue of inherited characteristics, rather than through individual effort or competition (e.g., The King of England is an ascribed status, while the President of the United States is not).

caste A group of people jointly assigned a position in the social hierarchy based upon inherited characteristics; in its extreme form, caste does not allow an individual to change this position.

class A group of people assigned a position in society based upon a combination of inherited characteristics and those traits earned through individual effort and competition. Individuals usually marry within this group and are generally able to move to a different ranking group.

conspicuous consumption The buying of goods and services as a means of demonstrating one's wealth and social position. This open exhibition of wealth is a form of impression management.

division of labor The degree of differentiation of tasks in society and their performance by different groups of specialists, rather than everyone doing the same work.

egalitarianism The doctrine advocating social equality for all members of a society, regardless of social and biological position at birth.

endogamy The practice that confines marriage to another member of an individual's group, or a proscription against marrying outside the group.

expectation and reciprocation Two factors of social behavior referring to the predictability and consistency of social interaction, and making the structuring of social behavior possible.

institution A pattern of behavior that focuses upon a central theme (e.g., economy: market place; politics: a political party in the United States; religion: a church).

latent function The effect or result of a pattern of behavior that is not apparent to the members of society who are engaging in it (e.g., funeral: to exhibit wealth, to support the solidarity of the group).

manifest function The effect or result of a pattern of behavior that is apparent to the members of a society (e.g., funeral: to remove the dead individual, to comfort the mourning family).

mechanical solidarity Durkheim's description of the binding force which holds a group together on the basis of the members' shared, uniform experience, and their consensus on values, attitudes and beliefs. This concept applies primarily to small-scale societies.

negative solidarity A force that holds people together because they are unable to leave the group due to geographical or language barriers, or cultural limitations upon mobility.

nouveau riche A group of people who have recently acquired great wealth, but have not yet developed the social characteristics to allow them entrance into the "upper crust" of society.

organic solidarity Durkheim's description of the binding force that holds a group together on the basis of their dependence upon each other. There is a maximum division of labor (tasks in society are specialized, and people are skilled at certain jobs), and the group's members rely upon each other for the goods and services that a single individual cannot provide for himself.

outcastes (also known as untouchables) The lowest-ranking group in the caste system of India.

role The appropriate and expected behavior attached to a social position in a particular situation.

role conflict The condition of an individual occupying several different positions in society, in which the appropriate behaviors do not coincide in a given situation.

social mobility The process of moving from one position to another in society, and adopting the appropriate behaviors attached to the new social position.

social solidarity The way a group is bound together through a shared system of values and the manner in which the group's members depend upon one another for each other's goods and services.

social stratification The ranking of the members of a group according to the sum total of an individual's inherited characteristics and those traits earned through individual effort and competition.

social structure The way groups are organized in a society, and the way the relationships between these groups are defined.

society An organized group of individuals engaging in social interaction and forming a unit bound together by their shared way of life or culture.

status The social position a person holds relative to a particular situation, and which is associated with a particular collection of rights and duties.

taboo (also tabu) A ritual prohibition against a specific behavior or contact with an object or person, usually punishable by supernatural sanctions.

Questions for Discussion

1 Pick a common activity in American culture, such as a football game, a business convention, or a wedding. What are the manifest functions of this activity? What might an anthropologist, as an outside observer, see as the latent functions of this activity?

2 What personal attributes combine to determine your own status? Which of these attributes are ascribed, and which are achieved? Which are more important in determining your overall status?

3 Give an example of role conflict from your own experiences. What were the expected patterns of behavior in the particular situation, and how did they conflict with each other? How did you resolve the conflict?

4 What are the most common means of achieving social mobility in Ameri-

can society? Are these avenues for mobility equally available to all members of our society? What restrictions do you see, and whom do they affect most?

5 Social stratification operates on many different levels. What is the system of social stratification in your college or university? Is it a closed or an open system; that is, how easy is it to move up or down within the system? How does this affect the attitudes of people at various levels toward the overall system?

6 What is the class affiliation of your family (i.e., lower, middle or upper)? What factors such as occupation, income, education, determine your class? How would you go about changing your class affiliation, and what barriers would you have to overcome?

Suggestions for Additional Reading

Berreman, Gerald D.

1968 Caste: The Concept of Caste. International Encyclopedia of the Social Sciences, volume 2, pp. 333–338.

A discussion of the various concepts of caste in the social sciences.

Dollard, John

1957 Caste and Class in a Southern Town. Third Edition. Garden City, N.Y.: Doubleday & Company.

An analysis of social stratification in the American South, applying the concepts of caste and class. The approach to caste is particularly valuable when read in conjunction with a study of caste in India, such as Mandelbaum's work cited below.

Durkheim, Emile

1964 The Division of Labor in Society. New York: The Free Press.

First published in 1893, this classic study of social solidarity outlines interrelationships between the division of labor, the moral codes and the legal codes of society. Recommended for the advanced student.

Farber, Jerry

1969 The Student as Nigger. North Hollywood, Calif.: Contact Books.

An interesting look at the nature of student status in American culture, in the context of social stratification both within the university and in the wider society.

Lundberg, Ferdinand
1968 The Rich and the Super-Rich. New York: Bantam Books.

Biographical sketches and histories of some of the leading families in the United States, documenting their acquisition of great wealth and power.

Mandelbaum, David G.
1970 Society in India. Volume 1, Continuity and Change. Berkeley: University of California Press.

A thorough study of the nature of social organization in traditional India. A second volume, *Society in India: Change and Continuity,* deals more with recent changes in the caste system.

Merton, Robert K.
1957 Social Theory and Social Structure. Second Edition. Glencoe: The Free Press.

A modern-day classic in sociology, this volume includes a thorough discussion of the concepts of structure and function as used in the social sciences.

Montagu, Ashley
1968 The Natural Superiority of Women. Revised Edition. New York: Collier Books.

A noted anthropologist debunks the myth of male superiority by drawing upon cross-cultural examples to present contradictions to the misconceptions about women.

Radcliffe-Brown, A. R.
1954 Structure and Function in Primitive Society. Glencoe: The Free Press.

A collection of papers following the classical "functionalist" approach to the study of society.

Warner, W. Lloyd, Marcia Meeker, and Kenneth Eels
1960 Social Class in America: A Manual of Procedure for the Measurement of Social Status. New York: Harper & Row.

Originally published in 1949, this is a classic work by an anthropologist on the concept of class in American society.

Wohl, R. Richard
1960 The Function of Myth in Modern Society. In Walter Goldschmidt, editor, Exploring the Ways of Mankind. New York: Holt, Rinehart and Winston.

An analysis of the Horatio Alger myth in American culture, and the assumptions and misunderstandings about the process of social mobility that Alger portrays.

Kinship, Marriage and the Family

Chapter Six

In the previous chapters we have surveyed the discipline of anthropology and some basic concepts used by cultural anthropologists in their work. We have dealt with the methods by which anthropologists conduct research in other cultures, and the means by which they seek to remain objective in their analysis of other peoples and their ways of life. And we have defined and elaborated upon the concepts of culture and society, illustrating how each is related to the other, and how each is structured so that its parts fit together into a unified whole. We are now ready to begin looking at some of the specific elements of culture that anthropologists concentrate upon, so that we can see how, in the course of studying a culture or comparing two or more cultures, the anthropologist is able to piece together the puzzle of life and better understand the incredible differences and surprising similarities he or she finds throughout the world.

Kinship Systems

We begin our discussion of the elements of social organization with kinship, for a number of very good reasons. *Kinship* is another word for the system of defining and organizing one's relatives. It provides the basis for social structure in all societies, and particularly in the traditional, non-Western societies that have been the focus of anthropological investigation for so long, kinship is the overriding principle upon which social relations rest. In our own modern industrial society this is less the case, for efficiency demands that a person fill a particular position not because of who he is, but based upon what he can do.

Marriage: the state or condition
of a community consisting of a master,
a mistress and two slaves, making in all two.
AMBROSE BIERCE *The Devil's Dictionary*

But we should recognize that this is the exception rather than the rule, and that in most societies throughout the world a person occupies a social position primarily as a result of his relationships to other individuals in the group.

Every culture provides its own system of relationships for dealing with the human biological necessities of reproduction, training, and passage from one generation to another. There are two fundamental types of relationships, those between people who are related biologically or genetically, whom we call "blood relatives" in our language, and those who are related by marriage. Of course, anthropologists have adopted the appropriate jargon terms for these two types of relationships (it seems we never pass up an opportunity to create a new scientific term, and kinship offers many such opportunities). We call blood relatives *consanguineal* relations, while those who are related by marriage we call *affinal* relations. People who are related to us by blood can trace their relationship back to a common ancestor, whether or not they are the same number of generations removed from that ancestor. Thus according to the American system of calculating biological relationships, we would include anyone who was descended from a common ancestor on any generational level, such as brother or sister, aunt or uncle, cousin, etc. Relatives by marriage usually cannot trace a relationship through a common ancestor, but have "married into" the family—for example, husband or wife, "in-laws," or an aunt or uncle who married a "blood" uncle or aunt, respectively

When we speak of kinship in any society, we generally refer to it as a *system*. This implies that the set of relationships recognized as significant among the members of the group are ordered and arranged systematically so that they are regular and predictable. To the degree that a particular society is kinship-oriented, this system of relations can serve as the basis for economic interaction such as the distribution of food and assignment of labor tasks, political interaction such as the distribution of power and authority over other individuals in the society, and many other aspects of life for members of the group. In addition, kinship can define the relationships between a group of people and the land they occupy, or the way in which land and other commodities are transferred from one member to another. It can determine who is to marry whom, as well as who may not marry whom. It provides the context within which new members of the society are trained in the culture they are to bear throughout their lives. In short, kinship organization can and does permeate every aspect of social behavior among some societies, and even in our own society which deemphasizes the importance of blood relations in most social contexts, our kinship system is crucial to our way of life.

The New York Public Library

Lewis Henry Morgan (1818–1881) *is perhaps the best known American anthropologist of the nineteenth century. Trained as a lawyer, Morgan developed an interest in anthropology through his experiences with the Iroquois Indians near his home in upstate New York. He began studying other Indian tribes, and in* Systems of Consanguinity and Affinity *(1871), he compared kinship systems and terminologies. As an outgrowth of his kinship studies, Morgan began to contemplate these differences in terms of an evolutionary sequence—he believed that the differences in kin terminologies could be explained by the fact that some societies represented an earlier stage of cultural evolution, and therefore their kinship systems were older, or in some cases simpler.*

Kinship Terminologies

By virtue of the fact that most people marry and most married couples have more than one child, we are related to a very large number of people, both living and dead. You may come from a very large family yourself, in which you know perhaps upwards of a hundred living relatives by name. Even if you come from a comparatively small family, with but a few living relatives close enough for you to know them well, you still have an enormous potential number of more distant relatives whom you do not know well enough to consider close, but who nevertheless can trace their descent from a common ancestor. If, for example, your great-great-grandfather had two children, each of whom had two children, and so on down to your generation, you would have one brother or sister, two first cousins, four second cousins, and eight third cousins, all in your generation, not to mention the aunts and uncles, first and second cousins once removed, and so on. And remember, you have had eight great-great-grandfathers! As you can see, the number of relatives accumulates rapidly with each new generation.

In every culture there is a set of terms used to describe relatives. But it is important to note that not every society uses the same categories to group relatives, or makes the same distinctions between different kinds of relationships. What is significant in one culture, and is therefore noted in the distinction of categories of relatives, could very well be completely insignificant in another culture, and therefore merged into a single category. Let us look at a specific example. In American culture we have a category described by the term "uncle." This group of people includes relatives of four kinds: (1) the brother of our father, (2) the husband of our father's sister, (3) the brother of our mother, and (4) the husband of our mother's sister. We can indicate this in Figure 6.1, which is a shorthand way of illustrating kinship relationships. In this diagram we use the following symbols: a triangle signifies a male, a circle a female, and a square an individual of either sex. In addition, an equal sign designates a marriage, a vertical line means descent, and a horizontal line indicates a brother-sister or sibling relationship. We use these symbols to designate the individuals as they are related to one central reference point, which we call "Ego." All relationships are calculated from that one individual's point of view. It helps if you put yourself in Ego's place when looking at the diagram, and it does not matter in this case whether you are male or female.

Now we may ask why it is that we put these four different types of relationship into the same category and call them by the same term. Does this happen in all cultures? The answer, of course, is that it does not, for as we shall see shortly, whereas for Americans the distinction between different kinds of uncles is relatively unimportant, for members of another culture this distinction can be crucial to the way the people organize their lives and their social interaction.

6.1

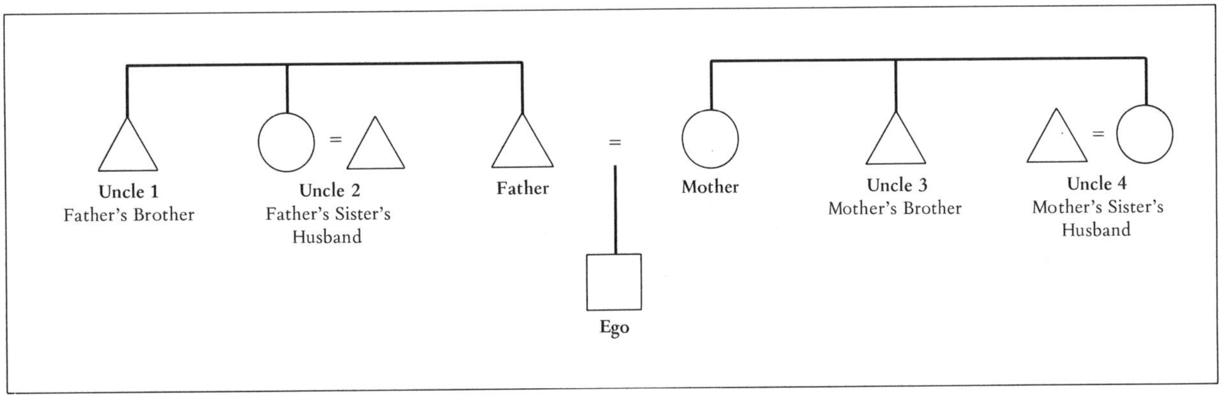

The reason that kinship terms vary from one culture to another (beyond the obvious differences in language) is that the system of organizing relations differs. The terms that people use are simply a handy device for putting that system into operation in everyday interaction with other people. A further reason for the variation in terms is that each category is based upon certain patterns of behavior expected from the individuals within that category. In other words, *kin terms are role terms,* that is, they designate not only a biological relationship but a *social relationship* as well. They vary from one culture to another because the behavior expected from certain individuals varies with each different culture.

Let us return to our example of the category "uncle" to see how this can be so. In American culture we generally expect the same treatment from all four kinds of uncles. For one thing, we do not make a legal distinction between our mother's brother and our father's brother. They are both expected to act toward us in the same way. While the husbands of our parents' sisters are not related by blood, they are married to people who are, and thus they are expected to adopt the behavior patterns of their spouses. This is not to say that every uncle will treat us exactly alike—obviously we all have favorites—but only that as our system operates, we would *expect* the same treatment from all.

In another society the situation might be quite different, however. Suppose, for example, that instead of tracing our line of descent through both parents equally, we tend to favor one over the other.

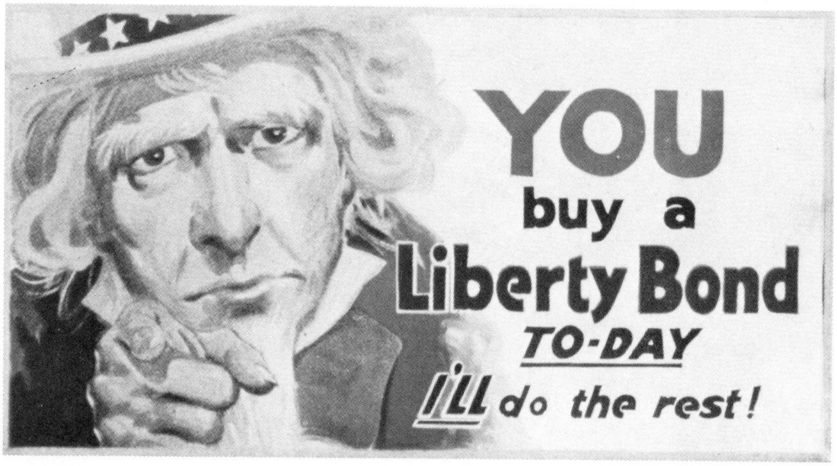

Kinship terms can designate more than just biological relationships.
(Culver Pictures)

This is not as farfetched as it might sound, for after all, in our society we do take our father's name and not our mother's in most cases. In some societies inheritance is even more one-sided than this, and when a child is born it inherits membership in a kinship group only through one side of the family—either the mother's side (called *matrilineal*) or the father's side *(patrilineal).* Let us assume, for the sake of simplicity, that there are two groups in a society, the Smiths and the Joneses. Furthermore, it is forbidden for a Smith to marry another Smith, and likewise for a Jones to marry another Jones. Finally, let us assume that the child inherits not only its surname, but also its kin group membership from its father. We can see why there might be a tendency to differentiate between types of uncles in such a society, for the distinction would become significant given the new set of rules for figuring relationships. This point is illustrated more clearly in Figure 6.2, where the dark figures designate Smiths, the light figures Joneses.

We can see what distinguishes between different kinds of uncles in this diagram. Uncle 1 is a Smith, the same as Ego; his children will be Smiths likewise. Uncle 2 is a Jones, a different kin group from Ego, and his children will also be members of a different kin group; thus he is significantly different from Uncle 1, both because of his own kin group affiliation and because his children belong to a pool of potential marriage partners for Ego, while the children of Uncle 1 do not. Uncle 3 is likewise a Jones, and in terms of kin group

6.2

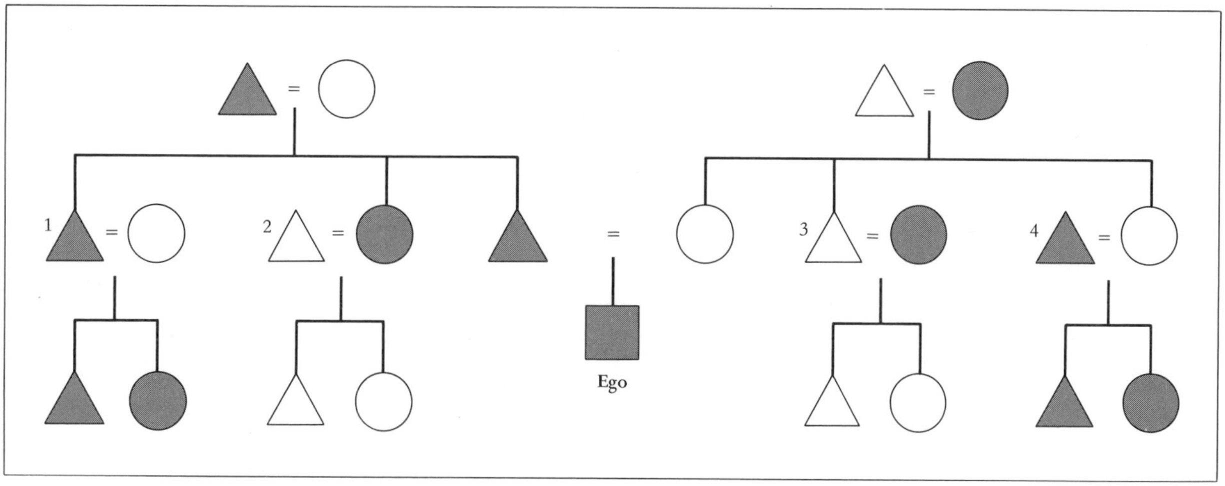

affiliation he is in the same category as Uncle 2. Note, however, that while 3 is a blood relative because he is the brother of Ego's mother, 2 is not a blood relative, but is related to Ego by marriage. Finally, Uncle 4 is a Smith, and in terms of kin group membership is of the same type as Uncle 1. Again, however, note that while Uncle 1 is a blood relative, Uncle 4 is not.

Now, how does this application of kinship terminology operate in real life? The Yąnomamö, a tribe located along the Orinoco River in Venezuela, are a patrilineal society, that is, a child inherits its kin group membership from its father, and not from its mother. The different types of uncles are significant in that not all are related to Ego to the same degree, and this difference is reflected in the kinship terminology. Ego calls his father by the term *Hayä;* he uses the same term for his father's brother, who belongs to the same clan, having inherited his membership from Ego's father's father. But Ego calls his mother's brother by a different term, *Shoaiyä,* indicating that he is in some way different from Ego's father and father's brother.

According to the terminology used among the Yąnomamö there is no difference between father and father's brother. This does not mean that people don't really recognize any difference—only that the kin term reflects an emphasis on group membership rather than biological parentage.

Another example of a distinction between types of uncles is found among a few societies in East Africa, who also maintain a separate term for father as opposed to father's brother, with a third term designating mother's brother. Thus, there are three terms used, where only two are found among the Yąnomamö, as well as in our own culture (father and uncle).

There is an important lesson to learn from this principle of ordering various people into categories. We tend to assume that because we organize relatives in a certain way in our own society, there is some fundamental principle of kinship organization that we follow, and that in cultures where our practices are not found the people are backward. However, this is clearly not the case. A kinship system can be ordered around any set of principles, and there is no right or wrong way to do it. The beliefs that a group of people share about what is significant in their kinship system do not have to be based upon some absolute rule of biological relationship. Otherwise, why would we lump all of our uncles into one category, and not distinguish between uncles by blood and uncles by marriage?

Whereas in our society it is generally not the custom to marry our cousin, in some societies this is not only allowed, but also it is the ideal. If we look back to Figure 6.2 once again, we can see why this is so. If Ego is a member of his father's kin group, but not his mother's, then he will have two types of cousins (in our sense of the term): those who belong to his own group and those who belong to another. Which cousins will belong to which group (in this example) can be determined by a simple rule: *parallel cousins* are members of the same group while *cross cousins* are not. By parallel cousins we mean those cousins who are related to Ego through relatives of the same (parallel) sex, namely mother and *mother's sister* or father and *father's brother*. Cross cousins, conversely, are those who are related to Ego through relatives of the opposite sex: mother and *mother's brother*, or father and *father's sister*. This distinction is illustrated in Figure 6.3.

6.3

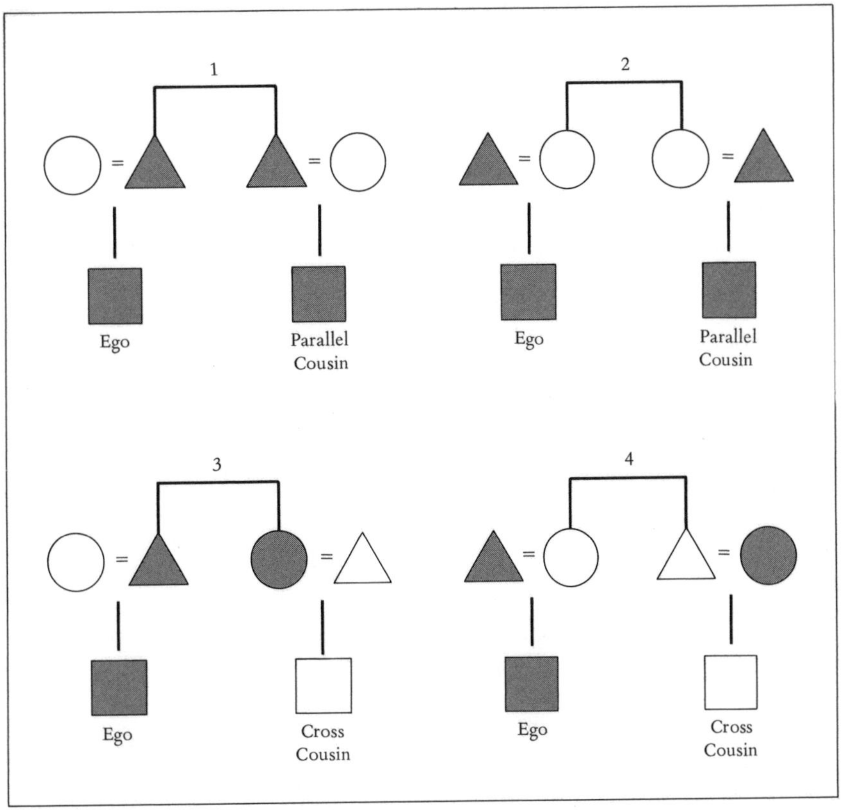

Now in our society with so many millions of people and so many different kinship groups, we have no trouble finding suitable marriage partners who are not related to us. But in many smaller societies, where the number of potential marriage partners is extremely limited, there can be complications involved in finding a husband or wife. Accordingly, a rule that designates that the ideal marriage partner is a cross-cousin insures that every individual will marry someone from a different kin group. Of course, such a system never works exactly, because nowhere does every married couple produce exactly two children, one of each sex, who grow up to marry and continue this process. But if the ideal is there in the minds of the people, then it instills in them a strong value associated with marrying outside the kin group. This is a way not only of maintaining the genetic diversity of the population by bringing in new people and avoiding heavy inbreeding, but at the same time it promotes the interaction of different kin groups within the society through the exchange of individuals for marriage partners, and thus promotes the solidarity of the society as a whole.

The Basis of Kin Terms

In American culture we rely upon four criteria in assigning kinship terms to individuals. First, we sometimes make a distinction based on the sex of the individual, so that we call a male sibling a brother and a female sibling a sister. Note that this is not true in all cases, since we have only one term for cousin regardless of sex. But in many categories we do have this distinction (e.g., mother/father, aunt/uncle, nephew/niece).

Second, we make a distinction based upon *generation.* Thus we have a distinct term for members of different generations, such as daughter, mother, grandmother, etc. Technically this distinction also exists for cousins, although it is not as rigidly used in everyday conversation. We tend to lump cousins of different generations together, especially as they grow more distant, although theoretically we could make a distinction between "first cousin," "first cousin once removed," "second cousin," and so on.

Third, we make a distinction in kin terms based upon the differences between a relative who is related to us in a direct line of *descent* from a common ancestor, and one who is not. Thus we distinguish between our father and our father's brother, or uncle. Other such distinctions include mother and aunt, son and nephew, grandfather and great-uncle, etc. This distinction is one between *lineal* relatives (because they are on the direct line of descent) and *collateral* relatives (because they are lateral branches of Ego's family tree, not part of the main trunk or line).

Finally, we make a distinction in some cases between relatives who are related by blood *(consanguineal)* and those related by marriage *(affinal)*. This distinction includes the different categories such as brother and brother-in-law, mother and mother-in-law, etc. But note that it is not valid for all categories in that we use the same term for consanguineal and affinal uncles or aunts.

A Zulu family in East Transvaal, South Africa. Kinship patterns may differ, but all children enjoy balloons! (Thea Detschek, DPI)

Additional factors are sometimes used in other cultures in determining kinship terms applied to individuals, although they do not come into play in the American system. One such consideration can be the sex of the linking relative. Using such a means of distinguishing kinship relationships, called *bifurcation,* we would make a distinction between a relative related through a female and the same general type of relative related through a male. For example, we would have one term for mother's brother and another for father's brother, or we might have separate terms for brother's children and sister's children. We do not make these distinctions in our society (in the first case all are uncles, in the second either nephews or nieces), but in many societies they are important in determining kinship system categories.

Another potentially important factor which we do not use in American society is the *sex of the speaker.* Many kinship terminologies have a different structure and a different set of categories depending upon whether the person speaking (Ego) is a male or a female. In our society the relative position of the sexes is basically equal (this may not seem true,but when compared to some non-Western societies the difference is astounding) and thus it does not make much difference whether it is a girl or a boy who uses the term "uncle." But in many societies it is significant to designate whether the speaker is male or female, and therefore girls are taught one set of kin terms and boys another. Such a distinction could reflect a fundamental principle of social inequality between the sexes. If a girl calls her uncle a different term from that used by a boy, it might indicate that the relationship between the uncle and the boy is expected to be completely different—with a different set of rights and obligations on the part of each—from the relationship between the uncle and the girl. Thus, within its own cultural context this practice makes sense.

Another factor used in distinguishing between kinship terms is the *relative age of the speaker,* that is, relative to the person designated by the term. Thus, a boy might use one kin term to refer to his older brother, and a second term to refer to his younger brother. Again, while this would not make much sense in American culture, in a society where age was of crucial importance in determining social relationships, it would be meaningful to recognize the importance of relative age in the kin terms used.

At this point you might ask, why is it necessary to know about all of these different factors in assigning kinship terms to various people in different societies around the world? We have stressed throughout this book that one of the best ways to learn to understand your own culture is to look outside it. If we accept the fact that there is a structure to our way of life, the task of uncovering that structure is made much easier by knowing what we are looking for.

Also, it is valuable to know just how important kinship can be in ordering the lives of people in other cultures. In American society we tend to minimize the importance of kinship because so many of its primary functions have been taken over by other institutions—the work group, the church group, the schools, etc. But in many non-Western societies kinship still operates as the major ordering force in the lives of the people, and for them almost everything is seen in the context of their kinship system.

Finally, terms carry social meanings as well as biological meanings, and as such they designate particular patterns of behavior that are appropriate to a particular situation. Frequently a kin term can be used as a cue to what is expected of an individual. The anthropologist Paul Bohannan gives an example from his fieldwork among the Tiv in Africa. He reports that if an informant wanted to give him a gift, he would call him "my father," because one bestowed gifts upon people whom one respected and honored. If the informant wanted to correct Bohannan's grammar or etiquette, he called him "my child," because it was expected that children would not know all the rules of proper social conduct, and were still in the process of learning the language. Thus, even though Bohannan was clearly an adult, his role in the Tiv society sometimes coincided with that of a child. On the other hand, if the informant wanted to include him on the same side in an argument, to lend support to his cause, he would call him "son of my mother." This term was used to indicate that there was an obligation to defend one another and to stick together, which was exactly the behavior called for in the argument. And finally, if the informant wanted to offer Bohannan a drink, he would use a non-kin term which meant "my age-mate," or a member of the same peer group but not a blood relative. This term thus designated that there was a common interest and a common bond that held the two together, but that the behavior associated with the situation was not kinship-oriented behavior, but was the interaction of friends. Drinking was appropriate for men of the same age, but was not related to kinship, and so the appropriate term was used, not only to inform Bohannan of the expectations of the speaker, but in more general terms to define the situation for all involved.

American Kinship Terminology

We have already mentioned some aspects of the American system of kinship and the terms for relatives in the standard usage of the English language. But it remains to look at it in more detail, and to demonstrate that American kinship is in fact a system, and that it is only one of many possibilities found in the world today.

In the American kinship system we trace our relationships equally through both sides of the family, rather than leaning heavily or entirely upon the mother's side or the father's side. This means that we tend to treat people related through our mother and through our father in the same manner, and we use the same kinship terms to designate relatives no matter which side of the family they are on. The formal system of terms used by Americans is similar to the general type known to anthropologists as the "Eskimo" kinship terminology. In this system, there is a separate term for "father" and "mother," while the categories of "father's brother" and "mother's brother" are merged under one term (uncle) and likewise "father's sister" and "mother's sister" are designated by a single term (aunt). Further, the children of parents' siblings are merged into a single category, designated by the same term (cousin).

But American kinship is more than just a set of formal terms, for there are a variety of informal words used to address or refer to individuals in a variety of situations. For example, although we have the formal term "mother," we may use any one of a number of alternate terms, such as "mom," "mommy," "ma," or we may use a first name, a nickname, a diminutive, or some other descriptive or joking term such as "old woman" or "old lady." The same holds true for the term "father," which can be replaced by a less authoritarian term such as "pop" or "daddy," or by "old man." These latter terms tend to be used in reference rather than in address—that is, we might refer to our father as "old man" when talking about him to someone else out of his earshot, but we would be less likely to use that term to address him personally. This points to a distinction between different kinds of terms used depending upon whether that individual is being addressed, referred to in his or her presence, or referred to in his or her absence. Thus we might use the term "mother" when referring to her in a discussion with our father, the term "ma" or "mom" when speaking to her personally, the term "my mother" when speaking to a member of our peer group about her when she is not there. These forms of reference and address vary considerably with the situation.

From this variation in the use of terms to designate an individual, we can see that each term has two basic functions: to organize relatives into categories or classify them, and to define or describe a role. Thus when we use the term "uncle" in standard American kinship terminology we are both categorizing an individual in terms of his relationship to us and at the same time we are defining a general set of behavior that it is understood that individual follows in interacting with us. It is important to note that these alternate terms are therefore not synonyms, that is, they do not have exactly the same meaning. It does not mean the same thing to say "father" and "daddy." One has a ring of formality and authority, while the other implies a closer and more informal relationship.

This use of kin terms to designate behavior rather than actual biological relationships points out another aspect of the flexibility of kinship systems, as well as their importance in the overall structure of society. In many situations in social interaction, we behave toward others in a way that corresponds to kinship behavior, even though we are not related. Sometimes people formalize that behavior through the creation of artificial, or *fictive,* kinship ties. For example, the anthropologist Elliot Liebow, in his book *Tally's Corner* about a black ghetto in Washington D.C., describes a relationship called "going for cousins." This is a way for two people of the opposite sex to establish a close personal relationship with no sexual overtones. By invoking the cousin relationship, which in American culture implies a taboo against sex, the two people can avoid suspicion by the rest of the community. The important aspect of this action from the anthropologist's point of view is that it is done within the context of kinship, indicating how crucial it is to the overall pattern of social relationships.

Descent

Having discussed the various relationships between individuals in a society and the meaning of those relationships, it remains to be seen how the members of a society determine who their relatives are. In every culture there are rules that establish how one defines one's kin, and who is to be included or excluded. The categories of relatives are arbitrarily limited according to these rules. One feature of the kinship system that serves to define the various categories of kinsmen is what we call *descent,* which represents the way in which two blood relatives trace their relationship to a common ancestor. This is not a biological consideration but a social one, for if the culture does not recognize the biological link between two individuals as significant, then according to the rules of that culture they are not related. It is not a question of how many physical characteristics they share as a result of having a common genetic heritage. It is simply a social fact.

Descent relationships can be reckoned through one line (either male or female) or through both. If descent is figured only through the mother's line, it is *matrilineal;* if only through the father's line, it is *patrilineal;* if through both, it is *bilateral.* As we noted earlier in this chapter, by excluding people related through one parent we divide our biologically related relatives into two groups, only one of which is recognized as part of our kin group. Frequently people related to a common ancestor will have a name, and will be considered as a corporate group with certain common rights and privileges. Perhaps the group will hold land in common for its members, or it might also be associated with a common religious shrine, or the possession of a common fund of knowledge such as a family ritual or myth. A *clan* is such a descent group, as is a *lineage,* the major difference being that a lineage consists of members who can trace their relationship to an actual common ancestor, while the members of a clan assume that they are related but cannot actually trace their links back far enough to reach that common ancestor.

In many cases there is a logical explanation among the people themselves, as well as for the anthropologist, for the particular type of descent. For example, the prevailing theory of conception might have something to do with whether descent is traced through the male or the female line, or both. Of course, in American culture we recognize the role of each parent in the process of conception, and biologically speaking we consider a child to be equally close to both parents. Thus it seems logical to us that descent in American culture is traced equally through both the male and female lines.

Among the Ashanti in West Africa, people believe that the blood of the child is contributed only by the mother, while the spiritual makeup of the child comes from the father. Since the Ashanti distinguish between two aspects of the self—the physical being and the spiritual being—the descent of each part of the individual is traced according to different principles. Biological descent among the Ashanti is therefore matrilineal, since it is the mother who contributes the physical essence to the infant, while spiritual descent is patrilineal, and the child becomes a member of his father's spiritual kin group.

To cite another example of the relationship between beliefs about conception and patterns of descent, in the Trobriand Islands in the Western Pacific it is believed that the child's spirit enters its mother's uterus by itself. The only role the male plays is to widen the path to the womb through intercourse, and to insure that the woman is married, since only married women may legitimately bear children. The actual biological role of the father is not considered. Thus in reckoning descent, the mother's line is the important one, for the child is born of the mother and not equally of both parents. Furthermore, the mother's brother is considered to have a closer relationship to

Sepik River tribesmen—young children join in a male-oriented activity. (Elliott Erwitt, Magnum)

the child than its biological father, because of his blood tie to the mother through a common ancestor.

Most societies in the world reckon descent through the male line, a fact that proves the importance of social considerations over biological factors. For even though it is obvious that the child is a part of its mother in a biological sense, in male-dominated societies (which include the vast majority) it is the male prerogative that wins out. Where men own property and hold power, they seek to retain that property and power as an exclusive right unto themselves. They can do this only if they are able to exclude women from positions of power, and it is through the descent system that they make sure that male children will carry on the tradition and female children will follow in the footsteps of their mothers.

Besides the prevailing theory of conception or the predominance of the male prerogative, there might be obvious economic reasons for one kind of descent existing in a particular society. Residence patterns are sometimes tied in with descent. In a matrilineal society the husband often comes to live in his wife's home village, thus reinforcing the pattern of descent, and conversely for a patrilineal society. If property is owned and distributed by men then patriliny is likely, whereas if it is owned and distributed by women (as is the case in some societies) then matriliny is more likely to be found. On the other hand, if a male skill such as hunting is based upon close knowledge of the area and experience in hunting it, then patrilineal descent is probable, because in that way men would retain rights over the hunting territory and be more likely to keep their place of residence over generations. This in effect maximizes the benefits of the experience of elders, who can pass along their specialized knowledge of the region and their skills in hunting the local game in the most efficient manner.

Marriage and the Family

If kinship is the basis for social organization in all societies in the world, then marriage is the basis for kinship. Of course, strictly speaking marriage is not an absolute necessity for human society. People could reproduce and train new members of society without the institution of marriage and without organizing society into family units to carry out these functions. Yet in no society in the world is this

A wedding party outside a church in Bolivia. Maybe the bride's shoes aren't so unusual after all. (Rothstein, United Nations)

completely the case; marriage and the family are cultural universals, found in some form everywhere. Marriage functions to control sexual activity within the society, following the rules upon which members of the group are organized. The family functions as a primary group in the socialization of the young, and it also defines the channels by which membership in a kinship group is transferred (descent) and by which material and nonmaterial possessions are passed down through the generations (inheritance).

Actually, marriage has several possible functions it can perform in different societies. Where society is concerned over the legitimacy of its new members, marriage establishes a set of legal parents. Where society is concerned about the restriction of sexual activity among its members, marriage provides guidelines for such activity. In some societies, marriage can be used to establish control over an individual's labor power, usually in the case of a woman who comes to live with her husband and his family. In many societies marriage carries with it a transfer of property, thus giving over the rights to that property—land, money, material goods, or whatever—to the family of one of the spouses.

An important element in any marriage, and one that should not be overlooked even in our own society, is the relationship that is established between two groups. A marriage is not simply an agreement between two people that they are in love and want to live together (although in modern society this is becoming more common); rather, a marriage in most societies is a contract that binds two families or even larger groups together socially, and sometimes economically. Among the nobility in traditional Europe, marriages were often arranged by heads of state in a way that would tie two countries together. The marriage of Phillip II of Spain and Mary Tudor, daughter of King Henry VIII and Catherine of Aragon, was a way of solidifying the relationship between Spain and England, forming a social, economic, and military bond between the two countries. Often inbreeding among the nobility was designed to prevent the division of royal estates as well, since by keeping the wealth within a small group there was less danger of spreading the royal fortunes and power too thinly.

Likewise in non-Western societies, marriage can be more of an economic contract than a bond between two individuals. Among the Tiwi in northern Australia, a man acquires a wife by promising his first-born daughter to his future father-in-law, or to the latter's close relatives. The more wives he can obtain, the more daughters he can promise, and thus the stronger his ties with other groups in his society. As he grows older, he begins to reap the rewards of his shrewd economic transactions, by acquiring more younger wives who will produce more daughters he can trade off for promises of future wives—a kind

Philip II of Spain and Mary Tudor of England—a political marriage. (New York Public Library)

of primitive social security system, at least from the male's point of view.

In traditional pre-revolution China, a wealthy family might acquire a wife for their son when she was just a child. They would bring her into the household at an early age so that she could be trained to work with her future mother-in-law, and when she reached the proper age she would be married to the son. However, the main function of the wife was to work in the household, and provide sons for her husband's lineage. Her role as a warm companion to her husband was minimized, as evidenced by the fact that marriages were arranged by the families and did not require the consent of either party.

This list of possible functions of marriage in different societies may be extended, and merely serves to indicate some of the basic ways in which marriage can be viewed: sexual access, parentage, labor, property and alliance. It is interesting to note that even though we assume that for us marriage is based solely upon the free choice of the two people involved, there are very strong pressures operating against this freedom. Our society erects a set of barriers to limit the opportunities for children to meet other children whose families do not have a great deal in common. As a result, the sheer probability of marrying someone very much like ourself is overwhelming. Segregation in neighborhoods and schools is one very effective way of insuring that children spend more time with "their own kind." Social functions arranged by a group such as a church or social club are another way of exerting subtle pressure upon people to interact with others who have much in common. Even the Greek system at colleges and universities—especially sororities—can be very effective in channeling members into the right social crowd.

The Family: Variations on a Theme

Every society recognizes the family as an important unit, but each places a different emphasis upon which members are most important and how that family unit should be structured. Thus the makeup of the family differs from one culture to another. In the United States, as in most industrial countries in the world, the family has grown smaller in response to the challenges of the industrial economy. Mobility, both social and geographical, has trimmed the family down to a small unit that can move about easily and does not present an economic burden to the breadwinner. Whereas on the farm a number of extra hands might be helpful, in the city the presence of uncles and aunts, grandparents and cousins, all under one roof, is most inefficient. As a result, the typical family in our culture has become what we call the *nuclear* family formed around the nucleus of parents and children with few, if any, others.

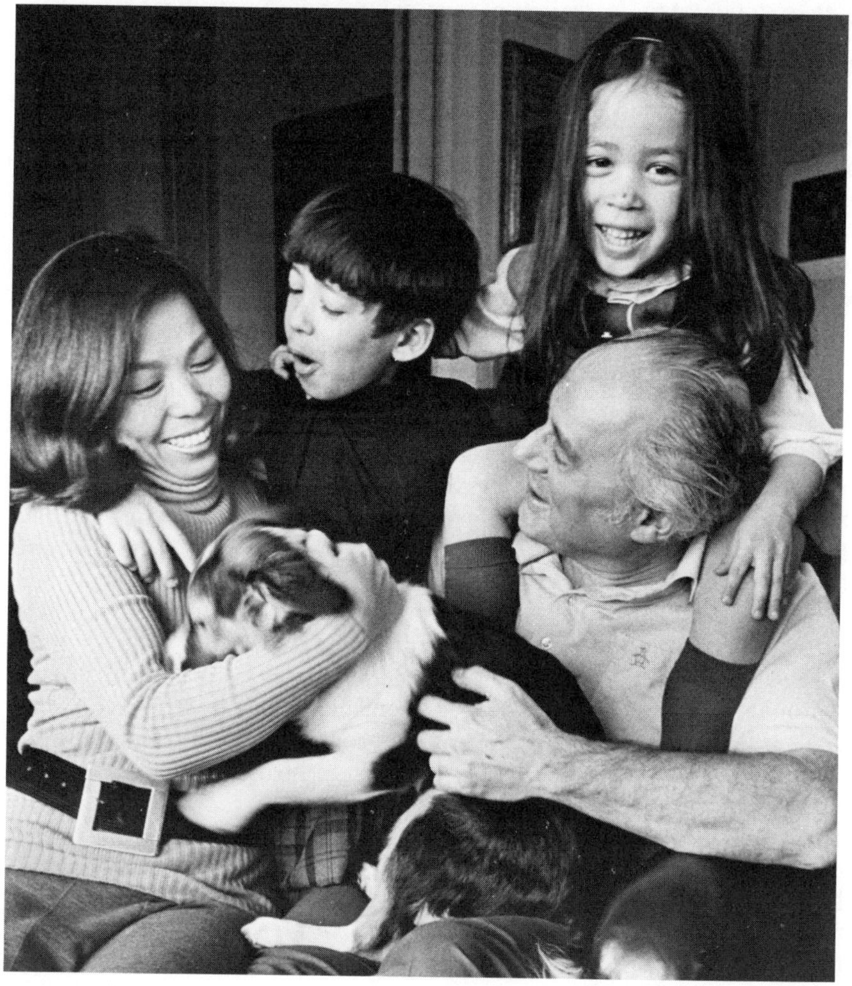

An American nuclear family: father, mother, son, daughter, and dog. This family also demonstrates an interracial marriage. (Alice S. Kandell, Rapho/Photo Researchers)

In contrast to the American family composed typically of a married couple and their offspring, many societies recognize the family as a residential unit which includes a wider circle of relatives. When more than two generations are represented, and particularly when collateral as well as lineal relatives reside in the household (e.g., aunts and uncles, or cousins), we speak of an *extended* family. This family type is more frequently found in agricultural peasant or tribal societies, and tends to disappear as the country becomes more urbanized. A variant of the extended family is what is called the *joint* family (or joint extended family), which consist of a married couple, their unmarried sons and daughters, and the nuclear families of their married sons.

An extended Minnesota farm family, effective in a rural setting but cumbersome in the city. (The Bettmann Archive)

Usually we think of the family not only in terms of biological and marital relationships, but also as an economic unit, a unit for socializing the young, and in general related to a number of different functions simultaneously. However, this is not always the case, and in some societies the biological family is not the equivalent of the social unit—that is, the satisfaction of sexual needs is separated from other functions of the family. Such was the case among the Nayar, a people of southern India, where the institution of marriage existed in a very different form from what we would consider normal. Around the time of puberty, each Nayar girl was ritually married according to the proper religious ceremony to a boy selected from a lineage linked to that of the girl by ties of mutual exchange. Following the ceremony the couple were secluded for a few days whereupon sexual activity might take place, but was not necessary. The couple then separated, with the boy returning to his home village and the girl to hers. Once they were separated, the girl had no further obligations to her husband until he died, when she and her children (by whatever man) had to observe a death ritual on his behalf.

After the ritual marriage and separation each party went his or her own way. The woman was free to engage in affairs with whomever she chose (provided the man was of the proper social position in Nayar society), and the man was likewise unhindered from entering into such relationships. Satisfaction of sexual desires and reproduction were thus fulfilled through a series of informal love affairs that established no permanent bond between a woman and her lover. A woman could have as many lovers as she wished at any one time, or she could restrict her attention to one man. They could be fleeting affairs, or they could be long-term relationships. The lover would visit after

supper and leave early the next morning, leaving his weapons outside her door as a sign to others. Anyone who arrived and found another's weapons there was free to sleep on the woman's porch.

The children of such unions called their mother's lovers by the term meaning "lord" or "leader," and such a term did not carry with it the implication of either biological or legal paternity. Even when paternity could definitely be established, the man had no obligations to his children other than paying for the expense of their birth. The children became the sole responsibility of the mother's kinship unit, or her *matrilineage*. This female-centered kinship unit included men, such as the brothers of the woman or her mother's brothers, and these men were obliged to contribute to the care and raising of the children born into the group, just as they were relieved of their obligations toward their own "biological" children born into another woman's matrilineage.

The explanation for this type of marriage—surely one of the most curious forms of that institution found anywhere in the world—lies in the general pattern of social organization among the Nayar. Traditional Indian society was divided into a number of distinct social groups, called *castes*. Each caste was ritually linked with a specific occupation, and along with it went a whole set of rules and a way of life appropriate only to that caste. The Nayars were traditionally a warrior caste, and it is thought that the lack of paternal responsibility and household obligations was functional in that it left the men free to follow their occupation. Of course the men were responsible for the children in their own matrilineage, but the matrilineage as a whole took care of the children and could take over the obligations in the man's absence. At the same time, the pattern of courtship and sexual activity seemed to fit in with the life style of the warrior caste, enabling men who were away from home (and women whose husbands might be away much of the time) to engage in a normal sex life with the approval of their society. As the need for warriors diminished and the caste system was finally abolished, this pattern also disappeared.

It has also been suggested that the Nayar marriage pattern had a function in maintaining the unity of the matrilineage. If a man became permanently devoted to one wife, his ties to his sisters and their children would diminish. By separating the marriage ritual from the actual performance of the biological functions of sexual activity and reproduction, the biological father is legally removed from playing an important role in his children's matrilineage, and at the same time he becomes closely aligned to his own matrilineage. Thus, while procreation is necessary for the continuance of the matrilineage, husbands are not. The Nayar marriage institution is one way of seeing that this distinction is maintained.

Nayar society shows the extreme range of variability of the family and marriage as social institutions, and as such it is of interest to the anthropologist. The Nayars represent a woman-centered family in a male-centered society, for while the matrilineage is the basic feature of social organization, the male-dominated warrior caste is the central focus of the group. Another variant on the family is the case of a woman-centered family in a woman-centered society. Bronislaw Malinowski's work in the Trobriand Islands in the Western Pacific describes this type of society.

In the Trobriands, descent is reckoned only through the mother's line. This fits in with the prevailing theory of conception and procreation, which we have discussed earlier. It is thought that the mother alone contributes to the makeup of the child, and the father is only a passive agent. Therefore, the child is closer to all members of its mother's kinship group, or matriline, and is not considered to be of the same group as its father, who belongs to another matriline. This pattern results in a different set of statuses and roles, with correspondingly different kinds of behavior between members of the family. For example, the term for "father" means, literally, "husband of my mother." The father is considered an outsider with regard to family affairs, and where male activity within the family is concerned, it is the mother's brother who bears the responsibility.

Nevertheless, the father is a close companion to his children, and the relationship between them is one of great warmth. However, the authoritarian role of father as head of the household and disciplinarian, which is so common in Western society, is not filled by the father in Trobriand society. Instead, it is the mother's brother who becomes the authority figure, due to his membership in the family group. He grants his sister's son permission to do things which would normally come from the father in other societies. A boy inherits property from his mother's brother, not from his father.

The Incest Taboo: A Universal Puzzle

Malinowski's description of the structure of the family in the Trobriands raises another interesting question regarding the institution known as the *incest taboo*. In every society there are rules which prohibit incest, i.e., sexual relations between certain relatives. The same rules are not found everywhere—what is important is that *some* rules exist in all societies. A number of theories have been proposed to explain why this should be the case, but as yet anthropologists have not arrived at a conclusive answer to this problem.

The reason for Malinowski's interest in the question of the incest taboo can be traced back to the work of Sigmund Freud, the noted founder of psychoanalysis. In *Totem and Taboo,* Freud suggested that the incest taboo originated when early man, in a fit of jealousy and rage over being denied access to the women of his group by a domineering father, banded together with his brothers and killed the father, ate him in cannibalistic style, and then engaged in sexual relations with his mother and sisters. But guilt caught up with him, and once he realized how horrible his crime had been, he renounced his sexual rights to the women of his family, thus creating the incest taboo. Freud argued that this was the first truly cultural act of mankind, for it represented an increased level of conscience and the thoughtful structuring of social (in this case sexual) relations as a result of that conscience.

Malinowski reacted strongly against Freud's discussion of the incest taboo, based upon his field experience in the Trobriands. Freud had suggested that the incest taboo that prohibited sexual relations between parents and children or between siblings was a result of this early struggle between father and sons—ultimately a question of power and authority.

Instead, Malinowski argued that the incest taboo was a way by which society could prevent a host of destructive tensions from arising between members of the family and the wider kinship unit. By prohibiting sexual relations between members of the nuclear family, the incest taboo insures that the jealousies and internal conflicts that could lead to the breakup of the family will be avoided. It has nothing to do with the history of the human race in the sense that Freud was referring to some long-forgotten act of early men, but instead can be seen in purely functional terms as a way of enabling society to continue to operate effectively.

A number of other theories have been proposed to account for the incest taboo, but each is equally unconvincing as a total explanation. According to some theorists, the incest taboo is a way of avoiding the harmful effects of inbreeding. But this argument does not explain why the incest taboo exists in nonliterate, non-Western societies where the science of genetics is unknown. Early human beings were surely not sophisticated enough in the knowledge of reproduction and transmission of genetic characteristics from one generation to the next to establish a law such as the incest taboo on a purely scientific basis. The explanation must lie elsewhere.

More recently, the theory has been proposed that the incest taboo is really a way in which human beings are able to form a society. The argument is that if men and women who are related by blood ties also form the family unit (through marriage and reproduction with each other), then the result is a self-sufficient group very small in size. The only way for that group to grow and become allied with others is to exchange marriage partners with another group and thus form a bond with them. But in order to do this, there must be a renunciation of sexual rights among the members of a group that forces them to exchange mates with others—otherwise this contract would not be necessary.

It is further suggested that this basic feature of reciprocity is a part of human nature, that is, that the human species is essentially sociable and has a built-in need to give and to receive. Where early men were able to exchange women with other groups nearby, the social bonds that arose between the two groups proved to be a strong advantage. As this practice spread, the success was so overwhelming that the rules preventing intercourse between members of the same family were made stronger. Thus, we can view the incest taboo, according to this theory, as the result of cultural evolution, whereby a cultural practice conferred a strong advantage upon those who adopted it. This theory of incest does seem more plausible than the others, but the trouble is we have no way of proving it conclusively. And it does not explain to our complete satisfaction why the incest taboo includes different sets of relatives in different societies (or even different degrees of relationships in our own society, as evidenced by the variety of laws found in different states in the United States).

Marriage

The question of incest prohibitions brings us to another major focus, the institution of marriage. Just as there are a number of different possibilities within a wide range of family structures, there is a great deal of variation in the structure of marriage and the rules that govern whom one may or may not marry. But we ought not confuse rules about marriage with rules prohibiting incest. The former deal with the establishment of a conjugal unit, whereas the latter deal strictly with sexual relations. A prohibition against marrying someone is not the same thing as a prohibition against having intercourse with them, although certainly both could be applied to the same individual. However, in many cases restrictions against marrying a certain type of individual go along with cultural expectations that one is entitled

A Zulu bride must keep her face covered for two days before the wedding ceremony. (From Photographic Collections in the University Museum, Philadelphia)

to, or at least allowed to, have intercourse with that type of individual. In India, for example, one is prohibited from marrying an individual who belongs to a caste on a lower social level than one's own. Thus a member of the farmer caste is not allowed to marry a member of the sweeper caste, and to do so would mean expulsion from the caste and probably from the village as well. Yet it is commonly expected that some men from the higher farmer caste will engage in sexual intercourse with some women of lower castes such as the sweeper caste (the opposite—men from a lower caste having intercourse with women from the higher caste—is not tolerated). Obviously, the similarity with other societies, ours included, is not remote. Consider, for instance, the recent sexual scandals of certain British politicians and prostitutes.

Marriage is a difficult institution to define so as to allow for all the possibilities and varieties found in the world. The example of the Nayar cited earlier points out one extreme of marriage, where the couple remains together for only a few days and sex is not a necessary part of the relationship. There are a number of factors that can vary in any marriage, and each society has its own set of rules to govern what form these factors will take.

Number of Mates

A marriage can be between any number of people of either sex. One man can be married to one woman, as is the case in our society. This variant is known as *monogamy,* derived from two Greek words, *mono-* (one) and *-gamy* (marriage). Lately, we have seen the onset of a new variant of monogamy, in which an individual of either sex takes a succession of spouses—an increasingly common practice as the divorce rate climbs. This pattern has been termed "serial monogamy," and except for the legal ceremony of marriage, it resembles the Nayar pattern described earlier.

The alternative to monogamy is the practice whereby an individual has more than one spouse at the same time, termed *polygamy,* again from the Greek, *poly-* (many). A man can have more than one wife *(polygyny—gyn-* is the Greek stem for "woman"), or a woman can have more than one husband *(polyandry—andr-* is related to *anthro-,* the Greek stem for "man"). Cases of polygyny are more frequent in the anthropological literature. Especially where the family is an economic unit and the women are called upon to contribute much of the labor, the addition of a wife can be seen as a contribution to the well-being of the entire family. The added wives are not looked upon simply for their sexual attributes or their child-bearing capability, but for their labor potential as well.

In traditional pre-revolution China we find an interesting example of polygyny. In some areas of China it was an acceptable practice for a man to bring into his household a second wife, usually with the first wife's permission, and only after the man had become wealthy enough to be able to support two wives. The second wife was a welcome addition to the family from the point of view of both the husband and the first wife. The husband was glad to have her as a sexual partner—the first marriage was arranged by the families, and the couple had no choice in their mate. Their sex life was supposed to come second to the woman's role in the man's household and in his lineage, and there was no guarantee that the couple ever would

Zsa Zsa Gabor obtains a quickie divorce in Mexico. Many Hollywood stars follow a pattern of "serial monogamy." (Wide World)

be personally compatible, nor was that of crucial importance. Thus, if the husband chose a second wife, it would be a woman who appealed to him in different ways and for different reasons. At the same time, the first wife would be glad to have another person around to share the household chores, and since the second wife was usually much younger than the first, the patterns of authority would be clearly defined. By bringing in a second wife, a couple could provide for themselves, each in his or her own way, for the future.

Degree of Authority

Since a marriage establishes ties between two or more individuals and sets up new roles, there must be new patterns of authority to go along with these new roles. In the Chinese example noted above, the society is male-dominated to the extreme. Men make all the important decisions and are the focus of attention. A woman can be divorced and returned to her family if she does not produce a male heir for her husband. (Ironically, we know now that it is the sperm cell contributed by the male and not the egg cell contributed by the female that determines the sex of the infant.) The woman in Chinese society is the head of her internal household and exercises authority over her children, but outwardly the marriage is based upon the principle of male dominance and authority.

Another example of an extremely male-dominated family is described by J.K. Campbell for the Sarakatsani of Greece. Among these rural pastoral people, it is important for a man to have many sons, for as Campbell says, "Sons bring prestige, daughters do not. When the husband enters the hut for the first time after the birth of a daughter, his wife turns her head away and lowers her eyes in shame."[1]

The opposite case, where the authority rests primarily with the women, is much less common. In societies where descent is through the female line, such as in the Trobriands or among the Nayar, females tend to have more authority simply because the children are members of their kin group and not that of their father. Yet even in such cases, we find that men have not relinquished all of their authority, for the role of the mother's brother becomes more important as that of the father diminishes.

1. J.K. Campbell, *Honour, Family and Patronage*. New York, Cambridge University Press, 1972, p. 56.

One of the clearest cases of authority resting with the woman is found in the so-called "matrifocal" family typical of lower-class ghetto life in the United States and in other industrializing countries. In this situation, because of the economic and social strains upon the family, the role of the father is minimized. The marriage bond becomes weak or nonexistent, and as a result the woman is not in a secure position as the wife of a single man, but rather she must form alliances with a succession of men for varying lengths of time. The result is that where the father is frequently absent, the only continuity in the family is that between the mother and her children, and the family life becomes centered around the mother rather than the father.

Residence

Where a couple lives after they are married is subject to variation from one culture to another. In American society the newlyweds are usually expected to go out and find a place of their own, rather than move in with the parents of either one. This pattern is called *neolocal* residence (*neo* = new), and it is typical of most industrial nations in the world. It fits in closely with the economic system that demands mobility, so that the family is not tied to one place or a larger group of people. It also fits in well with the prevalence of the nuclear family, although it should be pointed out that while the ideal of nuclear families and neolocal residence might exist in Western nations, they cannot be realized in many countries which are experiencing an acute housing shortage. In the nations of Eastern Europe, such as Czechoslovakia, Poland, and even Russia, the movement from the country to the city has been so rapid that housing facilities are simply inadequate to take care of all the people who want to move to the city. As a result, people are forced to double up with relatives in small apartments, while they sit patiently on a long waiting list for a place of their own.

Another possibility is to reside with the family of either the bride or the groom, a practice prescribed in some societies. If the new family is established in the household of the groom's father it is called *patrilocal,* and this practice is frequently found in patrilineal societies where descent is traced through the male line as well. If the new family is set up in the household of the bride's mother, it is called *matrilocal,* and while it is less common, it is usually found in conjunction with a matrilineal society.

Choice of Mate

In no society do people have an absolutely free reign when choosing a mate. Even in our own society, where the restrictions are almost nonexistent, there are clearly defined laws prohibiting a person from marrying a close relative. In addition, there are social rules that do not carry the weight of laws but operate just as effectively in limiting marriage choices. Thus, in spite of increasingly common mixed marriages, for most Americans the notion of interracial marriage is unacceptable, and to a lesser extent the idea of a marriage between two people of different religions is equally unpopular for some. Whether we recognize it or not, we are extremely likely to marry someone of the same social class, the same race, the same basic religious conviction—in short, someone just like us in almost all ways. We may think we are exercising our right of free choice, but we are really acting within the limitations imposed upon us by our culture, which we have

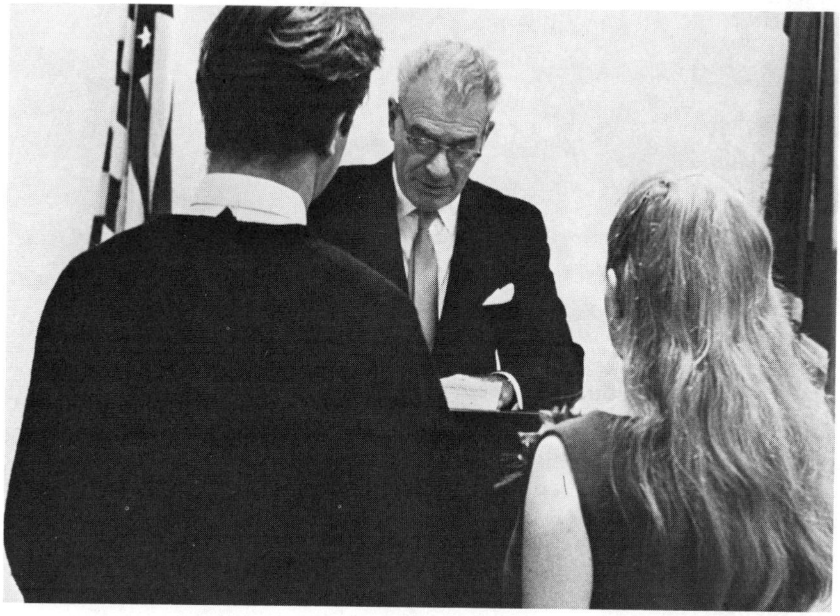

A simple marriage ceremony performed by a justice of the peace. (Anna Kaufman Moon, Frederic Lewis)

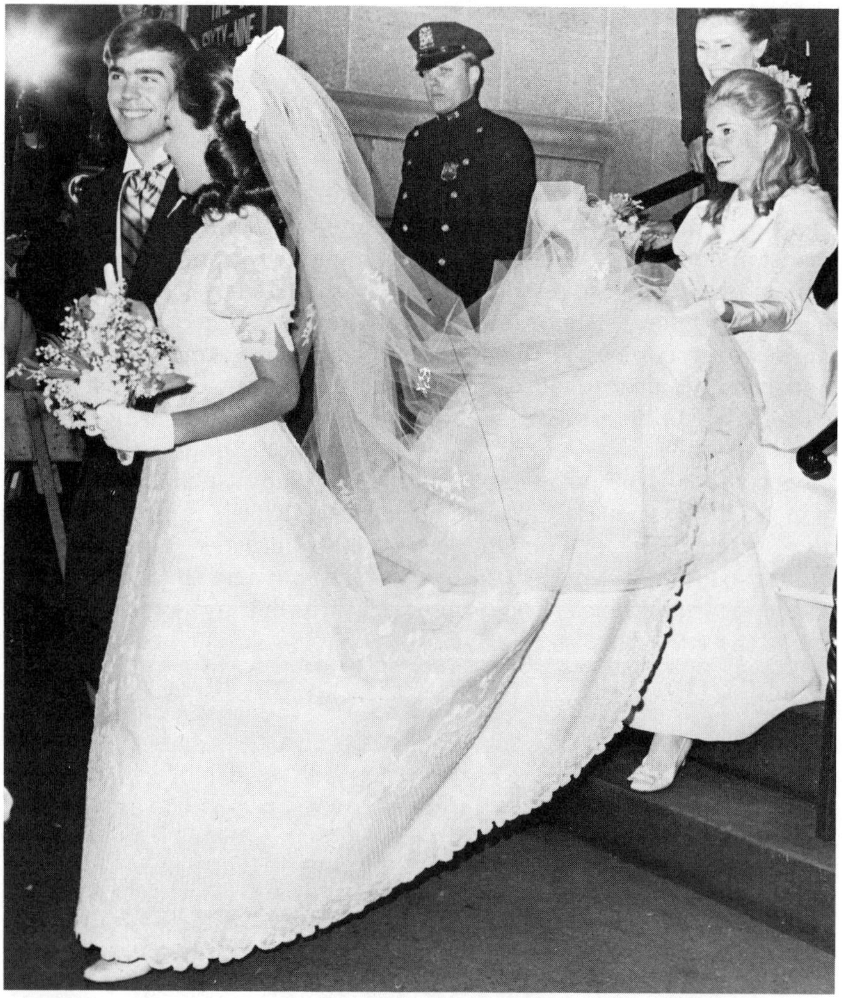

No one was surprised when David Eisenhower married Julie Nixon. (Wide World)

had drummed into our heads time and again as we grew up and learned what the appropriate patterns of behavior were in our culture.

Not every culture allows for any freedom in the choice of a mate. The rules restricting potential marriage partners can exclude or include a variety of different people, which immediately poses limits to the choice an individual can make. Usually there are rules that force an individual to marry *outside* the limits of a certain group (at least the nuclear family), while other rules define a different set of limits

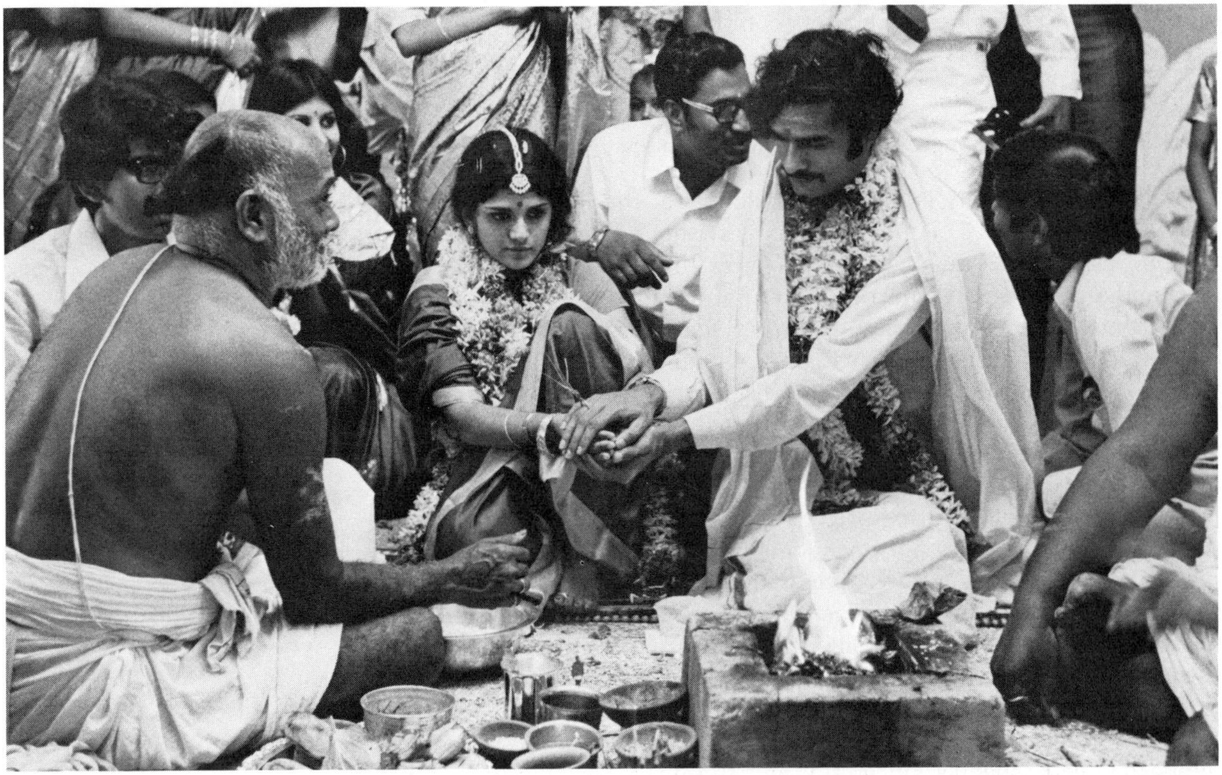

The bride and groom both wear flower garlands at their wedding in Madras, India. (Bernard Pierre Wolff, Photo Researchers)

for a group *within* which that individual should seek a partner. When marriage is *prohibited* within a group (however that group is defined) we call it *exogamy* (*exo:* outside; *gamy:* marriage). Conversely, when marriage is *confined* to a specific group, we have *endogamy* (*endo:* within). Sometimes these two principles can operate together to restrict marriage choices, while other times only one of the two will be in force. For example, in American culture we really don't have any strict rules of exogamy—that is, that we must marry outside of a particular group—except for the laws that govern what is defined as incest. (Note that actually exogamy and incest are two separate things. Incest deals with sexual relations, while marriage deals with conjugal relations; they are considered together because marriage and sex usually go together, but technically they are different.) However, in our society we do have very strong social prohibitions against interracial marriages (in some states these prohibitions actually take the form of legal restrictions). Thus we could say that America practices race endogamy.

Economic Exchange Accompanying Marriage

Not every society expects an exchange at the time of marriage. In the United States a couple may marry without any economic transaction at all. However, in many societies there is an exchange that accompanies the actual marriage ceremony, indicating that for most people marriage is much more than a social ceremony uniting two people. Two patterns emerge in the exchange, payments from the groom's family to the bride's, called *bride-price,* and payments from the bride's family to the groom's, called *dowry.* A marriage can be accompanied by one or both, and the exchanges can be equal or unequal.

The payment of bride-price seems to imply that a woman is viewed as a commodity; however, this is not always true. In general, where the woman comes to live with her husband in his father's household or at least in the same village, her labor potential is transferred from the household where she was born and raised to the one where she will live henceforth. Thus the bride-price can be seen as a way of compensating the girl's family for the loss of her services. In addition, the new role of the woman in her marriage is to produce heirs for her husband's kin group, and the girl's own family has no legal claim to her children.

The idea behind the opposite type of payment, dowry, is that the man brings into the marriage what wealth he has inherited, plus his labor and earning capacity. The woman, on the other hand, will probably not inherit much if anything from her parents, and her potential earning power is greatly reduced by the fact that she will be expected to bear and raise children and take care of the household chores. In some societies dowry is used as a means to acquire a more prestigious or higher class husband for a girl. In traditional Greek peasant society, for example, a girl's family would save up for many years to provide her with a suitable dowry to acquire a man who had some education, or worked in the city, or who owned a great deal of land. It is an old Greek saying that a man who has many sons has been blessed, while a man with many daughters has been cursed and faces a life of poverty and ruin.

A third alternative is the equal exchange between both families, so that the dowry and bride-price match each other in value. One might think that this would be unnecessary, except that it is once again a reaffirmation of the fact that marriage is an economic arrangement, not just a social ceremony. Also, by demanding equal exchange, a family can assure their son or daughter of a spouse of at least equal social standing, for by putting up a dowry or bride-price of a certain value they eliminate as future mates for their daughter or son anyone whose family cannot match that value. Equal exchange is thus another way of restricting the choice of mates in a subtle manner according to unwritten rules.

Age at Marriage

The age at which individuals of either sex are expected to marry is subject to great variation from one culture to another. For men, marriage is usually not appropriate until they are self-supporting, although here we must make a distinction between the actual marriage ceremony and the establishment of a household. In some areas of India, for example, a boy is married even before he reaches puberty, but his young bride then returns to her parents' home and the couple does not take up residence together for several years thereafter. At the other extreme is the case of the male in traditional Irish peasant society. A man was not supposed to marry until he had taken over the proprietorship of his father's farm. This meant that until his father died or retired, the boy was under his authority and did not have the means to support his own family. In many cases this situation extended until the son was well into his forties, and his position in the family was emphasized by the fact that other men in the community continued to refer to him as "boy," although he was in all other respects a fully grown man.

On the other hand, marriage for women is more closely related to the biological function of childbearing. Obviously any society that forced all of its women to wait until their forties to marry would soon die out. However, it is not unknown for women to postpone marriage (or for society to exert pressure upon women to marry later) in order to exert some measure of population control, especially where there are no artificial means of birth control available. Since a woman's fertile period usually lasts from her early teens until her forties, by

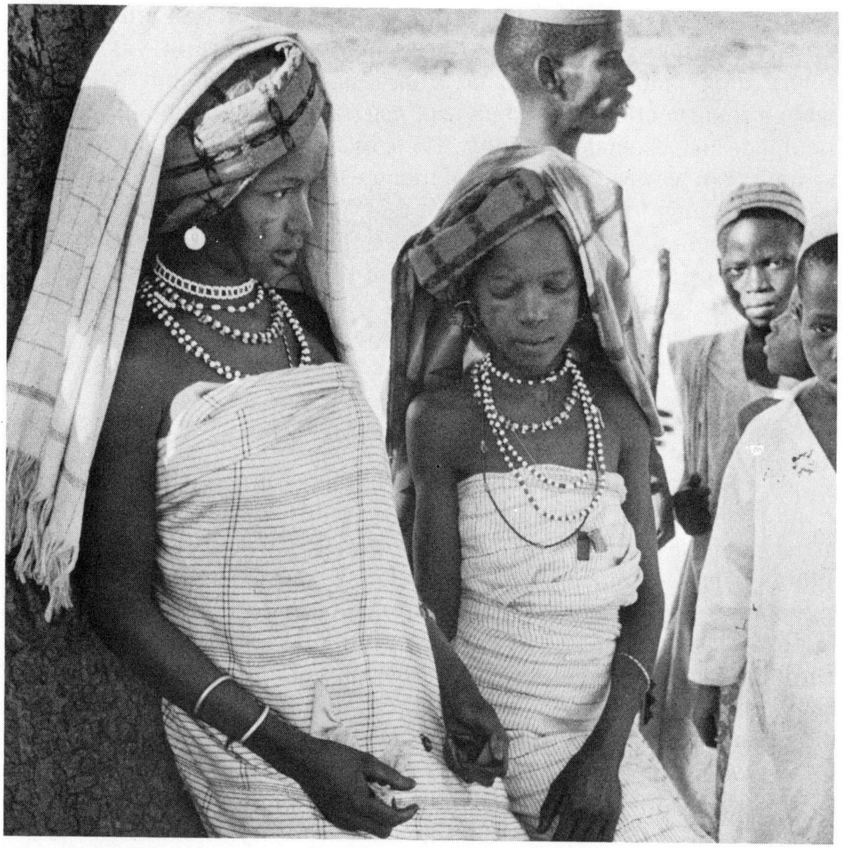

Pretty, marriageable Nigerian girls await beginning of beating ceremony, which will probably produce proud husbands for them. (Marilyn Silverstone, Magnum)

postponing marriage until the late twenties or thirties a woman can effectively limit the number of children she bears.

A rare case is found among the Tiwi, who have been mentioned several times in the last few chapters due to their rather unusual marriage practices. The Tiwi believe that a woman can become pregnant at any time (the fact that young girls and old women do not does not seem to matter), and they also believe that it is a very serious offense for a woman to become pregnant if she is not married. Therefore, a girl is betrothed even before she is born—that is, if the child is a girl, she already has had a husband selected for her by her father, and she is married from the day of her birth. If her husband should die, the woman is immediately transferred to another man, so that she never is unmarried throughout her entire life. Other societies have similar practices in which a couple is designated as future marriage partners in their early childhood, but the Tiwi must rank as the earliest in terms of the age of girls at their actual marriage.

Strength of Marriage Bond

Some marriages can be dissolved rather easily, while others cannot be terminated except by the death of one of the spouses. In Hollywood, it seems as if marriages have all but lost their meaning, while in Italy until a few years ago the thought of divorce was out of the question. Even today, under the "liberalized" divorce law in Italy, the couple must be separated for five years before a divorce can be granted. In some cases the practice of divorce and the strength of the marriage bond has to do with the economic exchange involved in the marriage. If the dowry or bride-price must be returned, the bond is stronger because the families are reluctant to give up what they have received.

In other cases, the strength of the bond is a one-sided affair, depending upon who has the power and authority in the society. A tradition in Islamic culture allows a man to divorce his wife simply by stating before a witness "I divorce you, I divorce you, I divorce you!" (If it were that easy in the United States, a lot of lawyers would be out of a job!) Usually the termination of a marriage is a part of the male prerogative that exists in most societies, although in our divorce courts the majority of cases are filed by women, apparently reflecting the different economic roles of men and women in that divorce frequently entails the payment of alimony by the man. The following short notice from a newspaper column gives a rather interesting example of how an Iranian woman managed to end her marriage:

> When Farideh Ghayebi, 22, of Tehran, found herself hoist on the wrong point of a marital triangle, she sold her husband to her rival for 700,000 rials (about $9,000). Divorce isn't easy in Iran, it seems, but when both parties reach a financial agreement, it is usually granted. "My husband wasn't such an extraordinary dish after all," said Mrs. Ghayebi. "I'm going on a long vacation with the price I got for him. I'm sure I'll find a better man later."[2]

2. International Herald Tribune, 1972.

Possibility of Remarriage

Whether a marriage is terminated by divorce or by the death of one of the spouses, the question of remarriage for one or both partners is another variable in the institution of marriage as it is found in different cultures. At one extreme is the case where no remarriage is possible. In India among the high castes a custom known as *suttee* dictated that when a man died, his wife was supposed to throw herself upon his funeral pyre and burn to death as he was being cremated. This practice, of course, is most effective in eliminating any possibility of remarriage for a woman, although there is (not surprisingly) no similar custom binding a man when his wife dies. In other cultures, when a woman's husband dies, it is considered the duty of the man's brother or brothers to provide for her, and she is married to one of them. It can also happen that when a woman dies, her husband obtains marital rights to an unmarried sister, if she has one. In both cases, the custom reflects once again the economic interest in the marriage, for the payment of a bride-price or dowry entitles the family to the services of the man or woman, and a premature death does not relieve the family of the deceased from that obligation.

Other cultures have different customs governing the remarriage of an individual, which could vary according to whether the marriage ended by death or by divorce, and according to the age of the individual. For example, in Swiss peasant villages it was very rare for a woman to remarry if she were widowed after her childbearing years had passed, but if she were still young it was perfectly acceptable for her to marry again. In the United States we generally expect people to go through a period of mourning—usually about a year—for a deceased spouse, but we have no similar expectations where the marriage ended in divorce. In fact, we are not very surprised when a man or woman remarries within a very short period after being divorced (it has been known to happen on the very same day).

Nature of the Marriage Union

The rights and duties of each marriage partner differ widely from one culture to another. Henry VIII used as a justification for at least one of his divorces the fact that his wife did not provide him with a male heir. In traditional China, providing a child was not enough.

It had to be a male heir, to carry on the tradition and name of the patrilineage. In our own society the traditional rights and duties of each spouse have been changing quite rapidly, and what were legitimate expectations a generation ago are no longer agreed upon by all. For example, a man can no longer expect that his wife will assume the traditional role of "housewife," which includes cooking, cleaning and raising a family. With the introduction of birth control and equal rights and employment opportunities for women, the traditional female roles are no longer so clearly defined; women have choices they did not have a few years ago. What this means for the institution of marriage in the United States is that the rights and duties of each partner will have to be redefined according to the wishes and preferences of both. Many more people are choosing not to have children today than a generation ago, and working wives are making it necessary for their husbands to assume a greater responsibility for the household maintenance. Also, with the traditional role of sexual consort no longer limited to a marriage partner (the pill had a lot to do with this), many people are preferring to assume much of the nature of married life without actually going through the official ceremony, which makes for a much more flexible, if somewhat less "stable," living arrangement.

Actually, recent statistics indicate that more people are getting married than ever. More couples may be living together before (or without) marriage, but eventually most do get married, though not necessarily to each other. What is really changing is the open acceptance of premarital sex, which in turn changes the nature of marriage as an institution and the expectations of a couple entering into it.

Not long ago I was interviewed by a local radio station concerning my thoughts on whether the institution of marriage was breaking down in the United States. My answer was that it was not breaking down, but going through a period of rapid adjustment to the many changes that we have experienced in the last generation in our society. It may be that if fewer people choose the formality of a marriage ceremony as a prerequisite to a married life style, we will have to redefine what we mean by marriage. But as long as there is a need for men and women to interact in order to reproduce, and as long as men and women seek out each other's company in any kind of permanent or even semipermanent relationship, there will be something that we can call marriage.

In the article that follows, Laura Bohannan describes her difficulty in trying to tell the Tiv, among whom she was working at the time, the story of *Hamlet.* She would describe a particular sequence in the play, only to be told by her audience that she was wrong, and that she did not understand the motives that led the characters to act as they did. In the end, she gave up in frustration, unable to convince them that her interpretation of *Hamlet* was correct.

The problem that Laura Bohannan encountered is directly related to the concepts of kinship and marriage and the family. She was telling her version of the story, based upon her own cultural interpretation of what was the proper behavior for each of the characters. A woman in mourning, for example, is not expected to remarry immediately. It looks particularly bad when her next husband is the brother of her recently deceased spouse. Yet among the Tiv, this is not only accepted, but *expected.* A younger brother will marry his older brother's widow immediately, so that he may protect her and provide a father for her children. The roles in the two societies are thus opposite each other, and this was why the Tiv elders could not agree with Bohannan's rendition of *Hamlet.*

Throughout the article the author cites examples of role conflict within a kinship situation, where the appropriate behavior according to the Shakespearean context was inappropriate according to Tiv culture. At the end, it is easy to see how if one does not start out with the same expectations, one is likely to react very differently to the behavior one observes.

Shakespeare in the Bush

Laura Bohannan

Just before I left Oxford for the Tiv in West Africa, conversation turned to the season at Stratford. "You Americans," said a friend, "often have difficulty with Shakespeare. He was, after all, a very English poet, and one can easily misinterpret the universal by misunderstanding the particular."

I protested that human nature is pretty much the same the whole world over; at least the general plot and motivation of the greater tragedies would always be clear—everywhere—although some details of custom might have to be explained and difficulties of translation might produce other slight changes. To end an argument we could not conclude, my friend gave me a copy of *Hamlet* to study in the African bush: it would, he hoped, lift my mind above its primitive surroundings, and possibly I might, by prolonged meditation, achieve the grace of correct interpretation.

It was my second field trip to the African tribe, and I thought myself ready to live in one of its remote sections—an area difficult to cross even on foot. I eventually settled on the hillock of a very knowledgeable old man, the head of a homestead of some hundred and forty people, all of whom were either his close relatives or their wives and children. Like the other elders of the vicinity, the old man spent most of his time performing ceremonies seldom seen these days in the more accessible parts of the tribe. I was delighted. Soon there would be three months of enforced isolation and leisure, between the harvest that takes place just before the rising of the swamps and the clearing of new farms when the water goes down. Then, I thought, they would have even more time to perform ceremonies and explain them to me.

I was quite mistaken. Most of the ceremonies demanded the presence of elders from several homesteads. As the swamps rose, the old men found it too difficult to walk from one homestead to the next, and the ceremonies gradually ceased. As the swamps rose even higher, all activities but one came to an end. The women brewed beer from maize and millet. Men, women, and children sat on their hillocks and drank it.

People began to drink at dawn. By midmorning the whole homestead was singing, dancing, and drumming. When it rained, people had to sit inside their huts: there they drank and sang or they drank and told stories. In any case, by noon or before, I either had to join the party or retire to my own hut and my books. "One does not discuss serious matters when there is beer. Come, drink with us." Since I lacked their capacity for the thick native beer, I spent more and more time with *Hamlet*. Before the end of the second month, grace descended on me. I was quite sure that *Hamlet* had only one possible

(Reprinted from *Natural History*, 75 (1966), by permission of the author.

interpretation, and that one universally obvious.

Early every morning, in the hope of having some serious talk before the beer party, I used to call on the old man at his reception hut—a circle of posts supporting a thatched roof above a low mud wall to keep out wind and rain. One day I crawled through the low doorway and found most of the men of the homestead sitting huddled in their ragged cloths on stools, low plank beds, and reclining chairs, warming themselves against the chill of the rain around a smoky fire. In the center were three pots of beer. The party had started.

The old man greeted me cordially. "Sit down and drink." I accepted a large calabash full of beer, poured some into a small drinking gourd, and tossed it down. Then I poured some more into the same gourd for the man second in seniority to my host before I handed my calabash over to a young man for further distribution. Important people shouldn't ladle beer themselves.

"It is better like this," the old man said, looking at me approvingly and plucking at the thatch that had caught in my hair. "You should sit and drink with us more often. Your servants tell me that when you are not with us, you sit inside your hut looking at a paper."

The old man was acquainted with four kinds of "papers": tax receipts, bride price receipts, court fee receipts, and letters. The messenger who brought him letters from the chief used them mainly as a badge of office, for he always knew what was in them and told the old man. Personal letters for the few who had relatives in the government or mission stations were kept until someone went to a large market where there was a letter writer and reader. Since my arrival, letters were brought to me to be read. A few men also brought me bride price receipts, privately, with requests to change the figures to a higher sum. I found moral arguments were of no avail, since in-laws are fair game, and the technical hazards of forgery difficult to explain to an illiterate people. I did not wish them to think me silly enough to look at any such papers for days on end, and I hastily explained that my "paper" was one of the "things of long ago" of my country.

"Ah," said the old man. "Tell us."

I protested that I was not a storyteller. Storytelling is a skilled art among them; their standards are high, and the audiences critical—and vocal in their criticism. I protested in vain. This morning they wanted to hear a story while they drank. They threatened to tell me no more stories until I told them one of mine. Finally, the old man promised that no one would criticize my style "for we know you are struggling with our language." "But," put in one of the elders, "you must explain what we do not understand, as we do when we tell you our stories." Realizing that here was my chance to prove *Hamlet* universally intelligible, I agreed.

The old man handed me some more beer to help me on with my storytelling. Men filled their long wooden pipes and knocked coals from the fire to place in the pipe bowls; then, puffing contentedly, they sat back to listen. I began in the proper style, "Not yesterday, not yesterday, but long ago, a thing occurred. One night three men were keeping watch outside the homestead of the great chief, when suddenly they saw the former chief approach them."

"Why was he no longer their chief?"

"He was dead," I explained. "That is why they were troubled and afraid when they saw him."

"Impossible," began one of the elders, handing his pipe on to his neighbor, who interrupted, "Of course it wasn't the dead chief. It was an omen sent by a witch. Go on."

Slightly shaken, I continued. "One of these three was a man who knew things"—the closest translation for scholar, but unfortunately it also meant witch. The second elder looked triumphantly at the first. "So he spoke to the dead chief saying, 'Tell us what we must do so you may rest in your grave,' but the dead chief did not answer. He vanished, and they could see him no more. Then the man who knew things—his name was Horatio—said this event was the affair of the dead chief's son, Hamlet."

There was a general shaking of heads round the circle. "Had the dead chief no living brothers? Or was this son the chief?"

"No," I replied. "That is, he had one living brother who became the chief when the elder brother died."

The old man muttered: such omens were matters for chiefs and elders, not for youngsters; no good could come of going behind a chief's back; clearly Horatio was not a man who knew things.

"Yes, he was," I insisted, shooing a chicken away from my beer. "In our country the son is next to the father. The dead chief's younger brother had become the great chief. He had also married his elder brother's widow only about a month after the funeral."

"He did well," the old man beamed and announced to the others, "I told you that if we knew more about Europeans, we would find they really were very like us. In our country also," he added to me, "the younger brother marries the elder brother's widow and becomes the father of his children. Now, if your uncle, who married your widowed mother, is your father's full brother, then he will be a real father to you. Did Hamlet's father and uncle have one mother?"

His question barely penetrated my mind; I was too upset and thrown too far off balance by having one of the most important elements of *Hamlet* knocked straight out of the picture. Rather uncertainly I said that I thought they had the same mother, but I wasn't sure—the story didn't say. The old man told me severely that these genealogical details made all the difference and that when I got home I must ask the elders about it. He shouted out the door to one of his younger wives to bring his goatskin bag.

Determined to save what I could of the mother motif, I took a deep breath and began again. "The son Hamlet was very sad because his mother had married again so quickly. There was no need for her to do so, and it is our custom for a widow not to go to her next husband until she has mourned for two years."

"Two years is too long," objected the wife, who had appeared with the old man's battered goatskin bag. "Who will hoe your farms for you while you have no husband?"

"Hamlet," I retorted without thinking, "was old enough to hoe his mother's farms himself. There was no need for her to remarry." No one looked convinced. I gave up. "His mother and the great chief told Hamlet not to be sad, for the great chief himself would be a father to Hamlet. Furthermore, Hamlet would be the next chief: therefore he must stay to learn the things of a chief. Hamlet agreed to remain, and all the rest went off to drink beer."

While I paused, perplexed at how to render Hamlet's disgusted soliloquy to an audience convinced that Claudius and Gertrude had behaved in the best possible manner, one of the younger men asked me who had married the other wives of the dead chief.

"He had no other wives," I told him.

"But a chief must have many wives! How else can he brew beer and prepare food for all his guests?"

I said firmly that in our country even chiefs had only one wife, that they had servants to do their work, and that they paid them from tax money.

It was better, they returned, for a chief to have many wives and sons who would help him hoe his farms and feed his people; then everyone loved the chief who gave much and took nothing—taxes were a bad thing.

I agreed with the last comment, but for the rest fell back on their favorite way of fobbing off my questions: "That is the way it is done, so that is how we do it."

I decided to skip the soliloquy. Even if Claudius was here thought quite right to marry his brother's widow, there remained the poison motif, and I knew they would disapprove of fratricide. More hopefully I resumed, "That night Hamlet kept watch with the three who had seen his dead father. The dead chief again appeared, and although the others were afraid, Hamlet followed his dead father off to one side. When they were alone, Hamlet's dead father spoke."

"Omens can't talk!" The old man was emphatic.

"Hamlet's dead father wasn't an omen. Seeing him might have been an omen, but he was not." My audience looked as confused as I sounded. "It *was* Hamlet's dead father. It was a thing we call a 'ghost.'" I had to use the English word, for unlike many of the neighboring tribes, these people didn't believe in the survival after death of any individuating part of the personality.

"What is a 'ghost?' An omen?"

"No, a 'ghost' is someone who is dead but who walks around and can talk, and people can hear him and see him but not touch him."

They objected. "One can touch zombis."

"No, no! It was not a dead body the witches had animated to sacrifice and eat. No one else made Hamlet's dead father walk. He did it himself."

"Dead men can't walk" protested my audience as one man.

I was quite willing to compromise. "A 'ghost' is the dead man's shadow."

But again they objected. "Dead men cast no shadows."

"They do in my country," I snapped.

The old man quelled the babble of disbelief that arose immediately and told me with that insincere, but courteous, agreement one extends to the fancies of the young, ignorant, and superstitious, "No doubt in your country the dead can also walk without being zombis." From the depths of his bag he produced a withered fragment of kola nut, bit off one end to show it wasn't poisoned, and handed me the rest as a peace offering.

"Anyhow," I resumed, "Hamlet's dead father said that his own brother, the one who became chief, had poisoned him. He wanted Hamlet to avenge him. Hamlet believed this in his heart, for he did not like his father's brother." I took another swallow of beer. "In the country of the great chief, living in the same homestead, for it was a very large one, was an important elder who was often with the chief to advise and help him. His name was Polonius. Hamlet was courting his daughter, but her father and her brother . . . [I cast hastily about for some tribal analogy] warned her not to let Hamlet visit her when she was alone on her farm, for he would be a great chief and so could not marry her."

"Why not?" asked the wife, who had settled down on the edge of the old man's chair. He frowned at her for asking stupid questions and growled, "They lived in the same homestead."

"That was not the reason," I informed them. "Polonius was a stranger who lived in the homestead because he helped the chief, not because he was a relative."

"Then why couldn't Hamlet marry her?"

"He could have," I explained, "but Polonius didn't think he would. After all, Hamlet was a man of great importance who ought to marry a chief's daughter, for in his country a man could have only one wife. Polonius was afraid that if Hamlet made love to his daughter, then no one else would give a high price for her."

"That might be true," remarked one of the shrewder elders, "but a chief's son would give his mistress's father enough presents and patronage to more than make up the difference. Polonius sounds like a fool to me."

"Many people think he was," I agreed. "Meanwhile Polonius sent his son Laertes off to Paris to learn the things of that country, for it was the homestead of a very great chief indeed. Because he was afraid that Laertes might waste a lot of money on beer and women and gambling, or get into trouble by fighting, he sent one of his servants to Paris secretly, to spy out what Laertes was doing. One day Hamlet came upon Polonius's daughter Ophelia. He behaved so oddly he frightened her. Indeed"—I was fumbling for words to express the dubious quality of Hamlet's madness—"the chief and many others had also noticed that when Hamlet talked one could understand the words but not what they meant. Many people thought that he had become mad." My audience suddenly became much more attentive. "The great chief wanted to know what was wrong with Hamlet, so he sent for two of Hamlet's age mates [school friends would have taken long explanation] to talk to Hamlet and find out what troubled his heart. Hamlet, seeing that they had been bribed by the chief to betray him, told them nothing. Polonius, however, insisted that Hamlet was mad because he had been forbidden to see Ophelia, whom he loved."

"Why," inquired a bewildered voice, "should anyone bewitch Hamlet on that account?"

"Bewitch him?"

"Yes, only witchcraft can make anyone mad, unless, of course, one sees the beings that lurk in the forest."

I stopped being a storyteller, took out my notebook and demanded to be told more about these two causes of madness. Even while they spoke and I jotted notes, I tried to calculate the effect of this new factor on the plot. Hamlet had not been exposed to the beings that lurk in the forests. Only his relatives in the male line could bewitch him. Barring relatives not mentioned by Shakespeare, it had to be Claudius who was attempting to harm him. And, of course, it was.

For the moment I staved off questions by saying that the great chief also refused to believe that Hamlet was mad for the love of Ophelia and nothing else. "He was sure that something much more important was troubling Hamlet's heart."

"Now Hamlet's age mates," I continued, "had brought with them a famous storyteller. Hamlet decided to have this man tell the chief and all his homestead a story about a man who had poisoned his brother because he desired his brother's wife and wished to be chief himself. Hamlet was sure the great chief could not hear the story without making a sign if he was indeed guilty, and then he would discover whether his dead father had told him the truth."

The old man interrupted, with deep cunning, "Why should a father lie to his son?" he asked.

I hedged: "Hamlet wasn't sure that it really was his dead father." It was impossible to say anything, in that language, about devil-inspired visions.

"You mean," he said "it actually was an omen, and he knew witches sometimes send false ones. Hamlet was a fool not to go to one skilled in reading omens and divining the truth in the first place. A man-who-sees-the-truth could have told him how his father died, if he really had been poisoned, and if there was witchcraft in it; then Hamlet could have called the elders to settle the matter."

The shrewd elder ventured to disagree. "Because his father's brother was a great chief, one-who-sees-the-truth might therefore have been afraid to tell it. I think it was for that reason that a friend of Hamlet's father—a witch and an elder—sent an omen so his friend's son would know. Was the omen true?"

"Yes," I said, abandoning ghosts and the devil; a witch-sent omen it would have to be. "It was true, for when the storyteller was telling his tale before all the homestead, the great chief rose in fear. Afraid that Hamlet knew his secret he planned to have him killed."

The stage set of the next bit presented some difficulties of translation. I began cautiously. "The great chief told Hamlet's mother to find out from her son what he knew. But because a woman's children are always first in her heart, he had the important elder Polonius hide behind a cloth that hung against the wall of Hamlet's mother's sleeping hut. Hamlet started to scold his mother for what she had done."

There was a shocked murmur from everyone. A man should never scold his mother.

"She called out in fear, and Polonius moved

behind the cloth. Shouting, 'A rat!' Hamlet took his machete and slashed through the cloth." I paused for dramatic effect. "He had killed Polonius!"

The old men looked at each other in supreme disgust. "That Polonius truly was a fool and a man who knew nothing! What child would not know enough to shout, 'It's me!'" With a pang, I remembered that these people are ardent hunters, always armed with bow, arrow, and machete; at the first rustle in the grass an arrow is aimed and ready, and the hunter shouts "Game!" If no human voice answers immediately, the arrow speeds on its way. Like a good hunter Hamlet had shouted, "A rat!"

I rushed in to save Polonius's reputation. "Polonius did speak. Hamlet heard him. But he thought it was the chief and wished to kill him to avenge his father. He had meant to kill him earlier that evening. . . ." I broke down, unable to describe to these pagans, who had no belief in individual afterlife, the difference between dying at one's prayers and dying "unhousell'd, disappointed, unaneled."

This time I had shocked my audience seriously. "For a man to raise his hand against his father's brother and the one who has become his father—that is a terrible thing. The elders ought to let such a man be bewitched."

I nibbled at my kola nut in some perplexity, then pointed out that after all the man had killed Hamlet's father.

"No," pronounced the old man, speaking less to me than to the young men sitting behind the elders. "If your father's brother has killed your father, you must appeal to your father's age mates; *they* may avenge him. No man may use violence against his senior relatives." Another thought struck him. "But if his father's brother had indeed been wicked enough to bewitch Hamlet and make him mad that would be a good story indeed, for it would be his fault that Hamlet, being mad, no longer had any sense and thus was ready to kill his father's brother."

There was a murmur of applause. *Hamlet* was again a good story to them, but it no longer seemed quite the same story to me. As I thought over the coming complications of plot and motive, I lost courage and decided to skim over dangerous ground quickly.

"The great chief," I went on, "was not sorry that Hamlet had killed Polonius. It gave him a reason to send Hamlet away, with his two treacherous age mates, with letters to a chief of a far country, saying that Hamlet should be killed. But Hamlet changed the writing on their papers, so that the chief killed his age mates instead." I encountered a reproachful glare from one of the men whom I had told undetectable forgery was not merely immoral but beyond human skill. I looked the other way.

"Before Hamlet could return, Laertes came back for his father's funeral. The great chief told him Hamlet had killed Polonius. Laertes swore to kill Hamlet because of this, and because his sister Ophelia, hearing her father had been killed by the man she loved, went mad and drowned in the river."

"Have you already forgotten what we told you?" The old man was reproachful. "One cannot take vengeance on a madman; Hamlet killed Polonius in his madness. As for the girl, she not only went mad, she was drowned. Only witches can make people drown. Water itself can't hurt anything. It is merely something one drinks and bathes in."

I began to get cross. "If you don't like the story, I'll stop."

The old man made soothing noises and himself poured me some more beer. "You tell the story well, and we are listening. But it is clear that the elders of your country have never told you what the story really means. No, don't interrupt! We believe you when you say your marriage customs are different, or your clothes and weapons. But people are the same everywhere; therefore, there are always witches and it is we, the elders, who know how witches work. We told you it was the great chief who wished to kill

Hamlet, and now your own words have proved us right. Who were Ophelia's male relatives?"

"There were only her father and her brother." Hamlet was clearly out of my hands.

"There must have been many more; this also you must ask of your elders when you get back to your country. From what you tell us, since Polonius was dead, it must have been Laertes who killed Ophelia, although I do not see the reason for it."

We had emptied one pot of beer, and the old men argued the point with slightly tipsy interest. Finally one of them demanded of me, "What did the servant of Polonius say on his return?"

With difficulty I recollected Reynaldo and his mission. "I don't think he did return before Polonius was killed."

"Listen," said the older, "and I will tell you how it was and how your story will go, then you may tell me if I am right. Polonius knew his son would get into trouble, and so he did. He had many fines to pay for fighting, and debts from gambling. But he had only two ways of getting money quickly. One was to marry off his sister at once, but it is difficult to find a man who will marry a woman desired by the son of a chief. For if the chief's heir commits adultery with your wife, what can you do? Only a fool calls a case against a man who will someday be his judge. Therefore Laertes had to take the second way: he killed his sister by witchcraft, drowning her so he could secretly sell her body to the witches."

I raised an objection. "They found her body and buried it. Indeed Laertes jumped into the grave to see his sister once more—so, you see, the body was truly there. Hamlet, who had just come back, jumped in after him."

"What did I tell you?" The elder appealed to the others. "Laertes was up to no good with his sister's body. Hamlet prevented him, because the chief's heir, like a chief, does not wish any other man to grow rich and powerful. Laertes would be angry, because he would have killed his sister without benefit to himself. In our country he would try to kill Hamlet for that reason. Is this not what happened?"

"More or less," I admitted. "When the great chief found Hamlet was still alive, he encouraged Laertes to try to kill Hamlet and arranged a fight with machetes between them. In the fight both the young men were wounded to death. Hamlet's mother drank the poisoned beer that the chief meant for Hamlet in case he won the fight. When he saw his mother die of poison, Hamlet, dying, managed to kill his father's brother with his machete."

"You see, I was right!" exclaimed the elder.

"That was a very good story," added the old man, "and you told it with very few mistakes. There was just one more error, at the very end. The poison Hamlet's mother drank was obviously meant for the survivor of the fight, whichever it was. If Laertes had won, the great chief would have poisoned him, for no one would know that he arranged Hamlet's death. Then, too, he need not fear Laertes' witchcraft; it takes a strong heart to kill one's only sister by witchcraft.

"Sometime," concluded the old man, gathering his ragged toga about him, "you must tell us some more stories of your country. We, who are elders, will instruct you in their true meaning, so that when you return to your own land your elders will see that you have not been sitting in the bush, but among those who know things and who have taught you wisdom."

Summary

Kinship is the system of defining relationships and organizing relatives into different categories. Although in American society it is relatively unimportant as a determinant of how we organize the rest of our life, for most people in the world kinship provides the basis for all other social relations. By studying kinship in other societies we are better able to understand our own system, and the role it plays in our lives.

Kinship terms are a way of categorizing relatives. Such terms are based not only upon biological relationships between individuals, but upon social relationships as well—that is, kinship terms designate certain patterns of behavior expected from individuals. Who a culture places in any particular category can vary, depending upon what the members of that culture consider to be significant factors in determining relationships. In American culture we use the factors of sex, generation, descent, and consanguineality in establishing kinship categories; other cultures do not necessarily follow this same pattern, but can instead rely upon additional features of kinship.

Marriage and the family are institutions that exist in every human society, although the form they take can differ greatly. Within the limits of what we consider to be a family, there can be anything from a nuclear family (parents and children) to a residential group, called an extended family, that includes many additional relatives. The Nayar of India provide an example of the minimal family unit, where the family is centered around the woman and the husband exists only in a formal sense. Among the Trobriand Islanders, a matrilineal society, the mother's brother takes over what we would consider to be the father's role as authority figure, and the father is cast in a more friendly and informal role comparable to that of an uncle in our society.

Marriage differs from one society to another in a number of ways. A man or woman can have more than one spouse. Authority can be equal or it can be vested on the male or (less frequently) on the female side. Residence after marriage can be with the husband's family, the wife's family, or in a new place independent of either. Mates can be selected by the parents in an arranged marriage, or there can be varying degrees of free choice. Economic exchange can accompany the marriage, in the form of dowry, bride-price, or both. Age at marriage can range from infancy to delayed marriages in one's thirties or forties. The marriage bond can be strong, or it can be broken relatively easily; remarriage may be allowed (and in fact required), or it can be forbidden. And the rights and duties of each spouse can differ as the roles are defined by society.

Glossary

affinal The term referring to the relationship between people through marriage.

bifurcation A term referring to the means of distinguishing kinship relationships on the basis of the sex of the linking relative. For example, ego uses one term for father's brother and a different term for mother's brother (as opposed to our system, in which both would be called by the same term, "uncle").

bilateral descent The system of tracing descent (inheriting kin group membership) through both parents equally, i.e., through both the male and female line.

bride-price A payment made by the groom's family to the bride's as a part of the marriage contract.

clan A descent group in which the members assume that they are related but cannot actually trace their links back far enough to reach a common ancestor.

collateral A term referring to individuals who are related to Ego, but are not on the direct line of descent (e.g., mother's brother, mother's sister, father's brother, father's sister are collateral relatives of Ego, while Ego's mother, father, grandmother, grandfather, etc., are lineal relatives).

consanguineal The term referring to the biological or genetic relationship between people.

cross cousins A term referring to those cousins who are related to Ego through relatives of the opposite sex (such as father's sister's children or mother's brother's children).

descent The rules by which kin group membership is defined, and the way in which two blood relatives trace their relationship to a common ancestor.

dowry A payment made from the bride's family to the groom's as a part of the marriage contract.

Ego The central reference point from which all relationships can be calculated on a kinship diagram.

endogamy The practice that confines marriage to another member of an individual's group, or a practice against marrying outside the group.

Eskimo kinship terminology A general type of kinship terminology and the formal system of terms employed in American kinship. In this system, there is a separate term for "father" and "mother," while the categories of "father's brother" and "mother's brother" are merged under one term *(uncle),* and likewise "father's sister" and "mother's sister" are designated by a single term *(aunt).* The children of parents' siblings are merged into a single category, designated by the same term *(cousin).*

exogamy The prohibition against marriage within a group, however that group is defined.

extended family The family unit in which more than two generations are represented, and particularly when collateral as well as lineal relatives reside in the household (e.g., aunts, uncles, cousins).

fictive kinship ties An artificial category of relationships that have been formalized in a kinship system between individuals who are not biologically related.

incest taboo A set of rules found in some form in every society, which prohibit sexual relations between certain relatives.

inheritance The means by which material and nonmaterial possessions are transferred from one generation to the next.

joint family (joint extended family) A variant of the extended family unit which consists of a married couple, their unmarried sons and daughters, and the nuclear families of their married sons.

kinship The system of defining and organizing one's relatives.

kinship terminology The set of terms people use to distinguish between different categories of relatives. These terms may designate both a biological and social relationship.

lineage A descent group in which the members can trace their relationship to an actual common ancestor.

lineal A term referring to individuals who are related to ego through the direct line of descent.

matrifocal family The family unit in which the strongest bonds are those between the mother and her children. Family life may be centered around the mother or the father and mother together.

matrilineal descent The system of tracing descent (inheriting kin group membership) through the female line—through the mother's side.

matrilocal residence The residence pattern in which the couple resides in the bride's mother's household after marriage. Societies that practice this residence pattern usually trace descent through the female line.

monogamy The marriage of one man and one woman.

neolocal residence The residence pattern in which the couple, after marriage, establish a household of their own, rather than moving in with the parents of either the bride or groom. This pattern of residence is usually found in association with the nuclear family unit.

nuclear family The family unit composed of a married couple and their offspring.

parallel cousins A term referring to those cousins who are related to Ego through relatives of the same (parallel) sex, such as father's brother's children or mother's sister's children.

patrilineal descent The system of tracing descent (inheriting kin group membership) through the male line—through the father's side.

patrilocal residence The residence pattern in which the couple resides in the groom's father's household after marriage. This practice is frequently found associated with patrilineal descent.

polyandry The marriage practice whereby a woman has more than one husband at the same time.

polygamy The marriage practice whereby an individual has more than one spouse at the same time.

polygyny The marriage practice whereby a man has more than one wife at the same time.

serial monogamy A variant of monogamy, in which an individual of either sex takes a succession of spouses, one at a time, divorcing in between.

suttee A custom formerly found among the high castes in India, in which a woman would throw herself upon her husband's funeral pyre and burn to death as he was being cremated.

Questions for Discussion

1 It has been said that when two Australian Aborigines meet for the first time in a neutral setting, the first thing they try to do is establish the fact that they have a common relative. If they are unable to find any link between them, they assume they are enemies and may eventually try to kill each other. What does this story tell us about the importance of kinship in Australian Aborigine society? What differences would you expect to find in comparing kinship in their society and ours?

2 In American culture we consider nepotism (using family ties as the basis for handing out favors, especially desirable positions) to be wrong. In a business setting, when the president's son is appointed vice-president over other more qualified candidates, there is grumbling about the favoritism being shown. Why has kinship become so unimportant in our society? Is there something inherent in our economic or political system that makes nepotism unacceptable?

3 In Japan, a factory is organized as one big, happy family. Workers and management feel a close relationship, and the thought of a strike is still unheard of in many Japanese factories. The owner and the executives take a very paternalistic attitude toward the workers, and try to promote a personal relationship that seems to be quite the opposite of the impersonal nature of the American business operation. If there is something about the American system that fosters this impersonality and promotes individual achievement rather than nepotism, how can we explain the apparent success of Japanese industry in recent years?

4 Can you think of some examples of fictive kinship in your own life? Do you use kin terms for people who are not really related to you? What kind of behavior do you expect from them? Does it parallel the behavior you expect of those who fit that term?

5 What have been some effects upon the nature of marriage in American culture as a result of women's liberation, improved birth control, abortion, affirmative action programs for hiring more women, and other changes that have led to greater equality for women?

Suggestions for Additional Reading

Bates, Marston
1967 Gluttons and Libertines: Human Problems of Being Natural. New York: Vintage Books.

A humorous and thoroughly enjoyable book that combines fascinating insights and a lot of good natured fun in looking at Western attitudes toward food and sex.

Bohannan, Paul
1963 Social Anthropology. New York: Holt, Rinehart and Winston.

A basic introductory textbook, this volume contains an excellent section on kinship and marriage.

Chagnon, Napoleon
1974 Studying the Yąnomamö. New York: Holt, Rinehart and Winston.

In this companion volume to the author's ethnography of the Yąnomamo, a tribe in South America, Chagnon describes in detail how the anthropologist goes about discovering the kinship system in the course of field work.

Elkin, A. P.
1964 The Australian Aborigines. Garden City, N.Y.: Doubleday & Company.

The classic study of a people who have perhaps the most complex kinship system known.

Fox, Robin
1967 Kinship and Marriage. An Anthropological Perspective. Baltimore: Pelican Books.

A more detailed analysis, dealing in greater detail with the major facets of kinship and marriage.

Freud, Sigmund
1918 Totem and Taboo: Resemblances Between the Psychic Lives of Savages and Neurotics. New York: Vintage Books.

Now available in a paperback edition, this classic work represents Freud's evolutionary theory of the incest taboo. Although much of the theoretical import of the book has since been discredited, it can still be read as an enlightening chapter in the history of anthropology.

Hart, C. W. M., and Arnold R. Pilling
1960 The Tiwi of North Australia. New York: Holt, Rinehart and Winston.

An ethnography of particular interest because of the unusual pattern of marriage found among this society.

Schneider, David M.
1968 American Kinship: A Cultural Account. Englewood Cliffs, N.J.: Prentice-Hall.

An interesting account of American kinship. The reader will be rewarded with many new insights into American culture, as well as some interesting and humorous perspectives about our kinship system.

Schneider, David M. and E. Kathleen Gough, editors
1961 Matrilineal Kinship. Berkeley: University of California Press.

A more specialized volume dealing with a specific type of kinship system.

Schusky, Ernest L.
1972 Manual for Kinship Analysis. Second Edition. New York: Holt, Rinehart and Winston.

A short but thorough handbook for understanding kinship systems and terminologies. The author explains kinship in simple language.

Religion, Magic and Witchcraft

Chapter Seven

To the newcomer to anthropology, it appears that most anthropological studies include at least a chapter on the religion of the people being studied, and often an entire book may be devoted to the subject. Why should this be the case? Are non-Western people innately more religious than we are? The answer lies in the fact that religious institutions in non-Western societies are more closely interrelated with the rest of the lives of those people than they are in our own society, making it difficult, if not impossible, to study any aspect of their life without touching upon their religious behavior. By virtue of our advanced technology, we have removed ourselves from the daily problems involved in wresting a living from the land. We have gained some degree of control over the natural environment, a control that does not exist in non-Western societies, and we are now dealing with an artificial, cultural environment. The problems that we face in our daily routines are problems of a man-made cultural system that can be manipulated. In other words, we are farther removed from nature than our contemporaries in non-Western societies, and our religious institutions reflect this distance by becoming more secularized. The effect that religion has upon molding economic, political, legal and other social institutions is therefore minimized.

As we will see, religion is not an easy phenomenon to study cross-culturally. It is especially difficult to understand the "why" of religious beliefs and practices in other societies. Compare the study of religion, for example, to the study of agricultural practices in another culture—an equally interesting and valuable topic for the anthropologist. The variety of agricultural practices and the reasons behind them cannot vary too much from one culture to another, due to the ecological limitations imposed by the environment. In contrast, with

Children know such a lot now.
Soon they don't believe in fairies,
and every time a child says
"I don't believe in fairies" there is a fairy
somewhere that falls down dead.
JAMES M. BARRIE *Peter Pan*

religion the variation is almost unlimited. Anything within the realm of the human imagination is possible. And, whereas we have scientific answers for the "why" of agriculture, we have no such answers for the "why" of religion.

Religion was first defined by Sir Edward Tylor over a hundred years ago as the belief in spiritual beings. In our discussion of the anthropological approach to the study of religion we will not limit our attention to such beliefs, however, for we also wish to include the basic assumptions that people make about other forces in the universe and the place of man in nature, and the practices that people carry out in an attempt to control their environment.

First, let us consider the relationship among religion, magic and science. Although these three categories seem to be quite distinct in our own culture, we find that for many non-Western peoples they tend to be fused together, and it is difficult for the observer to separate them. *Religion* is basically a belief system, which includes myths that explain the social and religious order and rituals through which the members of the religious community carry out their beliefs and act out the myths to explain the unknown. *Magic* is the attempt to manipulate the forces of nature to derive certain desired results. As such magic can be religious activity in some contexts, since it is part of a belief system dealing with forces of power and relating man to nature. The main difference is that magic assumes human power over the forces of the universe, whereas religion generally does not. *Science,* on the other hand, is different from both religion and magic in that it is based upon observed relationships in the knowable universe; its attempt to manipulate natural forces is based upon experiment and is not designed to call upon supernatural powers, as does magic.

Magic, science and religion exist together in all societies. American culture is characterized by the predominance of science, and our ability to control the environment by resorting to natural (as opposed to supernatural) forces. The American farmer, for example, uses fertilizers to increase his yield, irrigation to overcome the natural lack of rainfall, pesticides to kill off insects, and a host of scientific methods to insure his success. He probably also resorts to magic, but in our science-oriented culture he calls it "superstition." "Don't plant on Friday the 13th," for example, would be a superstitious dictum not unlike the magical practices of many non-Western peoples. The main difference is that although we bend to such superstitions, it is usually not with the same degree of conviction that one applies to magical practices.

In a society where people do not have this technological ability to control the environment, they must resort to magic and religion. They perform a rain dance to bring on the rain that is so vital to

Hopi Indian sun dance, calling on magic to influence the weather. (Wide World Photos)

survival, whereas our knowledge of meteorology would never lead us to perform a rain dance, because we "know" that rain is a natural phenomenon and not subject to supernatural control. In a technologically less advanced society, people might also employ magic to insure a good yield, such as not planting under a full moon or not allowing a woman to help with the harvest while she is menstruating. Such practices are ways of manipulating or appeasing the spirits or the supernatural forces that are seen as governing success in agriculture. But despite the predominance of religion, magic, or science, there will be elements of each in all cultures. Just as the American farmer might resort to cloud-seeding as a scientific solution, doesn't he also pray for rain occasionally, despite his scientific knowledge? If we pointed this out to him and asked why he thought prayer would help, even though he understood the meteorological causes of rain, we would probably get an answer something like "Well, it won't hurt, will it?" And there is some element of "science" in practices that appear magical to us. People probably would not perform a rain dance when rain was not normally expected, indicating that a certain amount of observation and "scientific" prediction is a prerequisite for expecting success from magical practices.

In this chapter we will first discuss religion as a cultural universal. We will be concerned especially with the relationship between religion and other aspects of the social order. We will then go on to discuss magic and witchcraft, illustrating how they too are related to the wider social context in which they exist.

Comparative Studies of Religion

People tend to take their religious beliefs for granted. They learn them as they grow up, and they develop understandings about them as a part of their culture. Recall our earlier discussion of the definition of culture, in which we pointed out that much of what we learn is on an unconscious level, and that we never really analyze our behavior. Thus if we call upon someone to articulate his religious beliefs, the results would probably be surprisingly unrewarding. Imagine a non-Western anthropologist asking an American Christian informant to explain how God could be one and three at the same time, or to describe to him what God looks like. We would find the same problem if we tried to investigate religion in another society. We are always bound by our own beliefs and concepts about religion, and even the questions we ask are necessarily limited to our own culturally determined religious framework.

The French sociologist, Emile Durkheim, emphasized three aspects of religion: (1) the social context of religious systems; (2) the sacred aspect of religion; and (3) the moral basis of religion in society.[1] Let us discuss each of these in order.

The real purpose of religion, according to Durkheim, is to express people's beliefs about the universe. Religion structures the universe, puts things in order, relates what is unknown to what is known. Other anthropologists have stated this same principle in different ways. Sir James Frazer noted the relationship between the religious order and the political structure of many societies, pointing out many parallels between the two.[2] Such an example might be more difficult to see in our own society because of strict separation of church and state, but elsewhere it is quite clear. In traditional China, for example, the Emperor was the incarnation of God, and the Imperial City was conceived as being an earthly duplication of the Heavenly City. In ancient Egypt, the Pharaoh was not only the head of state, but was descended from God. And in medieval Europe the church actively supported the feudal order through the operation of its land holdings. In each case, the holy order and the earthly order were one and the same, and religion was the link between the two. As Bronislaw Malinowski pointed out, the nature of the social order is justified in the myths that people create and in which they believe.[3] Thus myths not only explain things that cannot be otherwise understood, they explain why the world is the way it is and why it should remain that way. They serve, in Malinowski's words, as a charter for the social system.

Secondly, Durkheim divided things into the two categories of "sacred" and "profane." Some things in every society are set apart, and are considered special—either dangerous, or powerful, or imbued with a certain mystical aura. These things are sacred, in contrast with

1. Emile Durkheim, *The Elementary Forms of the Religious Life.* London: George Allen & Unwin, Ltd. 1915.

2. James G. Frazer, *The Golden Bough.* Abridged Edition. New York: The Macmillan Co., 1922.

3. Bronislaw Malinowski, *Myth in Primitive Psychology.* London: Routledge & Kegan Paul, 1926.

Temple of Ramses II, Egyptian Pharaoh around 1250 B.C. The Pharaoh's authority was derived from his divine origin. (George Holton, Photo Researchers)

the rest of the world, which is ordinary, or profane. Every society considers different things sacred according to the religious beliefs of the group, but the setting apart of sacred things is a cultural universal.

The third point made by Durkheim is that religion imposes a moral compulsion upon people to act in a certain way. As part of the system of beliefs about the nature of the universe, religion offers a guide to behavior among people, including a system of rules they must follow. Furthermore, because the religious beliefs are so deeply ingrained in the individual through his cultural training, religion offers a pattern of social control. When an individual violates a religious rule governing his behavior he feels guilty, whether or not he is actually caught and punished. At the same time, when he follows the rules he feels good about it and his beliefs are reinforced. We are all familiar with this notion in Western religions, in which a belief in salvation and an afterlife is directly linked to the proper adherence to a code of behavior during one's earthly life.

Thus we can say that religion fulfills basic, universal human needs, by enabling people to cope with the unknown and uncontrollable. It is difficult for us to comprehend the extent of many of these functions of religion, for in American culture we are used to exercising more control over our environment, and there is little that happens in our everyday life that science has not provided an explanation for. In the United States, religion has therefore become more secular in recent years. It still performs the same functions, but only to a limited extent. For example, Western religions have become more preoccupied with the path to salvation, and less with the control of supernatural power. We have no scientific knowledge about the concepts of the soul and afterlife, and these have become primary concerns of religion, replacing more mundane (to us) problems such as climate, illness and the like.

It is also interesting to note that in recent years we have heard much about a "crisis" in religion in the United States, referring to the drastic changes in the function of religion in our society. At the same time there has been a revival of religious fervor in the past decade in certain social circles. One explanation for this religious resurgence can be found in the rapidly changing morality of American society, for with it has come a strong plea for returning to a stronger moral

A typical Sunday at a Protestant church in New Jersey. (George Roos, DPI)

order. Religion is thus attempting to provide some stability in an era of otherwise uncontrollable change. As we have pointed out earlier, social life must be based upon rules of behavior. Religion can provide those rules so that human interaction can be based upon predictable responses and the expectation of certain patterns of behavior. Thus the religious response to the contemporary scene in American culture is basically a conservative one: seeking a return to an old morality rather than creating an adjustment to the new one.

In studying religion from a comparative perspective, it is helpful to keep this threefold definition in mind, both to guide our investigations and to avoid falling into our own cultural trap and becoming subjective in our analysis of non-Western religious behavior. We should concentrate on the integration of religion with the rest of the social order, the particular elements of the culture that are set off from the rest and treated as sacred, and the cohesion of the religious community based upon their shared set of values and rules of behavior as part of their religious tradition.

Types of Religious Beliefs

The most basic religious belief is the attribution of a spirit or soul to all living things, a belief which Edward Tylor called *animism*. Tylor found this type of belief to be universal, and it is easy to see why all peoples would arrive at basically the same kind of belief in an attempt to deal with the unknown or inexplicable. A belief in spirits or souls arises out of experiences such as dreaming or hallucinogenic trances, where despite the seemingly normal outward appearance of the individual, some inner "thing" leaves the body and engages in its own activities. What better way to explain the fact that a person can awake from a deep sleep, without having moved, and recount an adventure that occurred in a dream? How else can you explain the unconscious and unremembered actions of a person in a trance? And likewise in death the body remains, yet obviously something within the body has gone—that same "inner spirit." Sometimes the spirit is thought to dwell in the shadow of a person during the day, but to leave and wander about at night while he sleeps. At other times, the spirit is dissociated from the physical being; this is especially

A street scene in Calcutta, India, indicating the reverence with which people regard the sacred cow. (Nat Norman, Frederic Lewis)

true in death. If a person's wandering soul encounters (in a dream) the spirit of a dead ancestor, then there is the appearance of some kind of life after death, for despite the death of the physical portion of the relative, there is something that remains and lives on.

With the notion of two separate beings—one tangible and earthly and the other intangible and spiritual—such experiences make sense. Tylor thought this to be the most basic of all religious beliefs and set it forth as his minimal definition of religion. Animism, and its extension to inanimate objects, is religious in that the spirits are worshipped, and they are thought to have some kind of supernatural power. The attribution of a spirit and a supernatural power to animate and inanimate objects alike is a way of explaining the unknown and relating man to the universe.

Inherent in the notion of animism is the concept of power. Furthermore, it is a special kind of power that cannot be controlled, because it is supernatural in origin. It can only be observed and in some cases manipulated, but not created or destroyed. Belief in such power is characteristic of many different religious systems, and anthropologists have used the term *mana* to denote it in its various forms. Mana is a supernatural force which in itself is neither good nor bad, but simply exists in nature. It can be manipulated to good or bad ends, but at the same time it is frequently capricious, seeming to act in different ways at different times without any logical explanation. It is the nature of mana to be unpredictable and uncontrollable.

Closely associated with the concept of mana is *taboo* (also spelled *tabu*), a restriction on the behavior of humans to avoid contact with such power. (The words *mana* and *taboo* are derived from a Melanesian language where such beliefs are common and where they were first described by anthropologists.) Taboo is based upon the notion that power can be dangerous and that people need to follow a set of rules defining their behavior with respect to sacred beings and objects.

The concept of a special power such as mana can have many functions in a society. It can explain why some people are different than others—better hunters, better farmers, more successful lovers, or talented artists. The power can lie within the individual, or in some physical object he has at his disposal. A brave and successful warrior can excel because he himself is endowed with mana, or because he possesses objects which transfer their power to him, such as a magic charm worn around the neck, or a specially powerful bow or spear. Mana can also explain why much in nature is so unpredictable. If one garden produces a larger crop than an adjacent garden, it could be because its cultivator has more mana. If a normally successful witch doctor is suddenly unable to cure his patient, one explanation might be that he has lost his mana, or that there is a stronger force working against him.

A taboo is a prohibition against certain kinds of behavior. The authority behind this prohibition is often found in supernatural power, and in the danger inherent in the behavior itself. The prohibition can be completely arbitrary, with no "logical" explanation to back it up, or it can be directly based upon commonly understood and accepted principles. For example, in the Garden of Eden there was no reason given why the fruit could not be eaten. It was an arbitrary dictum set forth by the Lord, which was to be followed unquestioningly. Other taboos may have a clearer explanation behind them. In native Hawaiian culture, and also in ancient Egypt, it was the custom for people of royal blood (kings or pharaohs) to marry only with relatives, preferably sisters. Furthermore, it was taboo for king or pharaoh to have sexual intercourse with a commoner. The reason for this taboo was that these individuals were of divine origin, and as such they were embodied with a great deal of mana. While another member of the royal family also inherited this divine power, a commoner did not. Thus to produce offspring with a commoner would defile the power. Only by producing children within the royal line could the purity of the divine ruler be guaranteed. However, since there was no need to worry about the purity of the divine lineage among commoners, the prescribed pattern of incest among the royal family was not found in the rest of society; instead there were strong prohibitions against incestual relations.

A taboo is thus a kind of sacred law that replaces secular law in maintaining some form of social control. As Marston Bates points out in *Gluttons and Libertines*, our taboo against incest is much stronger than our laws might imply.[4] Whereas the punishment for incest is less severe than, say, for rape, there is often the assumption that along with the legal penalties comes dread supernatural retribution. The main difference is that the penalties for violating a taboo come mainly from supernatural agents, whereas transgressions against the law are punished by society. Mana and taboo can also explain the otherwise inexplicable. A predictable event does not occur, and it requires an explanation. A formerly successful warrior falls in battle, and the men sitting around the campfire afterward recall that he violated a taboo and was not able to purify himself. His death was not at the hands of the enemy, but was caused by supernatural power.

In analyzing these various types of religious beliefs, we might ask what creates and sustains them in a society. The answer can be found in the study of *myth*. Like animism and the belief in supernatural power, myth is a cultural universal. Myths are the vehicles through which a society expresses its beliefs about things it holds sacred. They are sacred stories that contain explanations of how things came to be the way they are, and how they should be maintained. There are creation myths that relate the story of the origin of society, and there are tales that convey prescriptions for how people are to act, and the justification for those actions. Thus the myths in a sense present a charter for society, and as such they not only relate to the sacred, but they are themselves sacred.

4. Marston Bates, *Gluttons and Libertines*. New York: Vintage Books, 1967.

Hare Krishna cult. Religious groups sometimes dramatize their beliefs by a symbolic separation from the rest of society. (Rhoda Galyn, Photo Researchers)

The historical verification of the "truth" of a myth is unimportant, and generally impossible. Since most myths are oral legends passed down from one generation to the next, after a short time they can no longer be verified anyway. Where myths are recorded in literate societies, they frequently relate to a time or an event for which there are no written records, so that historical verification is likewise impossible. The importance of a myth is in its "social truth," not its historical accuracy. Myths explain things not otherwise understood; their validity is maintained through the practices which they prescribe, carried out according to the instructions in the myth itself.

Earlier we discussed the caste system of India as a form of social organization with a rigid hierarchy of stratified social groupings, known as castes. This system finds its justification in the mythology embodied in Hindu theology, the basis for the religious belief of most Indian people. According to the Hindu teachings, when a person dies he or she goes on to another life through the process of reincarnation. Since a person is born into a particular caste and remains in it throughout his life, the only changes that occur in one's status come about through reincarnation—being born into a higher or lower caste in the next life. Furthermore, the way to achieve a higher status in the next life is not by emulating a high-caste life style in the present life, but by following exactly the rules of behavior for the station in which one is born. Any attempt to leave one's caste and achieve higher status within one's lifetime is a violation of this rule, and will result in returning in a lower caste (or possibly in a sub-human form, called transmigration of souls, rather than reincarnation) in the next life.

We can see how the myth of caste and reincarnation serves as a charter for the system of social stratification in India. In effect, it justifies the way things are and seeks to perpetuate them in the future. Throughout Hindu mythology there are stories of how these rules came to be and why they are to be followed. There are also tales of certain individuals who either broke the rules and were punished or who followed them and were rewarded. And the same is true for every culture. In America, for example, we have (to select but one from a vast array of myths) the series of stories told by Horatio Alger, in which the pattern of unlimited individual achievement is described. Alger's stories tell of a young boy (or girl) from humble origins who, through individual effort and initiative, "makes it" in the outside world. This has grown into a common system of beliefs in American culture, with the notion that anyone can achieve success up to the limits of his personal capabilities. Yet, as we all are aware, equality is not universal in our society, for there is discrimination practiced on the basis of race, sex, religion, and many other factors. The "equality of opportunity" myth serves as a justification for our system of free enterprise, but it does not describe reality.

As a further example of the role of mythology in the organization of society, consider The Dreaming, described by W.E.H. Stanner for the Australian tribes known as the Arunta. The Dreaming refers to an epoch when the mythical ancestors lived, and it includes both the act of dreaming or meditation, and the mythology upon which the people meditate. The Dreaming is difficult for Westerners to understand, because it does not conform to our notions of time. To quote Stanner,

> Although, as I have said, The Dreaming conjures up the notion of a sacred, heroic time of the indefinitely remote past, such a time is also, in a sense, still part of the present. One cannot "fix" The Dreaming *in* time: it was, and is, everywhen . . . . Clearly, The Dreaming is many

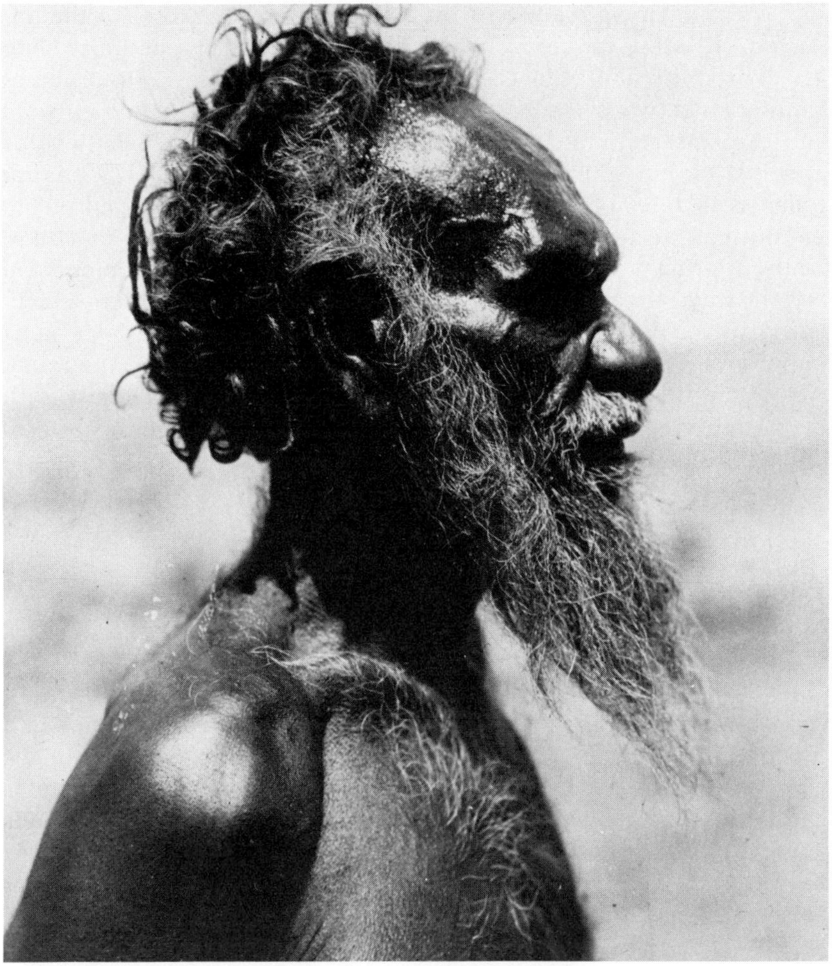

A member of the Arunta tribes of Australia. (American Museum of Natural History)

things in one. Among them, a kind of narrative of things that once happened; a kind of charter of things that still happen; and a kind of *logos* or principle of order transcending everything significant for aboriginal man.[5]

5. W.E.H. Stanner, *"The Dreaming."* In Australian Signpost, T.A.G. Hungerford, ed., Melbourne: F.W. Cheshire, 1956, pp. 51–65. Reprinted in William A. Lessa and Evon Z. Vogt, eds., *Reader in Comparative Religion.* Second Edition. New York: Harper & Row, 1965.

The Dreaming represents the Arunta attempt to explain the unknown. It is the means by which the individual attains unity with his own spirit and with the world in which he lives. It provides continuity between the past and the present, between the spiritual and the here-and-now. The Dreaming provides an explanation for creation, for how things came to be as they are. It deals with a moral order, with rules of conduct for how things are to be carried out in the present. It details the punishment for transgression of the rules, while offering a logical explanation for why people should act a certain way. It carries with it a sacred authority—Australian society is the way it is because The Dreaming says so. And perhaps most important of all, The Dreaming is the means by which the Australian Aborigines become one with nature, by being united spiritually with their environment and all its inhabitants, creating for them a philosophy of life that they carry out in their daily activities.

Types of Religious Practices

If myth presents society with the "why" of religious life, then *ritual* can be said to be the "how" by which those concepts are put into practice. A ritual is a prescribed way of carrying out a religious activity, such as a prayer, an act of worship, or a sacrifice. Rituals can be held in conjunction with regular events, such as the seasons in the agricultural cycle, or they can occur irregularly at birth, marriage, illness, or any unique or unplanned event. Rituals are important not only for their spiritual value, but for their symbolic meaning for the group. They signify that the proper actions have been performed so that the deities or spirits will be satisfied, but at the same time they have a deeper meaning to the members of the group, for they help to establish group boundaries by setting off those who have performed the necessary rituals, and who are therefore part of the select group, from those who have not. In examining several different types of rituals we can see how they reinforce the belief system of a society, and how a wide variety of rituals can perform the same basic functions for the group.

A typical collection of rituals with which we are all familiar are those surrounding the different stages of life: birth, entry into

Before you criticize this behavior as unusual, turn the page. (Abbott, Frederic Lewis)

Minister James Wade, of Cartersville, Georgia, holds three rattlesnakes in his bare hands during services, as a demonstration of his faith. (Wide World)

a religious community, adulthood, marriage, and so on until death. At each stage there is a particular ritual to signify the change in the individual (as much for society's benefit as for the individual's). Thus a typical progression of such rituals in American culture might be baptism, communion, confirmation, betrothal and marriage, and so on until the last rites or the funeral. Note that in our society the formal status of adulthood is conferred primarily through a secular rather than a religious ritual, and it is not as clearly defined as others. One might include in the process of achieving adulthood a number of significant events, such as obtaining a driver's license, registering for the draft (or attaining the age of 18), the twenty-first birthday and graduation from high school or college. In some cases even the wedding ceremony can be a confirmation of adult status.

Rituals of this type, which confer a new status upon an individual, are called *rites of passage,* referring to the fact that they involve the passage from one stage to another in the life cycle. Although every culture defines the limits of these stages somewhat differently, all cultures celebrate these changes through rites of passage. It is interesting also to note that in some cultures the passage from one stage to the next is a relatively informal, gradual process without much pressure or ceremony, whereas in others it can be an abrupt change surrounded by a great deal of anxiety, mystery, and even fear. As we noted for our own culture, achieving adulthood is a relatively gradual process. There are certain rights that a young man or woman obtains at several different ages along the way, so that by the time he or she is 21 years of age much activity defined by society as "adult" is already commonplace.

In contrast to the American pattern of achieving adulthood, in some societies this transition is much more abrupt, and is marked by a single important ceremony. Among many tribal societies, a boy's passage from childhood to adulthood is marked by ritual circumcision at puberty. As a child the boy is taught to fear this ritual, and the closer he comes to it the more intense his anxiety becomes. Yet at the same time, he is taught that only as an adult male can he participate in the meaningful religious activities of his tribe, so there is no alternative to the rite of passage. In the actual ceremony itself, the boy's fears are intensified even further by the older men who perform the circumcision. They may dance and sing of the "killing" they are about to do, or offer their condolences to the mothers of the initiates. The young boys are built up to a feverish pitch, and are often forced to

Baptism is a Christian ritual marking passage from one stage of religious life to another. (Bruce Roberts, Rapho/Photo Researchers)

fast and go without sleep for some time prior to the ceremony. During the circumcision they are removed from their families and from the rest of the group, and taken to an isolated place where the sacred operation will take place.

In many ways this type of circumcision ceremony is comparable to the old-fashioned fraternity initiation, with its hazing and its method of building up anxiety in the initiates. A "pledge" spends a year or more seeking admission to the chosen group, during which time he is taught the basics of fraternity life, but never allowed to share the "sacred" secrets of the group. The act of initiation itself is built up by the members, so that at the same time that the pledge increases his desire to gain this new status, he is instilled with fear, or at least discomfort, about what will be involved in the initiation ceremony

The rear of a fortified longhouse in New Guinea. Only the men may gather here, where they keep their weapons, and squat eating green bananas or chewing betel nuts. (Barbara Kirk, Peter Arnold)

itself. Rumors of corporal punishment, personal embarrassment and other forms of hazing merely add to his concern. When the time finally arrives for him to undergo initiation, he does so with a mixture of pride and anxiety, eagerness and hesitancy. And once the ceremony is over and he is accepted as a member of the group, he usually guards the secrets and the sacred knowledge he has obtained as jealously as his predecessors did before him.

Another type of rite of passage is known as a *vision quest.* In some Plains Indian tribes a boy could only become a man by acquiring spiritual power through a hallucinatory vision. Throughout his childhood a Crow Indian boy constantly heard from his peers and his elders that the only way he could acquire power in his society was through a vision. As he grew older, his desire for the good things in life—many

Interior of men's hut, Papua, New Guinea. Initiation into the ranks of adult males involves an elaborate rite of passage. (American Museum of Natural History)

horses, an important wife, and social recognition from his fellow tribesmen—ultimately drove him to seek a vision. First, he would go off alone, perhaps deep into the woods or to the top of a mountain. There he would beseech the spirits to bestow a vision upon him, a vision which would give him some of their supernatural power for his own use. He might fast for many days, induce exhaustion, or inflict pain upon himself in order to gain the sympathy of the gods. When this finally happened, he would have a vision in which valuable information was obtained to be used for success upon returning to the tribe. The benefits of the vision were of many kinds; they might include supernatural power as a curer or medicine man, or economic power, or perhaps some special ability as a warrior, or as a tribal leader.

Not only young initiates, but mature men and women would seek visions in times of emergency or personal stress. A woman with a sick child would seek a cure through a vision; a man who had lost a close relative would seek revenge through a vision. Thus vision quests existed both as rites of passage and as rituals designed for a specific occasion not associated with a change of status. The concept of a unique personal revelation is based upon the belief in the transfer of supernatural power through the hallucinatory vision, and frequently the vision also included instructions in how the individual could maintain the power, either through special magic to be practiced, or further rituals to be conducted. The occurrence of religious-based visions in Western society, such as that at Lourdes or Fatima, shows us that such things are not limited to so-called "primitives," but may play a similar role in industrial societies.

Whereas the vision quest is an individual act performed in isolation, away from the rest of the group, other rituals involving the transmission of supernatural power through a human agent can occur in a group situation. One such religious practice is *spirit possession,* in which a person becomes possessed by a supernatural spirit, usually in a state of trance. The individual then acts as a medium through which the spirit communicates to the people. The trance can be induced by ingesting drugs or other substances, or by dancing or some other physical activity. Messages can be transmitted concerning future events, the nature or cure of an illness, the cause of some evil event, or almost any question for which a supernatural answer would be suitable. Possession frequently spreads throughout the group, for the high-pitched excitement and frenzied activities are often contagious.

The recent popularity of the best-selling book and movie *The Exorcist* has revived interest in spirit possession in our society, once again illustrating the parallels between Western and non-Western cultures.

The examples given here are by no means an exhaustive list of the types of religious activities found throughout the world. They do, however, point out a few ways in which ritual is important to the religious life of a society as a whole, as well as to the individuals who practice it. In the following section we will attempt to draw together the elements of religion that we have discussed so far, to show how a particular belief system, coupled with a mythology and a collection of ritual activities, can act as an organizing principle around which people live their lives together and interact as members of a social group. For this we turn to a discussion of the religious system known as *totemism*.

Totemism

The term *totem*, derived from the Chippewa Indian language spoken in the Great Lakes area, refers to a natural item, either animate or inanimate, with which an individual or a group identifies. Although such identification is found among American Indian tribes, the most complete examples of religions based upon the relationship between a group of people and a totem are found in Australia. While the form of totemic religions varies considerably from one society to another, it is possible to speak of totemism in general terms, and to define some of its basic characteristics.

A totem can be an animal, a plant, or a natural inanimate object such as a rock, which is used as the symbol signifying the unity of the group. A society may be divided into many totemic groups, each identifying with a different totem. In its most extreme form, such as is found among Australian Aborigines, the totem is not merely a symbol of unity shared by a group of people; it is one with them. The identification is complete, not symbolic, and when a person says "I am a wallaby," he does not mean he is a member of the wallaby totemic group, or clan, but rather that he is of the same species as the wallaby, that there is a blood tie between him and all of the members of his group and the wallaby.

Totemism can be seen as a form of nature worship, where the spirit of the human and the spirit of the animal or plant that serves as the totem for the group are merged. Usually there are a number of taboos, or avoidances associated with totemism. It is common, for example, that a person will be strictly forbidden to eat any member of the totemic species, or to kill the totemic animal or plant, except on special ritual occasions when the unity of the group is celebrated in a special ceremony. Another common rule surrounds marriage: For a person to have sexual relations with another member of his or her totemic clan would be considered incestuous. Regardless of the actual degree of blood relationship between two individuals, the mystical relationship between all members of the clan is so strong that it overshadows the family. Thus the totemic clan usually determines the limits of the incest taboo.

Totemism not only forms the basis for a moral code among Australian Aborigines, but it is also the organizational principle around which society is ordered. A person inherits membership in a totemic clan from his or her parent (from the mother in a matrilineal society, the father in a patrilineal society). The relationship between an individual and others in his clan is clearly spelled out by their joint membership in the group. Likewise, the relationship between an indi-

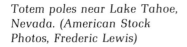

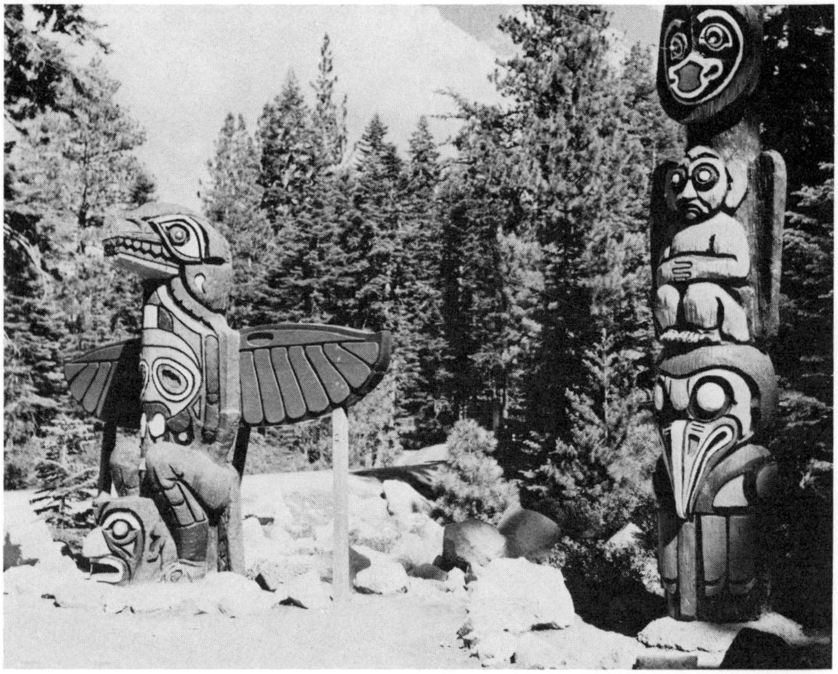

Totem poles near Lake Tahoe, Nevada. (American Stock Photos, Frederic Lewis)

vidual and others in his society who are members of other totemic groups is also a part of the knowledge he gains through membership in his own group. Thus the totemic system of classifying not only people, but also non-human elements of the environment, is an effective way of creating harmony between the social system and the universe, and defining every individual's place within that system.

We are all familiar with symbolic elements of totemism in our own culture. While we might not attach religious significance to the identification of a group with a particular animal, plant, or other natural object, we do recognize it as a principle of organization. Our sports teams, for example, are not simply referred to in terms of their locations or home towns, which would certainly be sufficient to distinguish among them, but also are identified with a mascot of some sort. The mascot can be human (San Francisco 49ers, Kansas City Chiefs, Cleveland Indians); it can be an animal (Boston Bruins, Baltimore Orioles, Detroit Lions); it can be a plant (Ohio State Buckeyes, Toronto

Frank Robinson of the Cleveland Indians. Team identification with a mascot (note the insignia on Robinson's arm) is similar to religious identification with a totem. (AP, Wide World)

Maple Leafs); or it can be some kind of inanimate object that serves as a unifying symbol (Chicago White Sox, Detroit Pistons, New York Jets). Ralph Linton documented the development of totemic groups in the United States Army during World War I, showing that although the religious significance does not exist, the apparent universal tendency to organize and categorize the universe extends to all societies, and is not just a phenomenon attributable to the so-called "primitive mentality."

Linton described the "Rainbow Division," the 42nd Division of the U.S. Army during World War I.[6] Shortly after the name was assigned to the division in 1918, members began to use the term "Rainbow" to refer to themselves, rather than the formal name of 42nd Division. Furthermore, the members of the Rainbow Division developed the idea that the actual appearance of a rainbow in the sky was a particularly good omen for them (but not necessarily for anyone else). This notion gained popularity until it became so strong that members of the division actually claimed seeing rainbows in the sky just before going into battle or after a victory, even though the weather conditions would have ruled out such an occurrence. The men in the division began to use the rainbow increasingly as their symbol, painting it on their equipment and even using it as a personal insignia worn on the shoulder—despite official regulations forbidding such actions. Eventually the idea spread to other divisions, which adopted different "totems" for themselves. Linton sums up the development of this form of totemism with the following observations:

1. A division of the personnel into a number of groups conscious of their individuality.
2. The possession by each of these groups of a distinctive name derived from some animal, object, or natural phenomenon.
3. The use of this name as a personal appellation in conversation with outsiders.
4. The use of representations of the group namesake for the decoration of group property and for personal adornment, with a taboo against its use by members of other groups.
5. A reverential attitude toward the group namesake and its representations.
6. In many cases, an unformulated belief that the group namesake was also a group guardian capable of giving omens.

6. Ralph Linton, "Totemism and the A.E.F." *American Anthropologist* 26:296–300, 1924.

Linton goes on to point out some of the differences between totemism in the army and forms of totemism found among Australian Aborigines. In the former version there are no regulations against marriage within the group, there is no idea of descent from the totem or blood relationship to it, and there are no special religious rituals involved in the relationship. However, he concludes that the same psychological processes that operate in non-Western societies in the development of totemism must also be operating in our own society, pointing to a basic similarity in the operation of the human mind in civilized and so-called "primitive" societies. And he concludes by pointing out how difficult it is to study totemism, or any religious belief system for that matter, for they are developed without any conscious direction on the part of members of society:

> It seems probable that in primitive groups also a whole series of attitudes and practices could be developed without the individual feeling any need for their rationalization until he was confronted by some anthropological investigator.[7]

Religious Specialists

While religious beliefs and practices might differ tremendously from one society to another, all are similar in that they include individuals who occupy positions as *religious specialists.* Such positions are based on the premise that there will always be an unequal distribution of knowledge and of personal ability, and that individuals with more than their share of these are in a better position to relate to the supernatural. They can be primarily religious in the sense that they seek help from the divine or spiritual world, or they can be more magical, in that they attempt to manipulate the spirits or the supernatural forces.

In our society, we have religious specialists who have undergone a training program to qualify them for their positions. A clergyman is a person who holds authority based upon his religious office. There is nothing inherent in his personality that attracts and maintains this authority. On the other hand, we also have lay preachers in some religious movements who hold their authority based upon their per-

7. Linton, *op. cit.*, p. 300.

sonal innate abilities, and not simply on their education. Thus we have two kinds of specialization—one where the power is in the office, and another where the power is in the individual. This same distinction holds true for religious specialists in other societies as well.

In contrast to the position of priest, who learns his religious knowledge through a formal training period, in many societies there is a religious specialist whose powers come directly from the supernatural forces, spirits, or gods. Of course, both types of specialists can exist together in the same society. This latter type, who serves as a vehicle for communication from the supernatural, is called a *shaman,* a Siberian term derived from a group of Eskimo societies

Zulu shaman sucking out the foreign spirit through the ear of a patient. (Ewing Galloway)

where such specialists are found. The Plains Indians also had such specialists, and there an individual aspiring to become a shaman had to seek the necessary power through a vision. In other societies, however, a shaman can be anyone who comes into direct contact with a spirit. Frequently this involves being possessed by the spirit, in which the individual loses (or seems to lose) control of himself and acts as if directed by the spirit itself.

Becoming a shaman can be the result of a mystical experience, such as a vision, or a period of special training, or both. It is interesting to note that many anthropologists have cast a skeptical eye toward shamans, noting how they use such tricks as ventriloquism, sleight of hand, and the creation of various optical illusions to achieve their results. Thus in a practical sense a shaman requires a certain kind of training, not in the religious doctrines which he interprets as a priest would, but in the methods he uses in his normal religious activities. Shamans are known in many societies as witch doctors or curers who are able to help their clients by using various supernatural powers to suck out the poison that is harming them, pull out the foreign matter in the "soul" of the client, or advise the person on rituals to perform in order to rid himself of the evil infesting his body or his spirit. But the important distinction between a shaman and another religious specialist such as a priest is that the shaman is not himself the actor, but is merely the medium for the supernatural spirit that performs the act.

Shamans can also act as diviners, individuals who are able to foresee future events or uncover the causes of past events. A diviner may attempt to discern the will of the gods, which enables the group to gain control over future events or to plan around them. A diviner can also discover the mysterious supernatural cause of an illness, when no other cause is readily apparent. He may do this by viewing some natural event, such as the flight of a flock of birds overhead, or the entrails of a slaughtered animal, or the design created by tea leaves in the bottom of a cup. Or he may act as a medium for a spirit which speaks through him and communicates directly with the members of the group. Divination thus takes many different forms, but in most societies it can be considered a religious activity in the sense that it deals with the supernatural, and involves an attempt to control the forces of the universe.

Priests, shamans and diviners are but a few of the many types of religious specialists found throughout the world. The important feature to note is not so much the tremendous variety of specialists that exist, but rather the fact that in most cases they perform many of the same functions for society. Whether we call him a guru, a priest or a minister, a shaman, medicine man or witch doctor, the religious specialist occupies his position because he is recognized as having some special knowledge or talent that carries with it a higher religious authority. His role in society becomes increasingly important as the religious beliefs and practices form the greater part of the basis for social behavior, as is the case in most non-Western societies studied by anthropologists. Where religion is fused with economic and political power, the religious specialist takes on added importance as a leader and an interpreter of custom and morality. In the United States there are a few such individuals—people like Billy Graham—who combine their religious position with a limited degree of political power. But Graham's political influence is not nearly so great as that of a leader whose position is grounded in the religious tradition of his or her country, such as the Pharaohs of ancient Egypt, or in modern times a religious-political leader like former King Faisal of Saudi Arabia, or Archbishop Makarios.

Magic and Witchcraft

As we have noted, all people seek to control their environment. They do this through manipulating the supernatural, through the practice of *magic;* through the explanation of how or why things happened the way they did, which is related to *witchcraft;* and through the prediction of future events, which is *divination.* We have discussed divination in the previous section, and we turn now to witchcraft and magic.

Magic is manipulative; it is like science in the sense that it seeks control over the forces of the universe, but it is unlike science in that it uses supernatural means to gain that control. Magic can be good or bad; it can be directed against an individual or an entire group; and it can be practiced by an individual or a group of people. When it succeeds it is proof that the magic is effective, that the spirits exist and that they can be manipulated. When it fails, however, it is not proof of the opposite. Rather, it is an indication that the proper rituals were not performed correctly, or that an important rule was broken,

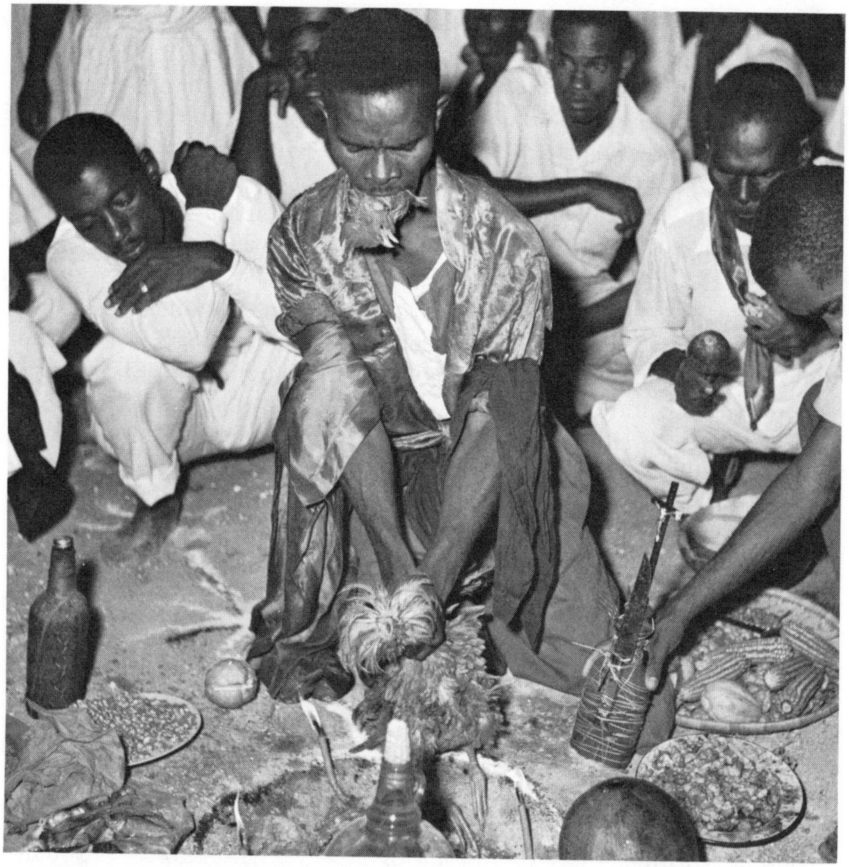

A houngan, a voodoo priest, possessed by a voodoo spirit during a ceremony. Notice the severed head of a rooster in the priest's mouth. (Odette Mennesson-Rigaud, Photo Researchers)

or that someone else also used magic to counteract the force. It is never the supernatural power that is at fault, but always the human practitioner.

In an early discussion of magic, Sir James Frazer isolated two basic principles: (1) Like produces like, which he called the *law of similarity*. (2) Things that have been in contact with each other continue to exert an effect upon one another after they have become separated, which he called the *law of contact*, or *contagious magic*.[8] A person who practices magic is likely to use one of these two laws as the basis for the actual manipulations he performs, and frequently these two principles are found together.

8. James G. Frazer, *The Golden Bough*, *op. cit.*, Chapter 3.

One of the best known examples of the law of similarity in magical practices is found in *voodoo*. A person first makes a doll in the image of the intended victim, then injures the doll image, such as by sticking a pin in it, or destroys it. By applying the principle of like producing like, the magic is supposed to be carried from the doll to the victim, producing the same result of injury or death. Voodoo has been shown to be very successful in some cases, and there are documented examples of people actually dying after they had been the victims of voodoo magic. Walter Cannon has shown that this results from the strength of beliefs about the effectiveness of voodoo.[9] Where the belief is deeply ingrained, the fear of voodoo is enough to cause death. He traces the physiological consequences of the reaction: the body becomes stimulated because of the initial fear; when this condition is prolonged, a subsequent state of shock can set in, which may result in reduced blood pressure, deterioration of the heart and other similar effects. The lack of food and water compounds the problem, and if it continues for more than a few days, the result can be fatal.

The law of similarity in magical practices can also be used for benevolent purposes. Eskimos of the Bering Strait region fashion dolls in the image of young babies, and give them to barren women to increase their ability to conceive. This law can also serve as a prevention or cure for illness, such as the use of a yellow substance to prevent jaundice, or something red to prevent bleeding. In medieval Germany, ashes were rubbed on the forehead of a person with a high fever, in the hope that just as the ashes had cooled, so would the patient's fever. Among the Dyak in Borneo, a medicine man will lie down and pretend to be dead. His fellow villagers wrap him up in mats and take him out to be buried, whereupon he will rise up, fully recovered and restored to life. The magic is supposedly transferred to the patient who lies near death, yet who should (if the magic is successful) recover and return from death as the medicine man did.

There are also negative practices or taboos based upon the law of similarity in magic. These taboos tell us what not to do in order for a desired effect to occur, or to avoid an unfavorable result. For example, among the Eskimos of Baffin Land, boys are forbidden to play the game of cat's cradle, because their fingers might later become

9. Walter B. Cannon, " 'Voodoo' Death." *American Anthropologist* 44:169–181, 1942.

entangled in the harpoon lines. This practice is taboo, despite the fact that it is a popular game among the girls. In contrast, among the Ainus of the Sakhalin Islands north of Japan, pregnant women may not spin thread for two months before delivery of the baby, lest the child become entangled in its umbilical cord. In our own society we have what we call superstitions, which are in many ways similar to taboos based upon the law of similarity, and although we might not be as convinced of their effectiveness we follow them nevertheless. For example, one of the best ways I know to insure a sunny day is to carry an umbrella to work! On the other hand, if I want it to rain, all I have to do is wash my car and leave it parked in the driveway—it never fails.

Regarding the second principle of magic, contagion, the most common practice is the belief that magic worked upon a severed portion of an individual will also affect the person himself. For example, the Navajo have a custom of burying their hair and nail clippings far away from the settlement, for they fear that these items could be used against them. In some tribes in Australia there is the belief that one can cause a man to become lame by placing a sharp piece of glass or bone in his footprint, which is considered to be part of him. This notion carries over to hunting, as in the old German practice of pounding a nail into the footprint of an animal being tracked, to prevent it from escaping.

Turning to witchcraft, we generally make a distinction between two different practices, witchcraft, which is an inherent trait, and sorcery, which can be learned. Witchcraft has many potential functions in society: it provides an outlet for aggression and hostility, a way of resolving tensions and conflicts, and it provides a convenient scapegoat for society. It can regulate the antagonisms that inevitably arise in any social situation. And it can explain otherwise inexplicable events, such as failure, disease, or misfortune. It has been pointed out frequently how witchcraft can act as a mechanism for social control, by regulating the behavior of certain members of the group. People can be forced to follow certain desired patterns of behavior, either because they are afraid of becoming the victims of a witch, or because they are afraid of being accused of being witches themselves. Thus if we are to study the social effects of witchcraft, we must also study the patterns of opposition to witchcraft, the way witches are dealt with in a society.

E.E. Evans-Pritchard, an anthropologist well-known for his studies

The New York Public Library

Sir James Frazer (1854–1941) *was one of the most influential anthropologists of his time, due primarily to his monumental work* The Golden Bough. *In this work, Frazer traced the evolution of human culture through the successive stages of reliance upon magic, religion, and science. It is one of the most detailed and complete accounts of various practices among human cultures, as well as one of the last truly classic evolutionary works of the period.*
One of Frazer's many important contributions to anthropology concerned the distinction between different types of magic—imitative magic, such as the use of a doll to imitate a desired result upon a person, and contagious magic, where a severed portion of a person (nail, hair, or clothing) could be used to practice magic upon that person.

Because adult males use harpoon lines to hunt seals, young Eskimo boys do not play cat's cradle, an example of the law of similarity in magic. (Ted Grant, DPI)

of African societies, discusses the ways in which witchcraft explains unfortunate events among the Azande, an African group living near the Congo River.[10] At the same time, witchcraft is an important aspect of other elements in the social life of the Azande, such as the way in which accusations prevent an individual from striving for success at the expense of others. A man who is too successful is likely to be accused of being a witch, and because men fear such accusations they tend to remain at a relatively even level with others in the group.

Evans-Pritchard points out that most of the Azande take witchcraft for granted. They expect to find it in their daily lives, and are

10. E.E. Evans-Pritchard, *Witchcraft, Oracles and Magic Among the Azande.* Oxford: Clarendon Press, 1937.

not surprised when it does occur, for it is a natural outgrowth of living together with other people in a social setting. Witchcraft is especially useful in explaining events that could not otherwise be explained to their satisfaction. How does an action repeated day after day suddenly produce an unfortunate result? For example, one day you are walking along a path and you bump into a stump, cutting your foot in the process. The next day the cut is infected. Here are several clear evidences of witchcraft. First, you have walked along the path every day for years, and never bumped your foot before. Why now? Second, you have bumped yourself many times before, but rarely does it produce a cut. Why now? Third, you have had cuts before, but rarely do they become infected. Why now? Clearly there was some evil force operating that caused you to suffer this mishap, making you blind to the stump and then causing the cut to become infected.

In what is perhaps the most thorough study of the relationship between witchcraft beliefs and practices and other aspects of the social order, S.F. Nadel compares witchcraft among four African societies.[11] He groups them into two pairs, the Nupe and Gwari in northern Nigeria and the Korongo and Mesakin in the Nuba Mountains of the central Sudan. Within each pair there is a great deal of cultural similarity, but a different pattern of witchcraft beliefs.

In comparing Nupe and Gwari witchcraft, Nadel points out that while the beliefs about the nature of witchcraft are similar (i.e., it is evil and destroys life), Nupe witches are always women, while in Gwari there is no sex distinction and witches and their victims can be of either sex. This can be explained by the strong sex antagonism in Nupe society, and by the fact that only women are accused of witchcraft, and only men have the power to defeat witchcraft. Among the Gwari no such sex antagonism exists. Digging deeper in the social factors involved, Nadel points to the economic and social independence of women in Nupe society. Women generally work as traders, and their agriculturalist husbands are frequently in debt to them. Women also are known to refuse to have children, thus freeing themselves for their jobs. This creates a role reversal so strong that it is reflected in the patterns of witchcraft.

In comparing witchcraft in Korongo and Mesakin societies, Nadel points out again how similar they are in so many ways, such as envi-

11. S.F. Nadel, "Witchcraft in Four African Societies: An Essay in Comparison." *American Anthropologist* 54:18–29, 1952.

ronment, language, economics, political organization, religious beliefs and kinship system. However, to understand witchcraft, he says, we must understand the system of age grading that occurs in both societies. Male adolescence revolves around a formal division into age groups, which in turn are centered around the exhibition of virility through athletic activities. At puberty this exhibition of virility is formalized in a ceremony and at the celebration, each boy receives as a present an animal from the herd of his mother's brother. Since the boy will eventually inherit the entire herd of the mother's brother, this pattern of gift giving is normal in both societies.

Regarding witchcraft in these groups, Nadel notes that the Korongo have no witchcraft beliefs at all, while the Mesakin are obsessed by fears of witchcraft and accusations of being a witch. These accusations frequently entail violent quarrels, and lead to physical attacks. Among the Mesakin, witchcraft operates most often between a boy and his mother's brother. Since witchcraft is seen as occurring only if there is some reason for resentment or anger, it is usually caused by an argument over the anticipated inheritance, that is, the gift at the initiation ceremony.

The distinction between these two societies seems to lie in the fact that while among the Korongo the duty of the mother's brother to give his sister's son an animal is never refused, the Mesakin mother's brother always refuses at first, and often the animal must be taken by force. Thus quarrels over the gift are frequent, and if by chance something should happen to the youth while such a quarrel is in progress, the mother's brother is usually accused of witchcraft.

Nadel assigns the difference between these two groups to cultural differences in adult attitudes toward life, and especially toward growing old. In both groups there is a hatred toward aging. Yet the Korongo men accept it, whereas the Mesakin attempt to avoid it, even to the point of concealing and denying sexual intercourse, believed to be the major cause of aging. Now in both societies the mother's brother sees in the demand for a gift the reminder that he is growing old. The gift anticipates the death of the donor, since upon his death the entire herd will be turned over to his heir, the sister's son. In Korongo society the men are prepared for a gradual decline and thus it is more acceptable, while for the Mesakin there is no gradual transition from youth to old age, and it is more difficult to accept when it arrives.

Clearly, then, there is more hostility toward the sister's son and toward the whole process of the gift giving in Mesakin society, which helps to explain their beliefs about witchcraft. Every man projects his frustrations into the allegations that others are guilty of witchcraft, and in punishing them he eliminates his own guilt feelings. Nadel also points out that the Korongo, who have no witchcraft, have a full mythology which explains the important things in the world in another way, whereas the Mesakin do not have such a well-developed mythology.

In conclusion, Nadel suggests that witchcraft beliefs are related to specific anxieties and stresses in social life. These anxieties can arise from childhood experiences, but they can also be the result of adult experiences, as in the Mesakin. Secondly, he suggests that witchcraft accusations tend to uphold the desired state of society by identifying the witch as the one who transgresses the values of the expected behavior. And finally, while it may be true that witchcraft beliefs serve to deflect hostilities in society, they may also create even greater tensions. The hostility may only be deflected in the sense that it is redirected toward a few convenient scapegoats.

Senator Joseph McCarthy during 1954 Senate hearings. He became famous for his witch hunt against Communists. (Wide World)

If we follow this line of reasoning about the social functions of witchcraft accusations, we can learn a great deal about the way our own society operates. For example, during the early 1950s the United States went through a period of witch hunting known as McCarthyism, in which an influential senator and his followers sought to cleanse the American people of the evil of Communism. There were Communists located in every corner of American society, and in many areas where this witch hunt got out of hand, the punishment for the victims of the movement was completely out of line with the crimes they were alleged to have committed. Today we have the same kind of witch hunt, in which a scapegoat is created to deflect the tensions and the aggressive impulses of various groups in our society. For many members of the group known as "Middle America," the politically conservative portion of the American population that came to be called the "silent majority," the cause of America's problems lies with the radical student groups scattered throughout the country. Many of the characteristics of witchcraft accusations in non-Western societies can be seen in legal proceedings against some of these people: the Chicago Seven, who were tried following the Democratic National Convention in Chicago in 1968; the Harrisburg Eight, alleged to have been involved in a conspiracy to kidnap Secretary of State Kissinger, but eventually acquitted of that charge; such avowed revolutionaries or dissidents as Angela Davis, Benjamin Spock and Jane Fonda. All of these incidents serve the same social function in American culture that witchcraft accusations do in others. Perhaps the best example is the recent series of accusations and counter-charges surrounding former President Nixon and the events known as "Watergate."

However, we should not look at witchcraft accusations as a one-sided process even in our own society. The very groups that are the victims of witch hunts are also the initiators of equally obvious witch hunts on their own, as witnessed by the fact that so many of the student and young revolutionary groups in our society blame specific institutions such as the police or the military for all the evils they suffer. To blame the police for carrying out the will of the people is as much a process of creating a scapegoat as to blame an old woman for the outbreak of an epidemic. Yet if society is to avoid an all-out war within itself and maintain some kind of internal order, such witch hunts can play a positive role. Indeed, the fact that they exist in so many different societies throughout the world indicates that they must have a function.

In the following article by Horace Miner, "Body Ritual Among the Nacirema," we are introduced to religious beliefs and a series of magical practices that are as different from our own way of life as night is from day. It may be difficult for us to comprehend how a people could be so involved with magic that it becomes obsessive and dominates their entire life style. On the other hand, for the people Miner describes it would be equally difficult to understand how we live from day to day. Perhaps this obsession of the Nacirema is at least a partial explanation of why they never were able to attain civilization, for with the domination of ritual they had to endure, they probably had little time to devote to technological advancement.

Body Ritual Among the Nacirema

Horace Miner

The anthropologist has become so familiar with the diversity of ways in which different peoples behave in similar situations that he is not apt to be surprised by even the most exotic customs. In fact, if all of the logically possible combinations of behavior have not been found somewhere in the world, he is apt to suspect that they must be present in some yet undescribed tribe. This point has, in fact, been expressed with respect to clan organization by Murdock. In this light, the magical beliefs and practices of the Nacirema present such unusual aspects that it seems desirable to describe them as an example of the extremes to which human behavior can go.

Professor Linton first brought the ritual of the Nacirema to the attention of anthropologists twenty years ago, but the culture of this people is still very poorly understood. They are a North American group living in the territory between the Canadian Cree, the Yaqui and Tarahumare of Mexico, and the Carib and Arawak of the Antilles. Little is known of their origin, although tradition states that they came from the east. According to Nacirema mythology, their nation was originated by a culture hero, Notgnihsaw, who is otherwise known for two great feats of strength—the throwing of a piece of wampum across the river Pa-To-Mac and the chopping down of a cherry tree in which the Spirit of Truth resided.

Nacirema culture is characterized by a highly developed market economy which has evolved in a rich natural habitat. While much of the people's time is devoted to economic pursuits, a large part of the fruits of these labors and a considerable portion of the day are spent in ritual activity. The focus of this activity is the human body, the appearance and health of which loom as a dominant concern in the ethos of the people. While such a concern is certainly not unusual, its ceremonial aspects and associated philosophy are unique.

The fundamental belief underlying the whole system appears to be that the human body is ugly and that its natural tendency is to debility and disease. Incarcerated in such a body, man's only hope is to avert these characteristics through the use of the powerful influences of ritual and ceremony. Every household has one or more shrines devoted to this purpose. The more powerful individuals in the society have several shrines in their houses and, in fact, the opulence of a house is often referred to in terms of the number of such ritual centers it possesses. Most houses are of wattle and daub construction, but the shrine rooms of the more wealthy are walled with stone. Poorer families imitate the rich by applying pottery plaques to their shrine walls.

While each family has at least one such shrine, the rituals associated with it are not family

Reprinted from *American Anthropologist,* **58** (1956).

ceremonies but are private and secret. The rites are normally only discussed with children, and then only during the period when they are being initiated into these mysteries. I was able, however, to establish sufficient rapport with the natives to examine these shrines and to have the rituals described to me.

The focal point of the shrine is a box or chest which is built into the wall. In this chest are kept the many charms and magical potions without which no native believes he could live. These preparations are secured from a variety of specialized practitioners. The most powerful of these are medicine men, whose assistance must be rewarded with substantial gifts. However, the medicine men do not provide the curative potions for their clients, but decide what the ingredients should be and then write them down in an ancient and secret language. This writing is understood only by the medicine men and by the herbalists who, for another gift, provide the required charm.

The charm is not disposed of after it has served its purpose, but is placed in the charm-box of the household shrine. As these magical materials are specific for certain ills, and the real or imagined maladies of the people are many, the charm-box is usually full to overflowing. The magical packets are so numerous that people forget what their purposes were and fear to use them again. While the natives are very vague on this point, we can only assume that the idea in returning all the old magical materials is that their presence in the charm-box, before which the body rituals are conducted, will in some way protect the worshipper.

Beneath the charm-box is a small font. Each day every member of the family, in succession, enters the shrine room, bows his head before the charmbox,mingles different sorts of holy water in the font, and proceeds with a brief rite of ablution. The holy waters are secured from the Water Temple of the community, where the priests conduct elaborate ceremonies to make the liquid ritually pure.

In the hierarchy of magical practitioners, and below the medicine men in prestige, are specialists whose designation is best translated "holy-mouth-men." The Nacirema have an almost pathological horror of and fascination with the mouth, the condition of which is believed to have a supernatural influence on all social relationships. Were it not for the rituals of the mouth, they believe that their teeth would fall out, their gums bleed, their jaws shrink, their friends desert them, and their lovers reject them. They also believe that a strong relationship exists between oral and moral characteristics. For example, there is a ritual ablution of the mouth for children which is supposed to improve their moral fiber.

The daily body ritual performed by everyone includes a mouth-rite. Despite the fact that these people are so punctilious about care of the mouth, this rite involves a practice which strikes the uninitiated stranger as revolting. It was reported to me that the ritual consists of inserting a small bundle of hog hairs into the mouth, along with certain magical powders, and then moving the bundle in a highly formalized series of gestures.

In addition to the private mouth-rite, the people seek out a holy-mouth-man once or twice a year. These practitioners have an impressive set of paraphernalia, consisting of a variety of augers, awls, probes, and prods. The use of these objects in the exorcism of the evils of the mouth involves almost unbelievable ritual torture of the client. The holy-mouth-man opens the client's mouth and, using the above mentioned tools, enlarges any holes which decay may have created in the teeth. Magical materials are put into these holes. If there are no naturally occurring holes in the teeth, large sections of one or more teeth are gouged out so that the supernatural substance can be applied. In the client's view, the purpose of these ministrations is to arrest decay and to draw friends. The extremely sacred and traditional character of the rite is evident in the fact that the natives return to the holy-mouth-man year after year, despite the fact that their teeth continue to decay.

It is to be hoped that, when a thorough study of the Nacirema is made there will be careful inquiry into the personality structure of these people. One has but to watch the gleam in the eye of a holy-mouth-man, as he jabs an awl into an exposed nerve, to suspect that a certain amount of sadism is involved. If this can be established, a very interesting pattern emerges, for most of the population shows definite masochistic tendencies. It was to these that Professor Linton referred in discussing a distinctive part of the daily body ritual which is performed only by men. This part of the rite involves scraping and lacerating the surface of the face with a sharp instrument. Special women's rites are performed only four times during each lunar month, but what they lack in frequency is made up in barbarity. As part of this ceremony, women bake their heads in small ovens for about an hour. The theoretically interesting point is that what seems to be a preponderantly masochistic people have developed sadistic specialists.

The medicine men have an imposing temple, or *latipso,* in every community of any size. The more elaborate ceremonies required to treat very sick patients can only be performed at this temple. These ceremonies involve not only the thaumaturge but a permanent group of vestal maidens who move sedately about the temple chambers in distinctive costume and headdress.

The *latipso* ceremonies are so harsh that it is phenomenal that a fair proportion of the really sick natives who enter the temple ever recover. Small children whose indoctrination is still incompleté have been known to resist attempts to take them to the temple because "that is where you go to die." Despite this fact, sick adults are not only willing but eager to undergo the protracted ritual purification, if they can afford to do so. No matter how ill the supplicant or how grave the emergency, the guardians of many temples will not admit a client if he cannot give a rich gift to the custodian. Even after one has gained admission and survived the ceremonies, the guardians will not permit the neophyte to leave until he makes still another gift.

The supplicant entering the temple is first stripped of all his or her clothes. In every-day life the Nacirema avoids exposure of his body and its natural functions. Bathing and excretory acts are performed only in the secrecy of the household shrine, where they are ritualized as part of the body-rites. Psychological shock results from the fact that body secrecy is suddenly lost upon entry into the *latipso.* A man, whose wife has never seen him in an excretory act, suddenly finds himself naked and assisted by a vestal maiden while he performs natural functions into a sacred vessel. This sort of ceremonial treatment is necessitated by the fact that the excreta are used by a diviner to ascertain the course and nature of the client's sickness. Female clients, on the other hand, find their naked bodies are subjected to the scrutiny, manipulation and prodding of the medicine men.

Few supplicants in the temple are well enough to do anything but lie on their hard beds. The daily ceremonies, like the rites of the holy-mouth-men, involve discomfort and torture. With ritual precision, the vestals awaken their miserable charges each dawn and roll them about on their beds of pain while performing ablutions, in the formal movements of which the maidens are highly trained. At other times they insert magic wands in the supplicant's mouth or force him to eat substances which are supposed to be healing. From time to time the medicine men come to their clients and jab magically treated needles into their flesh. The fact that these temple ceremonies may not cure and may even kill the neophyte, in no way decreases the people's faith in the medicine men.

There remains one other kind of practitioner, known as a "listener." This witch-doctor has the power to exorcise the devils that lodge in the heads of people who have been bewitched. The Nacirema believe that parents bewitch their own children. Mothers are particularly suspected of putting a curse on children while teaching them the secret body rituals. The counter-magic of the witch-doctor is unusual in its lack of ritual. The patient simply tells the "listener" all his troubles and fears, beginning with the earliest difficulties he can remember. The memory displayed by the Nacirema in these exorcism sessions is truly remarkable. It is not uncommon for the patient to bemoan the rejection he felt being weaned as a babe, and a few individuals even see their troubles going back to the traumatic effects of their own birth.

In conclusion, mention must be made of certain practices which have their base in native esthetics but which depend upon the pervasive aversion to the natural body and its functions. These are ritual fasts to make fat people thin and ceremonial feasts to make thin people fat. Still other rites are used to make women's breasts larger if they are small, and smaller if they are large. General dissatisfaction with breast shape is symbolized in the fact that the ideal form is virtually outside the range of human variation. A few women afflicted with almost inhuman hypermammary developments are so idolized that they make a handsome living by simply going from village to village and permitting the natives to stare at them for a fee.

Reference has already been made to the fact that excretory functions are ritualized, routinized, and relegated to secrecy. Natural reproductive functions are similarly distorted. Intercourse is taboo as a topic and scheduled as an act. Efforts are made to avoid pregnancy by the use of magical material or by limiting intercourse to certain phases of the moon. Conception is actually very infrequent. When pregnant, women dress so as to hide their condition. Parturition takes place in secret, without friends or relatives to assist, and the majority of women do not nurse their infants.

Our review of the ritual life of the Nacirema has certainly shown them to be a magic-ridden people. It is hard to understand how they have managed to exist so long under the burdens which they have imposed upon themselves. But even such exotic customs as these take on real meaning when they are viewed with the insight provided by Malinowski when he wrote:

"Looking from far and above, from our high places of safety in the developed civilization, it is easy to see all the crudity and irrelevance of magic. But without its power and guidance early man could not have mastered his practical difficulties as he has done, nor could men have advanced to the higher stages of civilization."

Summary

Religion has been one of the most studied aspects of non-Western societies, not because other people are more religious than we are, but rather because their religious behavior is not clearly divided from other aspects of their social life. We usually distinguish between *religion,* which is a belief system that explains the social and spiritual order, *magic,* an attempt to manipulate the forces of nature, and *science,* which is based upon experiment and does not call upon supernatural powers. Religion, magic and science exist together in all societies.

Religion exists in a social context, that is, religious beliefs are an expression of the way people order their lives. It is also a way of dividing up the universe into things *sacred* and things *profane,* and thereby setting apart those elements that are considered special. Religion also imposes a moral pressure upon people to act in accordance with what is believed to be right or proper.

One of the most basic religious beliefs is the attribution of a spirit or soul to all living things, called *animism.* Usually this takes the form of a belief in two separate beings, one tangible and earthly, the other intangible and spiritual. Another common belief is in the concept of supernatural power, frequently uncontrollable, which we call *mana.* Associated with this concept is that of *taboo,* a restriction on behavior to avoid contact with such power or to avoid certain actions that would cause the power to work against oneself. Religious beliefs are created and sustained by *myths,* or sacred stories that contain explanations of how things came to be the way they are and how they should be maintained. Myths are accepted on faith, and need not be verified in order to be considered valid.

A *ritual* is a prescribed way of carrying out a religious activity, such as a prayer, an act of worship, or a sacrifice. Rituals surrounding the different stages of life, such as birth, marriage or death, are called *rites of passage.* In some societies an individual could gain entry into adult status only by acquiring spiritual power through a hallucinatory vision, a ritual known as a *vision quest.* Another religious ritual is known as *spirit possession,* in which an individual is possessed by a supernatural spirit, usually in a state of trance.

Totemism is a religious system found among many peoples throughout the world. A *totem* is a natural item with which an individual or a group identifies. A society may be divided into many different totemic groups, each with its own totem. Totemism can form the basis for a moral code for the society by prescribing rules concerning eligible marriage partners, guidelines for interaction among members of the society, and even rules involving the interaction between people and their natural environment.

All societies include individuals who occupy positions as *religious specialists.* In some cases these are people who have undergone specialized training for their position, while in others a person occupies such a position as a result of innate personal qualities. A *priest* is an example of a religious specialist who must undertake a period of formal training. In contrast, a *shaman* is a religious specialist whose powers come directly from the supernatural forces; while there may be a training period involved in becoming a shaman, that in itself is not sufficient. A third type of religious specialist is a *diviner,* an individual who can foresee future events or uncover the causes of past events.

Magic is a practice designed to manipulate the supernatural forces, whereas *witchcraft* is used as an explanation of how or why things happen as they did. Magic can be good or bad, designed to benefit or harm a person or group of people. Sir James Frazer discussed two principles of magic: the *law of similarity,* which states that an action will produce a similar effect; and the *law of contact,* which states that things that have been in contact with each other continue to exert an effect upon one another after they have become separated. An example of the law of similarity is *voodoo,* in which a doll is made in the image of the intended victim and actions taken against the doll are believed to have a similar effect upon the victim. An example of a belief in the law of contact or contagion is found among people who following the custom of burying hair or nail clippings so that nobody can use them to cause the owner harm.

Witchcraft can be used to explain unfortunate events. If an accident occurs in an otherwise normal activity, it can be explained by witchcraft. Also, witchcraft can function as a way of relieving tensions that arise in a society. Nadel compared witchcraft in four African societies, and showed how in each case the pattern of witchcraft accusations could be understood by uncovering sources of tension between various groups within the society, such as antagonism between the sexes or between two categories of relatives. We can also see elements of witchcraft accusations operating to relieve tensions in our own society, by creating a class of scapegoats who can be blamed for various problems or otherwise inexplicable events.

Glossary

age grading The organization of groups in some societies based upon the association of individuals of similar age.

animism A religious belief in which a spirit or soul is attributed to all living things, and sometimes is extended to inanimate objects. The spirits are worshipped and, at times, thought to have supernatural power.

diviner A religious specialist who is able to foresee future events or uncover the causes of past events. Divination reflects an attempt to control the forces of the universe through the prediction of future events.

law of contact A principle in the use of magic stating that things that have been in contact with each other continue to exert an effect upon one another after they have become separated. Also known as *contagious magic,* it involves the manipulation of an individual's personal possessions or a severed portion of the body to create an effect upon that individual.

law of similarity A principle in the use of magic that involves manipulation of symbolic objects to produce the same effect upon an actual person or activity.

magic An attempt to manipulate the forces of nature to derive certain desired results. It may be religious in some contexts as a part of a belief system dealing with forces of power and relating people to nature. Magic, however, assumes human power over the forces of the universe, while religion does not.

mana A concept found in many religious systems, which refers to a supernatural force or power in nature. This power is not inherently good or bad, and it is both unpredictable and uncontrollable.

myth A sacred story that serves as an explanation for the natural environment, a group's relationship to the supernatural or spirit world, and their cultural customs and rituals. In nonliterate societies, these elaborate stories are part of an oral tradition passed on from one generation to the next. They also function as guidelines to explain how and why rituals are performed.

profane Those aspects of society that are considered ordinary, having no special religious significance.

reincarnation A concept found in the Hindu religion that refers to the rebirth of an individual into a higher or lower social position in the next life. In this sense it serves to support the system of social stratification in India. This concept is also found in various forms in other societies.

religion A belief system, which includes myths that explain the social and spiritual order, and rituals through which the members of the religious community carry out their beliefs and act out the myths.

religious specialist A position held in society by the individual considered most able to relate to the supernatural. Depending on the society, the position may be filled by an individual who has undergone specialized training, or by a person considered to have innate ability.

rite of passage (also called **life crisis rite**) A ceremony marking the change from one period or stage of life into another (e.g., baptism, bar mitzvah, marriage, funeral).

ritual A prescribed way of carrying out a religious activity, such as a prayer, an act of worship, or a sacrifice. Rituals reinforce the belief system of a society, and function both in terms of spiritual value and symbolic meaning for the group.

sacred Those aspects of society that are considered special (such as dangerous or powerful) and are thought of as having a certain mystical quality.

science A system of beliefs based upon observed relationships in the knowable universe, and an attempt to manipulate natural forces based upon experiment. It is not designed to call into question supernatural powers, as is magic.

secularization The process by which a society becomes more reliant upon civil attitudes and explanations, rather than religious attitudes and explanations.

shaman A religious specialist considered to have contact with spirits, and whose powers come directly from the supernatural forces. Communication with spirits usually takes place through possession, and the individual serves as a vehicle of contact for the rest of his group.

spirit possession A religious practice involving the transmission of supernatural power through a human agent. The ritual occurs in a group situation in which a person becomes possessed by a spirit through trance, induced by drugs or some physical activity, and then acts as a medium through which the spirit communicates to the other people

superstition A belief system lending support to certain activities, which is based upon supernatural explanations. As such, it has qualities similar to those of magic, but the participants have less conviction in their beliefs than does a practitioner of magic.

taboo (also **tabu**) A ritual prohibition against a specific behavior pattern, punishable by supernatural sanctions. In association with the concept *mana*, it refers to a restriction on the behavior of humans to avoid contact with such power, because it can be dangerous. It reflects a people's need to follow a set of rules defining their behavior with respect to sacred beings and objects.

totemism A religious system based upon the concept of totem, which may be an animal, a plant or a natural inanimate object signifying the symbolic unity of a group. A society may be divided into several totemic groups, each identifying with a particular totem, and in the extreme form, claiming a blood tie with the totem. As such it is both a type of nature worship, and a principle of organization in society.

vision quest A ritual, sometimes a rite of passage, found among many groups (including many American Indian tribes). An individual in isolation seeks the support of a spirit during a hallucinatory vision, usually induced through fasting and self-mutilation.

voodoo A form of magic based upon the law of similarity. A symbolic representation (doll) is made of an individual, and is manipulated in such a way as to produce similar effects on the individual.

witchcraft An explanation of how or why certain events occurred. Witchcraft functions as an outlet for aggression and hostitility, resolves tensions and conflicts, explains otherwise inexplicable events, and acts as a mechanism of social control by regulating behavior of certain members of the group.

Questions for Discussion

1. Emile Durkheim emphasized three aspects of religion: (1) the social context of religious systems; (2) the sacred aspect of religion; and (3) the moral basis of religion in society. How can you relate each of these features to your own religion? How does religion in this respect influence the other institutions of Western society? What are some of the sacred objects or concepts in our culture, and what is it that makes them sacred?
2. Under what conditions in American society do we rely upon supernatural help or support? What makes these situations different from those in which we rely upon science and technology?

3 There are certain behaviors surrounded by taboo in our society (e.g., talking about sex with one's parents). What are some examples of these behaviors or objects? What makes them taboo? Many of these attitudes are changing today; what effect will this have upon our beliefs?

4 There has been a religious revival in the United States in recent years. How would you account for this revival, and how is it associated with other aspects of our society, such as economics or politics?

5 While many Americans would scoff at the use of magic or witchcraft, you might be surprised at how often these beliefs are actually put to use. Think of some examples of your use of the law of similarity and the law of contact, or contagious magic. We may call it superstition, but the result is the same!

Suggestions for Additional Reading

Blatty, William Peter
1971 The Exorcist. New York: Harper & Row.

The best-seller dealing with possession and exorcism in Western society, an interesting contrast to similar religious beliefs and practices in non-Western societies.

Durkheim, Emile
1915 The Elementary Forms of the Religious Life. London: George Allen & Unwin, Ltd.

A classic study of primitive religion, in which the author looks at Australian totemism in an attempt to reconstruct the origins of religion in human society.

Elkin, A. P.
1954 Australian Aborigines. Third Edition. Garden City, N.Y.: Anchor Books.
A thorough analysis of totemism is included in this study of the cultures of native Australians.

Evans-Pritchard, E. E.
1937 Witchcraft, Oracles and Magic among the Azande. Oxford: Clarendon Press.

A classic account of religious beliefs and practices among this African society.

Frazer, Sir James G.
1922 The Golden Bough: A Study of Magic and Religion. Abridged Edition. New York: The Macmillan Co.

Originally published in 12 volumes, now available in abridged form, this is one of the best-known works in anthropology, valuable for its wide range of examples and sources.

LaBarre, Weston
1962 They Shall Take Up Serpents: Psychology of the Southern Snake-Handling Cult. New York: Schocken Books.

A study of a snake-handling Pentecostal church in the American South.

Lessa, William A., and Evon Z. Vogt (editors)
1972 Reader in Comparative Religion. Third Edition. New York: Harper & Row.

An excellent collection of articles on the anthropology of religion.

Lowie, Robert H.
1924 Primitive Religion. New York: Grosset and Dunlap.

An early cross-cultural analysis of religion in non-Western societies, still widely read today.

Mair, Lucy
1969 Witchcraft. New York: McGraw-Hill.

A British social anthropologist looks at witchcraft in its social context.

Malinowski, Bronislaw
1948 Magic, Science and Religion, and Other Essays. Glencoe: The Free Press.

A collection of papers, including the famous article distinguishing magic, science and religion.

Tylor, Sir Edward B.
1871 Primitive Culture: Researches into the Development of Mythology, Philosophy, Religion, Language, Art and Custom. London: John Murray.

Includes an early anthropological view of religion, and Tylor's analysis of animism as the most basic form of religious belief.

Wallace, Anthony F. C.
1966 Religion: An Anthropological View. New York: Random House.

One of many modern-day texts dealing with the anthropological approach to the study of religion.

Weller, Jack E.
1966 Yesterday's People. Lexington: University of Kentucky Press.

The author, himself a minister in Kentucky, portrays traditional Appalachian religious beliefs and practices.

Economics, Politics and Social Control

Chapter Eight

The anthropological approach to economics raises entirely different questions than the traditional approach of the economist. In this chapter we will face the problem of determining exactly what falls under the heading of economic behavior, political behavior or legal behavior. In our own society we usually have little difficulty differentiating between economic, political and legal behavior, but this is not the case among non-Western peoples. Instead, we find that in these societies there is no clear distinction between the various areas of social life. Institutions that in our society are neatly divided into different categories are so intricately tied together in some other societies that they cannot be separated. What may seem like a religious ceremony can also be a setting for economic exchange from another perspective, or a reaffirmation of the distribution of power and authority from a third. In this section we will review a number of different types of economic systems found in non-Western societies, demonstrating how they are fused with other types of behavior. Because of this fusion, the societies in question can be studied only in the context of the total social system.

The anthropological approach to economics attempts to show that if economic theory is to be considered valid, it must apply not only to Western industrial society, but to all societies. In the discussion that follows, we will first make a distinction between *primitive, peasant* and *industrial* economies. Then we will go on to consider three different modes of exchange—*reciprocity, redistribution,* and *market exchange* based upon supply and demand. Finally, we will indicate how the study of these different economic types and modes of exchange can lead us to a better understanding of the nature of social organization and the integration of culture.

A peasant father throws his hat
upon the ground.
"What did I do?" he asks one of his sons.
"You threw your hat upon the ground," the son answers,
whereupon the father strikes him.
He picks up his hat and asks another son, "What did I do?"
"You picked up your hat," the son
replies and gets a blow in his turn.
"What did I do?" the father asks the third son.
"I don't know," the smart one replies.
"Remember, sons," the father concludes,
"if someone asks you how many goats
your father has, the answer is, you don't know."

EDWARD C. BANFIELD *The Moral Basis of a Backward Society*

Primitive, Peasant and Industrial Economic Systems

Western economic theory is based on the premise that in a cash economy, people in a competitive situation will try to make as much money as they can. However, the anthropological approach to economics around the world cannot accept this as the guiding force in economic activity. In many non-Western societies other values influence the way people act. Prestige, or the obligations of kinship, or any of a number of outside factors might lead a person to disregard monetary gain and to make an economic decision that to us would seem "irrational." This is possible because not everyone is able to separate economic activity from other aspects of life to the extent that we do. For example, the American business ethic would have us believe that there is no place for favoritism in a competitive business situation. The boss's son has to earn his promotion like anyone else. (In reality, of course, we can easily cite instances where the boss's son or daughter received special considerations.) Yet in many societies a statement that denies such favoritism would be regarded as ridiculous. The son is entitled to special favors, and it would be foolish not to expect him to be treated differently.

The blending of economics with other aspects of social life, such as religion, marriage, or kinship is typical of traditional societies, in contrast to our own industrial society. What we call "primitive" economies are found in many non-Western societies studied by anthropologists, including not only hunters and gatherers, but some agricultural and horticultural groups as well. These are small-scale economies, found among relatively isolated, self-sufficient groups.

There is little division of labor within the society, which means that virtually everyone is engaged in the same economic activity. What little surplus the people are able to produce goes to their own fund to be used for ceremonies and special occasions; no surplus is produced to be exported or marketed. In sum, the primitive economy is one that is controlled exclusively by the local community. It is based upon a relatively simple technology using primarily human and animal power.

In contrast to the primitive system of production and limited pattern of consumption and exchange stands the modern industrial economy, with its advanced technology. Production in the industrial

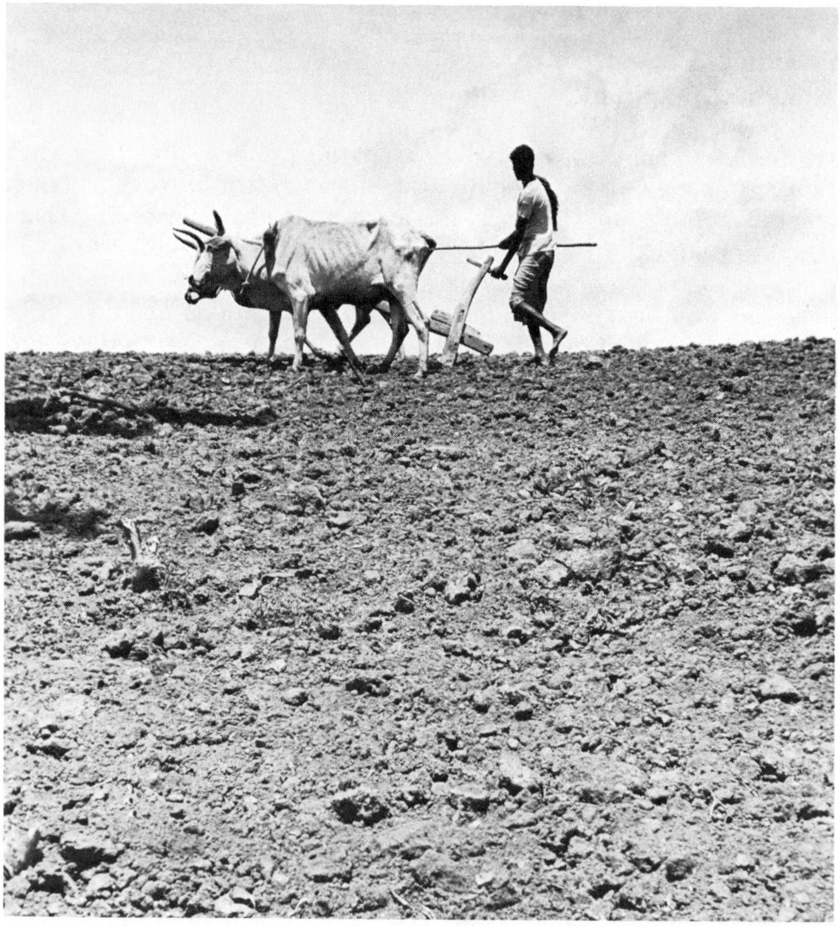

Agricultural practices in India are typical of a peasant economy, relying heavily on human and animal power. Left: A farmer plowing his field near Allahabad, Uttar Pradesh. (Raghubir Singh, Woodfin Camp) Right: Irrigating the rice crop in Madras. (United Nations)

economy is almost exclusively for exchange, which means that there is no self-sufficiency on the community level. The division of labor is extremely high, with specialists taking over almost every aspect of the society. The economy is controlled on the national or even the international level, and the individual producer is subject to pressures from the outside in his economic activity. Typical of the industrial economic system is our concept of the farmer as an agricultural businessman, a cultivator who is totally integrated into the market system and who produces crops for sale in a market system in return for a cash profit.

Midway between these two economic types is the peasant economy. Peasants are partly self-sufficient, and while they resemble producers in a primitive economic system in many ways, they also share characteristics with the modern farmer. There is no great division of labor in a peasant community, with almost every individual engaged in the production of food for consumption. Peasants rely upon a simple technology, with traditional tools made from locally available materials, and animal power yielding the major source of energy. But unlike the primitive economy, peasant producers are tied to a wider market system and are not completely autonomous in their production. The means and the results of production are controlled to some extent by an outside elite group, be it the state or a local sovereign or whatever, and they are forced to rely upon a politically and economically dominant town or city for their subsistence. They are taxed or in some other way do not have complete control over their land and labor. At the same time, peasants are distinguished from modern farmers in an industrial society by the fact that for the peasant cultivator, agriculture is a way of life and not simply an occupation. The

Threshing near the village of Abou El Namroos, outside Cairo, Egypt. Tractor in the background indicates a change from subsistence to market-oriented agriculture. (United Nations)

peasant tills the soil because it is a part of his tradition, while the farmer does so because it is a way to make a living.

With this brief distinction between three different economic systems in mind, let us turn to a discussion of the types of exchange to see how economic activity can be viewed in different societies. Note that most anthropological investigations have been concerned with societies characterized by primitive and peasant economic systems; only recently have anthropologists devoted any interest to modern industrial economies, and even then it has been with the idea of pointing out how on a microscopic level we can see elements of primitive and peasant economics in our own society.

Reciprocity

The economic historian Karl Polanyi, in his book *The Great Transformation,* has defined three patterns of exchange which can be considered as the basis for any economic system: *reciprocity, redistribution* and *market exchange.* Whereas Western economists tend to rely most heavily upon the nature of market exchange for an understanding of economics, anthropologists have found the other two types equally important in their studies of non-Western societies. Market exchange implies the law of supply and demand dictating who exchanges what with whom. Redistribution entails the collection of goods by a central authority, and then the reallocation of those goods according to some principle to members of the society. Reciprocity exists where people exchange goods without a market system and a law of supply and demand, and without an outside authority intervening.

Whereas redistribution implies stratification, reciprocity can occur in both highly stratified and basically egalitarian societies. It can be concerned with the exchange of goods such as agricultural products of handicrafts, or it can involve other items, such as the exchange of women between two groups. Frequently there are reciprocal arrangements among members of the same family or wider kinship group, and these arrangements are inherent in the kin obligations of the society. Among the Bushmen of the Kalahari Desert of South Africa, each individual does his or her part in hunting game or gathering roots, berries and other vegetable food during the day. When a hunter or a group of hunters are successful in a big kill, the meat they bring home is divided among their kinsmen, with the expectation that when someone else makes the kill the next time the debt will be repaid. It is not important that an exact balance ever be struck, so long as the obligations of reciprocation are maintained.

Bronislaw Malinowski, in his work on the Trobriand Islanders, describes a complex set of reciprocal relationships among the different island groups with whom the Trobrianders trade. One aspect of this economic system is called the *Kula Ring,* in which a series of island groups forming a ring engage in the exchange of shell ornaments and other ritually significant items. The trading ring is organized so that different items travel in different directions. For example, the Trobrianders trade arm bands for necklaces with the people from Dobu. This sequence would never be reversed, that is, the Dobuans would never give the Trobrianders arm bands, and the Trobrianders would never give the Dobuans necklaces. In addition, each Kula trader has a number of formally established trading partnerships with whom he may exchange these ritually important items.

The necklaces and arm bands and other treasures to be exchanged are held in very high esteem. They are used only on special ceremonial occasions, and each piece is well known to all traders, having its own name and history. Furthermore, these items cannot be used to buy anything other than ritual trade items. In other words, a Kula trader could not use a necklace to buy food, but only to buy an arm band. The value of each piece is established according to its qualities, and is generally agreed upon by all members of the trade ring. It has been suggested that the Kula Ring operates on the basis of a primitive form of currency, for these ritual items are used in much the same way that we use money.

On the surface it would seem that there is no rational explanation for this form of ritual exchange among members of the Kula Ring. The canoe trips required for trading expeditions cover long stretches of the open seas and entail a great deal of danger for the traders. We can see why certain items might be assigned ritual value, particularly when they are made of material, not locally available, that can only be acquired through trading with other island groups. But it is difficult to understand why these expeditions continue once a sufficient supply of these items has been secured. It would almost seem as if the Trobrianders and the others in the ring are inveterate traders who would go to any lengths to get together for an exchange.

Upon deeper analysis, however, the reason for the trade expeditions becomes clear. The Trobriand Islanders make a distinction between trade of ritual items such as arm bands and necklaces, and

(Courtesy Harcourt Brace Jovanovich, Inc.)

Bronislaw Malinowski (1884–1942) *spent six years studying the peoples of the Australian territories during World War I. His contribution to the field of anthropology rests not only with his emphasis upon field research and the method of participant observation (see Chapter 4); in his work in the Pacific, he produced many valuable accounts of the economic, religious and sexual lives of the people he studied. His analysis of the Kula Ring as an economic institution among the Trobriand Islanders offers a valuable insight into the function of trading expeditions for the people within the island ring. He also offered the view of a people's mythology as an explanation and justification for their social order—in his words, myth serves as a charter for society.*

the trade of practical items such as food and tools. When they set off on a trading excursion, it is with the expressed purpose of exchanging only ritual items. Yet this most emphasized activity, which possesses the most significance in terms of the motivation for trade, is actually the least significant in practical terms. The canoes used for Kula trade are laden with trade items of practical importance as well, and these items are exchanged as a preliminary to the Kula trade. The practical items do not have a ritual value attached to them, and they are the subject of much haggling back and forth among the traders. As long as all of the participants recognize that the mission really revolves around Kula trade, this kind of haggling can occur, although it is expressly forbidden to argue over the value of a Kula item. Trading partners who have a firmly established Kula relationship may not trade practical subsistence items with each other, which also prevents them from haggling with each other over any items at all.

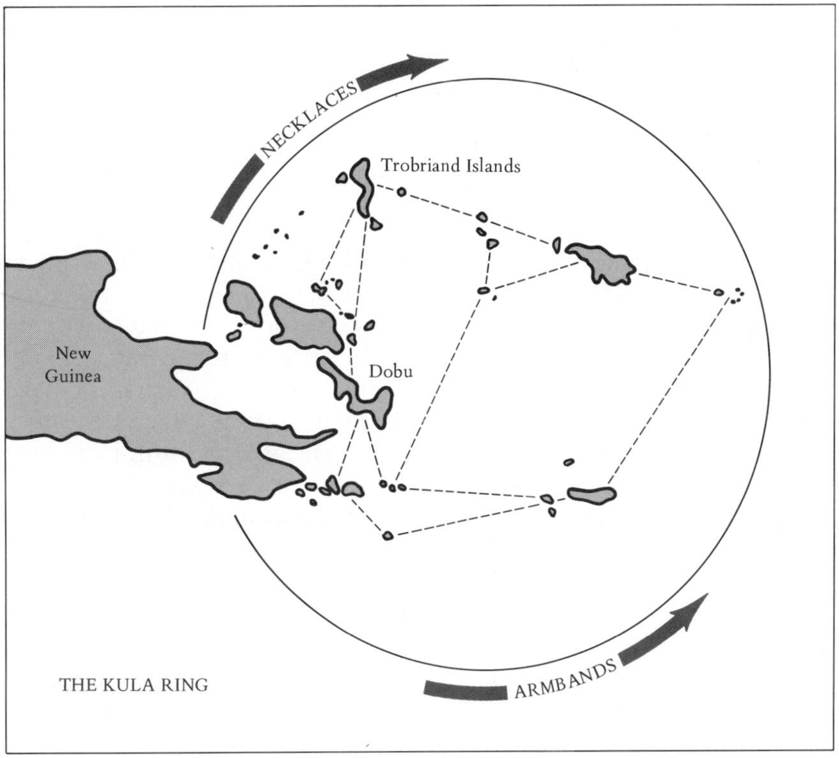

In other words, although the Trobrianders don't admit it, the Kula trade is really important for two reasons: not only does it bring about the exchange of ritually valuable items, but it also brings people together for the "incidental" exchange of more important subsistence items. Thus we can see two types of exchange operating at the same time, the Kula system which is basically a type of reciprocity, and the incidental trading which is a type of market exchange with fluctuating values depending upon supply and demand.

Both the Bushmen and the Trobriand patterns of reciprocity are examples of a primitive economic system, in which small-scale, relatively isolated societies control their own local economies and are basically self-sufficient. To illustrate the reciprocal type of exchange among a peasant society, we turn to the example of the *jajmani* system found in many peasant villages in India.

In a highly stratified society such as India, reciprocation is generally more carefully calculated. In the *jajmani* system, traditional payments are made for services. This is not a market system of exchange, however, because the values of the services are not based on supply and demand, but are fixed according to tradition. The *jajmani* system presents a means of reciprocation in the Indian village based upon the caste system and its implied occupational specialization.

Although most peasant villages in India are dependent primarily upon subsistence agriculture for their survival, not all families in these villages till the soil. Because of the complex system of stratification, only certain members of the community are land owners and farmers. Others who belong to different castes have various occupations according to their caste membership and its appropriate behavior. Some families practice specialized crafts, such as carpenters who make the farmers' tools or water carriers who provide water from the village wells for the rest of the residents. In return, each villager receives payments for his or her services in the form of agricultural produce from the farmer caste, and equivalent services or products from members of the other castes. Thus the land owner commands the services of a wide group of lower caste specialists. The *jajmani* system is the means which enables each specialist, including the cultivator, to obtain the goods and services of others in order to have the variety necessary for his existence. As such it is an institutionalized form of reciprocity among the villagers.

It is impossible, however, to separate the *jajmani* system as an economic institution from other institutions in Indian society. The

Farm hands build a shed for the wheat harvest in Punjab, India. (R. W. Young, DPI)

Hindu religion forms the basis for the *jajmani* system by providing the religious philosophy upon which the caste system is based. Clearly without the social stratification that the caste system implies, and the religious prohibition against people in certain levels of the social hierarchy performing various tasks, the *jajmani* system could not operate, since everyone in the village could cultivate his own land and provide his own products and specialized services. Thus the *jajmani* system is fused with religious practices, and is not simply economic. Likewise, the religion provides clear prescriptions for behavior for each caste, and thus forms the basis for the institutions of social control on the village level. Political and legal power and authority are delegated partly on the basis of religious tenets, and partly on the basis of economic power, both of which are supported by the *jajmani* system. Although it is in one sense an economic institution, we also define the *jajmani* primarily in social terms as a network of alliances between groups of individuals who practice different occupations. It enables them to exchange their goods and services, but not without bringing into play the entire context of Indian society.

Money is rarely important in the *jajmani* system. It is the exchange of goods and services with values defined according to tradition that has enabled the system to be maintained in the villages. Hereditary customs keep this system closed, unlike our open-market system with its free competition. In fact, where local village economies have become more dependent upon cash, the *jajmani* system has begun to break down. Consider, for example, what would be the result of translating a carpenter's payment of grain to a payment in cash. According to the traditional system, in return for his manufacture and repair of a farmer's tools, a carpenter would receive a payment of a certain amount of grain, which in terms of feeding his family has a fixed value over time. The grain payment will feed the same number of people today that it would have a hundred years ago. If we translate that to a cash payment, again with a fixed amount being recorded according to the tradition, the carpenter's actual payments in terms of how many mouths he can feed now fluctuates, as the value of the cash varies. And if the payment in cash is designed to rise and fall with the value of the currency so that a carpenter's payment maintains a steady relative value, then the traditional system of payments no longer holds.

Redistribution

Redistribution generally refers to some sort of enforced organization that replaces reciprocity, and at the same time increases output by requiring a surplus product to support a group of nonagriculturalists. In a redistributive system of exchange, products are collected and reallocated among the entire population. Obviously the reallocation changes the original distribution of goods in some way, otherwise there would be no need to collect them in the first place. Usually this change is in the form of support for a nonproducing elite, which retains the lion's share for itself, thus entrenching its power. Karl Wittfogel, in his book *Oriental Despotism,* has argued that this classic model of a redistributive form of exchange was characteristic of irrigation societies such as that of ancient Egypt. According to his theory, societies grew up around the riverbeds in otherwise arid regions of the world. The rivers afforded the people the necessary water and fertile soil to produce agricultural crops to support a relatively dense population. Eventually, however, the population outgrew the land, and in order to support greater numbers of people irrigation was necessary. As the irrigation system grew more complex, more intricate regulation and a greater concentration of power to enforce these regulations were required. The ultimate result was the organization of an elite group at the head of society, which solidified its power through laws and religious edicts.

Such was the case among the Pharaohs of ancient Egypt. Originally based upon the regulation of irrigation along the Nile River, the heads of state in the ancient Egyptian kingdoms eventually spread out their base of power and justified it through the religious doctrines adopted by the common people. They forced the agricultural population to produce a surplus, which was turned over to them, and then redistributed to nonagricultural workers and elites. In this way they were able to support the tremendous population of workers responsible for the construction of the pyramids.

As in the case of reciprocity, redistribution is frequently imbedded in a complex set of kinship relationships with other members of society. In some cases the central figure who collects and redistributes goods might be the head of a large extended household, or he might have only a fictive relationship to the producers, which he calls upon in his demand for surplus production. The Pharaoh was believed to be the divine incarnation on earth and thus related to all men symbolically. Likewise, a tribal chieftain, representing the spirit of all the ancestors of the tribe, could invoke his position as head of the tribe and symbolic leader of the people in collecting and reallocating the tribe's resources. Since all members of the tribe are considered to be related to one another through descent from a common ancestor, its leaders would be empowered to represent the group in such a way.

Redistribution as a form of exchange need not always involve the head of state collecting and reallocating goods from all members of society. Rather, we can find many examples of a combination of both redistribution and reciprocity operating together, in the sense that one individual might collect and then give away goods, with the expectation that those to whom he has given something will reciprocate in some fashion. Such is the case among the Kwakiutl Indians, in an institution known as the *potlatch*.

During the winter when little productive activity could be carried out, the Kwakiutl turned to ceremonial activities, in which redistribution was cloaked in the form of festivals and ritual gift giving. Vast feasts were held, sometimes accompanied by a potlatch, in which a man would give away his material possessions. A potlatch was an important ceremonial occasion used to validate a life crisis ceremony. A man would give a potlatch following his initiation into a secret society, or his marriage, or on any of a number of important ceremonial occasions. In the course of the potlatch he would seek to prove his worthiness of the position he claimed to hold, and to increase his prestige. The actual redistribution of his worldly possessions was quite ostentatious, and was designed to shame his guests and flaunt his own status. A man would spend months or even years preparing for this one occasion, borrowing and saving all he could, in order to have enough to give away. The principle of the potlatch

Pacific Northwest Indians display objects to be given away at a potlatch. (American Museum of Natural History)

was for a man to be able to give away more than his guests could reciprocate. By doing this he proved his importance and validated a higher status for himself. As a result, the guests at the potlatch now felt obligated to reciprocate with an even greater gift-giving festival.

Even more degrading to the guests than giving away wealth was the act of destroying it. A man giving a potlatch might end with a grand finale in which he literally burned blankets, canoes, valuable copper items and even food. Then, having achieved the ultimate in status, he would pay off the debts he had incurred in storing up all of this wealth, certain of the fact that he would be invited to the potlatches of others and receive payments from them. At the same time, he would begin amassing a new fortune for his next potlatch, for having achieved a particular status, he could never rest on his laurels. The higher the status he could achieve, the better off he would be at the potlatches of others; one did not gain any status at all by simply inviting a bunch of people to a potlatch, secure in the knowledge that they could be easily shamed.

Situations similar to the potlatch are not unknown in our own society. There is the case of a man who builds up an enormous estate and gives much of it away to charity in return for prestige, elevated social status, and perhaps even a prestigious and secure position in government or business—consider what it takes to become an ambassador! A debutante ball in our society is in some ways similar to a potlatch. First, it is something only for the wealthy, used to maintain or elevate their high status in society. Not everyone can have a coming-out party—it takes social position, not just money. In throwing such a party, an individual is actually redistributing some of his wealth to other members of the society. Also like the potlatch, he is doing this with the expectation that others will reciprocate. If they don't, he will make a note of it and not invite them to his next party. The point is that although cloaked in "strange" behavior, economic activity in other societies is not much different from our own.

We might also look at redistribution, as found in the potlatch, as a form of savings institution. A man acquires prestige through distributing a surplus. The prestige is shared by his clan or his family. Then if he or his family should have a bad year, or a river should run dry or a herd disappear, he can rely upon others who are indebted to him. In this sense, distributing a surplus, by whatever means, serves the same purpose as putting money in the bank.

Village market scene in India, indicating that market exchange exists along with the reciprocity of the jajmani system. (United Nations)

Market Exchange

We are all familiar with the typical American market system, ruled by the balance of supply and demand. In our economic behavior we tend to think in terms of calculated exchange in an impersonal setting. Each individual attempts to maximize his profit by calculating or estimating the return for labor and products. In other market systems, however, this is not always the case. Within the context of the Haitian market, for example, trade is bound up with a special personal relationship of intermediaries. This relationship is called *pratik,* and refers to the personal ties between an intermediary and those with whom she deals.

A *pratik* relationship is established between a woman trader and her customer. On the one side are the producers who use her as an intermediary in getting their goods to market, and on the other side are the retailers in the market who get their products from her. Bonds are established between the woman and her clients in various ways, but are always based upon a personalized relation, such as granting a "baker's dozen," extending credit, or lowering prices. This bond of *pratik* sets up obligations on the part of all participants, and in effect tends to lower profits while providing greater security. The reason for *pratik* existing can be seen in the nature of the rural economy of Haiti. Production is relatively high, yet comparatively few people are actually engaged in agriculture. As a result there are literally thousands of women who make a small living through trading. Admittedly this could be a high risk occupation, since the competition is so keen and the profit margin is so low. As a way of lowering the risk and increasing security, women establish personal bonds with both producers and retailers. For example, if you give a person a lower price consistently, you reduce your profit, but at the same time when the supply is such that he can go elsewhere for an even lower price, you still have a hold on him. Or, for example, as a trader you pay the producer slightly more than is necessary when the supply is high and the demand is low, with the result that when supply grows scarce, your *pratik* relationship means that he will hold some back for you, and you will not be shut out of the market.

Thus *pratik* relationships tend to stabilize what would otherwise be a highly fluctuating market situation due to the unstable nature of the Haitian agricultural economy. *Pratik* modifies pure competition by giving certain individuals priority in the market. As such, it appears on closer examination to be a highly practical, rational arrangement based upon the economic context in which it is found.

Economic and Social Organization

So far we have surveyed briefly several basic economic types and three modes of exchange that can occur within these economic systems. We have also seen that to characterize the economy of any society as based solely on reciprocity, redistribution or market exchange is incorrect. Any economy is a combination of all of these types of exchange, with one perhaps appearing as the dominant pattern. We must also be aware of the relationship between economics and other aspects of the social organization, that is, other basic institutions within the society. We pointed this out to a limited degree in the discussion of the *jajmani* system, indicating how it is reinforced through the religious doctrines found in India, and how it fits together with the system of social stratification that permeates all social relations in Indian villages.

We must also recognize that what appear to us as basic principles of economic activity in Western society are not followed by every society, and in fact are not even fundamental values associated with every culture. Our notion of maximizing individual profit, for example, is foreign to many people, who would prefer to engage in transactions which promoted solidarity (such as *pratik* relationships), calculating their profit in social as well as monetary terms. In previous chapters we have seen how marriage can be viewed as an economic exchange rather than a social activity, and in fact in most rural areas of non-Western societies the notion of a love object as the basis for a marriage runs counter to many basic values of the community. Also, we are accustomed to viewing our economic transactions in terms of calculating and weighing the alternatives. However, we must be aware of the fact that many values cannot be calculated, and many objects cannot have a value assigned to them. In a small, isolated community where everyone knows everyone else and all people interact with one another on a close, personal basis, getting ahead is rarely as important as fitting in with the group. Prestige and social approval of one's actions can be much more important than a higher material standard of living, and these factors will enter into any calculations made by a resident of the community. Coming from another culture, we tend to look at such economic activities as irrational because they violate our views on what is "rational" according to our system of values. But we must take into account the nonmaterial, intangible values that the people themselves assign to things. When we do this, their actions almost always turn out to be just as "rational" in their own context as ours.

Comparative Political Institutions

Just as with economics, we tend to look at politics as a separate aspect of life. If you were asked to describe politics in American society, you would probably begin by mentioning the structure of our system of government, the nature of political parties, the democratic system of free elections, and so forth. It is quite unlikely that you would bring in such nonpolitical institutions as the family, the church, or the school system. Yet just as we learned in looking at economics cross-culturally, in most societies political behavior is fused with many other aspects of social organization, and does not exist as a separate and distinguishable arena for social interaction.

We can define politics in a most elementary sense as the legitimate use of force or authority within a society. Thus we all engage in some sort of political behavior, for an essential ingredient in living together with other people is a recognized delegation of authority based on special capabilities, greater wisdom and experience, physical superiority, or whatever other criteria we choose. Politics is the way by which people maintain peace within a group and define their group relative to the outside world. Usually we define such a group by associating it with a geographical unit, as with a nation or a state, but this need not always be the case.

Band Organization

The form of political organization known as a *band* is found primarily among people who depend upon hunting and gathering. We can better understand how band organization works if we consider it in the context of the problems that a hunting and gathering society must face and the environment in which they live. People who live from the land without practicing agriculture, raising livestock, or in some other way increasing the amount of food available, may require a great deal of land to support them. This is because they may quickly exhaust the available food supply in a given area, and are forced to move on to a new source of food. Sometimes they follow migratory animals (which in turn are merely following the abundance of food and water for themselves), but more often the movement of a hunting and gathering band is based upon a combination of animal and plant food. Various trees ripen in different seasons, and the rainy season lasts longer or comes later in one area than another. All of these factors make for a unique life style, to which the band seems suited.

Hunting and gathering bands tend to be rather small throughout most of the year, with groups of perhaps 25 to 40 individuals forming the basic residential unit. Of course, the size of the group fluctuates, so that when food is plentiful several bands might join together for a feast, and when food is scarce a number of splinter groups will spread out over a larger area seeking water, animals and edible vegetation. Each band will consider a general area as its own, and while there are no specific boundaries that limit the movement of the group, members rarely go beyond what they consider to be their own territory in the normal course of events. Boundaries may overlap slightly, so that two groups might come into contact when each is on the fringe of its territory, but for the most part a band is isolated from its neighbors and goes about its daily activities alone.

Two elements of political organization operate in maintaining the band—the internal organization of the small group, and the external set of regulations governing the overall organization of a large number of neighboring groups in situations when they come into contact. On the level of the individual group, we can see how the combination of the environment and the way of life would lead to a loose-knit organization. Little in this way of life is permanent. Groups are frequently splitting up, with families going off to join another group, or larger factions forming their own band. Sometimes the group becomes too large to derive sufficient support from the surrounding area, and new land must be used. At other times, internal disputes may be solved by a division of a band into two or more groups. Moreover, a necessary aspect of life as a hunter/gatherer is that each person contribute something to the overall support of the group. There is no room for the nonproductive old or weak individuals when the food supply is so limited. As a result, each family tends to be self-sufficient, and does not rely as heavily upon the rest of the society for its existence as we are accustomed to doing. (Consider where you would be today if you had to grow your own food, make your own clothes and even manufacture your own automobile!)

The ties that bind people together in a band are necessarily of a different nature than the ties that bind people together in a modern industrial society. If a disagreement occurs, each party will feel free to leave the group if he cannot abide by the solution that is reached. To compare it to our own way of life, it is almost like membership in a club. One is free to drop out and join another such group if he does not get along, or if he disagrees with changes that are made. But very few of us would go so far as to drop out of American society just because we disagreed with some of its laws, or because the candidate we voted for lost the election. We have become so specialized that we rely upon others in our society to keep us alive, whereas the typical Bushman, or Australian Aborigine, or Eskimo—all members

Bushwomen in camp. In a band, leadership is normally informal and unstructured, based on consensus of the group. (Hubertus Kanus, Rapho/Photo Researchers)

of societies with band organization—is much better able to get along by himself or with only his family, despite the more hostile environment in which he lives.

Within such a group, the established form of governance tends to be based upon the principle of equality. This is not to say that there are no differences among members of the group, for every individual will be ranked and evaluated according to his or her own particular skill, as a hunter, a story teller, a successful curer, or whatever. But when decisions are made that affect the group as a whole, they are made on the basis of consensus, and are not imposed by one dominant king or chief. Cooperation in all endeavors is the best insurance for survival. If a hunter is successful, he shares his kill with the rest of the group, for he knows that the time will come when his luck will be down and someone else will share his success. This form of cooperation extends not just to the distribution of food, but to the very concept of ownership itself. The resources of the band belong to everyone equally, and are to be shared by all. If there is a leader in such a society, he achieves this status based upon his personal qualities and the respect of his fellow bandsmen. He has no authority to impose his own desires upon the rest of the group against their will, and should he attempt to do so, he will probably lose his position as leader.

A second type of political relationship regulates interaction among two or more small bands. Occasionally two groups will come into contact in areas where their territory overlaps. At other times several groups will gather to celebrate a special event, usually coinciding with a time of year when the food supply is abundant, such as the return of the migratory animals, the ripening of wild grains or other vegetation, the onset of the rainy season, or some other seasonal change in the environment. In such a setting, the bonds which hold these groups together in a political alliance can be most important, for they not only guard against warfare, but they help to integrate the groups and give them a common basis of interaction.

Although they are self-sufficient in the sense that they can obtain enough food to support themselves, bands cannot exist in total isolation from one another. A group of fewer than 40 or 50 people contains only a few families, and thus the number of potential mates for an individual is extremely limited. As we saw in the earlier chapter on kinship, every society has some form of incest taboo, restricting marriage to someone outside the immediate family. Over the years the inbreeding among a few families in a group of this size would mean that there would be no one left as an eligible marriage partner, and if a group remained isolated and continued to obey the incest taboo, it would soon die out. On the other hand, the incest taboo, which forces people to look beyond their own group, at the same time creates a combination of cooperation and dependency upon neighboring groups. It is an interesting question whether the incest taboo originated in the process of cultural evolution as a means of forcing potentially hostile neighbors to cooperate and overcome their differences in order to find marriage partners. Surely it is one of the most effective means of preventing warfare at the band level, for each individual has ties with many other groups through the marriages of his or her relatives, and who would want to engage in a battle with his relatives?

Meeting of the Dinka tribesmen of Sudan. (George Rodger, Magnum)

Tribes and Chiefdoms

There are very few hunting and gathering societies in the world today, and much of our information about band organizations is based upon reports of early contact with such groups in the past. Most

non-Western peoples live in larger groups and obtain their living by other means, which creates an entirely different set of problems requiring political solutions. One such form is *tribal organization.*

A tribe may contain hundreds or even thousands of people, making the delegation of authority and maintenance of order a much more complex process than in a band. Yet even at the tribal level, politics is not a separate institution, but is closely involved with the rest of the social organization. A family might exercise economic control over land, and thus engage in behavior that we would call "economic." It might also be engaged in an alliance with other families, to which we would apply the term "politics." Or it might be the center of a religious activity, such as ancestor worship. Thus when we consider political organization on the tribal level, as on the band level, we are really looking at political behavior of people in a wider social context, and not specifically political institutions that stand apart from the rest of society (as a political party is set apart in our own society).

A tribe can be generally defined as a confederation of groups who recognize a relationship with one another, usually in the form of common ethnic origin, common language, or a strong pattern of interaction based on intermarriage or presumed kinship. On a lower level of organization, a tribe is divided into smaller segments such as villages or regional groups, which in turn are divided into clans or lineages, and on the lowest level families and households. The tribe is considered political in the sense that it is the broadest base upon which joint activities can be organized and carried out by the group and in the name of the group.

Tribal political organization can be important in controlling behavior within the tribe, and in organizing activity in opposition to other outside groups. Of course, it can also operate to coordinate economic activity such as trading networks, or religious activity as in the pattern of worshipping a tribal deity—but this is part of the political process as well. Within the tribe, any dispute or opposition among smaller groups can be settled on the next higher level. If two families argue, the settlement can be reached by appealing to the clan dignitaries, whose authority is derived from and backed by the tribe itself. If two clans should engage in a feud, the ultimate solution may be handed down by the village headman. On the other hand, if there is opposition from some group outside the tribe, then it is the entire tribe that acts together in unison. This form of political organization is called *segmentary opposition,* and it is not unique to tribal societies. We have it in our own political system. For example, the southern Democrats and the northern Democrats might disagree over whom to nominate for the presidency, but once a nominee is chosen, both will support that candidate. Yet on a higher level, both Republicans and Democrats will support the American president, regardless of party, in opposition to the leader of another country. And if we should be invaded by creatures from outer space, we would probably overcome our differences with the Russians and join forces against what would be our common enemy. Segmentary opposition is merely a way of defining allegiance on different levels of organization, according to the scope of the problem.

The tribal form of segmentary political organization is perhaps the simplest type of political system, next to the egalitarian band. It offers an opportunity to organize behavior on different levels, but because it is so decentralized there is little power to enforce cooperation unless people themselves seek it out. As power becomes more concentrated in the hands of one or a few leaders, the political organization of the group becomes more complex. Such a system is frequently referred to as a *chiefdom,* where regional or tribal groups are organized under the authority of a single official. The chief can call upon the members of the group not just for political purposes, but usually he can organize economic activity or religious events as well. Thus the chief tends to be a strong force in bringing together the segments of the tribe, uniting them in a single group, while retaining a greater degree of authority over the activity of each member.

The chiefdom is a significant case of tribal political organization, for it is the beginning of centralized power which is so important in the ultimate evolution of the state-based society we are familiar with in the Western world. Also with the chiefdom comes the establishment of a system of ranking, or social stratification. In a band, all people are inherently equal, and while one man's greater skill as a hunter might give him more say in the organization of the hunt, it does not give him the right to more than his share of the kill. In a small tribal society the same holds true. A person might be recognized for some achievement or skill and obtain a certain amount of power or influence for it, but such power can change with the fortunes of the individual.

In a chiefdom, the headman is entitled to special treatment because of his position,and his family, lineage and village all the way down the line are able to share in his prestige and high position. The chief may be in a position to tax the population and allocate the goods in a program of redistribution. Such power can easily lead to an increase in the ranking differences within the society, for the reallocation of goods will entrench the chief and other higher ranking members in their elevated positions. It can also lead to an increase

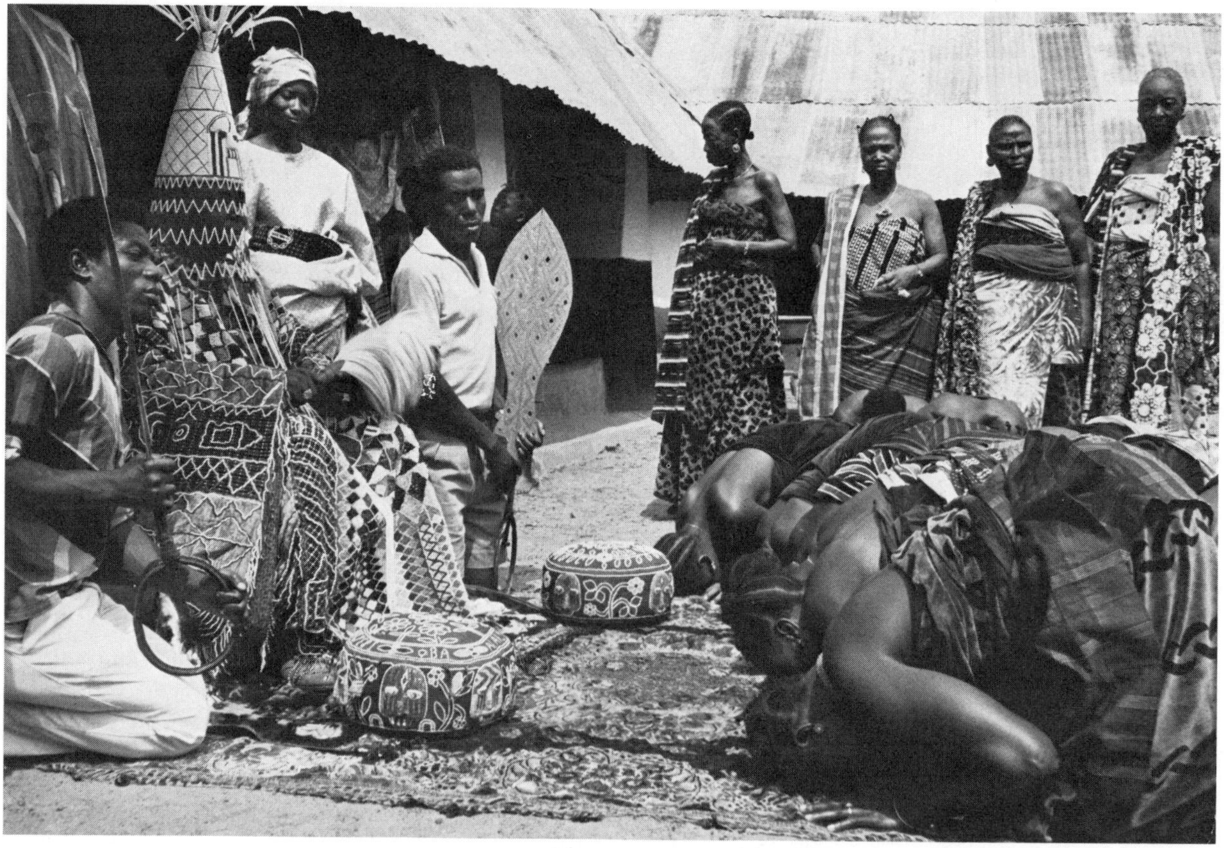

The King of the Yoruba tribe in Akure, West Nigeria being shown respect by several of his 156 wives. (Marc and Evelyne Bernheim, Woodfin Camp)

in the size of the society held together under one central authority. Traditional Hawaii was a chiefdom, with a population of over 100,000. As the chiefdom becomes more centralized, concentrating more power in the hands of a single individual, the society grows more like a state.

State Organization

A *state* is essentially a territorially based government with strong power to organize and carry out activity for the achievement of group goals. It is the most common form of political organization in Western societies, although as we have seen it is by no means the only type of political system that can exist. There is no sharp distinction between a chiefdom and a state, just as there is no clear line dividing a chiefdom from a tribe. Indeed, there can be elementary forms of state organization headed by someone whom we might call a chief, in that his position is not as a secular leader (such as a president or prime minister), but is a religious and perhaps even a kinship position as well.

The state is distinguished from other forms of political organization in the degree to which it can force people to act in certain ways. Its authority can be defined on religious grounds or it can be a secular authority, such as that in our own society where the coercive power of government rests with "the will of the people." The main feature setting the state apart from a chiefdom is the fact that the state is backed by the threat of force to coerce individuals. Along with this power goes a division into classes and, with more developed state governmental organizations, a bureaucracy as well, which distinguishes the political institutions from the rest of society.

Higher levels of economic and social organization are usually associated with a state. One such feature is urbanism, the concentration of people in towns and cities. Sanders and Price, in *Mesoamerica, The Evolution of a Civilization,* argue that the sheer size of cities requires a state-like political system to regulate behavior and integrate the individuals in the society. Moreover, the specialization of economic tasks in a large society not only creates a more complex social organization, but eventually leads to a social hierarchy of classes or castes.

Law and Social Control

Politics, as the legitimate use of force or authority in a society, is closely related to law and social control. The anthropologist who studies this area of social behavior is interested not only in the formal definitions of rules, but in the way people actually act, whether they conform to the rules or not. We assume that the rules people follow reflect their basic values, but at the same time we have to assume that the formal rules that they recognize are not always a true indicator of the way they behave. Since laws are a guide to what is appropriate behavior in a particular society, we can learn from them what kinds of actions people consider to be contrary to their values, and the degree of punishment can also indicate the extent of the transgression. In our own society we can get a clear picture of American values by looking at various actions that are defined as illegal, and comparing punishment generally associated with each crime. A minor traffic offense calls for a small fine, while petty theft might land the culprit in jail for a short time. In contrast, armed robbery would probably meet with a stiffer sentence than the white collar crime of embezzlement, even though the armed robber might net only a few dollars while the embezzler could get away with millions. Right away this tells us something about American values related to violence.

The same kinds of insights can help the anthropologist understand something about the values shared by people in other societies. We also recognize that not all legal sanctions are formal or written down in a code of laws. There are many rules that people are expected to follow, and for which they are punished in some sense if they do not. Social control can work in very subtle ways to mold the behavior of the members of a group, by such practices as exclusion from group activities, gossip, or even open criticism. The offense can be as simple as failure to observe proper table manners—by no means breaking the law, but nonetheless a transgression against the shared values of

Dugum Dani tribesmen of New Guinea engaged in ritual battle with neighboring tribes. The rules of warfare are carefully laid out and followed, keeping fatalities at a minimum. (Karl Heider)

the rest of society. We are all subject to such pressure, as you will recognize immediately in looking at the clothes you wear, the way you speak, the places you go and the people with whom you associate.

An example of how a legal system operates in a society different from our own will illustrate the basic assumptions that anthropologists make about the role of laws in the process of social control. Among Eskimos there are no specialized legal institutions such as we have in our courts, our police departments and the like. The prevailing principle in Eskimo law is that when someone violates your rights, you must take the law into your own hands and seek to correct the situation yourself. No matter who has the right on his side, the ultimate outcome usually depends upon who has the power and strength. This does not mean that the biggest and toughest individual can bully everyone else around, however, because if the offense is too blatant or repeated too often, he will find that his opponent's relatives step in against him, while his own kinsmen quietly turn the other way.

If a member of an Eskimo community is considered undesirable by the rest of the group, he may be removed either by exile or by execution. But even here, there is no strictly legal institution to deal with the situation; instead, an injured party can gather enough support for his cause, and then the offender's family will be asked to impose the sentence. In this way, no feuds can develop, an important factor to consider in an environment where people must cooperate in order to survive. Thus if we look closely at legal behavior in Eskimo society, we can see how the basic values of ruggedness, individuality and the struggle for survival are reinforced in the way people deal with behavior that violates the rules of conduct.

As with Eskimo society, in the Trobriand Islands most minor infractions are counteracted by self-help, that is, it is the individual's obligation to right any wrong that has been done to him. If a feud should start, there are recognized ways to end the disagreement without a great deal of bloodshed. The community can enforce a solution by first ending the fighting, and then mediating between the parties involved. One possibility is a "bloodwealth" to be paid by the offender—and the community may have to force the victim to accept such payment if he is unwilling. Another option is to resort to some kind of harmless contest, in which the disputants can settle their grievance without bloodshed. The Eskimos have a tradition known as a "song duel," in which each combatant tries to outdo the other in inventing songs that shame and ridicule the opponent. The group sits around and listens to the "duel," and eventually offers its judgment as to the victorious songster. Similar solutions can be reached through wrestling matches or other contests of strength in which no lasting damage is done. The alternative if the feud is allowed to continue is a situation in which the entire society is torn apart into warring camps, as in the famous legend of the Hatfields and McCoys.

An interesting aspect of the anthropological study of law occurs when two cultures come into contact and the legal system of one does not fit in with that of the other. Such a case was described by the columnist Anthony Lewis in a story reported in the International Herald Tribune several years ago. In this case, a man from a rural village in what used to be British East Africa (now Tanzania) was charged with murdering an old woman. He pleaded self-defense, claiming that she was a witch and had threatened to kill him through her use of magic. The man related to the court how one of his children became ill and eventually died. The old woman, who was a relative of the man, had been assigned the task of preparing the boy's funeral, but she had refused to do so, claiming she had cast a spell on the child. Instead, she had threatened to kill the man and his entire family. Shortly thereafter another child died, but when the man demanded that the woman cease her witchcraft, she had simply laughed at him and told him he was next. He left, and returned with an axe, which he used to kill her. Then he turned himself in.

The question for the anthropologist, or for any student of comparative law, is how to reconcile the interaction of two legal systems based upon two sets of values and moral codes. From the one standpoint, the man was clearly justified in killing the old woman, for his belief in witchcraft was genuine, and his fear was seemingly supported by the death of two of his children. However, from another point of view, there is a significant difference between the violent act of killing someone with an axe and the comparatively passive, and to some minds unsubstantiated, act of killing someone with witchcraft. Before reading on to see how the judges decided the case, you might stop and think what you would do if asked to sit on the jury.

Initially the man was convicted and sentenced to death. The case was then appealed to a panel of three judges, each of whom offered a different opinion. The first judge claimed that while the man's beliefs were unquestionably sincere, the law of the land had to be based upon reason, and a belief in witchcraft was simply unreasonable. If the newly developing country were to advance beyond its primitive background, such beliefs would have to be discouraged. The new law of the land was English common law, and witchcraft was unacceptable in that context. The second judge held that what was important was not the technicality of English law, but the motivation that drove the defendant to commit the murder. In this case, the man's motives were justifiable, and he should be judged not guilty. The third judge pulled the whole case together, rejecting the interpretations of the first two. While traditional beliefs were sincere, he argued that the country could not move ahead on that basis. And while English traditions were in many ways more "rational," they could not be strictly applied outside the cultural context in which they arose. Instead, the solution should be a compromise between the two systems: The man should be judged guilty, to emphasize the wrong he had committed, but he should be given a lighter sentence, in recognition of the basis for his crime.

The important lesson for students of anthropology is that law and social control are culture-bound, and reflect the system of which they are a part. There are no absolute truths that can form the basis for any legal system, and there are no rights or wrongs which can be argued in all cultural contexts. In traditional Eskimo society, when a person became too old and could no longer take care of himself, he might be left out on the ice to die. We may look at this as nothing less than murder, a cruel way to treat a close relative or lifelong friend. But for the Eskimo, who faces a difficult and tedious struggle for survival in a forbidding environment, feeding an extra mouth can mean the difference between survival and death. And remember, too, that it is easier to accept such a fate if you grow up knowing that it is the common practice, accepted by all. In reality, it is not significantly different from the practice of euthanasia, or "mercy killing," which has been widely debated and supported by many segments of our own society.

We can also learn much about the inequities in our own legal system from studying law in other cultures. If we recognize that American society is made up of many segments with vast cultural differences, we must be willing to apply this understanding to the way our own laws are interpreted. The values and moral codes of Americans are different according to the various life styles that we follow. The resident of an inner-city ghetto faces different problems than the suburban middle-class individual or the rural farmer, and thus must find different solutions to those problems. Yet many of

Demonstrators protesting outside Federal Building in Chicago, where eight persons are on trial for conspiracy during the 1968 Democratic National Convention. Civil disobedience and public protest are longstanding traditions in American culture. (UPI)

our laws are rigidly structured and do not take into account these cultural differences.

Let us consider, for example, the different ways of expressing disagreement or hostility in American culture—a linguistic question, but one that reflects cultural differences. If a middle-class white businessman were to say "I do not agree with the policies of the President," we would probably think nothing of it. However, if a militant Black Nationalist were to say something like "Off pig Ford," he might run the risk of being arrested for threatening the life of the President, even though in his cultural context the meaning of his words was the same. To prove that it is the culturally determined set of values and not the individual himself that is affected by the rigidity of the law, consider the typical ballgame taunt, "Kill the umpire!" Surely no one was ever arrested for threatening the life of another person with such a cheer. Literally speaking, it is every bit as threatening as "Off the pig!" but the cultural context is different, in that a sports event is an acceptable vehicle for expressing hostility and a public rally against a political figure sometimes is not.

Finally, if we are to study social control and understand the nature of law cross-culturally, we must recognize that there is a positive side to conflict. Opposition to an outside force can bind a group together by strengthening the group consciousness and promoting identity. Conflict can preserve the group by offering a safety valve for aggression and hostility. In fact, the absence of conflict does not necessarily imply stability, because there may be the potential for tremendous upheaval (as in a society ruled by a strong military dictatorship that allows no dissent). Moreover, conflict can serve to unite people who might otherwise never have come together in a joint venture. Every four years people find themselves working in support of a political candidate, side by side with others who are quite unlike themselves. An even stronger example occurs in time of war, when men and women from all walks of life are brought together in the armed services and forced to share a common life style and depend upon each other for their survival. The solidarity promoted by conflict in such an instance is perhaps the strongest possible bond.

In the following article, Elliot Liebow points out how in one segment of our society economic decisions are based upon a set of values quite different from what we normally assume to be the "American way." More important, he shows how these decisions are rational given the conditions affecting the people who make them. The unemployed male in a black ghetto faces problems that limit his aspirations, and by calculating the benefits of working at inferior jobs for lower pay, compared to not working at all and collecting welfare or unemployment, or even working only part time, he is able to maximize his income with a minimum of effort. In the eyes of a middle-class white businessman, who has few barriers to achieving his personal potential for success, such behavior appears "lazy" and "irresponsible." However, seen from the point of view of the inner-city black, who has little chance of ever reaching his potential in a society that discriminates against him and keeps him from finding a high-paying job, his behavior makes a great deal of sense.

Liebow's article gives us insight into some of the basic cultural differences within our own society. In addition, he points out how middle-class Americans are culture-bound in expecting all others to act as they do, and in criticizing them for acting differently, without bothering to go to the trouble of investigating and evaluating the different circumstances in which other people live.

Men and Jobs

Elliot Liebow

A pickup truck drives slowly down the street. The truck stops as it comes abreast of a man sitting on a cast-iron porch and the white driver calls out, asking if the man wants a day's work. The man shakes his head and the truck moves on up the block, stopping again whenever idling men come within calling distance of the driver. At the Carry-out corner, five men debate the question briefly and shake their heads no to the truck. The truck turns the corner and repeats the same performance up the next street. In the distance, one can see one man, then another, climb into the back of the truck and sit down. In starts and stops, the truck finally disappears.

What is it we have witnessed here? A labor scavenger rebuffed by his would-be prey? Lazy, irresponsible men turning down an honest day's pay for an honest day's work? Or a more complex phenomenon marking the intersection of economic forces, social values and individual states of mind and body?

Let us look again at the driver of the truck. He has been able to recruit only two or three men from each twenty or fifty he contacts. To him, it is clear that the others simply do not choose to work. Singly or in groups, belly-empty or belly-full, sullen or gregarious, drunk or sober, they confirm what he has read, heard and knows from his own experience: these men wouldn't take a job if it were handed to them on a platter.

Quite apart from the question of whether or not this is true of some of the men he sees on the street, it is clearly not true of all of them. If it were, he would not have come here in the first place; or having come, he would have left with an empty truck. It is not even true of most of them, for most of the men he sees on the street this weekday morning do, in fact, have jobs. But since, at the moment, they are neither working nor sleeping, and since they hate the depressing room or apartment they live in, or because there is nothing to do there,[1] or because they want to get away from their wives or anyone else living there, they are out on the street, indistinguishable from those who do not have jobs or do not want them. Some, like Boley, a member of a trash-collection crew in a suburban housing development, work Saturdays and are off on this weekday. Some, like Sweets, work nights cleaning up middle-class trash, dirt, dishes and garbage, and mopping the floors of the office buildings, hotels, restaurants, toilets and other public places dirtied during the day. Some men work for retail businesses such as liquor stores which do not begin the day until ten o'clock. Some laborers, like Tally, have already come back from the job

Reprinted from Elliot Liebow, *Tally's Corner.* Boston: Little, Brown and Company, Inc. (1967). Abridged with permission.

1. The comparison of sitting at home alone with being in jail is commonplace.

because the ground was too wet for pick and shovel or because the weather was too cold for pouring concrete. Other employed men stayed off the job today for personal reasons: Clarence to go to a funeral at eleven this morning and Sea Cat to answer a subpoena as a witness in a criminal proceeding.

Also on the street, unwitting contributors to the impression taken away by the truck driver, are the halt and the lame. The man on the cast-iron steps strokes one gnarled arthritic hand with the other and says he doesn't know whether or not he'll live long enough to be eligible for Social Security. He pauses, then adds matter-of-factly, "Most times, I don't care whether I do or don't." Stoopy's left leg was polio-withered in childhood. Raymond, who looks as if he could tear out a fire hydrant, coughs up blood if he bends or moves suddenly. The quiet man who hangs out in front of the Saratoga apartments has a steel hook strapped onto his left elbow. And had the man in the truck been able to look into the wine-clouded eyes of the man in the green cap, he would have realized that the man did not even understand he was being offered a day's work.

Others, having had jobs and been laid off, are drawing unemployment compensation (up to $44 per week) and have nothing to gain by accepting work which pays little more than this and frequently less.

Still others, like Bumdoodle the numbers man, are working hard at illegal ways of making money, hustlers who are on the street to turn a dollar any way they can: buying and selling sex, liquor, narcotics, stolen goods, or anything else that turns up.

Only a handful remains unaccounted for. There is Tonk, who cannot bring himself to take a job away from the corner, because, according to the other men, he suspects his wife will be unfaithful if given the opportunity. There is Stanton, who has not reported to work for four days now, not since Bernice disappeared. He bought a brand new knife against her return. She had done this twice before, he said, but not for so long and not without warning, and he had forgiven her. But this time, "I ain't got it in me to forgive her again." His rage and shame are there for all to see as he paces the Carry-out and the corner, day and night, hoping to catch a glimpse of her.

And finally, there are those like Arthur, able-bodied men who have no visible means of support, legal or illegal, who neither have jobs nor want them. The truck driver, among others, believes the Arthurs to be representative of all the men he sees idling on the street during his own working hours. They are not, but they cannot be dismissed simply because they are a small minority. It is not enough to explain them away as being lazy or irresponsible or both because an able-bodied man with responsibilities who refuses work is, by the truck driver's definition, lazy and irresponsible. Such an answer begs the question. It is descriptive of the facts; it does not explain them.

Putting aside, for the moment, what the men say and feel, and looking at what they actually do and the choices they make, getting a job, keeping a job, and doing well at it is clearly of low priority. Arthur will not take a job at all. Leroy is supposed to be on his job at 4:00 P.M. but it is already 4:10 and he still cannot bring himself to leave the free games he has accumulated on the pinball machine in the Carry-out. Tonk started a construction job on Wednesday, worked Thursday and Friday, then didn't go back again. On the same kind of job, Sea Cat quit in the second week. Sweets had been working three months as a bus-boy in a restaurant, then quit without notice, not sure himself why he did so. A real estate agent, saying he was more interested in getting the job done than in the cost, asked Richard to give him an estimate on repairing and painting the inside of a house, but Richard, after looking over the job, somehow never got around to submitting an estimate. During one period, Tonk would not leave the corner to take a job because his wife might prove unfaithful; Stanton would not take a job because his woman had been unfaithful.

Thus, the man-job relationship is a tenuous one. At any given moment, a job may occupy a relatively low position on the streetcorner scale of real values. Getting a job may be subordinated to relations with women or to other non-job considerations; the commitment to a job one already has is frequently shallow and tentative.

Objective economic considerations are frequently a controlling factor in a man's refusal to take a job. How much the job pays is a crucial question but seldom asked. He knows how much it pays. Working as a stock clerk, a delivery boy, or even behind the counter of liquor stores, drug stores and other retail businesses pays one dollar an hour. So, too, do most busboy, car-wash, janitorial and other jobs available to him. Some jobs, such as dishwasher, may dip as low as eighty cents an hour and others, such as elevator operator or work in a junk yard, may offer $1.15 or $1.25. Take-home pay for jobs such as these ranges from $35 to $50 a week, but a take-home pay of over $45 for a five-day week is the exception rather than the rule.

One of the principal advantages of these kinds of jobs is that they offer fairly regular work. Most of them involve essential services and are therefore somewhat less responsive to business conditions than are some higher paying, less menial jobs. Most of them are also inside jobs not dependent on the weather, as are construction jobs and other higher-paying outside work.

Another seemingly important advantage of working in hotels, restaurants, office and apartment buildings and retail establishments is that they frequently offer an opportunity for stealing on the job. But stealing can be a two-edged sword. Apart from increasing the cost of the goods or services to the general public, a less obvious result is that the practice usually acts as a depressant on the employee's own wage level. Owners of small retail establishments and other employers frequently anticipate employee stealing and adjust the wage rate accordingly. Tonk's employer explained why he was paying Tonk $35 for a 55–60 hour workweek. These men will all steal, he said. Although he keeps close watch on Tonk, he estimates that Tonk steals from $35 to $40 a week. What he steals, when added to his regular earnings, brings his take-home pay to $70 or $75 per week. The employer said he did not mind this because Tonk is worth that much to the business. But if he were to pay Tonk outright the full value of his labor, Tonk would still be stealing $35–$40 per week and this, he said, the business simply would not support.

This wage arrangement, with stealing built-in, was satisfactory to both parties, with each one independently expressing his satisfaction. Such a wage-theft system, however, is not as balanced and equitable as it appears. Since the wage level rests on the premise that the employee will steal the unpaid value of his labor, the man who does not steal on the job is penalized. And furthermore, even if he does not steal, no one would believe him; the employer and others believe he steals because the system presumes it.

Nor is the man who steals, as he is expected to, as well off as he believes himself to be. The employer may occasionally close his eyes to the worker's stealing but not often and not for long. He is, after all, a businessman and cannot always find it within himself to let a man steal from him, even if the man is stealing his own wages. Moreover, it is only by keeping close watch on the worker that the employer can control how much is stolen and thereby protect himself against the employee's stealing more than he is worth. From this viewpoint, then, the employer is not in wage-theft collusion with the employee. In the case of Tonk, for instance, the employer was not actively abetting the theft. His estimate of how much Tonk was stealing was based on what he thought Tonk was able to steal despite his own best efforts to prevent him from stealing anything at all. Were he to have caught Tonk in the act of stealing, he would, of course, have fired him from the job and perhaps called the police as well. Thus, in an actual if not in a legal sense, all the elements of entrapment are present. The employer knowingly provides the conditions which entice (force) the employee to steal the unpaid value of his labor, but at the same time he punishes him for theft if he catches him doing so.

Other consequences of the wage-theft system are even more damaging to the employee. Let us, for argument's sake, say that Tonk is in no danger of entrapment; that his employer is willing to wink at the stealing and that Tonk, for his part, is perfectly willing to earn a little, steal a little. Let us say, too, that he is paid $35 a week and allowed to steal $35. His money income—as measured by the goods and services he can purchase with it—is, of course, $70. But not all of his income is available to him for all purposes. He cannot draw on what he steals to build his self-respect or to measure his self-worth. For this, he can draw only on his earnings—the amount given him publicly and voluntarily in exchange for his labor. His "respect" and "self-worth" income remains at $35—only half that of the man who also receives $70 but all of it in the form of wages. His earnings publicly measure the worth of his labor to his employer, and they are important to others and to himself in taking the measure of his worth as a man.

With or without stealing, and quite apart from any interior processes going on in the man who refuses such a job or quits it casually and without apparent reason, the objective fact is that menial jobs in retailing or in the service trades simply do not pay enough to support a man and his family. This is not to say that the worker is underpaid; this may or may not be true. Whether he is or not, the plain fact is that, in such a job, he cannot make a living. Nor can he take much comfort in the fact that these jobs tend to offer more regular, steadier work. If he cannot live on the $45 or $50 he makes in one week, the longer he works, the longer he cannot live on what he makes.

Construction work, even for unskilled laborers, usually pays better, with the hourly rate ranging from $1.50 to $2.60 an hour. Importantly, too, good references, a good driving record, a tenth grade (or any high school) education, previous experience, the ability to "bring police clearance with you" are not normally required of laborers as they frequently are for some of the jobs in retailing or in the service trades.

Construction work, however, has its own objective disadvantages. It is, first of all, seasonal work for the great bulk of the laborers, beginning early in the spring and tapering off as winter weather sets in. And even during the season the work is frequently irregular. Early or late in the season, snow or temperatures too low for concrete frequently sends the laborers back home, and during late spring or summer, a heavy rain on Tuesday or Wednesday, leaving a lot of water and mud behind it, can mean a two or three day work-week for the pick-and-shovel men and other unskilled laborers.

The elements are not the only hazard. As the project moves from one construction stage to another, laborers—usually without warning—are laid off, sometimes permanently or sometimes for weeks at a time. The more fortunate or the better workers are told periodically to "take a walk for two, three days."

Both getting the construction job and getting to it are also relatively more difficult than is the case for the menial jobs in retailing and the service trades. Job competition is always fierce. In the city, the large construction projects are unionized. One has to have ready cash to get into the union to become eligible to work on these projects and, being eligible, one has to find an opening. Unless one "knows somebody," say a foreman or a laborer who knows the day before that they are going to take on new men in the morning, this can be a difficult and disheartening search.

Many of the nonunion jobs are in suburban Maryland or Virginia. The newspaper ads say, "Report ready to work to the trailer at the intersection of Rte. 11 and Old Bridge Rd., Bunston, Virginia (or Maryland)," but this location may be ten, fifteen, or even twenty-five miles from the Carry-out.

Heavy, backbreaking labor of the kind that used to be regularly associated with bull gangs or concrete gangs is no longer characteristic of laboring jobs, especially those with the larger, well-equipped construction companies. Brute strength is still required from time to time, as on smaller jobs where it is not economical to bring in heavy equipment or where the small, undercapitalized contractor has none to bring in. In many cases, however, the conveyor belt has replaced the wheelbarrow or the Georgia buggy, mechanized forklifts have eliminated heavy, manual lifting, and a variety of digging machines have replaced the pick and shovel. The result is fewer jobs for unskilled laborers and, in many cases, a work speed-up for those who do have jobs. Machines now set the pace formerly set by men. Formerly, a laborer pushed a wheelbarrow of wet cement to a particular spot, dumped it, and returned for another load. Another laborer, in hip boots, pushed the wet concrete around with a shovel or a hoe, getting it roughly level in preparation for the skilled finishers. He had relatively small loads to contend with and had only to keep up with the men pushing the wheelbarrows. Now, the job for the man pushing the wheelbarrow is gone and the wet concrete comes rushing down a chute at the man in the hip boots who must "spread it quick or drown."

Men who have been running an elevator, washing dishes, or "pulling trash" cannot easily move into laboring jobs. They lack the basic skills for "unskilled" construction labor, familiarity with tools and materials, and tricks of the trade without which hard jobs are made harder. Previously unused or untrained muscles rebel in pain against the new and insistent demands made upon them, seriously compromising the man's performance and testing his willingness to see the job through.

Sea Cat was "healthy, sturdy, active and of good intelligence." When a judge gave him six weeks in which to pay his wife $200 in back child-support payments, he left his grocery-store job in order to take a higher-paying job as a laborer, arranged for him by a foreman friend. During the first week the weather was bad and he worked only Wednesday and Friday, cursing the elements all the while for cheating him out of the money he could have made. The second week, the weather was fair but he quit at the end of the fourth day, saying frankly that the work was too hard for him. He went back to his job at the grocery store and took a second job working nights as a dishwasher in a restaurant, earning little if any more at the two jobs than he would have earned as a laborer, and keeping at both of them until he had paid off his debts.

Tonk did not last as long as Sea Cat. No one made any predictions when he got a job in a parking lot, but when the men on the corner learned he was to start on a road construction job, estimates of how long he would last ranged from one to three weeks. Wednesday was his first day. He spent that evening and night at home. He did the same on Thursday. He worked Friday and spent Friday evening and part of Saturday draped over the mailbox on the corner. Sunday afternoon, Tonk decided he was not going to report on the job the next morning. He explained that after working three days, he knew enough about the job to know that it was too hard for him. He knew he wouldn't be able to keep up and he'd just as soon quit now as get fired later.

Sometimes, the strain and effort is greater than the man is willing to admit, even to himself. In the early summer of 1963, Richard was rooming at Nancy's place. His wife and children were "in the country" (his grandmother's home in Carolina), waiting for him to save up enough money so that he could bring them back to Washington and start over again after a disastrous attempt to "make it" in Philadelphia. Richard had gotten a job with a fence company in Virginia. It paid $1.60 an hour. The first few evenings, when he came home from work, he looked ill from exhaustion and the heat. Stanton said Richard would have to quit, "he's too small [thin] for that kind of work." Richard said he was doing O.K. and would stick with the job.

At Nancy's one night, when Richard had been working about two weeks, Nancy and three or four others were sitting around talking, drinking, and listening to music. Someone asked Nancy when was Richard going to bring his wife and children up from the country. Nancy said she didn't know, but it probably depended on how long it would take him to save up enough money. She said she didn't think he could stay with the fence job much longer. This morning, she said, the man Richard rode to work with knocked on the door and Richard didn't answer. She looked in his room. Richard was still asleep. Nancy tried to shake him awake. "No more digging!" Richard cried out. "No more digging! I can't do no more God-damn digging!" When Nancy finally managed to wake him, he dressed quickly and went to work.

Richard stayed on the job two more weeks, then suddenly quit, ostensibly because his pay check was three dollars less than what he thought it should have been.

In summary of objective job considerations, then, the most important fact is that a man who is able and willing to work cannot earn enough money to support himself, his wife, and one or more children. A man's chances for working regularly are good only if he is willing to work for less than he can live on, and sometimes not even then. On some jobs, the wage rate is deceptively higher than on others, but the higher the wage rate, the more difficult it is to get the job, and the less the job security. Higher-paying construction work tends to be seasonal and, during the season, the amount of work available is highly sensitive to business and weather conditions and to the changing requirements of individual projects. Moreover, high-paying construction jobs are frequently beyond the physical capacity of some of the men, and some of the low-paying jobs are scaled down even lower in accordance with the self-fulfilling assumption that the man will steal part of his wages on the job.

Bernard assesses the objective job situation dispassionately over a cup of coffee, sometimes poking at the coffee with his spoon, sometimes staring at it as if, like a crystal ball, it holds tomorrow's secrets. He is twenty-seven years old. He and the woman with whom he lives have a baby son, and she has another child by another man. Bernard does odd jobs—mostly painting—but here it is the end of January, and his last job was with the Post Office during the Christmas mail rush. He would like postal work as a steady job, he says. It pays well (about $2.00 an hour) but he has twice failed the Post Office examination (he graduated from a Washington high school) and has given up the idea as an impractical one. He is supposed to see a man tonight about a job as a parking attendant for a large apartment house. The man told him to bring his birth certificate and driver's license, but his license was suspended because of a backlog of unpaid traffic fines. A friend promised to lend him some money this evening. If he gets it, he will pay the fines tomorrow morning and have his license reinstated. He hopes the man with the job will wait till tomorrow night.

A "security job" is what he really wants, he said. He would like to save up money for a taxicab. (But having twice failed the postal examination and having a bad driving record as well, it is highly doubtful that he could meet the qualifications or pass the written test.) That would be "a good life." He can always get a job in a restaurant or as a clerk in a drugstore but they don't pay enough, he said. He needs to take home at least $50 to $55 a week. He thinks he can get that much driving a truck somewhere . . . Sometimes he wishes he had stayed in the army . . . A security job, that's what he wants most of all, a real security job . . .

When we look at what the men bring to the job rather than at what the job offers the men, it is essential to keep in mind that we are not looking at men who come to the job fresh, just out of school perhaps, and newly prepared to undertake the task of making a living, or from another job where they earned a living and are prepared to do the same on this job. Each man comes to the job with a long job history characterized by his not being able to support himself and his family. Each man carries this knowledge, born of his experience, with him. He comes to the job flat and stale, wearied by the sameness of it all, convinced of his own incompetence, terrified of responsibility—of being tested still again and found wanting. Possible exceptions are the younger men not yet, or just, married. They suspect all this but have yet to have it confirmed by repeated personal experience over time. But those who are or have been married know it well. It is the experience of the individual and the group; of their fathers and probably their sons. Convinced of their inadequacies, not only do they not seek out those few better-paying jobs which test their resources, but they actively avoid them, gravitating in a mass to the menial, routine jobs which offer no challenge—and therefore pose no threat—to the already diminished images they have of themselves.

Thus Richard does not follow through on the real estate agent's offer. He is afraid to do on his own—minor plastering, replacing broken windows, other minor repairs and painting—exactly what he had been doing for months on a piecework basis under someone else (and which provided him with a solid base from which to derive a cost estimate).

Richard once offered an important clue to what may have gone on in his mind when the job offer was made. We were in the Carry-out, at a time when he was looking for work. He was talking about the kind of jobs available to him.

"I graduated from high school [Baltimore] but I don't know anything. I'm dumb. Most of the time I don't even say I graduated, 'cause then somebody asks me a question and I can't answer it, and they think I was lying about graduating. . . . They graduated me but I didn't know anything. I had lousy grades but I guess they wanted to get rid of me.

I was at Margaret's house the other night and her little sister asked me to help her with her homework. She showed me some fractions and I knew right away I couldn't do them. I was ashamed so I told her I had to go to the bathroom."

And so it must have been, surely, with the real estate agent's offer. Convinced that "I'm dumb . . . I don't know anything," he "knew right away" he couldn't do it, despite the fact that he had been doing just this sort of work all along.

Thus, the man's low self-esteem generates a fear of being tested and prevents him from accepting a job with responsibilities or, once on a job, from staying with it if responsibilities are thrust on him, even if the wages are commensurately higher. Richard refuses such a job, Leroy leaves one, and another man, given more responsibility and more pay, knows he will fail and proceeds to do so, proving he was right about himself all along. The self-fulfilling prophecy is everywhere at work. In a hallway, Stanton, Tonk and Boley are passing a bottle around. Stanton recalls the time he was in the service. Everything was fine until he attained the rank of corporal. He worried about everything he did then. Was he doing the right thing? Was he doing it well? When would they discover their mistake and take his stripes (and extra pay) away? When he finally lost his stripes, everything was all right again.

A crucial factor in the streetcorner man's lack of job commitment is the overall value he places on the job. *For his part, the streetcorner man puts no lower value on the job than does the larger society around him.* He knows the social value of the job by the amount of money the employer is willing to pay him for doing it. In a real sense, every pay day, he counts in dollars and cents the value placed on the job by society at large. He is no more (and frequently less) ready to quit and look for another job than his employer is ready to fire him and look for another man. Neither the streetcorner man who performs these jobs nor the society which requires him to perform them assesses the job as one "worth doing and worth doing well." Both employee and employer are contemptuous of the job. The employee shows his contempt by his reluctance to accept it or keep it, the employer by paying less than is required to support a family. Nor does the low-wage job offer prestige, respect, interesting work, opportunity for learning or advancement, or any other compensation. With few exceptions, jobs filled by the streetcorner men are at the bottom of the employment ladder in every respect, from wage level to prestige. Typically, they are hard, dirty, uninteresting and underpaid. The rest of society (whatever its ideal values regarding the dignity of labor) holds the job of the dishwasher or janitor or unskilled laborer in low esteem if not outright contempt. So does the streetcorner man. He cannot do otherwise. He cannot draw from a job those social values which other people do not put into it.

Only occasionally does spontaneous conversation touch on these matters directly. Talk about jobs is usually limited to isolated statements of intention, such as "I think I'll get me another gig [job]," "I'm going to look for a construction job when the weather breaks," or "I'm going to quit. I can't take no more of his shit." Job assessments typically consist of nothing more than a noncommittal shrug and "It's O.K." or "It's a job."

One reason for the relative absence of talk about one's job is, as suggested earlier, that the sameness of job experiences does not bear reiteration. Another and more important reason is the emptiness of the job experience itself. The man sees middle-class occupations as a primary source of prestige, pride and self-respect; his own job affords him none of these. To think about his job is to see himself as others see him, to remind him of just where he stands in this society. And because society's criteria for placement are generally the same as his own, to talk about his job can trigger a flush of shame and a deep, almost physical ache to change places with someone, almost anyone, else. The desire to be a person in his own right, to be noticed by the world he lives in, is shared by each of the men on the streetcorner. Whether they articulate this desire (as Tally does below) or not, one can see them position themselves to catch the attention of their fellows in much the same way as plants bend or stretch to catch the sunlight.[2]

Tally and I were in the Carry-out. It was summer, Tally's peak earning season as a cement finisher, a semiskilled job a cut or so above that of the unskilled laborer. His take-home pay during these weeks was well over a hundred dollars—"a lot of bread." But for Tally, who no longer had a family to support, bread was not enough.

"You know that boy came in last night? That Black Moozlem? That's what I ought to be doing. I ought to be in his place."

"What do you mean?"

"Dressed nice, going to [night] school, got a good job."

"He's no better off than you, Tally. You make more than he does."

"It's not the money. [Pause] It's position, I guess. He's got position. When he finish school

2. Sea Cat cuts his pants legs off at the calf and puts a fringe on the raggedy edges. Tonk breaks his "shades" and continues to wear the horn-rimmed frames minus the lenses. Richard cultivates a distinctive manner of speech. Lonny gives himself a birthday party. And so on.

he gonna be a supervisor. People respect him. . . . Thinking about people with position and education gives me a feeling right here [pressing his fingers into the pit of his stomach]."

"You're educated, too. You have a skill, a trade. You're a cement finisher. You can make a building, pour a sidewalk."

"That's different. Look, can anybody do what you're doing? Can anybody just come up and do your job? Well, in one week I can teach you cement finishing. You won't be as good as me 'cause you won't have the experience but you'll be a cement finisher. That's what I mean. Anybody can do what I'm doing and that's what gives me this feeling. [Long pause] Suppose I like this girl. I go over to her house and I meet her father. He starts talking about what he done today. He talks about operating on somebody and sewing them up and about surgery. I know he's a doctor 'cause of the way he talks. Then she starts talking about what she did. Maybe she's a boss or a supervisor. Maybe she's a lawyer and her father says to me, 'And what do you do, Mr. Jackson?' [Pause] You remember at the courthouse, Lonny's trial? You and the lawyer was talking in the hall? You remember? I just stood there listening. I didn't say a word. You know why? 'Cause I didn't even know what you was talking about. That's happened to me a lot."

"Hell, you're nothing special. That happens to everybody. Nobody knows everything. One man is a doctor, so he talks about surgery. Another man is a teacher, so he talks about books. But doctors and teachers don't know anything about concrete. You're a cement finisher and that's your specialty."

"Maybe so, but when was the last time you saw anybody standing around talking about concrete?"

The streetcorner man wants to be a person in his own right, to be noticed, to be taken account of, but in this respect, as well as in meeting his money needs, his job fails him. The job and the man are even. The job fails the man and the man fails the job.

Furthermore, the man does not have any reasonable expectation that, however bad it is, his job will lead to better things. Menial jobs are not, by and large, the starting point of a track system which leads to even better jobs for those who are able and willing to do them. The busboy or dishwasher in a restaurant is not on a job track which, if negotiated skillfully, leads to chef or manager of the restaurant. The busboy or dishwasher who works hard becomes, simply, a hard-working busboy or dishwasher. Neither hard work nor perseverance can conceivably carry the janitor to a sit-down job in the office building he cleans up. And it is the apprentice who becomes the journeyman electrician, plumber, steam fitter or bricklayer, not the common unskilled Negro laborer.

Thus, the job is not a stepping stone to something better. It is a dead end. It promises to deliver no more tomorrow, next month or next year than it does today.

Delivering little, and promising no more, the job is "no big thing." The man appears to treat the job in a cavalier fashion, working and not working as the spirit moves him, as if all that matters is the immediate satisfaction of his present appetites, the surrender to present moods, and the indulgence of whims with no thought for the cost, the consequences, the future. To the middle-class observer, this behavior reflects a "present-time orientation"—an "inability to defer gratification." It is this "present-time" orientation—as against the "future orientation" of the middle-class person—that "explains" to the outsider why Leroy chooses to spend the day at the Carry-out rather than report to work; why Richard, who was paid Friday, was drunk Saturday and Sunday and penniless Monday; why Sweets quit his job today because the boss looked at him "funny" yesterday.

As for the future, the young streetcorner man has a fairly good picture of it. In Richard or Sea Cat or Arthur he can see himself in his middle twenties; he can look at Tally to see himself at thirty, at Wee Tom to see himself in his middle thirties, and at Budder and Stanton to see himself in his forties. It is a future in which everything is uncertain except the ultimate destruction of his hopes and the eventual realization of his fears. The most he can reasonably look forward to is that these things do not come too soon. Thus, when Richard squanders a week's pay in two days it is not because, like an animal or a child, he is "present-time oriented," unaware of or unconcerned with his future. He does so precisely because he is aware of the future and the hopelessness of it all.

Sometimes this kind of response appears as a conscious, explicit choice. Richard had had a violent argument with his wife. He said he was going to leave her and the children, that he had had enough of everything and could not take any more, and he chased her out of the house. His chest still heaving, he leaned back against the wall in the hallway of his basement apartment.

"I've been scuffling for five years," he said. "I've been scuffling for five years from morning till night. And my kids still don't have anything, my wife don't have anything, and I don't have anything.

"There," he said, gesturing down the hall to a bed, a sofa, a couple of chairs, and a television set, all shabby, some broken. "There's everything I have and I'm having trouble holding onto that."

Leroy came in, presumably to petition Richard on behalf of Richard's wife, who was sitting outside on the steps, afraid to come in. Leroy started to say something but Richard cut him short.

"Look, Leroy, don't give me any of that action. You and me are entirely different people. Maybe I look like a boy and maybe I act like a boy sometimes but I got a man's mind. You and me don't want the same things out of life. Maybe some of the same, but you don't care how long you have to wait for yours and *I—want—mine—right—now.*"

Thus, apparent present-time concerns with consumption and indulgences—material and emotional—reflect a future-time orientation. "I want mine right now" is ultimately a cry of despair, a direct response to the future as he sees it.

In many instances, it is precisely the streetcorner man's orientation to the future—but to a future loaded with "trouble"—which not only leads to a greater emphasis on present concerns ("I want mine right now") but also contributes importantly to the instability of employment, family and friend relationships, and to the general transient quality of daily life.

Let me give some concrete examples. One day, after Tally had gotten paid, he gave me four twenty-dollar bills and asked me to keep them for him. Three days later he asked me for the money. I returned it and asked why he did not put his money in a bank. He said that the banks close at two o'clock. I argued that there were four or more banks within a two-block radius of where he was working at the time and that he could easily get to any one of them on his lunch hour. "No, man," he said, "you don't understand. They close at two o'clock and they closed Saturday and Sunday. Suppose I get into trouble and I got to make it [leave]. Me get out of town, and everything I got in the world layin' up in that bank? No good! No good!"

In another instance, Leroy and his girl friend were discussing "trouble." Leroy was trying to decide how best to go about getting his hands on some "long green" (a lot of money), and his girl friend cautioned him about "trouble." Leroy sneered at this, saying he had had "trouble" all his life and wasn't afraid of a little more. "Anyway," he said, "I'm famous for leaving town."

Thus, the constant awareness of a future

loaded with "trouble" results in a constant readiness to leave, to "make it," to "get out of town," and discourages the man from sinking roots into the world he lives in. Just as it discourages him from putting money in the bank, so it discourages him from committing himself to a job, especially one whose payoff lies in the promise of future rewards rather than in the present. In the same way, it discourages him from deep and lasting commitments to family and friends or to any other persons, places or things, since such commitments could hold him hostage, limiting his freedom of movement and thereby compromising his security which lies in that freedom.

What lies behind the response to the driver of the pickup truck, then, is a complex combination of attitudes and assessments. The streetcorner man is under continuous assault by his job experiences and job fears. His experiences and fears feed on one another. The kind of job he can get—and frequently only after fighting for it, if then—steadily confirms his fears, depresses his self-confidence and self-esteem until finally, terrified of an opportunity even if one presents itself, he stands defeated by his experiences, his belief in his own self-worth destroyed and his fears a confirmed reality.

Summary

The three topics of this chapter, economics, politics and social control, are not unrelated institutions, but are closely tied together. While in complex industrial states the political, economic and legal institutions are separate, in many societies economics, politics and law are three different types of behavior within the same institutional framework. People do not conceive of their actions in terms of whether they are political, as separate from economic.

In studying economic behavior, the anthropologist recognizes that different principles govern the decisions people make in other societies. While we consider maximization of profit to be the driving force in our own society, in another cultural context other factors might be more important—the obligations of kinship, the feelings one has about the environment, or the sentimental attachment one develops to the land or to cultural traditions. Interestingly enough, in recent years many critics of American society have cited just these typically "American" values as being the source of many of our current problems. We have long ignored family obligations in our emphasis upon achieved status over ascribed status; we have depleted our resources and polluted our environment with little concern for anything but the almighty dollar; we have fought off all the ways of the past that held us back from expanding our economy. Now we are recognizing the values that other people have followed, values that a few years ago we called backward and primitive. We have gained a new respect for the American Indian's interaction with his environment, and for the close family ties that many immigrants used to have but gradually lost in the attempt to get ahead in industrial society.

The same is true of the anthropological approach to politics. Through studying political organization in other societies we recognize the operation of principles that are in many ways foreign to our ideas about how to run a complex state organization. The band is made up of equals; decisions are derived from a consensus of the members, and feuding is avoided. The tribe contains more people, but still we find politics closely integrated with the rest of the social structure, not set off as a separate institution. In a chiefdom we begin to see the division of society into stratified groups and the centralization of power. But it is not until the state that we have a separate group whose task is to rule the society, vested with the authority to do so and backed up by the power to coerce people to behave in a certain way, even if it is against their will. It is only with the state that we have a truly separate political institution, distinguishable (at least to some degree) from religion, economics, the family and other social institutions.

Law and politics can be distinguished in that law is a way of organizing society to deal with internal matters, whereas politics organizes the society to deal with outside groups. The anthropologist who studies law is concerned both with formal rules defining appropriate behavior and with informal or unwritten rules, which can be just as powerful and effective in regulating the way people act. We recognize that while all societies have some form of law, there are no absolute laws that exist in every society throughout the world. A law is a statement about culturally determined values, and it can exist on a formal level or through the more subtle means of social control that are acted out in countless situations in everyday life. In our own society, where there is a great deal of cultural diversity, we find many problems in our written legal system, which ignores cultural differences. The cross-cultural perspective of the anthropologist offers us a better understanding of these problems, and the hope of finding a workable solution.

Glossary

ancestor worship A religious system based upon the belief that one's dead ancestors can have an effect in determining the lives of a group's living members. The living descendants follow certain rituals to seek their ancestors' help and to avoid offending them and thus keep them from bringing harm.

band A form of political organization found primarily among hunting and gathering peoples. These groups, usually composed of between 25 and 40 individuals, are loosely organized and tend to be based on a principle of equality. Leadership rests upon the qualities of an individual, rather than in a formalized position of authority. Several bands are usually associated in an alliance for the purpose of seasonal subsistence and the exchange of marriage partners.

bloodwealth A social sanction found in Trobriand society to settle disputes and avoid feuding between individuals or groups. The bloodwealth is a payment made by an offender to a victim, and the latter may be forced to accept the fee even if he is unwilling.

chiefdom A political system in which regional or tribal groups are organized under a centralized position of authority. The chief acquires authority by virtue of the position, rather than on the basis of his personal qualities, and he may organize his group for political, economic and religious functions. The chiefdom is associated with a system of ranking or social stratification, and the chief therefore receives special privileges and has special duties.

euthanasia The practice of mercy killing.

headman The leader of a group in which the authority is based upon the personal qualities of the individual, rather than in a formal position of authority.

hunting and gathering The subsistence activity based upon the hunting of animals and the gathering of plants. This subsistence may also include fishing. Although it requires a low level of technology, it usually provides a relatively secure existence.

industrial economy An economy based upon an advanced technology in a society where tasks are specialized and people perform different jobs. Production is almost exclusively for exchange and there is no self-sufficiency on the community level.

jajmani system An economic system found in many peasant villages in India, based upon the caste system and its implied occupational specialization. In this highly stratified society, it is an institutionalized form of reciprocity. Payments made for services are determined by tradition, allowing for the exchange of goods and services between the various castes or occupational groups.

Kula ring A pattern of exchange found in some of the islands of Melanesia. The pattern combines an exchange of both ritual trade items and practical items in a yearly cycle between the islands. It represents a primitive economy in a small-scale, relatively isolated society that is basically self-sufficient.

law A formal system of rules that are a guide to the appropriate behavior in a particular society, backed by the threat of force.

market exchange A pattern of exchange based upon the law of supply and demand in which each individual attempts to maximize his profits by placing a value on labor and products.

peasant economy An economy in which there is a certain degree of self-sufficiency, and almost every individual is engaged in the production of food for consumption. The economy is based upon a simple technology, but peasant producers are tied into a wider market system and are not completely independent in their production. Agriculture is a way of life, and not just an occupation.

politics The legitimate use of force or authority within a society. It is also the way by which people maintain peace within a group and define their group relative to the outside world.

potlatch A form of exchange combining redistribution and reciprocity, found among the aboriginal populations of the Pacific Northwest Coast of North America. Associated with the winter ceremonial season, the potlatch serves as a vehicle to gain prestige through both the giving away of gifts and the destruction of material goods. The individual thus challenges his guests to match his wealth and failure to reciprocate means an increase in prestige and a demonstration of high status and wealth for the individual.

pratik The special personal relationship between a woman trader and her customers in the rural market system of Haiti. The trader lowers her own profits and makes special concessions to her customers in order to insure her own security in a competitive and highly fluctuating agricultural market economy.

primitive economy Small-scale economies, found among relatively isolated, self-sufficient groups in which the members share uniform experiences. The economy is not separated from the other institutions in society (as it is in the United States, where politics, economics and religion have their own well-defined institutions). There is a small surplus usually used to support ceremonials and special occasions, and it is based upon a simple technology, primarily using human and animal power.

reciprocity The exchange of goods, services, and in some cases even marriage partners. The form of exchange involves an arrangement between groups in which items are given and expected in return. The exchange takes place without a market system, without a law of supply and demand, and without outside intervention.

redistribution A pattern of exchange in a stratified society in which there is a collection of goods by a central authority and then a reallocation of those goods to members of the society.

segmentary opposition A form of political organization in which a society is divided into groups, each subdivided into hierarchical units. Alliances are formed within each unit and they provide a mechanism for settling disputes either within the group or between groups.

social control The legal sanctions of a particular society that ensure conformity to the values of that society. These sanctions may be in the form of laws, their transgression being punishable by force, or they may be less formal and unwritten, transgression being punishable through gossip, criticism or shame.

song duel A contest found among Eskimos that is designed to settle disputes without actual fighting. The duel consists of the combatants' inventing songs to shame and ridicule each other, and the witnesses decide who is the victor.

state A territorially-based government, characterized by a centralization of authority in which people may be directed to follow certain rules by threat of force. There is a specialization of economic tasks and an associated stratification of society. The state is usually associated with urbanism, which in turn means a very large population and a high population density.

subsistence agriculture The production of food for one's own consumption.

tribe A confederation of groups who recognize a relationship to one another, usually in the form of common ethnic origin, common language, or a strong pattern of interaction based on intermarriage or presumed kinship. These groups, ranging from hundreds to thousands of people, provide the broadest base upon which joint activities can be organized and carried out by the group and in the name of the group.

Questions for Discussion

1 One of the characteristics of economic behavior in a small-scale society is the importance of personal relationships over the attempt to gain every last penny of profit from a transaction. Can you think of situations in your own society where personal factors enter in to reduce profit (such as the difference between the neighborhood grocer who throws in an extra item to make a "baker's dozen," as opposed to the formal and impersonal climate of a large supermarket)?

2 Can we view the American system of income-tax assessment as a form of redistribution similar to that found in non-Western societies? How does it compare to the redistributive economies discussed in this chapter?

3 In the American political scene, many activities that would be unacceptable if done to a fellow American are praiseworthy if done to an outsider. For example, in war we condone the killing of others, and we promote spying against agents from other countries, but deny the right to pry into the private affairs of our own citizens. How does such behavior reflect the notion of segmentary opposition in a tribal society?

4 Recently there has been much controversy about the legality of abortion.

Recognizing that there are no absolute standards of conduct that are valid in all cultures, how can the anthropological study of other cultures help us understand this and other similar issues in our own society?

5 A classic hypothetical legal case, called "The Case of the Speluncean Explorers," describes a group of scientists trapped in a cave. They calculate the amount of air available, and the time it will take for the workers on the outside to rescue them, and determine that there is not enough oxygen for all to survive. Accordingly, they draw lots and the loser is killed. In the end, their calculations prove accurate. They are rescued just in time, and had they allowed one additional person to live, all would have suffocated. Are the survivors guilty of murder? Why or why not?

Suggestions for Additional Reading

Economics

Belshaw, Cyril S.
1965 Traditional Exchange and Modern Markets. Englewood Cliffs, N.J.: Prentice-Hall.

A short survey of different types of exchange and the impact of modernization upon traditional peasant market exchange.

Dalton, George (editor)
1967 Tribal and Peasant Economies. Readings in Economic Anthropology. Garden City, N.Y.: Natural History Press.

A collection of articles on the anthropological approach to economics, including studies of the potlatch, jajmani system, and peasant markets, all discussed in this chapter.

Gamst, Frederick C.
1974 Peasants in Complex Society. New York: Holt, Rinehart and Winston. A short analysis of peasant economics and social organization around the world.

LeClair, Edward E., Jr., and Harold K. Schneider (editors)
1968 Economic Anthropology. New York: Holt, Rinehart and Winston. A collection of articles dealing with the major issues in economic anthropology, including the major theoretical division between the substantivist and formalist approaches.

Liebow, Elliot
1967 Tally's Corner. Boston: Little, Brown.
A study of the black ghetto of Washington, D.C., with a valuable perspective on the economics of ghetto life from an insider's point of view.

Nash, Manning
1966 Primitive and Peasant Economic Systems. San Francisco: Chandler.
A short analysis of the differences in economic organization among most tribal and peasant societies.

Polanyi, Karl
1944 The Great Transformation. New York: Rinehart & Co.
A detailed analysis of the three types of exchange—reciprocity, redistribution and market exchange—discussed in this chapter.

Weber, Max
1958 The Protestant Ethic and the Spirit of Capitalism. Translated by Talcott Parsons. (orig. 1904) New York: Charles Scribner's Sons.
The classic study by the German sociologist of the relationship between the teachings of Protestantism and the inner drive and work ethic that is the foundation of capitalism.

Political Organization

Balandier, Georges
1970 Political Anthropology. New York: Random House.

Fried, Morton H.
1967 The Evolution of Political Society: An Essay in Political Anthropology. New York: Random House.
Two textbooks dealing with the anthropological study of political organization in non-Western societies.

Heider, Karl
1970 The Dugum Dani. Chicago: Aldine.
A study of a tribal society in highland New Guinea, particularly interesting in contrast to the Kalahari Bushmen described by Thomas (see below). The Dugum Dani are perhaps best known for their ritualized warfare, which is depicted in the excellent ethnographic movie, *Dead Birds.*

Sahlins, Marshall D.
1968 Tribesmen. Englewood Cliffs, N.J.: Prentice-Hall.

Service, Elman R.
1966 The Hunters. Englewood Cliffs, N.J.: Prentice-Hall.
These two books, part of the Foundations of Modern Anthropology series, offer an interesting contrast of two types of social and political organization.

Sanders, William T., and Barbara Price
1968 Mesoamerica: The Evolution of a Civilization. New York: Random House.
Includes a discussion of the different forms of political organization: band, tribe, chiefdom and state.

Swartz, Marc J., Victor Turner, and A. Tuden (editors)
1966 Political Anthropology. Chicago: Aldine.
A collection of articles on political organization from a cross-cultural perspective.

Thomas, Elizabeth Marshall
1959 The Harmless People. New York: Alfred A. Knopf.
A study of the Kalahari Bushmen, a hunting and gathering band.

Law and Social Control

Bohannan, Paul (editor)
1967 Law and Warfare: Studies in the Anthropology of Conflict. Garden City, N.Y.: Natural History Press.
A collection of articles on law and warfare in non-Western societies.

Hoebel, E. Adamson
1954 The Law of Primitive Man. Cambridge, Mass.: Harvard University Press.
One of the earliest studies of legal anthropology, a survey of different forms of legal institutions around the world, emphasizing non-Western "primitive" societies.

Nader, Laura (editor)
1965 The Ethnography of Law. American Anthropologist, Special Publication, volume 67, number 6, part 2.

1968 Law in Culture and Society. Chicago: Aldine.
Two collections of articles by anthropologists dealing with law and social control in cross-cultural perspective.

Social and Cultural Change

Chapter Nine

There has been life on the earth for some six hundred million years. In this span, the human species is a relative latecomer. Recent findings have pushed the existence of humanlike animals back to perhaps four million years ago, but it was not until about one million years ago that the first members of the genus *Homo* came into being. It is not our purpose here to trace human evolution through the various species of cavemen down to the present species, for such a study lies in the realm of physical anthropology or human biology. But it is relevant to note here, in a chapter on social and cultural change, how recently modern *Homo sapiens* has come onto the scene and how quickly changes have resulted. Only within the last hundred thousand years or so has culture begun to expand beyond the limits of caveman society; agriculture, the basis for any kind of permanent settlement, is less than ten thousand years old; urbanism, even in its earliest forms, is perhaps six thousand years old; and as we all know, the industrial revolution has occurred only within the last 250 years. If we were to compress the entire span of human life on the earth into a single day, agriculture would be invented around 11:56 P.M., people would begin to settle in towns and cities at 11:57, and the industrial revolution would begin shortly after 11:59:30. More change has occurred during the last 30 seconds of this "human day" than in all the time leading up to it. We might ask two very logical questions: What were people doing all that time? And why has so much change occurred in such a short time?

I was born in the middle
of human history. . . . Almost as much has happened
since I was born as happened before.
KENNETH BOULDING, *1966*

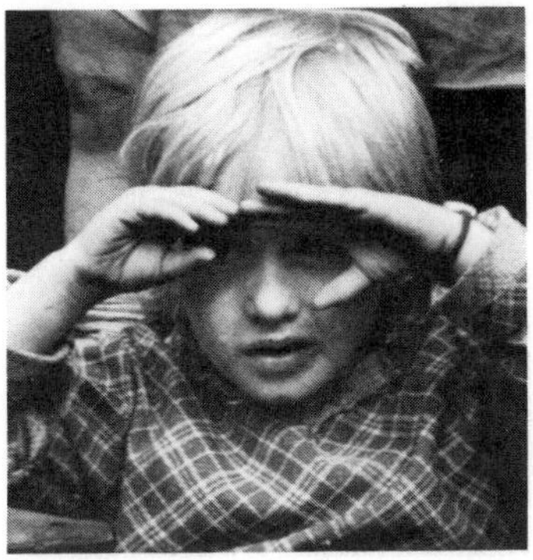

The Rise of Civilization

For most of their history, men and women lived by hunting and gathering food to keep themselves and their families alive. Indeed, some hunting and gathering societies have continued into the twentieth century, and much of what we know about human prehistory is based upon a combination of inference from the way modern tribes live and from the archeological record of the past. Using a simple technology, these people obtain most of their food by gathering roots and berries, fruits and any other vegetation available. Frequently they migrate from one region to another with seasonal climatic changes. Hunting is of secondary importance in terms of caloric intake, although meat is an important source of protein and animals provide them with other materials as well. The existence of hunting and gathering societies sounds rather precarious, but as anthropologist Richard Lee has pointed out, even in the most barren of surroundings, a band can survive without much fear of starvation. Lee studied the Bushmen of the Kalahari Desert, in South Africa. Here he found that by relying heavily upon nuts and roots, with occasional successes at hunting, the Bushmen can obtain enough of the right kinds of food to provide them with a well-balanced diet all year round. In fact, Lee suggests, their food supply is so secure that they need to spend less than half their working day providing for their meals, and have the rest of the time free to do whatever they like. He describes them as if they were the original leisure class, certainly not the picture we would have of a wandering band seeking food in the desert.

But for all their leisure time, hunters and gatherers could not really be expected to change very rapidly—certainly not at the pace that we have experienced in the past few thousand years. Technology tends to increase geometrically: The more you have, the faster it grows. Technological change is like compound interest, and hunters and gatherers don't have very much in the bank. Although they find enough food for themselves, surviving is still a day-to-day task for everyone. The band cannot afford to carry non-food-producing members who do not work to support themselves. Furthermore, the development and exchange of new ideas is extremely limited. A given area can only support a limited number of people, and this tends to create isolated pockets of hunters and gatherers who in time grow more unlike their neighbors. They become not only physically isolated but culturally separate as well. These two conditions—living from day to day and being isolated from others—were strong factors in inhibiting any major changes for literally hundreds of thousands of years. Moreover, since they enjoyed a relatively successful and secure life style, hunters and gatherers were really under no pressure to seek radical changes.

Natives of Girianga, northern Kenya, hunting with bow and arrow. Hunting and gathering societies have experienced little technological change, but this does not mean their cultures are static. (Africa Pix, Peter Arnold)

Agriculture

It was not until about ten thousand years ago that human groups began to give up hunting and gathering as a way of making a living. Hunting and gathering groups in the Near East (and later in other areas of the world) began to rely rather heavily upon wild grains that grew in the region, and in time they eventually learned to domesticate these grains. This was the first step toward agriculture, which was the necessary prerequisite for civilization. As people were able to combine the domestication of plants and animals, many other changes occurred in their life as well. No longer did they have to move around a wide area to find enough food. The size of the group could expand, since the land could support many more people through agriculture than through hunting and gathering. Equally important was the fact that agriculture allowed a family to produce more food than it could consume, and this surplus could be used to feed other people who were freed for other occupations than food producing. More important, surplus food could be stored for future use, or exchanged in trade networks, or used in many different ways. This was crucial to the development of civilization, as we shall see. For the first time a class

Kikuyu women cultivating with traditional njembe tool. (Marc and Evelyne Bernheim, Woodfin Camp)

of people emerged who could turn their attentions to other aspects of life without worrying where their next meal was coming from.

Urbanism

The next great step toward civilization was the formation of urban centers. Indeed, the word *civilization* is derived from the Latin word for city, and we tend to think of civilization and urbanism as going hand in hand. Although most of the early urban centers were so small that they would barely deserve the name "city" in today's meaning of the term, still they were important in the process of culture change. The concentration of people in urban centers was a natural outgrowth of the increase in population that resulted from agriculture, combined with the growing number of people who no longer were required to engage directly in food production. Such people congregated in a single community where they could perform other crafts and services, which they at first exchanged directly with the agriculturalists of the region. In fact, early cities were small enough to accommodate both farmers and nonfarmers. But as the size of the city grew, it became more and more a center for specialists in other activities, and its populations became increasingly heterogeneous, that is, composed of people who were unlike each other.

It is easy to see how such an atmosphere can play a major role in culture change: Where everyone in a community is engaged in the same occupation and shares the same basic experiences (as in a farming community), there is a great deal of pressure to conform; on the other hand, where there is more diversity in a community and people do not share the majority of their experiences (as in an urban community made up of specialists in different crafts and services), there is less pressure to conform to a single standard. As a result, there is greater freedom to innovate, and more likelihood that the innovations will be accepted by others in the community. In other words, the very nature of the city as a collection of different kinds of people is a basic force in promoting change. Thus it is with agriculture as a prerequisite for urban life, and then ultimately with urbanism itself, that the snowballing effect of cultural and social change begins. Compared to the overall span of life on the earth, this transitional period is quite rapid. But compared to the life span of a single individual, it is still rather slow. It took several thousand years for the development of agriculture and the stabilization of production to lead to urbanism.

Literacy

A third major step in the chain of events that led toward modern civilization was the invention of writing. In fact, for many scholars it is not urbanism but the invention of writing that signifies the beginning of civilization. The importance of writing cannot be exaggerated for the overall process of change, and particularly for the problem that confronts us most often today, the *rate* of change. Prior to the era of widespread literacy, the limitations upon knowledge were most severe. Relying upon oral communication meant that one could only learn what was passed down from one generation to the next by word of mouth. It was very difficult to build upon traditions, and communication was limited to people with whom one came in direct contact. Of course, there was change over time, and oral communication was not completely ineffective. After all, it is this basic ability to communicate that is fundamental to the origin of culture in the first place, and to the differentiation between human beings (who learn) and animals (who must rely for the most part on instinct).

Writing was important because it gave people the opportunity to store up knowledge and communicate over a much wider area. It also enabled an exactness of communication that was not possible through verbal teaching alone, which relied so heavily upon the memory. Traditions that had been passed on through the generations orally could now be written down, so that the next generation no longer had to commit them to memory, but could learn them quickly, keep them in a convenient form for reference, and thus begin to modify them and pass along new ideas as well as old ones. Records could be kept, names and dates and places could be noted, and countless other uses of writing could be made to expand knowledge in ways that previously were impossible.

Another important aspect of literacy was the power it conferred upon those who had it over those who did not. In the early days of writing one of its main functions was to record the religious doctrines that until then had been a part of the oral tradition. Recording and interpreting the holy scriptures became a task of the priestly class, and it tended to create a sharper distinction between them and the rest of society. By making this class the ultimate authority on religious doctrine, it placed them in a position to assume leadership of the entire society. Moreover, because those who were literate could record and reinterpret the religious doctrines, they were in a position to solidify their power and justify their goals for society and programs to carry out those goals. In short, literacy created the conditions for the earliest forms of complex state organization, which in turn became the most efficient means of utilizing human energy for purposes beyond the immediate satisfaction of the material needs of people. As long as people were interested only in getting enough to eat and to survive in relative comfort, there was little incentive to seek change. But once the state enters into the picture, with political and economic goals that extend beyond the comforts of its citizens—and especially once it has the power to coerce its citizens to cooperate to achieve those goals—the incentive for change is enormous. And while it is not absolutely essential that there be literacy in order to achieve a state organization, the early history of the first literate societies demonstrates its importance.

We could continue with this thumbnail sketch of the fundamentals of civilization and their role in social and cultural change, but as we approach the present these factors become more well-known: the origin of the concept of the corporate body of citizens, the development of a secular legal code that made government a public institution rather than a religiously based seat of power, and so on into the Industrial Revolution and even the atomic age of the past three decades. The combination of material inventions and new ideas that has accelerated the process of change is discussed by modern historians, and although they may disagree on the relative importance of one invention or idea over another, they do not disagree on the basic trends toward change. Material inventions such as the printing press, gunpowder, the automobile, the harnessing of electrical and then atomic energy—the list could go on forever—have helped to make the world grow smaller as they have brought us into the twentieth century. Likewise, new idea systems in religion, politics, economics, law, science and the arts have all contributed to the rapid change characteristic of our age.

The subject of this chapter is how cultural anthropologists approach the question of social and cultural change. We have outlined briefly what the process of change was by which civilization came into being, although this is primarily the province of archeology and ancient history. What we are concerned with, and what we will deal with in the rest of the chapter, is how cultural anthropologists have studied change and what they have learned about it in the past century, especially in the past few decades.

Early Anthropological Interest In Change

As we pointed out in Chapter 1, people have been interested in change at least as far back as we have written records. The ancient Greeks compared their own society to that of the barbarians surrounding them and postulated an evolutionary scheme whereby they had emerged from a similar lower stage themselves. Ever since then, as Western societies have come into contact with other peoples who were perhaps not as advanced technologically or who were different in some other way, writers have tried to explain the causes of these differences, that is, why Western society has advanced (or why non-Western society has declined). This attempt at understanding social change has gone through many phases, each era developing its own theoretical assumptions about the nature of society and the basis for change. In the rest of this chapter we will summarize several of these approaches as they have appeared in the works of anthropologists in the century since the discipline became formally recognized as a social science.

Perhaps the most dominant intellectual tradition in the nineteenth century was evolution. Charles Darwin's earth-shaking work *The Origin of Species* (published in 1859), while recognized by many to be the first major step toward the development of an evolutionary theory, was really the culmination of a long period of interest in evolution, the processes by which it worked, and the proof of its effect upon life. It is not surprising, then, that a similar trend should develop in anthropology, parallel to Darwin's work in biology, to describe social and cultural change in evolutionary terms. Differences between Western and non-Western cultures were explained as being the result of varying rates of change, or climbing up the evolutionary ladder toward civilization at different speeds. According to one prominent American anthropologist of that period, Lewis Henry Morgan, all peoples were given the same potential for achieving civilization at Creation. How-

Charles Darwin's voyage on the H.M.S. Beagle, shown here at anchor in the Straits of Magellan at the tip of South America, led to his discovery of the principle of natural selection. (The Bettmann Archive)

ever, due to natural impediments such as climate or physical isolation, or any of a number of other factors, not all cultures exercised that potential at the same rate. Thus change was seen as inherent in human society, and differences were explained by the changes that each society experienced.

Toward the end of the nineteenth century this approach to the study of social and cultural change was challenged, with the attack being led by Franz Boas, a German immigrant who founded the first department of anthropology in America at Clark University in 1888. Boas was originally trained as a physicist, then turned to geography, and while on a field trip became interested in anthropology. His background in science was important, however, for it led him to question the methods of the nineteenth century anthropologists as unscientific. Perhaps because of his foreign heritage and upbringing, he also reacted strongly to what he felt were strong racist overtones in the theory of cultural evolution, which placed Western societies at the pinnacle of evolutionary advancement while the Third-World countries remained at the bottom, hopelessly stagnant.

Thus Boas mounted a two-pronged attack against evolutionism, one based upon scientific principles of investigation, and the other upon the implicit racism and the lack of cultural relativity. In scientific terms Boas did not agree with the theory of cultural evolution as it was expressed by nineteenth-century anthropologists, for he felt that it ignored the most fundamental and clearly observable source of change—the contact between two cultures. Evolutionists had tended to minimize the role of *diffusion* (the spread of an innovation from its point of origin throughout an area and ultimately, through contact with other cultures, to neighboring regions). But Boas, who was to become a dominant figure in American anthropology in the early twentieth century, held firmly that rather than looking at change as the unfolding of the potential for civilization, we must focus upon those changes that we can observe and document as we study the effects of contact between two or more groups with different cultures.

Boas' attack on evolutionism led to a new method in cultural anthropology in the United States, with an emphasis upon collecting minute facts rather than constructing grand theories. He and his students set out to investigate the diffusion of culture through historically documented contact between cultures. Most of the early work was done in American Indian societies, not only because they were a handy subject for American anthropologists, but also because there was a great deal of concern for recording (if not preserving) the traditions of what appeared to be a disappearing culture. The goal was to reconstruct the past, establishing the origin, development and spread of every aspect of a culture—not just material objects such as weapons, tools, ornaments, and the like, but the intangible aspects such as folk tales, dances, magical practices and religious beliefs. If this seemed rather tedious and at times unproductive (which it certainly does in retrospect), Boas justified such a method by claiming that if anthropology was to become a science it had to have a firm basis in fact, not just conjecture. By examining the form and geographical distribution of any aspect of a culture, he felt he was on the way to understanding how it came into being, and ultimately how it spread from one culture to another. This understanding was the key to formulating a law of cultural change.

Acculturation

Boas never produced any major theory of culture change, for he had embarked upon a never-ending search for detail that would not lead him to any conclusions until it was all gathered. He is an important figure in the study of change, however, for two reasons. First, he led the battle against applying an evolutionary theory to culture change as it had been applied to biological change, and his criticisms were so effective that he literally laid evolutionism to rest for more than half a century in cultural anthropology. Secondly, Boas is an influential figure because of the important role he played in training a large number of students who in turn became the leaders of anthropology in the early twentieth century. Many of these students followed Boas' interest in the study of change, but applied their efforts in a more effective way. Where Boas had been concerned with documenting the fact that an innovation had diffused, his followers in the next generation of anthropological investigations became aware of the importance of contact between two or more groups for the diffusion of culture. The result was that between about 1920 and 1950, a major school of anthropology arose, based upon the study of social and cultural change through culture contact, a process known as *acculturation.*

Acculturation can be defined as change that occurs when groups of individuals having different cultures come into continuous first-hand contact. This is a rather broad definition, taking into account many different kinds of change and situations of contact. It may help to examine acculturation studies in more detail, with specific examples, to see how anthropologists have viewed change arising out of contact between different groups.

One factor that can affect the exchange of elements of culture is the type of contact between two or more groups. For example, in some situations the contact is between two entire societies, or at least a representative cross-section of each. Thus, where two nonhostile Indian tribes moved into the same region we might expect a blending of culture as members of the two tribes interacted, perhaps intermarried, and in general shared their ways of life. On the other hand, many other situations involve only a selected segment of one society in contact with another. The contact between the Spanish conquerors and the Mexican Indians involved only a small portion of Spanish society, surely not representative of the entire culture. Similarly, American contact with the peoples of the Pacific Islands during World War II was also limited to a small part of American culture, the military. Other examples might affect the cultural exchange differently, as in the case of contact between missionaries from

Eugene Ray

Melville Jean Herskovits
(1895–1963)
is known widely as the first American anthropologist to specialize in African studies, particularly Afro-American cultures in the New World. At a time when American anthropology was concerned primarily with native American cultures, Herskovits applied the same principles of analysis to Africa. After conducting fieldwork in Africa, he turned his attention to Afro-American cultures, particularly in the Caribbean, pointing out how African traditions are reworked into the way of life forced upon them in the New World. Herskovits' study of Afro-American culture led him to an interest in culture change, and he was a leading figure in the development of a school of anthropology concerned with the process of acculturation, or culture change through contact.

one culture and an entire group in another area, or between traders, miners, or other equally marginal members of a society.

Other interests in acculturation studies have to do with the process of change. What traits were ultimately borrowed by one culture, in what order, and with what resistance? Was a new innovation adopted exactly as it existed in the original culture, or was it changed to fit in better with the borrowers' culture? Was there an element of prestige involved in borrowing? Answers to these and other questions were sought in an attempt to understand the process of cultural and social change, not only for interpreting events in the past, but to predict future change as well.

Eskimo mother nursing infant with a bottle, introduced through contact with white culture. (Burt Glinn, Magnum)

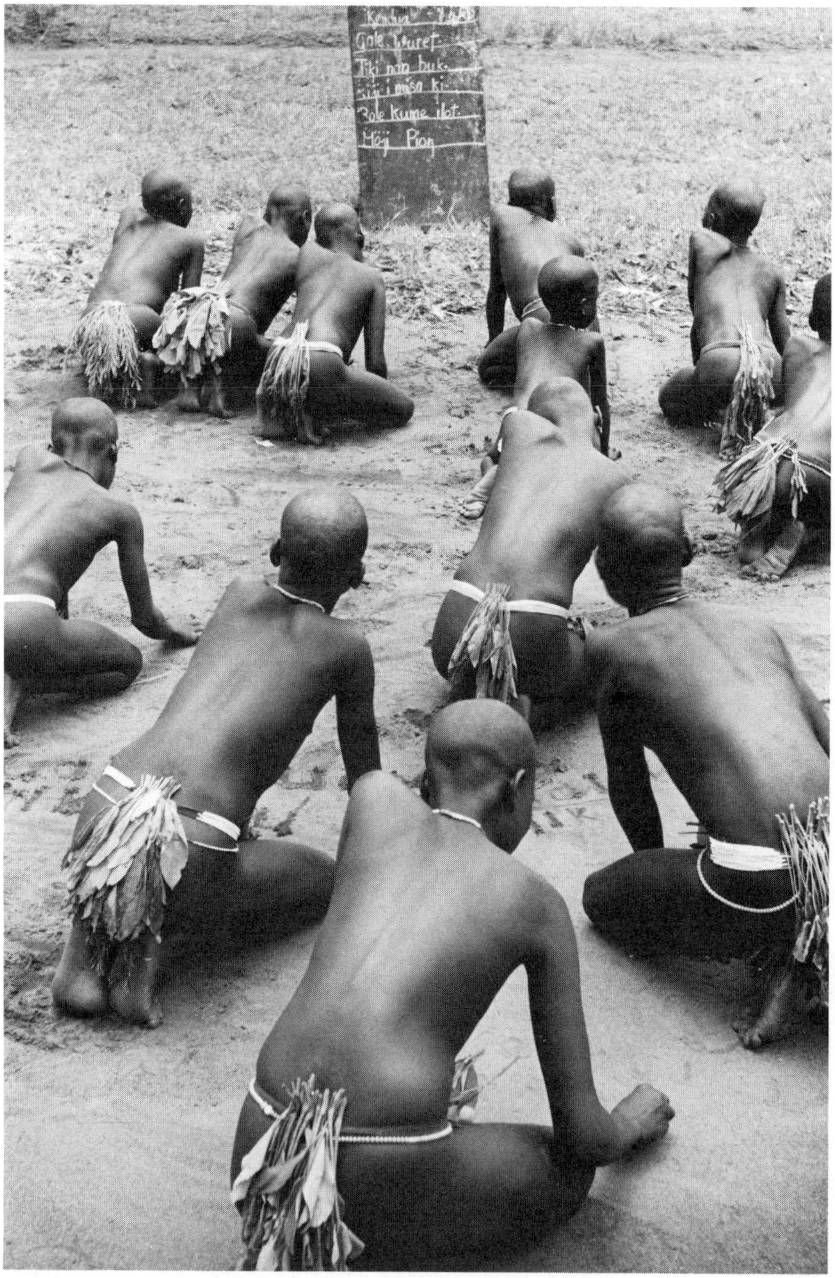

Through contact with white missionaries and school teachers, many children such as these in Africa, attended "schools" for the first time. (George Rodger, Magnum)

Plains Indian Culture: The Decline of Tradition

One early study of acculturation was carried out by Margaret Mead, who described the changing culture of a Plains Indian people who had been in contact with white society. At the time of her study in the early 1930s, the contact had been so recent and cataclysmic that adjustment had not been possible, and therefore her study concentrated on the problems of disorganization that resulted from the contact.

The Indians' initial contact with white culture was through fur traders, who introduced guns and steel traps to Indian culture. The second phase of contact was marked by white settlers in the region, the establishment of an Indian agency, a Presbyterian mission, and the disappearance of the buffalo. Finally, in the third phase, the Indians were pressured to abandon their traditional way of life (e.g., living in tipis, hunting, trapping, and fishing) and were encouraged to adopt the way of life of the typical rural white American. Mead points out that even with all these changes, the Indians might have been able to get by, but after a period of about 25 years they had to face the problem of increased white settlement which took their land away from them. The white settlers did not mingle with the Indians, but maintained separate cultures which kept them from getting along with one another. While the Indians were encouraged to adopt the white people's ways, at the same time they were prevented by white prejudice from participating in joint cultural ventures.

As Mead shows in her study of this culture contact, Indian religion broke down almost entirely under the pressure by white contact. Initially all the Indians converted to Presbyterianism as a result of the efforts of the white missionaries. But the new religion failed to provide them with the rewards it preached, and they soon turned to peyote cults for their religious needs. Peyotism also provided an outlet for their traditional ritual ceremonies which did not fit into the Presbyterian service. At the time Mead wrote of this situation, the peyote religion was still the predominant form among the tribe, and very little of either the original religious beliefs or the recently adopted white people's religion had been retained. Thus she describes a situation of cultural breakdown, where contact between two cultures leads not to the sharing of elements of the cultures but to the disorganization and disintegration of a traditional way of life, and at the same time a rejection of much of the new way that is offered.

As a postscript to this study, Mead points to a positive result of the contact between whites and Indians. Because this process of subjugation of Indian culture to the way of the whites was common across the country, and not just among this one tribe, the various Indian tribes began to develop an identity with one another. Whereas formerly they had considered themselves culturally distinct, they now faced a common enemy that drew them together as allies. Thus as a result of acculturation with whites, a class consciousness arose among Indians, which has built up over the last century to a peak today. In the days before white contact such a common identity would have been unthinkable, but when faced with a common threat, Indians of all tribes began to look at one another in a new light, ignoring their differences and stressing their similarities.

Caribbean Culture: The Blending of Traditions

In a study of acculturation in the Caribbean, Melville Herskovits describes the process of *syncretism,* the reinterpretation of new cultural elements to fit them in with the already existing traditions. Herskovits studied the introduction of Christian ideas into the religion of blacks in the New World, particularly the relationship between African gods and Catholic saints. He emphasizes that non-European people do not easily abandon their native religious beliefs and practices when confronted with Christianity. Rather, they usually react in one of two ways: they either try to perpetuate the old way and reject anything new; or else they take over the external form of the new elements but reinterpret them to fit into the old way, keeping the old values and meanings alive.

Herskovits cites examples of New World blacks in Cuba, Brazil and Haiti to illustrate this process. He says that while they profess nominal Catholicism, they still belong to cults that are under the direction of priests whose functions are essentially African and whose training follows traditional patterns of instruction and initiation. He also points to specific identifications between African gods and Catholic saints, showing how the content of the old religion is carried over into the form of the new.

Brought over to the New World as slaves, the Africans were baptized into the Catholic church in these countries. The whites tried to eliminate the traditional cults of the blacks, which they feared would serve as a focus for organizing revolutionary activities. Although the groups were broken up to a certain extent, they did manage to continue on local levels. However, since they were officially banned, they were forced to take on a new appearance to hide their real nature. Thus in many of these cults, although the Catholic practices were adopted to placate the whites, they were only a mask for the continuation of traditional rituals.

Luo warrior from Lake Victoria region of Kenya with feathered headdress, cigarette and tin can bracelet. (Marc and Evelyne Bernheim, Woodfin Camp)

Herskovits points to some examples of traditional African deities which have been reinterpreted in terms of the Catholic hierarchy of saints. *Legba* is a god in Dahomey who guards the crossroads and entrances to temples, residence compounds and villages. He is also widely worshipped in Haiti, where he must open the path for the supernatural powers. *Legba* is believed by most people from Dahomey who live in Haiti to be the same deity as St. Anthony. The reason for this identification is that the pictures commonly used to depict St. Anthony show him to be an old man, poorly dressed, carrying a cane to support him as he walks. The use of such a cane or wand is frequently attributed to *Legba* as well, who uses it to enforce his watch of the path, and to open the path to supernatural powers.

Damballa is a Dahomean rainbow serpent deity. He is widely associated with the serpent cult, which is said to be rather popular in Haiti. Yet in Haiti he is generally identified with St. Patrick, who is also closely associated with snakes in the Catholic tradition, allegedly driving the serpents out of Ireland. Following this logic even further, Moses is said to be the father of *Damballa*. This is because of the description in the Bible of Moses throwing down his staff on the ground in front of the Pharaoh, whereby it turned into a serpent.

In a like manner, many other traditional deities are worked into the newly imposed Catholic tradition. Sometimes the saints are even equated with natural phenomena, such as the sun, moon and stars, rather than simply personified. St. John the Baptist, for example, is in some areas of the Caribbean worshipped as the deity who controls thunder and lightning. This is because in pictures of him he is frequently seen holding a lamb, and in traditional Dahomean mythology the ram is the emblem of the god of thunder. In the same vein, saints are added to the Catholic tradition to cover certain areas of the Old World tradition which are otherwise omitted in the Christian scriptures. For example, many blacks in the Caribbean worship such deities as *St. Soleil* (St. Sun), *Ste. la Lune* (St. Moon), *Sts. Etoiles* (Sts. Stars), and *Ste. la Terre* (St. Earth).

Herskovits' study of the contact between traditional African and white cultures in the Caribbean illustrates how flexible people can be in adopting new ways. However, such flexibility is not always possible, and instead culture contact may lead to irreparable breaks in the continuity of traditional patterns, as is illustrated by the following example.

Australian Aborigine Culture: The Reversal of Tradition

The Yir Yoront are a tribe located on the northern peninsula of Australia, described in a study by Lauriston Sharp. Before white contact, technologically their culture was of the old stone age type, which meant that they supported themselves by hunting and fishing, and gathering fruits and vegetables. The most important tool in their culture was a polished stone axe with a short handle, and this was important not only in their economy, but in their social ranking system as well. The axe was a masterpiece produced only by men. It required specialized knowledge of the natural resources of the area, such as wood for the handle, bark for cord for the binding, and the right kind of stone. While the axe could be used by anyone, man, woman, or child, it could only be obtained by trading. Thus elaborate trade networks arose among men (and only men) to acquire stones for the axes. Since only men owned the axes, even though women did most of the work with them, they constantly had to ask the men to borrow the axes, setting up an elaborate means of reinforcing male superiority and dominance in the group and clearly marking out the patterns of authority.

This traditional pattern of ownership and use of the stone axe and the resulting social relationships it created were shattered when the Yir Yoront came into contact with white culture. Around the turn of the century the Australian government established three mission stations in the Yir Yoront territory, and through them many items of Western culture were dispensed. The missionaries encouraged members of the tribe to work for the mission, and they were paid in what were considered to be useful goods, including steel axes. However, the steel axe was introduced in large numbers and indiscriminately among the Yir Yoront, to anyone who worked for the mission. The new axe proved to be much more efficient than the old stone axe, and it soon replaced its predecessor as an item of prestige and importance in Yir Yoront culture.

It is easy to see how the introduction of the steel axe might affect the Yir Yoront. For one thing, axes were no longer only the property of men, for women and children acquired them from the mission. The dependence that the stone axe created upon the men was transferred to the mission through the steel axe. Men who were formerly independent lost their power over women and children, especially those men who were too proud and independent to work for the mission in return for an axe for themselves. In short, the introduction of the steel axe upset most of the traditional patterns associated with the stone axe. Men sometimes became so desirous of the steel axe that they would sell their wives or daughters into prostitution to acquire one from a Westerner, or even from one of their own tribesmen. The values associated with age, sex and kinship ties were no longer reinforced through the use of the steel axe. Furthermore, along with the decline in the clear ownership patterns surrounding the axe came a decline in patterns of ownership in general, with a resulting increase in stealing and crime in general. The old culture lost much of its meaning and began to die out (and all because of an axe!).

The author of this study does not offer any value judgments about the changes that took place in Yir Yoront culture. He does not suggest that a male-centered society such as existed prior to white contact is necessarily better (or worse) than a society where women have a measure of equality, such as the post-contact Yir Yoront achieved. He notes that while crime increased, the standard of living also rose. His main purpose is to illustrate how complex the process of change can be, with unanticipated consequences in other areas of life. As such, he presents us with a valuable study of acculturation as a process of cultural and social change.

Nativism and Revitalization Movements

As an offshoot of acculturation studies, anthropologists in the 1940s and 1950s turned their attention to a particular result of culture contact. As Western culture intruded more and more into the far corners of the world, bringing with it immense wealth and impressive technological mastery, many isolated and relatively unknown peoples saw their old way of life eroded. Helpless in the face of the pressure exerted by the new masters, formerly free and proud people found their traditions no longer effective. Frustration became a widespread social problem. One response was to give up the old ways and try to be like the white man, in the hope of gaining the desired elements of Western culture. Another alternative, practiced by many in response to their powerlessness, was to reject everything new and to preach a return to the "pure" culture of the good old days. Such efforts have been called "revitalization" movements in reference to their attempt to revitalize, or breathe new life into the old cultural patterns and traditions.

Early interest in revitalization movements among anthropologists began with the study of such phenomena as the Ghost Dance of the

Amish culture represents an attempt to retain the traditional way of life in the midst of a changing society. Though tractors and automobiles are more efficient, the Amish stick with the horse-drawn plow and cart. (Mark Chester, Monkmeyer)

North American Indians in the late nineteenth century and the Cargo Cults of Melanesia in the twentieth century. Both types of movements arose primarily in response to the disintegration of the former way of life due to contact with white culture. One of the earliest discussions of these movements, as a particular type of response to similar conditions in different parts of the world and at different times, was offered by Anthony Wallace, who actually coined the term "revitalization." He attempted to bring together a variety of movements and describe them in similar structural terms, demonstrating that such widely different occurrences as the rise of Christianity, the Ghost Dance of 1890, the Taiping Rebellion in China, and the Russian Revolution were all variations of the same process of social change.

The process of revitalization is based on dissatisfaction with the present system, and is an attempt by people to create more satisfactory conditions in which to live. What is so special about revitalization is that it is a conscious process designed to produce change, thus making it different from diffusion or acculturation as types of cultural change. Wallace views revitalization as a reaction to stress: When an individual is faced with a problem, he must either change himself to be able to tolerate it, or else change the stress at its source. But when a group of people experience the same stress, and they choose to do something about it, they are in effect seeking to revitalize their way of life, their culture. They can accomplish this either by changing the physical reality or by altering the psychological reality (that is, their perception of the problem, rather than the root of the problem itself). In this way we can see basic similarities in such seemingly different responses as a passive religious movement that offers a new doctrine (thus changing the psychological reality of the problem) and a revolution, which seeks to change the actual physical cause of the stress through violent means.

The Ghost Dance: Return to the Good Old Days

Revitalization movements can be classified into a number of different subtypes, which enables us to see even greater similarities, as well as to understand the different causes and reactions on the part of the people affected. First, there are what have been called "nativistic" movements, which place a strong emphasis on the elimination of alien persons, customs, values and materials from the culture. The term *nativism* refers to the attempt to return to the traditional or native cultural patterns and expel anything that is foreign from the culture. In such a movement, frequently certain aspects of the traditional culture are selected as being especially important, and are given symbolic value; rarely is the rejection of *all* new elements accomplished.

The Ghost Dance of the North American Indians is an excellent example of a nativistic movement. It arose out of the frustration experienced by many Indian tribes as a result of contact with the westward-moving whites. Forced to give up their traditional way of life, and stunned by the drastic change in the environment caused by the intrusion of white culture (such as the virtual extermination of the buffalo, which had been so important to Indian culture), the Indians did not know where to turn. Many were forced onto reservations, and began to adopt white culture. They soon found that this was not the answer, for they shared more of the negative aspects of that new way of life than the benefits. They inherited alcoholism, racial discrimination, poverty and illiteracy, but no wealth, power or freedom. In short, the time was ripe for a new solution, one that did not require acquiescence to the authority of the white man.

An Indian prophet named Wovoka provided the answer. He experienced a religious vision, in which he saw into the future. The answer he conveyed to his people, which ultimately spread throughout the Great Plains to a number of Indian tribes, was for the Indian to reject the ways of the white man, return to the old traditions, and practice the new ritual of the Ghost Dance. When this task had been accomplished, that is, when Indian culture had once again become purified of the evil ways of the white man, the buffalo would return, and the dead ancestors of the Indians would ride out of heaven into battle to help them drive the whites from the earth. In some more radical versions of this prophecy it was claimed that those who adhered to the faith would be immune to the bullets of the white man's gun, and could ride into battle without fear of injury or death. It must have been a tragic sight to see a band of Indians riding up to a cavalry troop, armed only with bows and arrows yet secure in their belief that they would not be harmed.

Cargo Cults: Imitating the New Ways

A second type of revitalization movement is what has been called a "cargo cult," a term derived from a series of cults found in the Pacific Islands during and after World Wars I and II. Natives on many of these islands saw huge amounts of cargo being delivered to military and mission installations established by Western nations, but at the same time they realized that they were not sharing in the new wealth. They came to believe that if they adopted the ways of the foreigners, they too would be able to receive the cargo. Obviously they did not correctly perceive the relationship between the foreign customs and the delivery of the cargo, and the result was that they adopted Western dress patterns, built imitation air strips and boat docks, and waited for the planes and ships to deliver their reward.

Cargo cults are thus different from nativistic movements in that they seek to adopt new cultural patterns in order to revitalize their culture, rather than return to traditional ways of life. The earliest anthropological interest in cargo cults was Francis Williams' report in 1923 of such a movement among the native people in New Guinea. The movement was called the *Vailala Madness,* named after a town in the southern coast of New Guinea where it began in 1919. Faced with the technological and military superiority of the white culture, the people sought to adopt many of the alien ways. They destroyed many sacred objects and discontinued earlier ritual practices, substituting Christian elements for them. The actual "madness" was a dance involving frenzied, uncontrolled excitement, along with the destruction of religious and art treasures.

The doctrine of the Vailala Madness centered around two main themes. First, there was the expectation of the imminent return of the dead, primarily through the vehicle of a cargo ship similar to the steamers which were seen bringing goods to the whites. Second, probably as a result of their perception of the superiority of white culture, the natives adopted the belief that their ancestors were themselves white, and that the deceased who would return on cargo ships would thus be white. There were also many Christian elements in the doctrine of the movement, and many prominent leaders claimed they were Jesus Christ, and that the heavenly state they were expecting would be Jehovah's Land, as described in the Christian teachings.

From descriptions of this and other cargo cults in the Pacific

Swimming at Lake Rudolf in northern Kenya. Tourism has been a powerful force in bringing cultures of the world into contact. (Peter Beard)

Islands, we can understand many of the forces that seem to lead people to join such movements. A number of similar movements have occurred in widely scattered places and many years apart, leading us to conclude that rather than being the result of the diffusion of an idea, they have arisen out of similar conditions. A common element among all the movements is that they occur in areas where there has been considerable contact with Western culture. In addition, they have occurred where people have not been able to participate in the higher standard of living that they have witnessed in the white community. Thus in the port towns, where the standard of living is higher, such movements have not arisen. Nor have they occurred in the more isolated areas of the Pacific, such as the interior of New Guinea where European influence has not spread. Cyril Belshaw, an anthropologist who has investigated these movements throughout Melanesia (an area in the Pacific Islands), has concluded that the cults are caused by a change to a position halfway between the old and the new, coupled with the inability to change further. In other words, the people experience enough of the benefits of Western culture to want more, but just as their expectations rise ever higher, they are cut off. One result is that they imitate the ways of the white man, either out of respect or out of jealousy or hatred. It is interesting to compare this type of movement with the concept of nativism, to see how opposite responses to the same basic problem can arise, both generated by culture contact and the prospects of rapid change.

Millenarian Movements: Looking to the Future

A third type of revitalization movement is a *millenarian movement,* which emphasizes a transformation of the world designed and carried out by a supernatural power. Such a movement is based upon the belief in the coming of the millennium, when all wrongs will be set right. Frequently the millenarian movement takes on a messianic quality, inspired by a charismatic leader who generates a great deal of emotional involvement on the part of the followers. Most radical millenarian movements occur among oppressed peoples, indicating a correlation between social and economic conditions and this type of revitalization attempt.

The functions of these movements, as pointed out by the Italian anthropologist Vittorio Lanternari, tend to be quite varied. They serve as potent agents of change, creating a bridge between the future and the past. They connect religion and politics, for they often can serve as a prototype of a modern revolutionary movement. Revolutions, much like millenarian movements, are brought about by a combination of deprivation and frustration on the part of a large number of people, who have seen their culture disintegrate. In many cases what started out as a local and small-scale millenarian movement mushroomed into a full-scale revolution.

The idea of a millennium is most often associated with the period of one thousand years found in the Judeo-Christian tradition referring to the second coming of Christ. In a wider sense, however, it can be applied to any conception of a perfect age to come, or a perfect place to be attained. In addition, these movements usually demand of their followers some ordeal which will make them worthy, such as a difficult journey or pilgrimage, a ritual purification, or an act of violence. The idea of a millennium which will bring with it a Golden Age is especially popular in situations of culture contact, but it can be the basis for a movement in a crisis situation which was not necessarily caused by the intrusion of a foreign culture. Famines, plagues, or other natural disasters can lead to a religion-based movement seeking to revitalize the culture, as can a major political upheaval.

Millenarian movements frequently anticipate the coming of a new age in the near future, and although they are vague about the actual mechanisms by which it will become a reality, they offer a plan for bringing it about. We can see an element of millenarianism in many of the major political movements in recent history. Communism, with its utopian view of the future, fits this model, and the Communist movement can be seen as the active force for such a change. Likewise, Nazism advocated a ritual purification that ultimately would lead to a new Golden Age. In these and other cases there are a number of similarities: the importance of charismatic leaders (e.g., Lenin, Hitler); the reliance upon magical properties, or symbolically important beliefs (the assumed invincibility of the German army in World War II closely parallels the notion of the immunity of the Indians to the white man's bullets); the elimination of foreign or unwanted elements from the culture, particularly symbolically important groups (the Russian aristocracy, the German Jews).

Relative Deprivation: A Cause of Revitalization Movements

It is interesting to reflect on the causes of millenarian movements, and revitalization movements in general. What must happen to a group of people, or to their way of life, before they will actively seek to change things? How severely must their traditions be challenged and their values be negated before they are moved to act? One of the most plausible explanations has been presented by David Aberle, who suggests that the phenomenon of revitalization movements can be understood through the concept of what he calls "relative deprivation." He defines this as "a negative discrepancy between legitimate expectation and actuality"—that is, a change over time that leads a group of people to feel deprived relative to some other standard. We can measure relative deprivation by comparing the past to the present circumstances of a single group of people, such as the impact that the disappearance of the buffalo had upon the Indian. Thus the Indians of the late nineteenth century felt deprived relative to the conditions in which they themselves lived not so many years earlier. Or we can compare the present situation of one group to that of another contemporary group, noting a difference which causes the disadvantaged group to feel relatively deprived.

It is important to stress the notion of relativity, for as Aberle notes, it is not so much the discomfort as the dissatisfaction that is a cause of revitalization movements. For a hunting and gathering society with an expectation (based on experience) of going hungry one out of four days, the failure to find game is not a relative deprivation. However, for a middle class American not to be able to afford meat every day is a relative deprivation, not when compared to the hunters and gatherers, but when compared to the past circumstances in American society. For a multi-millionaire to lose all but his last million dollars in a stock market crash would be relative deprivation, for even though he would be living the same way as many other millionaires, he would be comparing his situation to his past, and not to their present. A more powerful example can be seen in the case of poor people in America. The standard of living of the poorest people in the United States is higher than probably 75 percent of all the people in the world. Yet there is a very strong feeling of relative deprivation among America's poor, for the important relative factor is not how peasants live in India or China, but how the rest of Americans live. They feel deprived because although they receive a relatively large slice of the world's pie, they receive a relatively small slice of the American pie.

Relative deprivation can occur not only in a material sense, such as a comparative lack of wealth or possessions, but also in a symbolic sense. Thus when a group considers itself to have higher status than it is accorded by the prevailing customs (as in the case of Indians after white contact), this is a case of relative deprivation. In a study of dissatisfaction within the ranks of the army, for example, it was found that men in lower-ranking groups were more content with their status than men in higher-ranking groups. The reason for this apparently confusing result can be seen in the concept of relative depri-

A coal miner's family in eastern Kentucky—poverty in the land of plenty. (David Campbell, Photo Researchers)

vation. Promotion was much less frequent on the lower levels (that is, proportionately fewer low-ranking men were promoted) than on the higher levels. Thus if a low-ranking soldier was passed over for promotion several times, although he might be disappointed, he did not feel relatively deprived compared to the rest of the men at his level. On the other hand, the higher a man went in the system, the greater the expectation of promotion, and thus the greater the feeling of relative deprivation when promotion did not come. This was expressed as dissatisfaction with the system, jealousy, anxiety, uncertainty and frequent complaints.

It is important to emphasize that relative deprivation must exist on a group level for it to be a significant force in bringing about a revitalization movement. If you or I as individuals feel we are not accorded a high enough status or that we are denied our fair share of the things we strive for, while we might feel deprived on an individual level, this is not a solid basis for a social movement. But when conditions promoting dissatisfaction are widespread enough that the feeling is common among a large proportion of the population, the potential exists for a strong movement advocating social change. The concept of relative deprivation thus has a great deal of relevance for understanding many of our own social problems today, and we should be able to apply it, along with other concepts derived from the study of culture, to the solution of those problems.

Philip C. Davis

Leslie A. White (1900–1975) *is an important figure in the study of culture change, and is generally known as the leader in the revival of the doctrine of cultural evolutionism. Although originally trained in the anti-evolutionist approach common throughout American anthropology in the early part of this century, White turned to evolutionism after rereading the works of Lewis Henry Morgan.*
White suggests that advancement along an evolutionary scale can be measured according to the amount of energy a society harnesses and utilizes, allowing us to quantify the difference between a society with a stone-age technology and a modern industrial society.

Modernization

Modernization is the major theme in recent history, encompassing the social and cultural changes resulting from the Agricultural Revolution, the Industrial Revolution, and more recently the Atomic Revolution. It is a process that has occurred first in Western societies, but which has spread throughout the world, both by design and by chance. Although many of the earlier factors that contributed to modernization were not in fact of Western origin, the culmination of the various processes that have produced the industrial societies of the twentieth century has taken place primarily in Europe and the United States, and only very recently in non-Western countries such as Japan.

Anthropology has an important stake in the study of modernization. Since it is a process occurring in every country in some way or another, there is an urgent need for comparative studies to give us a cross-cultural perspective on the problems encountered in various parts of the world. Moreover, in most societies traditionally studied by anthropologists (tribal and peasant peoples), cultural patterns are changed through contact with the West. Changes ultimately influence the technology, economic order, patterns of social relationships, ideologies, every aspect of traditional life. However, we also recognize that whereas industrial technology grew up in Western countries, and thus was molded to fit the cultural patterns peculiar to those countries, when it is transplanted to the Third World it does not always fit in with the existing patterns in those cultures. As a result, anthropologists who have studied the traditional way of life of these peoples are now interested in how it is being changed through contact with the West. Frequently they find that the changes in non-Western countries do not follow the pattern of industrialization in Europe and the United States, as the new technology must be modified to fit in with the existing values and traditions.

Modernization is a broad term covering a number of separate processes. It is usually assumed that these processes occur together, and that they are necessarily interrelated. By modernization we usually mean at least the following: economic growth, or industrialization; urbanization; and Westernization. In this section we shall look at each of these processes separately, comparing the original changes that took place in the West with examples of contemporary changes in the so-called "developing nations" of the Third World.

Industrialization

The growth of industry in any society cannot occur without related changes in agriculture. By the very fact that industry requires a large number of people to work in factories rather than on farms, there must be a transformation of agriculture so that fewer people can produce more food in order to supply the nonagricultural work force. Thus the conditions of the Industrial Revolution were not really laid down until the seventeenth century, when the application of science to agricultural production began to take effect. (This period has been called the Second Agricultural Revolution; the first was the original domestication of plants, which occurred in prehistoric times in the Near East.) But increasing production is not enough in itself, for there must be a way to make the surplus available to the work force. Thus along with the industrialization of a country must come a commercialization of agriculture, so that surplus products can be transported to markets.

The significance of this process for the anthropologist who studies rural people in non-Western countries is obvious. Traditionally such people were *subsistence agriculturalists,* that is, they produced food primarily for their own consumption, with only a little surplus to take care of a few basic needs. They were not integrated into a national or international market system, and many of them even got along without cash, by trading their surplus directly for other products they needed. Industrialization also meant a major change in the structure of the rural population, because at least in its early stages it required a larger work force than was available in the cities. Mass migration from rural areas to towns and cities has thus been a trend in industrializing countries. But more than that, it has been selective migration of people in a narrow age group, usually about 15 to 35 years of age, which has left the countryside with a rather uneven proportion of old people. Here the implications for rural life are evident, for without the input of new ideas and the pressure for change from the young, traditions become solidified and the relatively conservative rural communities take on an even more conservative character.

Another important change resulting from industrialization has affected the nature of the family. In a rural farm community the typical family is a large unit made up of several generations, not limited to parents and children. The farm is an ideal place for such a family unit, where there are a variety of tasks for persons of both sexes and all ages, and in a subsistence operation designed merely to produce food for the members of the group, all members of an extended family can carry their weight on the farm. But when the family moves to the city and enters into the industrial work force this is no longer the case. Here the crucial factor affecting the family becomes *mobility:* both geographical (or physical) mobility and social mobility, the ability to rise in the system of social stratification. The urban industrial family is frequently on the move, and the members on the fringe merely hold it back. In addition, the work situation in the city does not offer opportunities for extra members to contribute their share to the family economy, as they could on the farm, and they become a liability to the nuclear family unit that must support them. As a result, the process of modernization has caused a clear shift from the extended family pattern toward the norm of a nuclear family made up of parents and their unmarried offspring.

Other factors accompanying the increase in industry and the decline in subsistence farming have included the growing independence of young people, the rising status of women, a trend toward individually arranged marriages as opposed to marriages arranged by the parents, a decline in plural marriage, and the prevalence of neolocal residence, that is, the establishment after marriage of a new household independent of either spouse's parents. All of these basic cultural changes can be traced directly to the economic effects of industrialization upon a formerly rural, agrarian population. For example, as land is no longer the key economic concern, young people who can offer their labor potential on the open market gain a measure of economic security at a much earlier age, and thus become independent of the constraints of their parents and families. Women also enter the labor force and through their newly won economic position they experience a rise in status, coupled with an independence from the mastery of their husbands or fathers. Further, in a rural farm community a marriage was based primarily upon economic considerations, such as how much land a potential spouse was likely to inherit, where it was located, and how it would fit in with the plans and assets of the individual to be married. For members of the industrial labor force, however, these questions no longer have much meaning, and as a result marriage becomes a personal bond between the two principal individuals, rather than an economic arrangement between two families. In addition, the independence of the couple from the constraints of the family enterprises leads them to separate themselves physically as well as emotionally, and this is reflected in residence patterns after marriage.

Urbanization

Urbanization includes not only the growth in the actual size of cities, but the growth in the number of cities and in the proportion of the population living in urban locations. It is generally considered closely related to industrialization because industry is usually located in cities, and people who work in industry must live nearby. In addition to the demographic (population) factors involved in the growth of cities, we generally mean something more by the term *urbanization,* a change not only in the physical nature of the city but in the psychological and cultural makeup of the people who move to the city. Of course, with the growth of cities there must be parallel growth in networks of communication and transportation, market systems, new technological advances, and a growing specialization of labor.

Anthropologists who study urbanization, however, are not only concerned with these broad-scale changes in the city, but also with the effects of city life upon formerly rural people. For example, in rural areas the identification of an individual is generally seen in terms of his family first, then his community. Rarely does an isolated rural resident think in terms of nationalistic goals, or identify with the nation as a whole. Yet when he moves to the city he finds that his local orientation is no longer useful, and he must change his entire outlook toward the country of which he is a part, rather than the village or even the city. This change from localism to nationalism is connected with a major transformation of the values of the rural migrant, and can be seen as one of the most sweeping effects of urbanization.

Another difference between life in a small village and in the city is the nature of personal interaction. In a rural community every-

Urbanization draws people to the cities even when they cannot find work. One result has been the growth of squatter settlements, such as this slum neighborhood on the outskirts of Rio de Janeiro, Brazil. (Paul Conklin, Monkmeyer)

one knows everyone else personally. People know about each other's pasts, about their interests, their peculiarities; it is hard to keep anything secret in a small village. On the other hand, the city is an anonymous place where a person can literally disappear. People are thrust into situations where they must interact with others whom they have never met. Personalism can no longer serve as the basis for such interaction, and instead people develop ways of dealing with each other in a formal manner according to prescribed rules of behavior. For the new migrant to the city this can be very difficult to adjust to, and can be a source of great frustration. To some extent it can be avoided by the creation of stronger neighborhood ties in areas where there is a high concentration of migrants. Thus we frequently find sections of large cities that are solidly ethnic, where a different language is spoken from the rest of the city, and where people still seem to have the kind of personal relationships that we might expect to find in a village. Such ethnic neighborhoods are adaptations to the city, attempts to maintain some of the old traditions and offer some sense of comfort and security to newcomers who are turned off by the impersonal nature of the rest of the city.

Another feature of this impersonality of the city and the reaction to it by urbanites is the attempt to create smaller groups in which an individual can maintain strong personal ties. Whereas in a village this is not necessary because everyone is thrown together by the nature of village life, in the city a person must actively go out and look for such a group. Thus it is typical of the social organization of city life that there are large numbers of what we call *voluntary associations*, or groups that an individual member must seek out and join. Such associations are commonly based upon shared interests rather than factors such as residence in the same neighborhood, over which most people have relatively less control. A voluntary association might be formed by people who share the same occupation, or the same interest in leisure-time activities. The basis for such a group can be almost anything.

Thus in moving from the country to the city, the migrant experiences a change from what anthropologists call the "folk" culture to the "urban" culture. He moves from a small, relatively isolated, homogeneous village to a large, impersonal, individualistic community. His family becomes less important as he is integrated into the industrial economy, and he turns instead to secular institutions and groups of people who share the same specialized interests. Of course, this does not all happen overnight. In many cases studied by anthropologists it has been found that even second generation immigrants still cling to many of the traditions found in the rural areas from which their parents came. In his classic study, Oscar Lewis followed Mexican migrants from a small village to Mexico City, in an attempt to see how the pressures of city life affected their rural "folk" culture. In fact, he found that there was very little breakdown of traditional culture among first-generation migrants. Family ties remained strong, and the people formed what might be called an "urban village," an attempt to create an artificial folk culture in the midst of the city.

In other studies similar trends have been observed. Even in the United States today, rural migrants to cities have been known to resist the pressures of urbanization and maintain many folk traditions. For example, in the past two decades there has been a massive migration of Appalachians to urban areas in the midwest, prompted by the decline in the two basic economic activities of the region, subsistence agriculture and coal mining. In countless studies of Appalachian migrants to the city it has been found that they maintain very strong ties with their families "back home." The migrants tend to live in parts of the city known as "Little Appalachia," such as the section known as "Uptown" Chicago, where an estimated 50,000 Appalachian migrants reside. They work together in the same factories, worship at the same churches, and in general resist the intrusion of urban culture into their lives wherever possible. Many migrants still communicate regularly with their families in Appalachia; on any Friday evening you can see an almost endless stream of cars heading south across the Ohio River at Cincinnati, Portsmouth or any other city along the river.

What do these two apparently contradictory trends—the simultaneous breakdown and maintenance of folk culture among urban migrants—tell us about the process of urbanization? For one thing, we can see how the traditional way of life that is functional in a small community setting can be a disadvantage to a person living in the city. Thus there will be pressure for the migrant to give up his old ways if he is to succeed in his new home. But at the same time, we can learn a valuable lesson about the nature of culture itself. Culture is basically conservative. We learn patterns of behavior easily in our childhood, but we give them up only with great difficulty as adults. This is why it takes at least one generation, usually more, to see a complete change from folk to urban culture. The migrants themselves tend to hold steadfastly to their traditions, fighting off any newfangled, "citified" ideas. Their children grow up in a kind of dualistic environment: Their parents teach them the old values, and their peers and others with whom they come in contact in the city teach them a new and different set of values. Sometimes they make the transition to urbanites smoothly in one generation, but, depending upon the strength of the urban village in which they are raised and the conservatism of their own cultural heritage, it can take much longer.

The city is a place for rapid social change, even as ethnic communities fight to retain their traditional cultures. (Sam Falk, Monkmeyer)

Westernization

Of all the aspects of modernization, the concept of Westernization is the most difficult to define. By this term we generally refer to the adoption of cultural patterns characteristic of Western society. Many of these changes have already been discussed, such as the predominance of the nuclear family, the rising status of women, or the growth of a market economy and an accompanying market mentality. But Westernization can occur without movement to the city, or without taking a job in industry, and at least as I use the term here, it refers to changes in the values, attitudes, beliefs—the whole psychological makeup of individuals in non-Western societies.

One of the most important influences in this process is the mass media. Through communication with the outside world, people in formerly isolated areas become aware of a new prestigious model. New products and materials are made available to people, and high prestige is attached to them. At the same time, although people are unaware of it, it is impossible to adopt a new material culture, including the products and increased standard of living of a newly industrialized and urbanized society, without some of the values associated with industrialization and urbanization rubbing off. For example, a man who used to work on his family farm cannot take a job in a factory without adopting some of the values that go with industrial labor. He will develop a new conception of time and efficiency, something that never had to be exact on the farm. He will begin to calculate the cash value of his labor, whereas on a subsistence-oriented farm his labor had no cash value. Punctuality and precision are basically Western values that were not found in most agricultural societies prior to the spread of Western culture and the beginning of modernization. This is not necessarily because Westerners are so different from people in the rest of the world, but rather because there are certain requirements (we might call them constraints) imposed by the conditions of industrial labor that bring about these values. And the same might be said for city life, with its anonymity and specialization: It is not that these cultural patterns are something innate in the nature of the people who live in Western countries, but rather that the urban industrial centers where these values and patterns were functional were initially located in the West.

Another important factor in the spread of Western culture is the uneven rate at which elements of it are adopted. This is a phenomenon

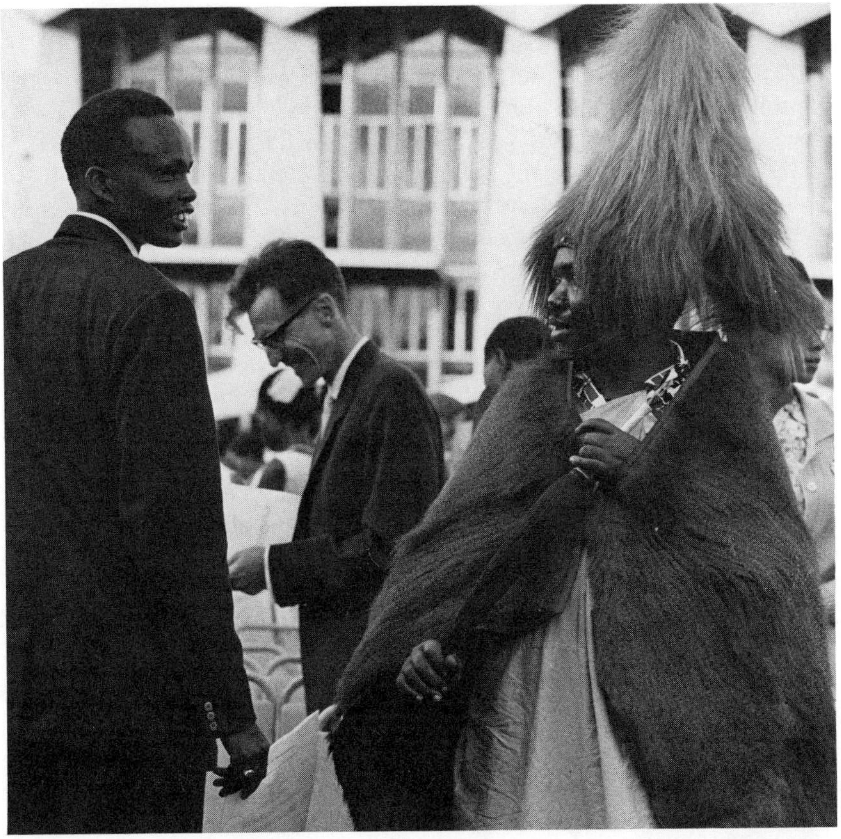

Masai chief in robes and monkey-skin coat chats with Western-dressed Kenyan at Royal College, Nairobi. (Marc and Evelyne Bernheim, Woodfin Camp)

known as *culture lag,* a term referring to the fact that certain kinds of ideas and innovations are adopted more readily than others. This is true not only of cross-cultural change, but within a single society. For example, ever since the invention of the atomic bomb, social commentators in America have suggested that although we have the capacity to kill the entire population of the world ten times over, we still have not developed the technological and moral capabilities to ensure that we will not do so accidentally. The well-known novel *Fail Safe,* and many similar stories, have illustrated the danger in which we live, whereby a relatively simple mechanical failure, or the actions of an all-too-powerful but mentally unbalanced individual, could launch the world into nuclear war. This is a clear example of culture lag, where values lag behind technological advances.

Andre Simić, an anthropologist who has studied urbanization in Yugoslavia, reports of rural peasants who attempt to become Westernized but are unable to do so because of the technological barriers. He tells of a family that purchased a refrigerator because of the enormous prestige associated with such an innovation, but was unable to put it to use because the village had no electricity. Other anthropologists have noted similar cases in which refrigerators were used as storage vaults, clothes closets, even illicit stills, in each case because of the lack of electricity. And Simić tells of another family in the village he studied that had purchased a radio and placed it conspicuously in the living room of the house for all visitors to admire, despite the fact that it would not operate without current.

We should recognize that Westernization is not an absolute necessity in industrialization. There is no single model of an industrial society that must be followed by all countries. Each culture has its own traditions, and its own particular history and direction, and these differences will affect the form that modernization takes in any society. For example, it is generally assumed that part of the process of

Watusi men enjoy ice cream for the first time. They prefer the refrigerator door open, since it is cooler. (Ace Williams, Frederic Lewis)

Westernization is the change from ascribed to achieved status—the introduction of the "merit system" and the elimination of personalism in an impersonal industrial setting. In our own society the idea of nepotism is unacceptable, for it is considered inefficient to promote someone on any basis other than merit. However, in Japanese society, where industrialization has been every bit as successful, this is not the case. A Japanese factory is conceived of as a family, and people are brought into it on that basis. The factory management is very paternalistic in the way it treats the workers, a far cry from our own system where benefits have been won only through sometimes bitter battles between management and labor unions. The Japanese example proves that industry can operate without a total transformation of the native value system to conform to a Western model. While it is true that Western values usually make for more efficient production in industry, and thus are commonly adopted by the people of newly industrializing nations (although sometimes unknowingly), it is important to recognize the flexibility of any culture, and its ability to accept change without undergoing a total transformation.

Modernization: A Case Study

The village of Kippel is nestled in a cul-de-sac valley high in the Swiss Alps, surrounded on four sides by mountains. Until recently traffic in and out of the valley was almost nonexistent, and the way of life of its few hundred residents was much the same as when the valley was first settled in the Middle Ages. Almost everyone practiced a mixed economy of agriculture and livestock raising, growing enough grain and potatoes to provide for their needs, and relying mainly upon dairy cattle for the remainder of their diet. Marriage was generally with someone from one of the four villages in the valley, for it was necessary to combine the inheritance of two individuals to provide enough land to support a family, and in addition the limited experience of young people with the outside world almost forced them to look for a spouse at home. Village life was marked by a great deal of cooperation in tasks which required more labor than one household could supply, and there were many such tasks due to the difficulties of farming steep slopes and transporting crops or building materials

Kippel, an alpine village in the process of modernization.

vertically. Also typical of the traditional era of the valley was the dominance of the church (Roman Catholic) over every aspect of life, with many festivals and a great deal of ceremony surrounding daily activities.

Following World War II the Swiss government undertook a program of industrialization in the mountainous regions of the country. Railroad lines were extended into more isolated areas, water power projects required a large labor force to construct and then maintain dams, and many factories were built in mountain regions to promote industry there. A number of men from Kippel left agriculture during these years to take jobs in industry, at first constructing railroad lines, dams and factories, later working there. In 1961 a large aluminum factory was built less than an hour's drive from Kippel, and today more than twenty men from the village work in the factory. Most other men between 35 and 55 work as unskilled or semi-skilled laborers at similar jobs, and commute to work daily, or sometimes weekly, from their homes in Kippel.

The shift from agriculture to industry shortly after World War II led to many drastic changes in Kippel. The younger generation all at once became free to advance and get away from agriculture. Whereas formerly it was expected that when a boy finished primary school he would go to work on his father's farm, he was now expected to continue on in school and learn a trade, or in rare cases obtain even more training and take up a white collar job. Agriculture became something of a hobby for the old men, who were the only full-time farmers left in the village. But the new working class did not give up farming altogether, for there was still a strong feeling of insecurity in the new industrial jobs, and an attachment to the land and to the values of subsistence agriculture. As a result, these men became what

An elderly farmer using the traditional scythe to mow hay. (John Friedl)

is known as *worker-peasants,* that is, people who have gone to work in factories but who have maintained a small agricultural operation on the side. In Kippel, the majority of the work done on these small-scale farming operations is performed by women and young girls, relatives of the male head of the household. The man will help out on weekends and during his vacation, but the main responsibility for farming has definitely shifted. Younger men who have completed school and have better paying employment than their parents now have completely given up the idea of farming, and do not even maintain a small agricultural operation to qualify them as worker-peasants. Thus within one generation Kippel has gone from an agricultural village to a working-class suburb.

Other major economic changes have affected the village life style as well. About ten years ago a group of investigators purchased a large tract of land above the neighboring village and began plans to develop a ski resort. In all over $1 million was paid to the owners of this land, many of them from Kippel. Within a few short years the tourist industry in Kippel and throughout the valley has mushroomed. Villagers now obtain low-interest, government subsidized

The summer pastures take on new importance as winter ski slopes, representing a major change in the village economy. (John Friedl)

Young women wear their formal dresses on festive occasions, but more for the tourist value than out of a sense of tradition. (John Friedl)

loans to build new houses, and the typical house includes one flat for the owner's family and at least one or two additional flats to be rented to tourists. A man with such a house can earn as much from the rent he collects as he does from his unskilled job. Several new tourist-oriented projects have sprung up in the villages below the planned ski resort, including a new hotel in Kippel. And of course all of these projects create jobs for local residents, thus transforming the village economic scene once again from a working-class community to a tourist center whose main source of income is rapidly becoming the provision of services.

These economic changes have spelled the end of many traditional aspects of village culture. The communal labor that used to be such an important part of village life, promoting solidarity among the members of the community, now is almost nonexistent. Since there is no labor force engaged in agriculture, there is no interest in maintaining community projects, and when someone needs help today he usually has to pay for it. There is a new emphasis upon inheritance. Whereas formerly everyone sought to put together a complete agricultural unit including land in various parts of the valley and at various altitudes, today the heirs vie for land near the village that can be used as house sites. Formerly valuable agricultural land outside the village limits now has little value.

Marriage patterns have changed in recent years as a result of the economic transformation of the village. Improved transportation facilities and increased experience outside the village have led to a greater proportion of marriage with outsiders. People tend to marry younger today than they did a generation ago, for they are able to gain financial security much earlier than they could when they were planning to become farmers and had to wait for their share of the inheritance. There is a growing trend toward emigration, with young people finding that they cannot practice the skills they have learned without going to the city. Finally, there has been a steady decline in the authority and influence of the church upon many younger people, as they broaden their outlook on life through their experiences away from the village.

What has happened in Kippel in the past 30 years is typical of the effects of modernization on small communities throughout the world. Industrialization reaches out and draws these communities into the mainstream of national culture, overcoming the differences that were such an important source of identity for the villagers. Some are pulled into the city, attracted by the promise of fame and fortune. Others, such as the people of Kippel, remain in their village, only to find that it, too, is becoming urbanized, if not in size then at least in its culture. What we are seeing in Europe, and to a lesser extent in the Third World, is the spread of a mass culture, a unifying influence that affects rural people as well as city dwellers. As the world becomes

In the past, masks such as this were worn as part of a pre-Lenten festival similar to Mardi Gras. Now they are carved for sale to tourists. (John Friedl)

smaller, media intrude into even the most isolated village, farmers are uprooted and drawn into factories or forced to become rural businessmen, and the process of modernization continues to obliterate the traditional cultures that for so long have been the subject of anthropological investigations.

In the following article, adapted from his best-selling book, *Future Shock,* Alvin Toffler paints a picture of technology running rampant in modern society. Change has gotten out of hand, he claims, and the rate of change has increased so drastically that we are no longer able to cope with it, let alone plan for it. The result is "future shock," a psychological state characteristic of the contemporary American scene.

It is not surprising that change should be so prevalent in our society today, given what we know about the past. In this chapter we have seen how, beginning with agriculture and then urbanism and literacy, each new rung in the ladder of cultural evolution has increasingly transformed it into a revolution. The rate of change has many parallels in the modern world too. Since we are now experiencing a population explosion, and if necessity is the mother of invention, has there ever been a greater need for change in our world society than there is today?

These are questions Toffler raises, and for which he suggests a few initial answers. His article carries us well beyond the present concern in anthropology for the study of change. Perhaps the next generation of anthropologists will have a sense of urgency about their work that the present generation has only begun to experience.

The Accelerative Thrust

Alvin Toffler

Early in March, 1967, in eastern Canada, an eleven-year-old child died of old age.

Ricky Gallant was only eleven years old chronologically, but he suffered from an odd disease called progeria—advanced aging—and he exhibited many of the characteristics of a ninety-year-old person. The symptoms of progeria are senility, hardened arteries, baldness, slack, and wrinkled skin. In effect, Ricky was an old man when he died, a long lifetime of biological change having been packed into his eleven short years.

Cases of progeria are extremely rare. Yet in a metaphorical sense the high technology societies all suffer from this peculiar ailment. They are not growing old or senile. But they *are* experiencing super-normal rates of change.

Many of us have a vague "feeling" that things are moving faster. Doctors and executives alike complain that they cannot keep up with the latest developments in their fields. Hardly a meeting or conference takes place today without some ritualistic oratory about "the challenge of change." Among many there is an uneasy mood —a suspicion that change is out of control.

Not everyone, however, shares this anxiety. Millions sleepwalk their way through their lives as if nothing had changed since the 1930's, and as if nothing ever will. Living in what is certainly one of the most exciting periods in human history, they attempt to withdraw from it, to block it out, as if it were possible to make it go away by ignoring it. They seek a "separate peace," a diplomatic immunity from change.

One sees them everywhere: Old people, resigned to living out their years, attempting to avoid, at any cost, the intrusions of the new. Already-old people of thirty-five and forty-five, nervous about student riots, sex, LSD, or miniskirts, feverishly attempting to persuade themselves that, after all, youth was always rebellious, and that what is happening today is no different from the past. Even among the young we find an incomprehension of change: students so ignorant of the past that they see nothing unusual about the present.

The disturbing fact is that the vast majority of people, including educated and otherwise sophisticated people, find the idea of change so threatening that they attempt to deny its existence. Even many people who understand intellectually that change is accelerating, have not internalized that knowledge, do not take this critical social fact into account in planning their own personal lives.

Time and Change

How do we *know* that change is accelerating? There is, after all, no absolute way to measure change. In the awesome complexity of the

Reprinted from Alvin Toffler, *Future Shock*. New York: Random House, Inc. (1970). Abridged with permission.

universe, even within any given society, a virtually infinite number of streams of change occur simultaneously. All "things"— from the tiniest virus to the greatest galaxy—are, in reality, not things at all, but processes. There is no static point, no nirvana-like un-change, against which to measure change. Change is, therefore, necessarily relative.

It is also uneven. If all processes occurred at the same speed, or even if they accelerated or decelerated in unison, it would be impossible to observe change. The future, however, invades the present at differing speeds. Thus it becomes possible to compare the speed of different processes as they unfold. We know, for example, that compared with the biological evolution of the species, cultural and social evolution is extremely rapid. We know that some societies transform themselves technologically or economically more rapidly than others. We also know that different sectors within the same society exhibit different rates of change—the disparity that William Ogburn labeled "cultural lag." It is precisely the unevenness of change that makes it measurable.

We need, however, a yardstick that makes it possible to compare highly diverse processes, and this yardstick is time. Without time, change has no meaning. And without change, time would stop. Time can be conceived as the intervals during which events occur. Just as money permits us to place a value on both apples and oranges, time permits us to compare unlike processes. When we say that it takes three years to build a dam, we are really saying it takes three times as long as it takes the earth to circle the sun or 31,000,000 times as long as it takes to sharpen a pencil. Time is the currency of exchange that makes it possible to compare the rates at which very different processes play themselves out.

Subterranean Cities

Painting with the broadest of brush strokes, biologist Julian Huxley informs us that "the tempo of human evolution during recorded history is at least 100,000 times as rapid as that of pre-human evolution." Inventions or improvements of a magnitude that took perhaps 50,000 years to accomplish during the early Paleolithic era were, he says, "run through in a mere millennium toward its close; and with the advent of settled civilization, the unit of change soon became reduced to the century." The rate of change, accelerating throughout the past 5000 years, has become, in his words, "particularly noticeable during the past 300 years."

C. P. Snow, the novelist and scientist, also comments on the new visibility of change. "Until this century . . ." he writes, social change was "so slow, that it would pass unnoticed in one person's lifetime. That is no longer so. The rate of change has increased so much that our imagination can't keep up." Indeed, says social psychologist Warren Bennis, the throttle has been pushed so far forward in recent years that "No exaggeration, no hyperbole, no outrage can realistically describe the extent and pace of change. . . . In fact, only the exaggerations appear to be true."

What changes justify such super-charged language? Let us look at a few—change in the process by which man forms cities, for example. We are now undergoing the most extensive and rapid urbanization the world has ever seen. In 1850 only four cities on the face of the earth had a population of 1,000,000 or more. By 1900 the number had increased to nineteen. But by 1960, there were 141, and today world urban population is rocketing upward at a rate of 6.5 percent per year, according to Edgar de Vries and J. P. Thysse of the Institute of Social Science in The Hague. This single stark statistic means a doubling of the earth's urban population within eleven years.

One way to grasp the meaning of change on so phenomenal a scale is to imagine what would happen if all existing cities, instead of expanding, retained their present size. If this were so, in order to accommodate the new urban millions we would have to build a duplicate city for each of the hundreds that already dot the globe. A new

Tokyo, a new Hamburg, a new Rome and Rangoon —and all within eleven years. (This explains why French urban planners are sketching subterranean cities—stores, museums, warehouses and factories to be built under the earth, and why a Japanese architect has blueprinted a city to be built on stilts out over the ocean.)

The same accelerative tendency is instantly apparent in man's consumption of energy. Dr. Homi Bhabha, the late Indian atomic scientist who chaired the first International Conference on the Peaceful Uses of Atomic Energy, once analyzed this trend. "To illustrate," he said, "let us use the letter 'Q' to stand for the energy derived from burning some 33,000 million tons of coal. In the eighteen and one half centuries after Christ, the total energy consumed averaged less than one half Q per century. But by 1850, the rate had risen to one Q per century. Today, the rate is about ten Q per century." This means, roughly speaking, that half of all the energy consumed by man in the past 2,000 years has been consumed in the last one hundred.

Also dramatically evident is the acceleration of economic growth in the nations now racing toward super-industrialism. Despite the fact that they start from a large industrial base, the annual percentage increases in production in these countries are formidable. And the rate of increase is itself increasing.

In France, for example, in the twenty-nine years between 1910 and the outbreak of the second world war, industrial production rose only 5 percent. Yet between 1948 and 1965, in only seventeen years, it increased by roughly 220 percent.

Thus for the twenty-one countries belonging to the Organization for Economic Cooperation and Development—by and large, the "have" nations—the average annual rate of increase in gross national product in the years 1960-1968 ran between 4.5 and 5.0 percent. The United States grew at a rate of 4.5 percent, and Japan led the rest with annual increases averaging 9.8 percent.

What such numbers imply is nothing less revolutionary than a doubling of the total output of goods and services in the advanced societies about every fifteen years—and the doubling times are shrinking. This means, generally speaking, that the child reaching teen age in any of these societies is literally surrounded by twice as much of everything newly man-made as his parents were at the time he was an infant. It means that by the time today's teen-ager reaches age thirty, perhaps earlier, a second doubling will have occurred. Within a seventy-year lifetime, perhaps five such doublings will take place—meaning, since the increases are compounded, that by the time the individual reaches old age the society around him will be producing thirty-two times as much as when he was born.

Never in previous history has this ratio been transformed so radically in so brief a flick of time.

The Technological Engine

Behind such prodigious economic facts lies that great, growling engine of change—technology. This is not to say that technology is the only source of change in society. Social upheavals can be touched off by a change in the chemical composition of the atmosphere, by alterations in climate, by changes in fertility, and many other factors. Yet technology is indisputably a major force behind the accelerative thrust.

To most people, the term technology conjures up images of smoky steel mills or clanking machines. Perhaps the classic symbol of technology is still the assembly line created by Henry Ford half a century ago and made into a potent social icon by Charlie Chaplin in *Modern Times.* This symbol, however, has always been inadequate, indeed, misleading, for technology has always been more than factories and machines. The invention of the horse collar in the middle ages led to major changes in agricultural methods and was as much a technological advance as the invention of the Bessemer furnace centuries later. Moreover, technology includes techniques, as well as the machines that may or may not be necessary to apply them. It includes ways to make chemical reactions occur, ways to breed fish, plant forests, light theaters, count votes or teach history.

This acceleration is frequently dramatized by a thumbnail account of the progress in transportation. It has been pointed out, for example, that in 6000 B.C. the fastest transportation available to man over long distances was the camel caravan, averaging eight miles per hour. It was not until about 1600 B.C. when the chariot was invented that the maximum speed was raised to roughly twenty miles per hour.

So impressive was this invention, so difficult was it to exceed this speed limit, that nearly 3,500 years later, when the first mail coach began operating in England in 1784, it averaged a mere ten mph. The first steam locomotive, introduced in 1825, could muster a top speed of only thirteen mph, and the great sailing ships of the time labored along at less than half that speed. It was probably not until the 1880s that man, with the help of a more advanced steam locomotive, managed to reach a speed of one hundred mph. It took the human race millions of years to attain that record.

It took only fifty-eight years, however, to quadruple the limit, so that by 1938 airborne man was cracking the 400-mph line. It took a mere twenty-year flick of time to double the limit again. And by the 1960's rocket planes approached speeds of 4000 mph, and men in space capsules were circling the earth at 18,000 mph. Plotted on a graph, the line representing progress in the past generation would leap vertically off the page.

The pattern, here and in a thousand other statistical series, is absolutely clear and unmistakable. Millennia or centuries go by, and then, in our own times, a sudden bursting of the limits, a fantastic spurt forward.

The reason for this is that technology feeds on itself. Technology makes more technology possible, as we can see if we look for a moment at the process of innovation. Technological innovation consists of three stages, linked together into a self-reinforcing cycle. First, there is the creative, feasible idea. Second, its practical application. Third, its diffusion through society.

The process is completed, the loop closed, when the diffusion of technology embodying the new idea, in turn, helps generate new creative ideas. Today there is evidence that the time between each of the steps in this cycle has been shortened.

Thus it is not merely true, as frequently noted, that 90 percent of all the scientists who ever lived are now alive, and that new scientific discoveries are being made every day. These new ideas are put to work much more quickly than ever before. The time between original concept and practical use has been radically reduced. This is a striking difference between ourselves and our ancestors. Appollonius of Perga discovered conic sections, but it was 2000 years before they were applied to engineering problems. It was literally centuries between the time Paracelsus discovered that ether could be used as an anaesthetic and the time it began to be used for that purpose.

Even in more recent times the same pattern of delay was present. In 1836 a machine was invented that mowed, threshed, tied straw into sheaves and poured grain into sacks. This machine was itself based on technology at least twenty years old at the time. Yet it was not until a century later, in the 1930's, that such a combine was actually marketed. The first English patent for a typewriter was issued in 1714. But a century and a half elapsed before typewriters became commercially available. A full century passed between the time Nicholas Appert discovered how to can food and the time canning became important in the food industry.

Today such delays between idea and application are almost unthinkable. It is not that we are more eager or less lazy than our ancestors, but we have, with the passage of time, invented all sorts of social devices to hasten the process.

Thus we find that the time between the first and second stages of the innovative cycle—between idea and application—has been cut radically.

The stepped up pace of invention, exploitation, and diffusion, in turn, accelerates the whole cycle still further. For new machines or techniques are not merely a product, but a source, of fresh creative ideas.

Each new machine or technique, in a sense, changes all existing machines and techniques, by permitting us to put them together into new combinations. The number of possible combinations rises exponentially as the number of new machines or techniques rises arithmetically. Indeed, each new combination may, itself, be regarded as a new super-machine.

The computer, for example, made possible a sophisticated space effort. Linked with sensing devices, communications equipment, and power sources, the computer became part of a configuration that in aggregate forms a single new super-machine—a machine for reaching into and probing outer space. But for machines or techniques to be combined in new ways, they have to be altered, adapted, refined or otherwise changed. So that the very effort to integrate machines into super-machines compels us to make still further technological innovations.

It is vital to understand, moreover, that technological innovation does not merely combine and recombine machines and techniques. Important new machines do more than suggest or compel changes in other machines—they suggest novel solutions to social, philosophical, even personal problems. They alter man's total intellectual environment—the way he thinks and looks at the world.

Recently, the computer has touched off a storm of fresh ideas about man as an interacting part of larger systems, about his physiology, the way he learns, the way he remembers, the way he makes decisions. Virtually every intellectual discipline from political science to family psychology has been hit by a wave of imaginative hypotheses triggered by the invention and diffusion of the computer—and its full impact has not yet struck. And so the innovative cycle, feeding on itself, speeds up.

If technology, however, is to be regarded as a great engine, a mighty accelerator, then knowledge must be regarded as its fuel. And we thus come to the crux of the accelerative process in society, for the engine is being fed a richer and richer fuel every day.

Knowledge as Fuel

The rate at which man has been storing up useful knowledge about himself and the universe has been spiraling upward for 10,000 years. The rate took a sharp upward leap with the invention of writing, but even so it remained painfully slow over centuries of time. The next great leap forward in knowledge-acquisition did not occur until the invention of movable type in the fifteenth century by Gutenberg and others. Prior to 1500, by the most optimistic estimates, Europe was producing books at a rate of 1000 titles per year. This means, give or take a bit, that it would take a full century to produce a library of 100,000 titles. By 1950, four and a half centuries later, the rate had accelerated so sharply that Europe was producing 120,000 titles a year. What once took a century now took only ten months. By 1960, a single decade later, the rate had made another significant jump, so that a century's work could be completed in seven and a half months. And, by the mid-sixties, the output of books on a world scale, Europe included, approached the prodigious figure of 1000 titles per *day*.

One can hardly argue that every book is a net gain for the advancement of knowledge. Nevertheless, we find that the accelerative curve in book publication does, in fact, crudely parallel the rate at which man discovered new knowledge. For example, prior to Gutenberg only 11 chemical elements were known. Antimony, the 12th, was discovered at about the time he was working on his invention. It was fully 200 years since the 11th, arsenic, had been discovered. Had the same rate of discovery continued, we would by now have added only two or three additional elements to the periodic table since Gutenberg. Instead, in the 450 years after his time, some seventy additional elements were discovered. And since 1900 we have been isolating the remaining elements not at a rate of one every two centuries, but of one every three years.

Furthermore, there is reason to believe that the rate is still rising sharply. Today, for example, the number of scientific journals and articles is doubling, like industrial production in the advanced countries, about every fifteen years, and according to biochemist Philip Siekevitz, "what has been learned in the last three decades about the nature of living beings dwarfs in extent of knowledge any comparable period of scientific discovery in the history of mankind." Today the United States government alone generates 100,000 reports each year, plus 450,000 articles, books and papers. On a worldwide basis, scientific and technical literature mounts at a rate of some 60,000,000 pages a year.

Francis Bacon told us that "Knowledge . . . is power." This can now be translated into contemporary terms. In our social setting, "Knowledge is change"—and accelerating knowledge-acquisition, fueling the great engine of technology, means accelerating change.

The Flow of Situations

Discovery. Application. Impact. Discovery. We see here a chain reaction of change, a long, sharply rising curve of acceleration in human social development. This accelerative thrust has now reached a level at which it can no longer, by any stretch of the imagination, be regarded as "normal." The normal institutions of industrial society can no longer contain it, and its impact is shaking up all our social institutions. Acceleration is one of the most important and least understood of all social forces.

This, however, is only half the story. For the speed-up of change is a psychological force as well. Although it has been almost totally ignored by psychology, the rising rate of change in the world around us disturbs our inner equilibrium, altering the very way in which we experience life. Acceleration without translates into acceleration within.

This can be illustrated, though in a highly oversimplified fashion, if we think of an individual life as a great channel through which experience flows. This flow of experience consists—or is conceived of consisting—of innumerable "situations." Acceleration of change in the surrounding society drastically alters the flow of situations through this channel.

Two situations alike in all other respects are not the same at all if one lasts longer than another. For time enters into the mix in a crucial way, changing the meaning or content of situations. Just as the funeral march played at too high a speed becomes a merry tinkle of sounds, so a situation that is dragged out has a distinctly different flavor or meaning than one that strikes us in staccato fashion, erupting suddenly and subsiding as quickly.

Here, then, is the first delicate point at which the accelerative thrust in the larger society crashes up against the ordinary daily experience of the contemporary individual. For the acceleration of change, as we shall show, shortens the duration of many situations. This not only drastically alters their "flavor," but hastens their passage through the experiential channel. Compared with life in a less rapidly changing society, more situations now flow through the channel in any given interval of time—and this implies profound changes in human psychology.

For while we tend to focus on only one situation at a time, the increased rate at which situations flow past us vastly complicates the entire structure of life, multiplying the number of roles we must play and the number of choices we are forced to make. This, in turn, accounts for the choking sense of complexity about contemporary life.

Moreover, the speeded-up flow-through of situations demands much more work from the complex focusing mechanisms by which we shift our attention from one situation to another. There is more switching back and forth, less time for extended, peaceful attention to one problem or situation at a time. This is what lies behind the vague feeling noted earlier that "Things are moving faster." They are. Around us. And through us.

There is, however, still another, even more powerfully significant way in which the acceleration of change in society increases the difficulty of coping with life. This stems from the fantastic intrusion of novelty, newness into our existence. Each situation is unique. But situations often resemble one another. This, in fact, is what makes it possible to learn from experience. If each situation were wholly novel, without some resemblance to previously experienced situations, our ability to cope would be hopelessly crippled.

"When things start changing outside, you are going to have a parallel change taking place inside," says Christopher Wright of the Institute for the Study of Science and Human Affairs. The nature of these inner changes is so profound, however, that, as the accelerative thrust picks up speed, it will test our ability to live within the parameters that have until now defined man and society. In the words of psychoanalyst Erik Erikson, "In our society at present, the 'natural course of events' is precisely that the rate of change should continue to accelerate up to the as-yet-unreached limits of human and institutional adaptability."

To survive, to avert what we have termed future shock, the individual must become infinitely more adaptable and capable than ever before. He must search out totally new ways to anchor himself, for all the old roots—religion, nation, community, family, or profession—are now shaking under the hurricane impact of the accelerative thrust. Before he can do so, however, he must understand in greater detail how the effects of acceleration penetrate his personal life, creep into his behavior and alter the quality of existence. He must, in other words, understand transience.

Summary

For millions of years human beings survived by hunting and gathering their food, employing a relatively simple technology. Although there was cultural change during this period, it occurred at a slow rate compared to more recent times. With the introduction of agriculture, then cities and writing, culture began to change at an ever increasing rate, until now in the twentieth century change has become a matter of course.

Anthropologists of the nineteenth and early twentieth centuries first became interested in culture change as a result of contact with peoples who were different from the Western cultures with which they were familiar. They sought an explanation for these differences, and arrived at an evolutionary theory to account for the apparent change that led to cultural diversity. Then, as anthropology concentrated upon the study of so-called primitive peoples who changed as a result of contact with Western society, they narrowed their field of investigation to the actual processes by which non-Western cultures were transformed through such contact, a process called *acculturation.* Later, they began to see similarities in certain kinds of social movements that arose in contact situations, and focused upon a study of revitalization movements brought about in part by the creation of expectations that could not be met.

More recently, interest has centered upon the process of modernization that has been occurring in Third-World countries, where the introduction of industrial economies, the movement of people to cities, and the adoption of Western patterns of behavior have led to major cultural changes. Although these processes frequently occur together, they can also occur independently of one another. Kippel, a small village in the Swiss Alps which has recently undergone a great deal of modernization, offers an example of how industrialization and Westernization can take place without a movement of people to the city, but rather by the transmission of urban mass culture to the rural countryside through the effects of the modern media.

Glossary

acculturation A process of culture change that occurs when groups of individuals having different cultures come into continuous first-hand contact.

Cargo Cult An attempt to adopt new cultural patterns in order for a group to renew their culture, rather than return to traditional ways of life. These movements took place in the Pacific islands where there was considerable contact with Western culture, but where the people were unable to participate in the higher standard of living they witnessed in the white community.

civilization The stage of society usually associated with agriculture, urbanism and a written language.

culture lag A term referrring to the fact that certain kinds of ideas and innovations are adopted at a different rate than others. This differential rate of change may occur between cultures, and within a single culture as well.

diffusion The spread of an innovation from its point of origin throughout an area and ultimately, through contact with other cultures, to neighboring regions.

domestication The process whereby people brought the production of plants and animals under their direct control.

folk culture A society characterized by its personalism, smallness, homogeneity and relative isolation.

Ghost Dance An attempt to return to traditional cultural patterns, as a result of the frustration experienced by many North American Indian tribes through contact with Western culture.

Homo The genus in the Linnaean taxonomy that includes both fossil and living man and woman.

hunting and gathering The subsistence activity based upon the hunting of animals and gathering of plants. This subsistence may also include fishing. Although it requires a low level of technology, it usually provides a relatively secure existence.

industrialization The growth of industry in any society. This process has prompted concurrent changes in agriculture, the family, and various aspects of the social structure.

millenarian movement A revitalization movement in which an oppressed and frustrated people believe in the coming of a new age. Such a movement relies upon symbolically important beliefs, usually has a charismatic leader, and is an attempt to eliminate foreign or unwanted elements from the culture.

modernization A broad term covering at least the following separate processes: economic growth, or industrialization; urbanization; and Westernization. It is usually assumed that these processes occur together, and that they are interrelated, although this is not always the case.

nativistic movements An attempt to return to the traditional or native cultural patterns and to eliminate alien persons, customs, values, and materials from the culture.

relative deprivation A change over time that leads a group of people to feel deprived relative to some other standard (relative to another group, or to their own past situation). The resultant dissatisfaction may be a cause of revitalization movements.

revitalization movement A conscious process on the part of a people designed to produce change through the renewal of their old cultural patterns and traditions, which have disintegrated due to contact with Western culture.

social mobility The process of moving from one position to another in society, and adopting the appropriate role behaviors attached to the new social position.

subsistence agriculture Producing food primarily for one's own consumption.

syncretism The process of reinterpreting new cultural elements to fit them in with the already existing traditions in a culture.

urbanism The development of cities along with a growth in population size and density. There is usually a specialization of tasks and the division of the work among people trained for special jobs.

urbanization The growth in the size of cities, the number of cities, and the proportion of the population living in urban locations. Urbanization has frequently been associated with the characterization of heterogeneity, impersonalization, and individualism.

Vailala Madness A movement among the native people in New Guinea that began in 1919. Faced with the technological and military superiority of the white culture, the people sought to adopt many of the alien ways.

voluntary associations Groups in which membership is based upon any common interest (e.g., similar occupation, leisure-time activities, etc.). These associations are often a reaction to the impersonalization of city life.

Westernization The adoption of cultural patterns characteristic of Western society. Changes in non-Western societies include the predominance of the nuclear family, the rising status of women, growth of a market economy and an accompanying market mentality, as well as changes in their values, attitudes and beliefs.

worker-peasants People who have gone to work in factories, but have retained a small agricultural operation on the side.

Questions for Discussion

1 When we speak of the "melting pot" in American culture, we generally think of the assimilation of immigrants into a traditional American way of life. But at the same time, these groups have had a part in changing American culture in the process of acculturation. Discuss some of the everyday aspects of your life that are foreign in origin and have resulted from contact with immigrants in recent American history.

2 It has been suggested that Christianity began as a locally based revitalization movement. How was early Christianity similar to other revitalization movements mentioned in this chapter? Was it nativistic in seeking a return to past conditions, or millenarian in seeking a transformation of the world (or was it both)? What conditions of relative deprivation might have fostered the spread of Christianity?

3 Can there be modernization without adopting certain Western values and patterns of behavior? Can you conceive of a factory where workers showed up whenever they felt like it, or a market that opened and closed whenever the traders decided they wanted to work? What is it about our way of life that requires punctuality and efficiency?

4 In recent years the rate of technological change has increased so rapidly that we are now faced with numerous social problems, such as the energy shortage, the spiraling rate of inflation, or the threat of nuclear annihilation. Can the rate of change continue to increase, and if it does, what will be the consequences? Do you see any efforts in our society to slow down change?

Suggestions for Additional Reading

Aberle, David F.
1966 The Peyote Religion among the Navaho. Chicago: Aldine.

A more detailed account of the rise of Peyotism among the Navaho following the breakdown of traditions in the face of contact with white culture. Also included is a chapter on the notion of relative deprivation as a cause of certain kinds of revitalization movements.

Friedl, John
1974 Kippel: A Changing Village in the Alps. New York: Holt, Rinehart and Winston.

A case study of modernization and its effects upon a small village in the Swiss Alps.

Herskovits, Melville J.
1938 Acculturation: The Study of Culture Contact. New York: J. J. Augustin.

A thorough discussion of the field of acculturation studies, including short summaries of a number of important works conducted in the 1920s and 1930s.

Lanternari, Vittorio
1963 The Religions of the Oppressed: A Study of Modern Messianic Cults. New York: Alfred A. Knopf.

In another approach to modern religious movements, the author attempts to correlate the rise of messianic movements with the increase in oppression as a result of culture contact.

Lee, Richard B., and Irven DeVore (editors)
1968 Man the Hunter. Chicago: Aldine.

A collection of articles dealing with hunting and gathering societies. This volume is valuable as a guide to contemporary differences in human societies of today, and provides an indication of the enormous change that has occurred in recent years.

Mayer, Philip
1971 Townsmen or Tribesmen: Conservatism and the Process of Urbanization in a South African City. Second Edition. New York: Oxford University Press.

A comparison of urbanization and culture change among two groups of Bantu migrants to East London, South Africa. The Townsmen are those who have adopted the urban life-style and values, while the Tribesmen are those who have rejected them and continue to maintain their traditional way of life, despite the pressures of the city.

Mead, Margaret
1932 The Changing Culture of an Indian Tribe. New York: Columbia University Press.

An early study of acculturation among a Plains Indian tribe, discussed briefly in this chapter.

Moore, Wilbert E.
1965 The Impact of Industry. Englewood Cliffs, N.J.: Prentice-Hall.

A short summary of the changes brought about through the process of industrialization, summarizing not only the conditions necessary for the process of industrialization to occur, but also the consequences.

Sharp, Lauriston
1952 Steel Axes for Stone-Age Australians. Human Organization 11:17–22.

A more detailed account of the Yir Yoront, discussed in the preceding chapter.

Simić, Andre
1973 The Peasant Urbanites: A Study of Rural-Urban Mobility in Serbia. New York: Seminar Press.

An interesting account of the changes brought about by industrialization and urbanization. Particularly valuable is the discussion of value changes, or Westernization, in a formerly peasant population as the culture of the city spreads to the countryside or the people move to the cities.

Toffler, Alvin
1970 Future Shock. New York: Bantam Books.

The fascinating best-seller dealing with our runaway technology and the failure of the rest of our culture to keep up with it.

Waddell, Jack O., and O. Michael Watson (editors)
1971 The American Indian in Urban Society. Boston: Little, Brown.

A collection of articles dealing with the problems of cultural breakdown and adjustment among Indians in modern American urban society.

Worsley, Peter
1968 The Trumpet Shall Sound: A Study of Cargo Cults in Melanesia. Second Edition. New York: Schocken Books.

The most thorough analysis of Cargo Cults as a response to culture contact. The author traces the history of these movements, and places them in the context of the changing political and economic scene in the Pacific Islands.

Applied Anthropology

Chapter Ten

One of the most important justifications for any scientific investigation is the applicability of the information that scientists obtain. Indeed, it is the potential for application that separates science from art. We study music, literature, and philosophy to expand our knowledge and to gain a different perspective on life. But when we seek to apply the knowledge we have gained to solve the problems that beset us, we turn from the humanities to the sciences.

Applied Anthropology and Culture Change

Anthropology has been called the most humanistic social science, and for many years there was a debate among members of the profession concerning whether anthropology was not in fact an art, rather than a science. Perhaps this difference of opinion derives from the very beginnings of anthropology as an academic discipline, when anthropologists were just as often interested in expanding their knowledge of the exotic as in applying that knowledge to the betterment of their own society or of the people they studied. Some nineteenth-century social scientists studied society in order to use their specialized insights in proposing and carrying out future programs of change. August Comte, one of the founding fathers of sociology, even suggested that sociologists should be charged with governing society, since only they had the training required to understand how the inner dynamics of society operate.

But in its early days anthropology was much more descriptive

Many administrators tend to use
social science the way a drunk uses a lamppost—
for support rather than for illumination.

ALEXANDER LEIGHTON

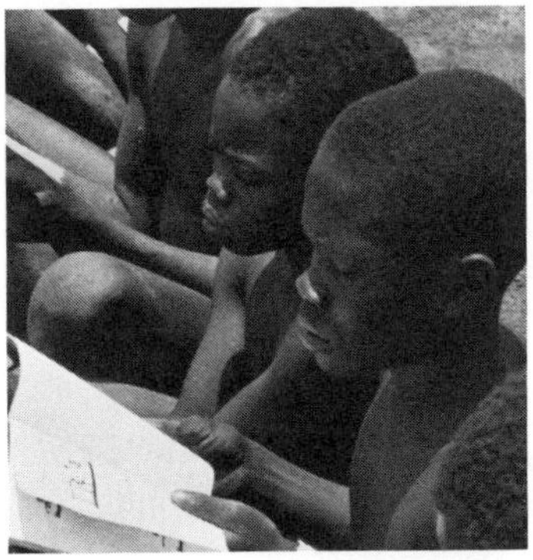

than analytical. It was the study of strange and bizarre cultures in as yet uncivilized areas of the world, where simple description of the native practices was the main objective. Occasionally comparisons were made between practices in different societies, but rarely was there any deeper analysis of the practices themselves, or the ways in which they fit into the rest of the culture. It was not until the late nineteenth century that anthropology was considered useful as a science, and government officials began to inquire into the application of anthropological investigations. In Europe, anthropology became the tool of colonial governments, for it was recognized that by gaining greater knowledge and understanding of the native peoples and their cultures, a more efficient colonial policy could be created. Colonial administrators and officials in Africa, Asia and the Pacific applied anthropological insights to local policies (although rarely did they think of themselves as anthropologists), working within the structure of the native culture to achieve their government's aims.

If the people had a strong tradition of hereditary chiefdoms, the colonial government would try to set up an administrative system that maintained the continuity of the line of chiefs, incorporating them into the new administrative order. Where a large migrant labor force was required to support the economic enterprises of the colonial government (as in the diamond and copper mines in South Africa or the plantations of Latin America), migration was encouraged and even forced in each region in a different manner, depending upon the particular traditions of the native people. For example, in a region where men customarily migrated for trade, in herding their animals, or for any of a number of other reasons, the colonial officials merely redirected the migration routes to lead to the mines or the plantations.

On the other hand, if the population was made up of primarily sedentary agriculturalists, another means would have to be found to get them to move, such as instituting a tax on the land that would force them to work for cash wages, to the ultimate benefit of the new administration. In each case, adopting policies that fit in with the local culture is really practicing applied anthropology by using the knowledge gained in studying another culture toward the solution of a problem.

In the United States the early application of anthropological investigations was tied in with the so-called Indian problem toward the end of the nineteenth century. There were various views on how to deal with the Indians—whether to help them assimilate into white society, or force them to maintain their own independent culture and actively prevent them from coming into contact with white society. Given the history of violence in the westward movement, and the frequent and often fanatic hatred of the Indians by some whites, it was not likely that the Indians would be left alone to do as they wished. Nor was it widely proposed that they be forced to maintain their own separate culture and identity, for such independence was feared by many whites. The dominant opinion, and the ultimate policy of the American government, was to facilitate the cultural assimilation of Indians into white society. This was a difficult policy to carry out, however, for it had to be combined with a policy of racial segregation. The task for the government officials, therefore, was to find a way to make the Indians conform to white standards while keeping them from intruding upon white society. Anthropologists employed by the Bureau of Indian Affairs and other government agencies were assigned to study Indian culture and find out how it could be altered most efficiently to speed the process of assimilation.

The American concern with the "Indian problem" continued into the twentieth century, until it was overtaken by the "immigrant problem." Large numbers of Europeans, Latin Americans and Asians poured into the United States, settling mainly in the major cities on the east and west coasts and around the Great Lakes. While immigration was nothing new, the problems that arose in the cities, and especially in the ethnic communities within those cities, were alarming. One need only recall the turbulent situation among warring ethnic groups in Chicago during the Prohibition Era to comprehend the dramatic effect of immigration upon American culture. As specialists in foreign cultures, anthropologists were called upon once again to

Immigrants streamed into New York and other American cities in the early twentieth century, raising new questions of culture change for a generation of anthropologists. (J. Jay Hirz, Frederic Lewis)

contribute their insights and knowledge to the solution of the "immigrant problem." In fact, however, very little concrete use was made of the contributions of anthropology to the social problems in America, either in the nineteenth century with the Indians or in the twentieth century with the urban ethnic communities. This was not entirely the fault of anthropology as a discipline, but more of the public officials who distrusted social science and social scientists, and who consistently ignored their suggestions and acted on political grounds in response to the vested economic interests of those who voted them into power. Clearly anthropologists had much to contribute to the questions that were raised, just as they do today. This is a serious problem for the future of anthropology, one we shall discuss in detail in the concluding chapter.

During World War II anthropologists contributed their knowledge of foreign cultures to the war effort. Both allies and enemies were subjected to the scrutiny of students of culture in the hope of learning more about them, and thus about how to deal with them. Where actual fieldwork was impossible, studies were made through the available literary sources. Immigrants were interviewed, radio broadcasts and newspapers were analyzed, and even novels were included in an attempt to gain some insight on what policies would be most effective in dealing with the countries in question. Ultimately some benefits were derived from this effort; our study of Japanese culture helped in the formulation of a surrender policy for the Japanese in the Pacific that took into account the role of the Emperor, and the strong feelings of loyalty and respect for authority among the soldiers, who identified directly with him. The decision to allow the Emperor to remain in that capacity (though stripped of all his power), and to have him give the order of surrender directly to his soldiers, probably saved countless lives. Had the American army attempted to force a surrender without the order of the Emperor, no doubt many Japanese soldiers who did surrender would have fought to their deaths, ignoring any command of a foreign leader whose authority they did not recognize.

Following World War II the focus of applied anthropology changed once again. Two very important tasks were undertaken by the United States and the Western world in general: the reconstruction of those countries whose losses in the war had been devastating, and the attempts to raise the standard of living in the so-called developing countries of the Third World, where the level of poverty and suffering grow even faster than the already overflowing populations. In both cases, but especially in the latter, anthropologists had valuable information to contribute, and in the years immediately following the war a number of professionally trained anthropologists occupied government positions. The primary concern of the programs instituted in this era was how best to plan and carry out the social and cultural change that was required to build or rebuild the economies and societies of the Third-World and war-torn countries. Particular emphasis was placed upon planned improvements in agriculture, health, medical services, education, and social welfare programs. It should not be forgotten that the period following the war was one of political tension and conflict between the capitalist countries of the West and the socialist countries of the East, and Western development programs, especially in the heavily populated Third World, were carried out in a situation of intense competition with similar attempts financed by the Soviet Union. Even today, the foreign aid program of the United

States is frequently prompted at least as much by political purposes as by humanitarian goals, which means that what the anthropologist can contribute is usually tempered by the political conditions under which the program is to be carried out.

Planned Change

The study of applied anthropology is frequently the study of problems in planned change. The applied anthropologist must start out with some basic assumptions about the people he is working with and the changes he is proposing. First of all, he must assume that something which originates in one culture and is molded to fit the ideals and patterns of that culture will not necessarily be acceptable to people who have a different way of life. Instead, people tend to accept innovations from another culture in bits and pieces, reworking them to fit into their own way of life, discarding aspects of a program that they find objectionable. The result might be that the most important aspect of the program is not accepted, while the more trivial or unnecessary elements are adopted enthusiastically and wholeheartedly. For example, one of the most prominent changes to take place in the early period of self-government of many countries in the Third World is the institution of a national airline. If we examined the way these airlines function in the context of Western society, we would probably conclude that they are "irrational" and "unnecessary." For us, an airline is a means of transportation; in a country with no need for mass air transportation and relatively little wealth to support such a system, it would seem superfluous. Yet we must recognize that the newly emerging countries have borrowed only part of a Western innovation. They perceive the airline as an important symbol of their entry into the modern world, and they have discounted the transportation factor. In this new context we can better understand other functions of a national airline.

Armed with this assumption that innovations must fit a new context, it is the task of the applied anthropologist to see that the program is reworked before it is presented to the people, so that it can be organized in a manner acceptable to them, while at the same time accomplishing the goals of the original plan. There is obviously an ethical question involved in the position of an applied anthropologist. To whom does he owe his allegiance? To the government who pays him to do a job? To the set of values that he holds about what is best for the people he is working with? Or to the people's own values? In a sense, many an applied anthropologist is placed in the role of a counselor whose job it is to convince people to accept something they might otherwise reject. He is required to use his knowledge of their way of life to get them to accept it, by hook or by crook, even if he has to engage in a small-scale con game to accomplish his goal. Yet at the same time the applied anthropologist is placed in such a position because he can operate between two cultures. He is not only aware of how people live in a small community halfway around the world; he is also familiar with the technological advances in the United States and elsewhere. By virtue of his education and knowledge he has a certain responsibility to help those who are less educated and less knowledgable. Certainly there is an ethical question involved in the use of power vested in the anthropologist

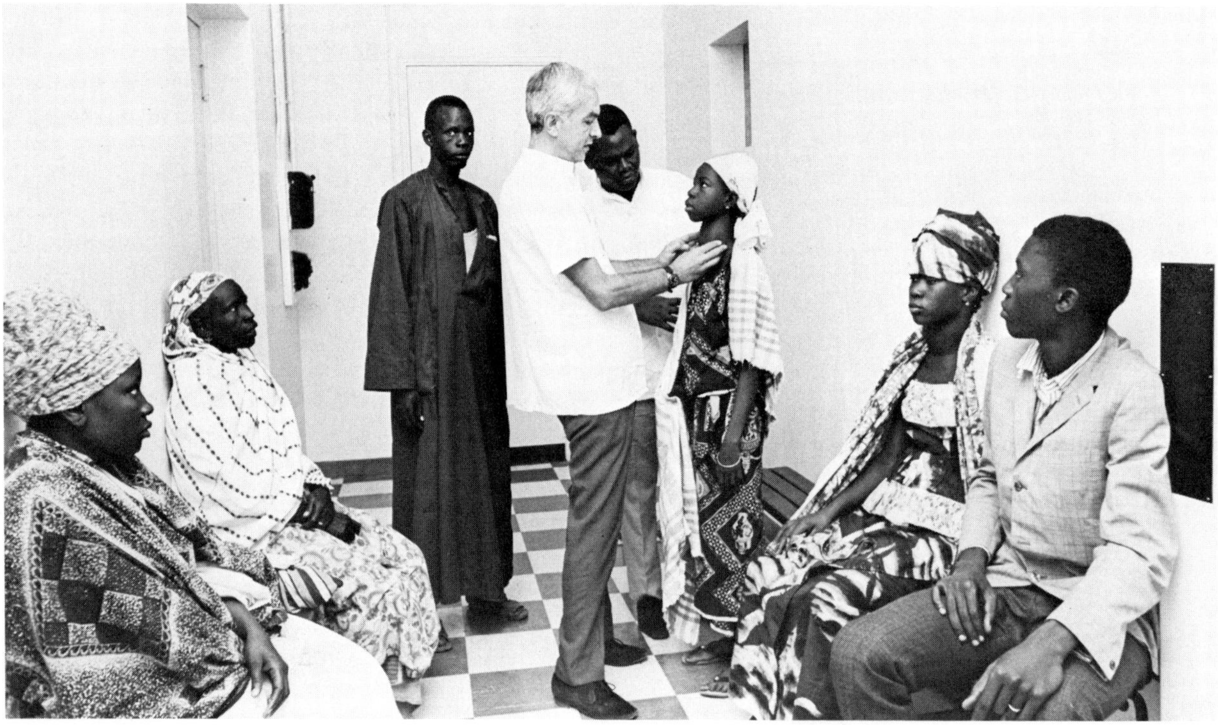

The West African Cancer Research Institute at Dantec Hospital in Dakar, Senegal, diagnoses and treats cancer and thyroid disorders. Public Health programs such as this are a major goal in planned change. (United Nations)

in such a situation, but if we accept the assumption that there are some basic values we must adhere to in carrying out such programs, then their benefits outweigh accusations of intrusion upon another people and unduly influencing their way of life. Such values include the preference of health over sickness, or the belief that a full stomach is better than an empty stomach, or the right of every individual to an education.

A second assumption made by applied anthropologists is that all change operates within a cultural context. Earlier we defined culture as an integrated system, so that a change in one aspect would have an effect upon others. Consider, for example, what the invention of the automobile has meant to American culture. It has not only facilitated transportation; it has become the focal point of the American economy. People have moved from the cities to suburbs, changing the whole pattern of residence in America from what it was a century ago. With upwards of 40,000 people dying in traffic accidents on our highways each year, most of them still at the age of active reproduction, the population structure of our country has been changed. Farming has become more commercialized, and different crops can be grown and transported to markets more quickly. Recreation patterns have responded to the new method of transportation. And, of course, the automobile has extracted a heavy toll from our environment, polluting the air in our cities and depleting the resources of our land. It is amusing to ask "What if Henry Ford had known what was going to come of his great invention? Would he still have carried it through?"

But this is precisely the question that the applied anthropologist must ask of himself when placed in a position of evaluating a proposed program of planned change. He knows that there is no such thing as "simple" change—that any change will produce other changes, and that many of those secondary changes will be unanticipated. His job is to try to anticipate as many of them as possible, and to evaluate the overall results of the program, not just the immediate goals. Perhaps after weighing all the relevant factors he can suggest adjustments to head off an undesired consequence, but his responsibility and his ethical duty are always to consider the project in terms of its overall effect upon other people—to reject a program, no matter how noble and defensible its goal might be, if the means to achieving that goal cannot be justified. It is especially important in the sense that an anthropologist almost always works with other specialists in programs of planned change, specialists who are not trained to consider the

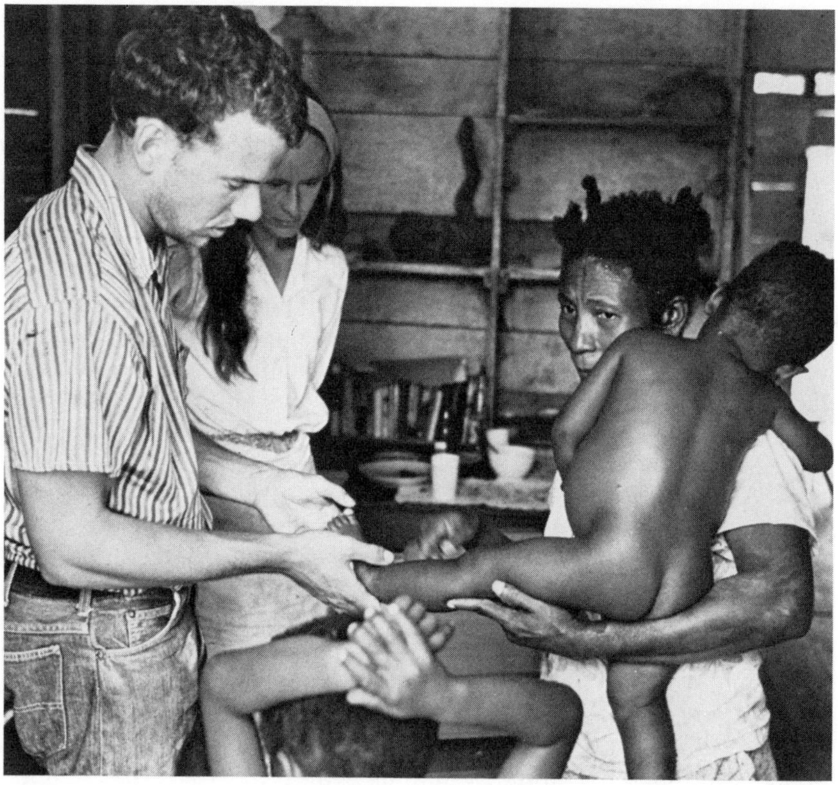

The Peace Corps uses many anthropological insights in its work. Here a young boy is examined in a Peace Corps station in rural Colombia. (Francis Laping, DPI)

native culture and to plan around it. Someone trained in the mechanics of administration can easily lose sight of the consequences of the program in his striving to complete it most efficiently. It is the anthropologist's responsibility to counsel those who carry out such a program on the price that will be paid in reaching the desired goals, and on alternatives that would avoid such problems while not seriously compromising the overall achievements of the program.

Many planned change programs have been merely programs of Westernization, the introduction of Western technology, along with the necessary training in the use of that technology. However, through the experience in another way of life that an anthropologist acquires in his training, he learns that it is not always desirable, let alone possible, to change the way of life of a people just to raise their standard of living. If we adhere to our value of cultural relativism, by which we grant every culture an integrity of its own, then we are bound to look for ways of helping others without completely remaking them into people just like us. Whether the planned change be in the form of introducing tractors into rural farming practices, health clinics in areas of high disease, or birth-control programs in overpopulated countries, we must recognize the right of each culture to retain its own traditions. We must find ways to introduce these changes without completely transforming everything else about them.

Some programs with which you are probably familiar have taken this approach with great success. The Peace Corps, for example, has adopted a policy of working with the people of Third-World countries to solve the problems that they themselves consider serious. Peace Corps volunteers follow closely the basic requirements laid out by Malinowski for anthropological fieldwork that we discussed in Chapter 4: As part of their training and preparation they learn the language of the people with whom they are to work; they live among the people, preferably in the same village or community; they observe the customs of those people and try to fit in with their way of life as much as possible. In short, they do not force their ways upon others, so much as they try to determine what the people want for themselves. While I do not mean to imply that the Peace Corps is totally without its problems, clearly these methods (which have also been adopted by other agencies with similar goals, such as ACTION and VISTA, to name but two) are preferable to those of many earlier planned change programs that operated in complete ignorance of local culture.

Barriers to Change

Books on applied anthropology frequently contain story after story of how a planned change program failed, and how in the analysis of the failure it was discovered that a minor adjustment in the program would have led to improved results, if not total success. George Foster, in *Traditional Cultures and the Impact of Technological Change*, discusses applied anthropology programs in terms of two factors: barriers to change that exist within the traditional cultures, which must be overcome if the program is to succeed; and stimulants to change that can be injected into the program, taking into account the nature of the native culture and the design of the planned change. Many of the examples that follow are cited in Foster's book, an excellent introduction to the study of applied anthropology.

In describing the situation in which many applied anthropologists find themselves, Foster cites an ancient oriental fable:

> Once upon a time a monkey and a fish were caught up in a great flood. The monkey, agile and experienced, had the good fortune to scramble up a tree to safety. As he looked down into the raging waters, he saw a fish struggling against the swift current. Filled with a humanitarian desire to help his less fortunate fellow, he reached down and scooped the fish from the water. To the monkey's surprise, the fish was not very grateful for this aid.[1]

The anthropologist who is not aware of the cultural differences to be overcome in instituting a program of planned change might feel very much hurt and surprised, much like the monkey in the fable. It may seem to us that we are rescuing people from the problems that plague them, while to them it appears that we are forcing unwanted changes upon them that threaten to destroy their traditions and the way of life that has been a part of their culture for generations. Is it any wonder that they are not grateful?

The anthropologist must recognize that the changes he sees as good and beneficial might not be interpreted as such by the people with whom he is working. If the program is to be a success, he must overcome a number of barriers to the change, and this usually means altering the program rather than forcing the people to alter their way of life. Sometimes this requires only a minor adjustment to avoid a relatively easily solved problem. For example, in instituting a rural health program the planners might begin by offering the services and medicines free of charge to rural people who are known to be extremely poor. However, in many countries, especially among rural peasants who have had a history of exploitation at the hands of landlords, police and various government officials known collectively as "outsiders," such free assistance is likely to be viewed as some kind of trick. Why would the government, which has only taken from them in the past, suddenly develop a humanitarian interest in the peasants and decide to give them something for nothing? An easy way around this problem, requiring very little change in the original plan, is to institute a small charge for services and medicines dispensed at the rural health clinic.

1. George M. Foster, *Traditional Cultures and the Impact of Technological Change.* New York: Harper & Row, 1962, p. 1.

George M. Foster (1913–) *is active in the field of applied anthropology, and has served in that capacity throughout the world.* Traditional Cultures and the Impact of Technological Change *(1962, revised 1973) is a detailed analysis of the barriers and stimulants to planned change encountered by the applied anthropologist in the field. He is also the author of* Applied Anthropology *(1969), and has been instrumental in the development of a program of medical anthropology. Foster is also recognized as a leading figure in the rapidly growing field of peasant studies in anthropology. In "What is Folk Culture?" (1953) he raised some important issues concerning the definition of peasants as a valid topic of anthropological investigation.*

The fee should be enough to dispel any suspicion that the government might have something up its sleeve in offering such services, but it should not be so high as to discourage those people who can least afford it.

Other times the planned change program might require a drastic reorganization to overcome a barrier to change, and while such major alterations are certainly not popular with administrators, they are nonetheless necessary if the program is to have a chance of success. To continue with our example of a rural health clinic, in many countries there is a severe shortage of trained medical personnel, but especially of female doctors. At the same time, cultural values of rural peasant women are generally quite conservative. Thus a woman might not submit to an intimate physical examination by a male doctor (or her husband might not permit such an examination, even if his wife were willing). Given the shortage of female physicians and the norms of the potential patients, obviously a drastic reorganization of the program is necessary if it is to reach the majority of the people for whom it is intended. It might mean that before the program starts there should be a preliminary effort to train more women doctors. Or it could be designed to operate with a minimum of MDs, replacing them wherever possible with specially trained female nurses. Clearly the alternative of forcing women to undergo examinations by male physicians offers little hope of success.

Cultural values can act as very strong barriers to change, and it is frequently the task of the applied anthropologist to find a way to present the program of planned change so that it is not perceived as being in conflict with those values. For example, in the United States we tend to place a positive value upon change—any change—for its own sake. We are constantly subjected to advertisements for "new, improved" detergents, foods and almost any other kind of product. Our cars look different every year, as do our clothing styles. One major American company has as its slogan "progress is our most important product." Indeed, it seems we are more willing to accept change than anyone else in the world. And that is exactly the point. In most societies, and especially in nonindustrial areas of the world, people tend to rely just as heavily upon tradition as we do upon change. They feel a strong attachment to the ways of their ancestors, and any attempt to replace their traditions with some newfangled contraption will be rejected without any consideration for its merit. Thus if he is to be successful in having a program accepted, the applied

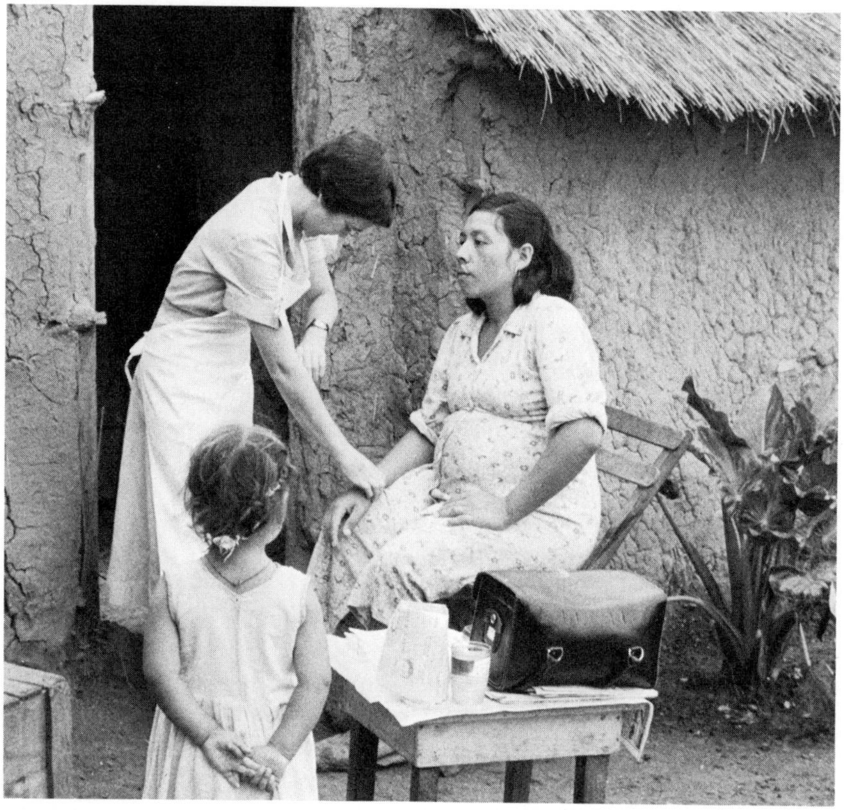

Prenatal examinations are especially difficult to promote. Here a student nurse from a public health project in the Chaco region of Argentina examines an expectant mother. (United Nations)

anthropologist must find some way of introducing it to people so that it will be perceived as compatible with a part of their tradition. Christian missionaries found this out when they learned to work their Christian teachings gradually into the existing system of beliefs of the people, rather than abruptly replacing an entire religious tradition with a new one. The same principle can be applied by anthropologists to other kinds of change.

Other cultural values, such as pride and dignity, can enter into the success of such a program. For example, Americans would offer little resistance to adult education programs. Most American corporations encourage their employees to seek additional training, and many even require it. We admire people who return to school after long absences, and at my own university, as at many others throughout the country, there is a program which seeks to attract senior citizens to attend classes by offering them student status without the customary tuition fee. Yet not all cultures hold the same views on adult education. In some societies school is perceived as something for children, and the suggestion that adults should return to school would meet with complete disapproval. If adult education is to be successful in such a setting, it must be presented as something other than a return to school—perhaps by offering instruction informally, outside of the school building, and in a manner as different from the traditional schoolroom pattern as possible.[2]

Questions of pride and dignity can be recognized in advance and dealt with, provided there is someone working in the program who has a thorough knowledge of the local culture. For example, a program to sell improved seed to farmers in a village in India failed because, although the poorer villagers participated, the wealthier and more influential farmers in the village would have nothing to do with it. The reason, it turned out, was that the best farmers were able to raise enough seed by themselves to feed their families and provide for next year's crop. To buy or borrow seed was a sign that one could not raise a sufficient crop, and for the most successful farmers in the village this would mean a loss of face.[3] Had someone in the program realized this in advance, an alternative could have been worked out, perhaps by trading some of the new, improved seed for some of the old seed from the farmers' last crop. But the assumption that everyone would immediately recognize the value of the new seed ignored the cultural barriers to change in this village.

Very simple cultural values such as taste can serve as barriers to change. In a program to introduce a new hybrid corn to farmers in New Mexico, the farmers immediately recognized the economic advantage of the new seed, which increased their yield substantially. However, despite the increase in income that the new corn afforded them, within a few years all the farmers had gone back to planting the old seed. The reason was that the new corn had a different texture, color and taste. For the Mexican-Americans of the area, the tortilla was a staple in their diet. However, the women found that the new

2. For an example of this problem in India, see S. C. Dube, *India's Changing Villages*. London: Routledge & Kegan Paul, 1958.

3. Morris E. Opler and R. D. Singh, "Economic, Political and Social Change in Villages of North Central India." *Human Organization* 11:2:5-12, 1952.

corn was inferior for making tortillas.[4] In this case the farmers were willing to sacrifice economic gain from the increased yield for better corn for their own use. Since they farmed primarily for subsistence, that is for their own consumption, they could not continue using both types of corn, and thus reverted to the one that fit in better with their dietary preferences. Had the administrators of the change program foreseen this problem, they might have spent more time looking for a hybrid seed that would increase the yield but would not be so different in taste and texture from the one already in use.

Finally, it is interesting to note that even something as simple as a body position, or what we call a motor pattern, can vary from one culture to another and can be a barrier to change. The introduction of latrines into rural villages, for example, might seem to be a simple task to which no one would object. But the fact is that for people who are not used to sitting down while defecating, such a contraption appears comical and useless. People who have become accustomed to squatting would find the seat on a latrine most uncomfortable. It would be a simple matter to construct a latrine built lower to the ground, so that it enabled people to assume a more comfortable position, yet if we are not aware of the potential for such a problem we probably will not even think about ways of averting it until it is too late. Thus there is much we can learn from the study of cultural differences, even on the most minute level, that can aid us in applying the knowledge gained by anthropologists to the solution of practical problems.

Besides the problems encountered in introducing changes that conflict with basic cultural values, norms, tastes, and the like, there is also a potential series of barriers on what we might term the "social" level—that is, in the area of group relations within a community. For example, in many small, tightly knit communities the traditional tasks are carried out in groups so that people interact closely and form strong bonds associated with their work. In a village where there is no running water and no bakery, women will gather together to do their washing at the central fountain or the stream, and they will bake their bread at the communal oven. Facilities such as the fountain and the oven thereby become important not only for their obvious

4. Anacleto Apodaca, "Corn and Custom: the Introduction of Hybrid Corn to Spanish Farmers in New Mexico." In Edward Spicer, ed., *Human Problems in Technological Change*. New York: The Russell Sage Foundation, 1952.

function in these tasks, but also for the opportunity they afford for women to gather together, talk and gossip, and pass the time while doing their work. It might seem to an outsider that an innovation such as piping running water into the home or supplying ovens for each household would improve the standard of living, but for these women it would not improve the *quality* of living. Indeed, it would have the opposite effect, for it would break up an important peer group from which they receive much satisfaction.

Authority is another aspect of the social structure of a community that can serve as a barrier to change. An innovation, if it is to be accepted, must be introduced to those in authority within the community, and their leadership must be seen as an important factor in its overall acceptance. In a village in Peru, several wells were dug to supply water to the villagers. However, the project failed and the villagers did not take advantage of the wells because they were drilled on private land owned by people who were not leaders in the community, and those who did hold high positions of authority were not consulted. As a result, they used their influence to reject the plan.[5]

Along similar lines, one often finds that a community will be divided into two or more factions—groups that oppose each other in many aspects of village life. If the object is to get the entire community to adopt an innovation, then it must be introduced carefully to avoid falling victim to the interests of any one faction. If it is introduced only to members of one faction, it will probably be summarily rejected by members of the other groups. Instead, if before the program is begun a study is made of the community so that such problems can be taken into account, then the introduction of the innovation can be made to members of each group at the same time. This is another example of how an anthropologist with a knowledge of community dynamics can apply his knowledge to the solution of community problems.

A third kind of barrier, in addition to cultural and social aspects of the people who are to participate in the program, is what Foster calls a "psychological" barrier to change. Such problems can frequently be seen as a failure in communication. In an attempt to communicate the nature of the planned change and the proposed benefits, the anthropologist must realize that the message the people

5. Allan R. Holmberg, "The Wells That Failed." In Edward H. Spicer, ed., *Human Problems in Technological Change.* New York: The Russell Sage Foundation, 1952.

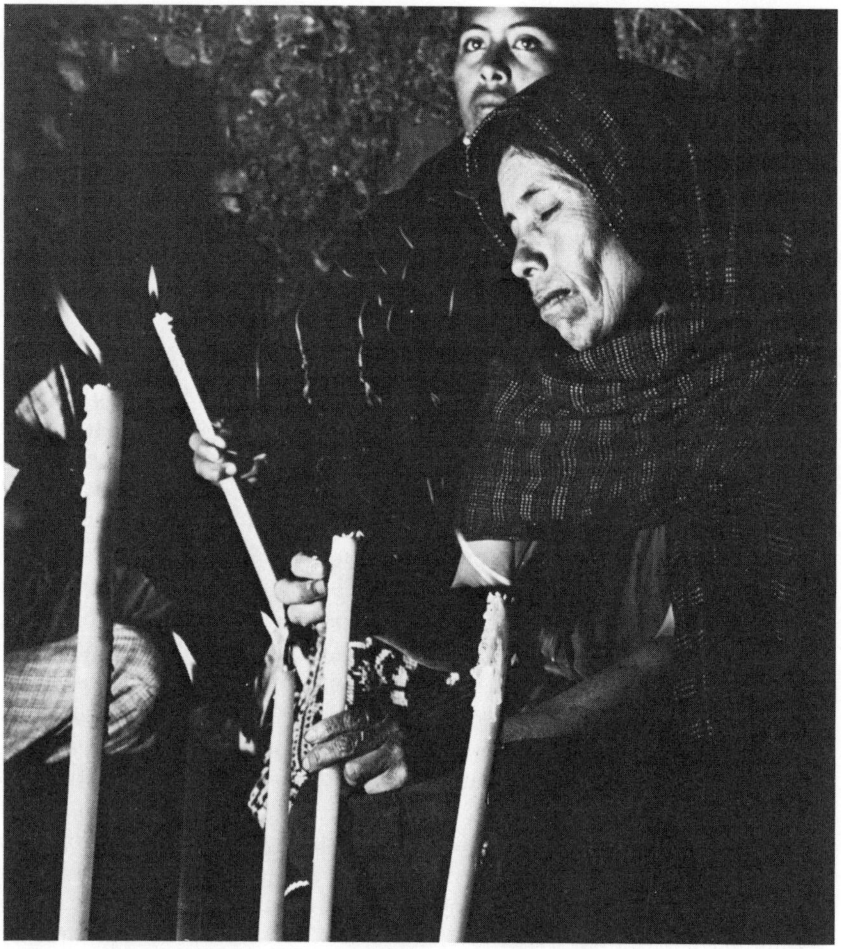

Mexican mourners light candles in remembrance of their dead relatives. (Mexican National Tourist Council)

receive is not the same as the message he intended to convey. Or, there might be other elements of the program that convey a message to the people without the project administrators ever realizing it. For example, it has been said that Mexican Indians are reluctant to call the priest for the last rites of the church when a relative is gravely ill, despite the fact that they are devout Catholics.[6] However, when seen from their point of view, their reluctance makes perfect sense: They have observed from past experience that almost every time the

6. Georgetta Soustelle, cited in Foster, *op. cit.* 1973, p. 130.

priest is called, the patient dies shortly thereafter. Thus the message conveyed by the Church, which seeks to have all its members receive the last rites before dying, is not the message understood by the Indians.

A similar but more relevant problem for the applied anthropologist deals with the role of the hospital as perceived by the residents of a rural community (or an urban community, for that matter). Usually when people are relatively isolated and hospital care is far away and too expensive for them, they are taken to a hospital only in the most serious cases. As a result, fewer people who enter a hospital survive, for they do not make more casual use of the facilities like most city dwellers. It is easy to see how such conditions could lead to the belief that a hospital is where someone goes to die, and that confinement (like the last rites of the Church, noted above) should be avoided. If a rural health care program is to succeed in the face of such psychological barriers, it must proceed cautiously with a program of education and demonstration to relieve the people of such fears. It may be necessary to take people into a hospital when there is nothing seriously wrong with them, simply to demonstrate to their fellow villagers that they can survive the experience of hospitalization. Such practices would normally meet with extreme resistance from doctors and program administrators who lack anthropological insight into the problem, but in the long run it would be much easier and more efficient to make such a concession than to expect the people to adapt to the program.

Another such failure to communicate can be seen in the perceptions people have of various roles. People in one culture might view a specialist as having a different role than he perceives himself to have. For example, in some cultures a folk curer is expected not only to cure a patient, but first to diagnose the illness by discovering the symptoms without the aid of the patient. Consider the plight of a person who is used to a medical specialist of this type when he enters a modern Western clinic, and the first thing the doctor asks him is to describe his symptoms! If he is used to the "doctor" finding out through some magical means what is wrong with him, he is not likely to hold the modern physician in high esteem when he can't even get past the first step in the diagnosis. Obviously such a doctor must be incompetent.[7]

7. Foster, *op. cit.* 1973, pp. 138–139.

Women of rural India attend a family planning course given by a social worker. In many cases it is necessary to do more than simply explain how birth control works—other cultural considerations must be taken into account. (United Nations)

The use of media in communication can also cause problems. For example, Indians in Peru were shown movies of medical interest to illustrate how lice transmit typhus, a disease prevalent in their area. When they were interviewed after the movie, it was found that they had not gotten the message at all. The reasons were twofold: first, the movie had been made on a Pacific island, and they could not identify with the setting. It was difficult for them to perceive how the message of the movie could be relevant for them, when they lived in the mountains and the people affected by typhus in the movie lived on tropical islands. Secondly, in the movie the lice were shown in close-up shots in which they filled the entire screen. Being unfamiliar with camera techniques and movies in general, the people had taken the demonstration literally. They concluded that since there were no insects as large as the enormous full-screen close-ups they had witnessed, the problem did not exist for them. It would seem a simple matter to communicate using movies, but as this example illustrates we can take nothing for granted in cross-cultural programs of planned change, or even between groups with different levels of education and experience within a single culture.

Stimulants to Change

So far it appears as if any attempt to introduce change will automatically be rejected in the face of so many barriers. In part the problem of rejection can be tempered by a thorough study of the subject culture with an eye toward uncovering potential barriers and taking them into account in the planning stage. Yet even the most observant anthropologist will come up against unanticipated barriers, for there will always be unforeseen consequences, new problems that arise after an innovation is introduced. To counter the effects of such barriers, the anthropologist can advocate the use of a number of elements in the program that will stimulate the acceptance of the change, regardless of the potential problems that might be encountered.

We have already mentioned a few such stimulants in other contexts. In some societies, particularly where industrialization has already begun and where consequently Western culture has become a prestige model, many innovations are accepted simply because they are identified with the West, which is synonymous with progress, wealth, and power. Even though people do not perceive a need for latrines or smallpox vaccinations or any similar Western item, they can sometimes be induced to accept them simply because they are a symbol of advancement. While the reasons for the success of the program might not be as valid in the eyes of the administrators, the results are every bit as effective.

Economic gain and competition can serve as stimulants for change. If it can be shown that an innovation will mean more money or a higher standard of living, it is more likely to be accepted. Likewise, promoting competition between individuals, between factions in a community, or even between communities in a region, can often spur people on to accept innovations that they might otherwise have rejected. The competitive instinct can thus be used to overcome the strong tendency on the part of many people throughout the world to cling to their time-tested traditions.

Friendship or a close personal relationship between a member of the program staff and the people for whom it is designed can serve as a stimulant to change. It is not enough to send in trained personnel to administer a project, for if they are not trusted and they cannot relate to the people, chances are their suggestions will not be heeded. On the other hand, if a project worker has a close tie with a community member, he can get that person to try the innovation as an act of trust. This is an important aspect of training programs for such groups as the Peace Corps, where the personal relationship between the volunteer and the people with whom he is working is stressed as a factor in the overall success or failure of the program.

Religious appeal may help to stimulate an innovation, for by appealing to the authority and the tradition of religion one can arouse interest and concern where it might not otherwise exist. If an innovation can be justified by reference to sacred scriptures it has a better chance of being adopted. In one case in India an area of otherwise deserted land was planted with a grove of trees. In an attempt to get the villagers to water the trees and care for them, the grove was dedicated to Krishna, whereby the villagers felt obligated to take care of it.[8] Religion can also be used effectively in promoting education, with the goal of teaching people to read the holy scriptures of their faith.

Finally, it is important to point out that any innovation will have a better chance of success if it can be shown to fit in with already existing cultural patterns. It is important to maintain traditional values, and to adjust the roles of people engaged in the program so that they fit in with the local conditions. For example, many rural health programs aim not only at curing sick individuals, but also at teaching them the value of preventive techniques. In such a situation a doctor may assume the role of instructor rather than curer. Thus it is important to examine the roles of teacher, curer, and doctor in each community to ascertain which role would have the best chance of stimulating the desired change toward a practice of preventive medicine. If there are no schools, or if adult education is unpopular, then perhaps the role of curer would be the best one in which to present the doctor. If the villagers' experience with doctors has been negative, then perhaps he should be presented as a teacher. If there is a fear or mistrust

8. Albert Mayer and Associates, *Pilot Project India*. Berkeley: University of California Press, 1958.

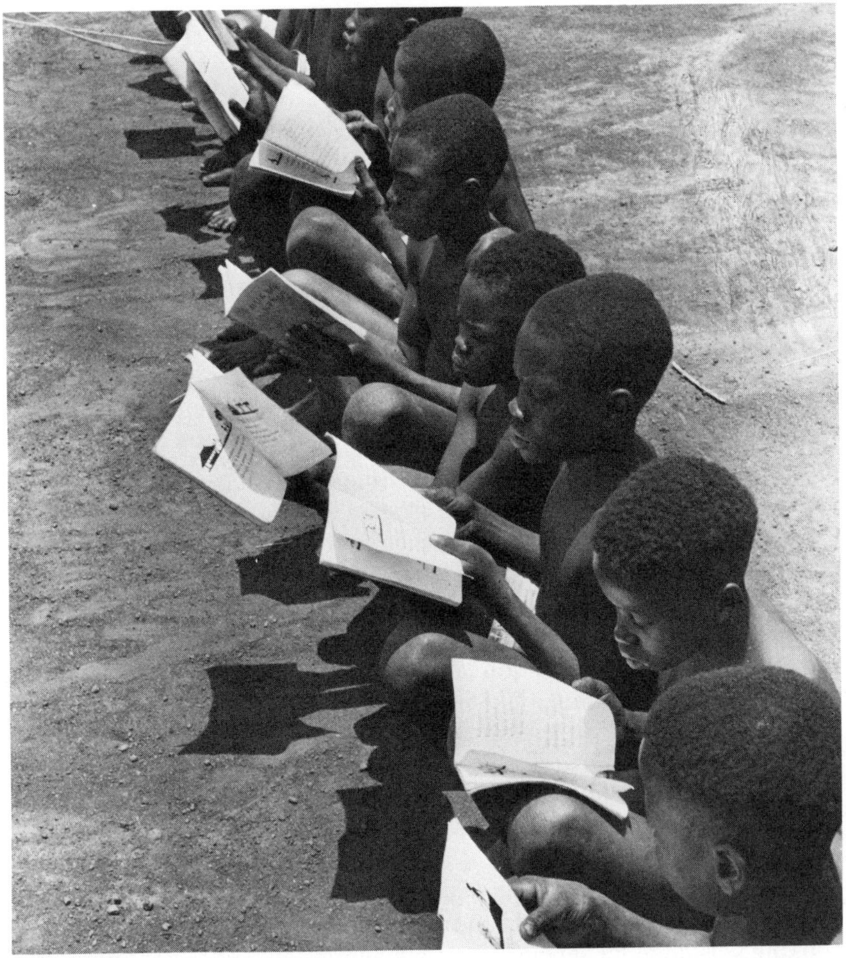

Sudanese children learning to read in a formal educational system. (George Rodger, Magnum)

of government, the program should dissociate itself from any official governmental agency. If there are definite patterns of authority already existing in the village, they should be utilized to stimulate acceptance of the change. In sum, it must be recognized that every innovation introduced into a new cultural setting will have to exist in a new context, and no matter how well it might have fit in the culture where it originated, it must be reworked to fit somewhere else. To demonstrate how well it fits can act as a stimulant for its adoption, by overcoming the universal tendency to stick with what is familiar and accept what is new only after a very cautious trial.

Unanticipated Consequences: The Pitfalls of Planned Change

Throughout the discussion of applied anthropology and the problems that programs of planned change must face, we have stressed the point that by introducing an innovation into another culture we unleash a whole series of changes, not all of which we can predict in advance. Knowing that there will be unanticipated consequences of such actions, the applied anthropologist takes on the additional responsibility of evaluating the program as it progresses, and determining whether its ultimate success will not be at a price that he considers to be too high. If he is lucky he may even anticipate some secondary consequences, and if he is experienced he will apply the results of other similar programs to predict some secondary changes and call them to the attention of those who are running the program.

Anthropologists and others engaged in public health programs have long been aware of the hazards of programs involving dietary change. For example, in an area supported almost entirely by a diet of raw fish, it is known that many people suffer from tapeworms. Thus at first sight it might seem a logical conclusion to introduce a program (including education and the necessary materials) so that people will begin to cook their fish, thus killing the tapeworms before they are consumed. But what about the secondary consequences of cooking fish? We have also learned that where people eat mainly fish and have few additional sources of vitamins, this practice can have negative consequences, for cooking lowers the food value of the fish. Thus we might simply be trading the problem of tapeworms for the problem of vitamin deficiency or even malnutrition.

Public health officials in India found that in many villages where cooking was done inside the hut with no chimney and poor ventilation, there was a high incidence of respiratory and eye ailments. They set out to solve this problem, assuming that it would be a simple matter to introduce chimneys and windows and a new kind of stove that would eliminate the smoke from the house. But they did not take into account the secondary consequences of such a change. The huts in many of these villages were made with thatched roofs, and the roofs were infested with wood-boring ants. The high level of smoke, although it caused eye and lung ailments, also kept the ants under control. When a new, low-cost smokeless stove was introduced, the ants began to multiply and ate up the roofs more rapidly. Now this in itself might not seem serious, except that the cost of a new roof for an Indian peasant is a considerable portion of his income—income that he would otherwise spend to maintain his already meager standard of living. By causing him to replace his roof more frequently, the innovation had the unanticipated consequence of lowering his standard of living in other ways. In effect, he traded respiratory and eye diseases for a poorer diet and fewer clothes, which ultimately also affected his health.

In Iran a similar situation developed, only this time it was not the wood-boring ants that were kept under control by the smoke, but the anopheles mosquito which carries the dread disease malaria. By keeping a high level of smoke in the house, the family was relatively safe from malaria.[9] With the introduction of a smokeless stove also came the rise in the rate of illness. Again, the unanticipated consequence was to trade one problem for another. The lesson we can learn from such experiences is not to abandon all hope of helping people, but rather to try to anticipate the consequences of any program of planned change that we intend to introduce, and to look to the experiences of other similar programs in other parts of the world to avoid making the same mistakes over again.

Applied Anthropology and the Future

Most applied anthropology has dealt with planned change in the Third-World countries, and this is perhaps as it should be. Attempts to spread the wealth and knowledge of the Western world and put them to use in raising the standard of living in other less wealthy countries, helping less fortunate people, have been all too few and infrequent. Thus it is a tragedy when the attempts fail because of the lack of knowledge of foreign cultures, knowledge that anthropologists are better equipped to provide than perhaps anyone else. If anthropology as a discipline is to be criticized, it is not for the role it has played in planned change—the benefits have far outweighed the abuses that have occurred—but rather for its failure to take a stronger stand and to force itself upon programs where no use was

9. Foster, *op. cit.* 1973, pp. 96–97.

made of basic anthropological insights. This is a problem that continues today, and anthropology is still a misunderstood and relatively little-known field, making its use by government and private agencies far less frequent and efficient than it should be.

The challenge for applied anthropology in the future lies not only in the Third World, but here at home with the problems that beset us today. It is time to abolish the distinction between anthropologists

Poverty exists in this country too. Welfare permits this mother of six children to buy flour and beans, but her house has no water or electricity. (Arthur Tress, Photo Researchers)

who study foreign cultures and other social scientists who study their own society. We are all students of culture and if our discipline is to have any validity it must be applicable to our own culture as well. If we have learned from our study of others, we ought to be able to apply that knowledge to ourselves. I look forward to anthropology becoming increasingly important in dealing with the cultural differences behind many of the more severe problems in our society, including race relations, sexism, drug addiction, alcoholism and crime. To do this, it is not necessary that every government employee be a trained anthropologist, or that every poverty program be administered by someone with a Ph.D. But it is important that the message that anthropology has to convey—and it is an important message—be made available to as many people as possible, as clearly as possible. This goal for the discipline of anthropology is the subject of the final chapter of this book.

In the following article, Richard B. Lee describes a situation in which all of his theory and classroom training could not help him overcome a basic gap in communication across cultural boundaries. The author was making a special effort to share his resources with his hosts, and not only misunderstood their response to his kindness, but was insulted by it. Had the story ended there, it would simply have been another case of cultural limitations preventing people from growing closer together and learning about each other.

However, Lee was able to penetrate the cultural patterns of the Bushmen and learn the true meaning of their apparent unfriendliness and ungratefulness. In doing so, he was performing the task of an applied anthropologist, as it has been described in this chapter. Most of the problems applied anthropologists are called upon to deal with are basically problems of lack of knowledge, understanding or communication in a cross-cultural setting. While Lee was not engaged in a development program, as an applied anthropologist might be, the basic lesson of this experience can be useful to us in understanding how anthropological methods and insights can be put to use in a wide variety of situations.

Eating Christmas in the Kalahari

Richard Borshay Lee

The !Kung Bushmen's knowledge of Christmas is thirdhand. The London Missionary Society brought the holiday to the southern Tswana tribes in the early nineteenth century. Later, native catechists spread the idea far and wide among the Bantu-speaking pastoralists, even in the remotest corners of the Kalahari Desert. The Bushmen's idea of the Christmas story, stripped to its essentials, is "praise the birth of white man's god-chief"; what keeps their interest in the holiday high is the Tswana-Herero custom of slaughtering an ox for his Bushmen neighbors as an annual goodwill gesture. Since the 1930s, part of the Bushmen's annual round of activities has included a December congregation at the cattle posts for trading, marriage brokering, and several days of trance-dance feasting at which the local Tswana headman is host.

As a social anthropologist working with !Kung Bushmen, I found that the Christmas ox custom suited my purposes. I had come to the Kalahari to study the hunting and gathering subsistence economy of the !Kung, and to accomplish that it was essential not to provide them with food, share my own food, or interfere in any way with their food-gathering activities. While liberal handouts of tobacco and medical supplies were appreciated, they were scarcely adequate to erase the glaring disparity in wealth between the anthropologist, who maintained a two-month inventory of canned goods, and the Bushmen, who rarely had a day's supply of food on hand. My approach, while paying off in terms of data, left me open to frequent accusations of stinginess and hard-heartedness. By their lights, was a miser.

The Christmas ox was to be my way of saying thank you for the cooperation of the past year; and since it was to be our last Christmas in the field, I determined to slaughter the largest, meatiest ox that money could buy, insuring that the feast and trance dance would be a success.

Through December I kept my eyes open at the wells as the cattle were brought down for watering. Several animals were offered, but none had quite the grossness that I had in mind. Then, ten days before the holiday, a Herero friend led an ox of astonishing size and mass up to our camp. It was solid black, stood five feet high at the shoulder, had a five-foot span of horns, and must have weighed 1,200 pounds on the

Editor's Note: The !Kung and other Bushmen speak click languages. In the story, three different clicks are used:

1. The dental click (/), as in /ai/ai, /ontah, and /gaugo. The click is sometimes written in English as tsk-tsk.
2. The alveopalatal click (!), as in Ben!a and !Kung.
3. The lateral click (//), as in //gom. Clicks function as consonants; a word may have more than one, as in /n!au.

Reprinted from *Natural History,* **78,** December 1969.

hoof. Food consumption calculations are my specialty, and I quickly figured that bones and viscera aside, there was enough meat—at least four pounds—for every man, woman, and child of the 150 Bushmen in the vicinity of /ai/ai who were expected at the feast.

Having found the right animal at last, I paid the Herero £20 ($56) and asked him to keep the beast with his herd until Christmas day. The next morning word spread among the people that the big solid black one was the ox chosen by /ontah (my Bushman name; it means, roughly, "whitey") for the Christmas feast. That afternoon I received the first delegation. Ben!a, an outspoken sixty-year-old mother of five, came to the point slowly.

"Where were you planning to eat Christmas?"

"Right here at /ai/ai," I replied.

"Alone or with others?"

"I expect to invite all the people to eat Christmas with me."

"Eat what?"

"I have purchased Yehave's black ox, and I am going to slaughter and cook it."

"That's what we were told at the well but refused to believe it until we heard it from yourself."

"Well, it's the black one," I replied expansively, although wondering what she was driving at.

"Oh, no!" Ben!a groaned, turning to her group. "They were right." Turning back to me she asked, "Do you expect us to eat that bag of bones?"

"Bag of bones! It's the biggest ox at /ai/ai."

"Big, yes, but old. And thin. Everybody knows there's no meat on that old ox. What did you expect us to eat off it, the horns?"

Everybody chuckled at Ben!a's one-liner as they walked away, but all I could manage was a weak grin.

That evening it was the turn of the young men. They came to sit at our evening fire. /gaugo, about my age, spoke to me man-to-man.

"/ontah, you have always been square with us," he lied. "What has happened to change your heart? That sack of guts and bones of Yehave's will hardly feed one camp, let alone all the Bushmen around /ai/ai." And he proceeded to enumerate the seven camps in the /ai/ai vicinity, family by family. "Perhaps you have forgotten that we are not few, but many. Or are you too blind to tell the difference between a proper cow and an old wreck? That ox is thin to the point of death."

"Look, you guys," I retorted, "that is a beautiful animal, and I'm sure you will eat it with pleasure at Christmas."

"Of course we will eat it; it's food. But it won't fill us up to the point where we will have enough strength to dance. We will eat and go home with stomachs rumbling."

That night as we turned in, I asked my wife, Nancy: "What did you think of the black ox?"

"It looked enormous to me. Why?"

"Well, about eight different people have told me I got gypped; that the ox is nothing but bones."

"What's the angle?" Nancy asked. "Did they have a better one to sell?"

"No, they just said that it was going to be a grim Christmas because there won't be enough meat to go around. Maybe I'll get an independent judge to look at the beast in the morning."

Bright and early, Halingisi, a Tswana cattle owner, appeared at our camp. But before I could ask him to give me his opinion on Yehave's black ox, he gave me the eye signal that indicated a confidential chat. We left the camp and sat down.

"/ontah, I'm surprised at you; you've lived here for three years and still haven't learned anything about cattle."

"But what else can a person do but choose the biggest, strongest animal one can find?" I retorted.

"Look, just because an animal is big doesn't mean that it has plenty of meat on it. The black one was a beauty when it was younger, but now it is thin to the point of death."

"Well I've already bought it. What can I do at this stage?"

"Bought it already? I thought you were just considering it. Well, you'll have to kill it and serve it, I suppose. But don't expect much of a dance to follow."

My spirits dropped rapidly. I could believe that Ben!a and /gaugo just might be putting me on about the black ox, but Halingisi seemed to be an impartial critic. I went around that day feeling as though I had bought a lemon of a used car.

In the afternoon it was Tomazo's turn. Tomazo is a fine hunter, a top trance performer and one of my most reliable informants. He approached the subject of the Christmas cow as part of my continuing Bushmen education.

"My friend, the way it is with us Bushmen," he began, "is that we love meat. And even more than that, we love fat. When we hunt we always search for the fat ones, the ones dripping with layers of white fat: fat that turns into a clear, thick oil in the cooking pot, fat that slides down your gullet, fills your stomach and gives you a roaring diarrhea," he rhapsodized.

"So, feeling as we do," he continued, "it gives us pain to be served such a scrawny thing as Yehave's black ox. It is big, yes, and no doubt its giant bones are good for soup, but fat is what we really crave and so we will eat Christmas this year with a heavy heart."

The prospect of a gloomy Christmas now had me worried, so I asked Tomazo what I could do about it.

"Look for a fat one, a young one . . . smaller, but fat. Fat enough to make us *//gom* ('evacuate the bowels'), then we will be happy."

My suspicions were aroused when Tomazo said that he happened to know of a young, fat, barren cow that the owner was willing to part with. Was Toma working on commission, I wondered? But I dispelled this unworthy thought when we approached the Herero owner of the cow in question and found that he had decided not to sell.

The scrawny wreck of a Christmas ox now became the talk of the /ai/ai water hole and was the first news told to the outlying groups as they began to come in from the bush for the feast. What finally convinced me that real trouble might be brewing was the visit from u!au, an old conservative with a reputation for fierceness. His nickname meant spear and referred to an incident thirty years ago in which he had speared a man to death. He had an intense manner; fixing me with his eyes, he said in clipped tones:

"I have only just heard about the black ox today, or else I would have come here earlier. /ontah, do you honestly think you can serve meat like that to people and avoid a fight?" He paused, letting the implications sink in. "I don't mean fight you, /ontah; you are a white man. I mean a fight between Bushmen. There are many fierce ones here, and with such a small quantity of meat to distribute, how can you give everybody a fair share? Someone is sure to accuse another of taking too much or hogging all the choice pieces. Then you will see what happens when some go hungry while others eat."

The possibility of at least a serious argument struck me as all too real. I had witnessed the tension that surrounds the distribution of meat from a kudu or gemsbok kill, and had documented many arguments that sprang up from a real or imagined slight in meat distribution. The owners of a kill may spend up to two hours arranging and rearranging the piles of meat under the gaze of a circle of recipients before handing them out. And I also knew that the Christmas feast at /ai/ai would be bringing together groups that had feuded in the past.

Convinced now of the gravity of the situation, I went in earnest to search for a second cow; but all my inquiries failed to turn one up.

The Christmas feast was evidently going to be a disaster, and the incessant complaints about the meagerness of the ox had already taken the fun out of it for me. Moreover, I was getting bored with the wisecracks, and after losing my temper a few times, I resolved to serve the beast anyway. If the meat fell short, the hell with it. In the Bushmen idiom, I announced to all who would listen:

"I am a poor man and blind. If I have chosen one that is too old and too thin, we will eat it anyway and see if there is enough meat there to quiet the rumbling of our stomachs."

On hearing this speech, Ben!a offered me a rare word of comfort. "It's thin," she said philosophically, "but the bones will make a good soup."

At dawn Christmas morning, instinct told me to turn over the butchering and cooking to a friend and take off with Nancy to spend Christmas alone in the bush. But curiosity kept me from retreating. I wanted to see what such a scrawny ox looked like on butchering, and if there *was* going to be a fight, I wanted to catch every word of it. Anthropologists are incurable that way.

The great beast was driven up to our dancing ground, and a shot in the forehead dropped it in its tracks. Then, freshly cut branches were heaped around the fallen carcass to receive the meat. Ten men volunteered to help with the cutting. I asked /gaugo to make the breast bone cut. This cut, which begins the butchering process for most large game, offers easy access for removal of the viscera. But it also allows the hunter to spot-check the amount of fat on the animal. A fat game animal carries a white layer up to an inch thick on the chest, while in a thin one, the knife will quickly cut to bone. All eyes fixed on his hand as /gaugo, dwarfed by the great carcass, knelt to the breast. The first cut opened a pool of solid white in the black skin. The second and third cut widened and deepened the creamy white. Still no bone. It was pure fat; it must have been two inches thick.

"Hey /gau," I burst out, "that ox is loaded with fat. What's this about the ox being too thin to bother eating? Are you out of your mind?"

"Fat?" /gau shot back, "You call that fat? This wreck is thin, sick, dead!" And he broke out laughing. So did everyone else. They rolled on the ground, paralyzed with laughter. Everybody laughed except me; I was thinking.

I ran back to the tent and burst in just as Nancy was getting up. "Hey, the black ox. It's fat as hell! They were kidding about it being too thin to eat. It was a joke or something. A put-on. Everyone is really delighted with it!"

"Some joke," my wife replied. "It was so funny that you were ready to pack up and leave /ai/ai."

If it had indeed been a joke, it had been an extraordinarily convincing one, and tinged, I thought, with more than a touch of malice as many jokes are. Nevertheless, that it was a joke lifted my spirits considerably, and I returned to the butchering site where the shape of the ox was rapidly disappearing under the axes and knives of the butchers. The atmosphere had become festive. Grinning broadly, their arms covered with blood well past the elbow, men packed chunks of meat into the big cast-iron cooking pots, fifty pounds to the load, and muttered and chuckled all the while about the thinness and worthlessness of the animal and /ontah's poor judgment.

We danced and ate that ox two days and two nights; we cooked and distributed fourteen potfuls of meat and no one went home hungry and no fights broke out.

But the "joke" stayed in my mind. I had a growing feeling that something important had happened in my relationship with the Bushmen and that the clue lay in the meaning of the joke. Several days later, when most of the people had dispersed back to the bush camps, I raised the question with Hakekgose, a Tswana man who had grown up among the !Kung, married a !Kung girl, and who probably knew their culture better than any other non-Bushman.

"With us whites," I began, "Christmas is supposed to be the day of friendship and brotherly love. What I can't figure out is why the

Bushmen went to such lengths to criticize and belittle the ox I had bought for the feast. The animal was perfectly good and their jokes and wisecracks practically ruined the holiday for me."

"So it really did bother you," said Hakekgose. "Well, that's the way they always talk. When I take my rifle and go hunting with them, if I miss, they laugh at me for the rest of the day. But even if I hit and bring one down, it's no better. To them, the kill is always too small or too old or too thin; and as we sit down on the kill site to cook and eat the liver, they keep grumbling, even with their mouths full of meat. They say things like, 'Oh this is awful! What a worthless animal! Whatever made me think that this Tswana rascal could hunt!' "

"Is this the way outsiders are treated?" I asked.

"No, it is their custom; they talk that way to each other too. Go and ask them."

/gaugo had been one of the most enthusiastic in making me feel bad about the merit of the Christmas ox. I sought him out first.

"Why did you tell me the black ox was worthless, when you could see that it was loaded with fat and meat?"

"It is our way," he said smiling. "We always like to fool people about that. Say there is a Bushman who has been hunting. He must not come home and announce like a braggard, 'I have killed a big one in the bush!' He must first sit down in silence until I or someone else comes up to his fire and asks, 'What did you see today?' He replies quietly, 'Ah, I'm no good for hunting. I saw nothing at all [pause] just a little tiny one.' Then I smile to myself," /gaugo continued, "because I know he has killed something big.

"In the morning we make up a party of four or five people to cut up and carry the meat back to the camp. When we arrive at the kill we examine it and cry out, 'You mean to say you have dragged us all the way out here in order to make us cart home your pile of bones? Oh, if I had known it was this thin I wouldn't have come.' Another one pipes up, 'People, to think I gave up a nice day in the shade for this. At home we may be hungry but at least we have nice cool water to drink.' If the horns are big, someone says, 'Did you think that somehow you were going to boil down the horns for soup?'

"To all this you must respond in kind. 'I agree,' you say, 'this one is not worth the effort; let's just cook the liver for strength and leave the rest for the hyenas. It is not too late to hunt today and even a duiker or a steenbok would be better than this mess.'

"Then you set to work nevertheless; butcher the animal, carry the meat back to the camp and everyone eats," /gaugo concluded.

Things were beginning to make sense. Next, I went to Tomazo. He corroborated /gaugo's story of the obligatory insults over a kill and added a few details of his own.

"But," I asked, "why insult a man after he has gone to all that trouble to track and kill an animal and when he is going to share the meat with you so that your children will have something to eat?"

"Arrogance," was his cryptic answer.

"Arrogance?"

"Yes, when a young man kills much meat he comes to think of himself as a chief or a big man, and he thinks of the rest of us as his servants or inferiors. We can't accept this. We refuse one who boasts, for someday his pride will make him kill somebody. So we always speak of his meat as worthless. This way we cool his heart and make him gentle."

Summary

Applied anthropology is the use of insights gained in the study of other cultures to solve pressing social problems throughout the world, but particularly in non-Western or technologically less advanced societies that have been the main focus of anthropological research. In the United States, applied anthropology grew out of the concern with cultural differences between whites and Indians, and later became concerned with problems surrounding cultural differences among various immigrant groups. More recently, anthropologists have contributed to the programs of planned change following World War II, and they continue to make important contributions to the planning and hopefully the ultimate success of programs of change in the developing countries of the world.

In any attempt to introduce new cultural elements to people, there will be barriers to change. Values such as modesty, conservatism, pride and even taste, can spell the doom of a program of planned change if they are not taken into account. Authority patterns must be considered, and factions or group dynamics cannot be overlooked in the administration of such a program. Psychological factors such as people's perception of the changes and of their traditional way of life may also serve as barriers to change.

To overcome the barriers to change, the applied anthropologist can call upon stimulants to achieve the aims of the program. Occasionally the changes can be made to appear prestigious in order to get people to adopt them. Economic gain can be a strong motivation for change, as can close personal friendship or rapport between the change agent and the people of the community. Religious appeal may also be used to gain greater acceptance of a new innovation.

In every case of change, there will be secondary consequences, many of them unanticipated. It is the role of the applied anthropologist to try to predict these secondary changes, and to plan for them in advance. The elimination of one problem may create another problem even more serious than the first, thus threatening the success of the entire program.

The ability of anthropology to aid in the solution to the world's pressing problems will be the key to the success of the discipline in the future. Our understanding of other cultures has enabled us to make valuable contributions toward improving the living conditions of countless people throughout the world. At the same time, we are recognizing the growing need to contribute our knowledge and understanding toward the solution of problems on the home front as well.

Glossary

applied anthropology The use of the knowledge gained in studying other cultures toward the solution of practical problems.

assimilation The process by which a group becomes culturally incorporated into a larger society through contact and the adoption of the larger society's cultural traits.

sedentary A term referring to a group's residence at the same location for an entire year. *Nomadism* is an alternative form of residence in which a group migrates seasonally from one location to another depending upon the natural resources available at a given time and place.

Questions for Discussion

1 American society is currently undergoing some drastic changes and is facing some rather awesome problems, i.e., pollution of the environment, the breakdown of family life, ambiguity of morals, depletion of resources and economic troubles. From what you have learned about the field of anthropology, how might you apply some of its techniques to help solve these problems?

2 How do the Peace Corps and Vista affect the lives of the people who are given aid by the American government? Does this work have any similarities to or differences from applied anthropology.

3 The applied anthropologist attempts to solve practical problems through solutions generated from anthropological knowledge. The anthropologist tries to anticipate the long-range effects of changes in one part of the culture upon other institutions. If you were an applied anthropologist given the task of solving our nation's economic problems, what repercussions would you anticipate in other aspects of our society and how would you plan for these? (For example, there is a relationship between high unemployment, a large number of people dependent upon public assistance, and changing attitudes concerning the work ethic.)

4 There are numerous subcultures in American society. Each of these groups (American Indians, Chicanos, etc.) shares a way of life that in many respects sets it apart from the dominant society. American society has attempted to assimilate these groups, in many cases, into the mainstream of society, but often with very little success. What are the cultural, social, and psychological barriers to change that keep many of these groups separated from American society? How much of this can be accounted for by negative solidarity (see Chapter 5)? Is it a good idea for the American government to continue its attempt to assimilate these subcultures? Why or why not?

Suggestions for Additional Reading

Clifton, James A. (editor)
1970 Applied Anthropology: Readings in the Uses of the Science of Man. Boston: Houghton Mifflin.

An excellent collection of articles dealing with applied anthropology, discussing many of the problems and ethical issues raised in this chapter.

Erasmus, Charles
1961 Man Takes Control. Minneapolis: University of Minnesota Press.

An analysis of social change and the potential for applied anthropology from the point of view of economic stimulants to change.

Foster, George M.
1969 Applied Anthropology. Boston: Little, Brown.

An expanded analysis of applied anthropology, its methods and goals, which grew out of the original 1962 version of *Traditional Societies*.

1973 Traditional Societies and Technological Change. Second Edition. New York: Harper & Row.

A summary of the barriers to planned change and stimulants that can be used by the applied anthropologist to overcome some of these barriers.

Goodenough, Ward H.
1963 Cooperation in Change. New York: Russell Sage Foundation.

A manual designed to be used by applied anthropologists in the field.

Niehoff, Arthur H. (editor)
1966 A Casebook of Social Change. Chicago: Aldine.

A critical evaluation of attempts to introduce change in the major developing areas of the world.

Paul, Benjamin D. (editor)
1955 Health, Culture & Community. Case Studies of Public Reactions to Health Programs. New York: Russell Sage Foundation.

A collection of articles dealing with a specific type of applied anthropological program, analyzing some of the general problems encountered in health programs.

Spicer, Edward H. (editor)
1952 Human Problems in Technological Change. New York: John Wiley & Sons.

A collection of articles on various programs of planned change, particularly valuable for classroom use because of the format of each article: first the problem is presented, then a series of questions are posed before the outcome is discussed to uncover the hidden causes or barriers to change.

The Meaning of Anthropology in Our Society

Chapter Eleven

In a sense, social science is caught in a paradoxical situation in the 1970s. In this age of specialists, the average person wouldn't dream of pulling his own teeth—he automatically goes to a dentist. We certainly wouldn't think of cutting ourselves open to remove an appendix—we would go to a surgeon. Even for the minor task of unstopping a clogged drain we call a plumber. If our car breaks down we call a mechanic, and if we get busted we call a lawyer for legal assistance.

Yet society and its problems are at least as complex as any of these others. Still, if you stop the man on the street, he will almost invariably feel competent to offer his solution to all the social problems that confront us. Every average Joe is an expert on drugs, crime, racial policies, the economy, and our country's military and political foreign policy. How many people call a sociologist when their kids get busted? How many call an anthropologist when a black wants to move into their white neighborhood? More likely they call a real estate agent, who in some neighborhoods doubles as an expert on the racial inferiority of blacks due to his long and hard training in the field of not selling them houses.

On a national level, although social scientists are indeed consulted, they are consulted with the foregone conclusion that their findings will fit in with present policies. Scientists are requested to give opinions on scientific matters, not moral questions. On occasion, when their findings do not jibe with official policies, they are summarily rejected. Consider, for example, the commission on pornography established by former President Lyndon Johnson. It presented him (and later his successor, former President Richard Nixon) with a report concluding that our pornography laws (or better said, our anti-pornography laws) should be relaxed, revised and even elimi-

It is not important what social scientists say, so much as how one uses what they say.

GERALD BERREMAN *Is Anthropology Alive?*

nated in some cases. Of course, this was an answer based upon the analysis of data subjected to scrutiny by trained social scientists. But it could not be defended when it did not fall in line with the Nixon administration's moral views on the so-called pornography "problem." As a result, the report was swept under the rug and no official action was taken. One wonders what the results would have been had the report concluded the opposite!

In case after case, the recommendations of social scientists are rejected because they are found to be politically unacceptable. What are the reasons for this callous treatment of science? As it appears to me, it is rooted in the notion of science as being "value-free." Scholars in this country do research, but are not supposed to make moral decisions. Such decisions are left up to the moralists who "represent" the people. Thus, when scientists come up with conclusions, the moralists still retain the power of veto, which they frequently exercise. And to some degree that is indeed as it should be. Science should not be allowed to impose its findings upon the people without being checked by the people.

But the situation is rarely reversed. No one questioned the moral leaders of the country regarding whether it would be proper to drop an atom bomb. Scientists working on the Manhattan Project, which ultimately produced the bomb in the early 1940s, were asked only to contribute their scientific expertise. They were requested to provide the formula to create an atomic explosion. But when later some of them criticized the way in which this formula was being used, they were branded as incompetent to deal with moral judgments. In those days, the critics were called Communists. No one asked them how to use the bomb—that was a question for another kind of specialist, a military expert.

The notion of a value-free science applies to anthropology as well. It does not mean that the anthropologist has no values, for as we have pointed out throughout this book, everyone by virtue of his culture, has a set of values that he shares to a greater or lesser degree with the remainder of his countrymen. What it does mean is that anthropology as a discipline is not supposed to be oriented toward a particular set of values, but only toward objectivity—truth, if you will. Of course, it is impossible for the anthropologist to avoid injecting his own views into his work, and this is why his training is so important, for it teaches him to recognize this cultural bias and to work around it whenever possible. But the reason that science has not played a stronger role in molding society is that anthropologists, along with scientists in other fields, have used the excuse of a value-free science to avoid taking a stand on major social issues, even where their training and experience make them the most likely and most qualified people to do so. We have failed to make a distinction between our scientific investigations and educated opinions, and have hidden behind the wall of objectivity. It is, indeed, as Gerald Berreman has said,

> . . . science has no responsibility, but scientists do. Scientists are people. They cannot escape values in the choices they make or in the effects of their acts.
>
> If we choose to collect our data and make our analyses without regard to their use—leaving that choice to others—we may believe that we are adhering to the most rigorous scientific canons (and hence the most highly *valued* canons) by not intervening in society. But to say nothing is not to be neutral. To say *nothing* is as much a significant act as to say *something*. . . . To be uncommitted is not to be neutral, but to be committed—consciously or not—to the *status quo*. . . .[1]

Let me offer an example of the use and continued misuse of social science to perpetuate a wrong and harmful myth. Early notions concerning race and intelligence in this country assumed that intelligence was fixed at birth, and could not be affected by an individual's life experience and his culture. This notion fit in well with the existing racist theories, for races exhibited different intelligence levels in terms of academic achievement and IQ testing. Moreover, IQ tests were

1. Gerald D. Berreman, "Is Anthropology Alive?" In *Readings in Anthropology*, Volume 2, Second Edition. Morton H. Fried, ed. New York: T.Y. Crowell, 1968.

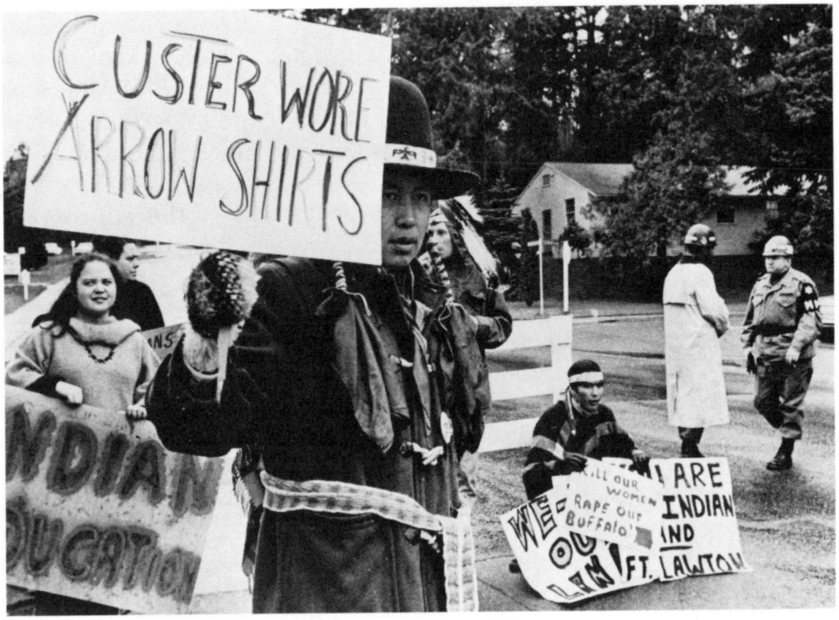

Assimilation is not always the answer. Indians picketing outside Fort Lawton in Seattle want to establish a cultural center on land declared surplus by the federal government. (Wide World)

obviously geared to perpetuate this situation, by testing for adherence to middle-class values and standards.

Massive IQ testing began early in the twentieth century. During World War I a large number of draftees were given these tests to determine their aptitudes for various assignments, and in general to rank them according to intelligence, as measured by the standard IQ test. After the war people began to analyze the test results, and especially to sort them out according to race. They found that there was a significant difference between whites and blacks, with whites scoring much higher on the average. These findings were then used to perpetuate the myth of racial inferiority.

Fortunately, more recently these results have been analyzed once again, and we have drawn a different set of conclusions. Until social scientists were willing and able to stand up against the racist onslaught, however, American blacks suffered from the misapplication of so-called "scientific" findings in an attempt to perpetuate the popular notions of white superiority. It has now been demonstrated that IQ tests are not in fact an accurate measure of intelligence, for they ignore many contributing factors affecting the performance of the individual—cultural factors such as home environment, school environment and level of education of parents. Also, it has been shown that the questions on such tests are specifically designed to elicit answers that conform to the standards of middle-class white culture. A black person from a lower-class background would not have the experience necessary to perform well, despite the fact that he might have a superior intelligence. For example, a question found on some IQ tests for young children asked them to select from a list of colors the appropriate color for milk. If the child selected the answer "white," he got the question right. Any other answer was marked wrong. However, designers of the test completely ignored class distinctions in grading the examinations. During the Depression, many poor families had to purchase an inferior quality of milk that had a bluish tint. Thus, many ghetto children grew up drinking milk that was not really white, and although their answer "blue" on the test was both accurate and intelligent, they were marked down for it.

In addition to discoveries of the bias of IQ testing and the application of the inaccurate results to racist ideologies, subsequent studies of the results of tests upon World War I GIs indicated that if the scores were looked at from a different perspective, the results could be interpreted in a very different manner. For example, if we compare the scores of northern blacks and southern blacks in these tests, we find that the northerners score much higher, indicating a definite environmental factor influencing the test score. Likewise, the longer blacks had been in the north, the higher their scores. Blacks from New York City scored higher in direct proportion to the length of time they had been living there. Thus it could not be claimed that northern blacks scored higher because they were not a representative sample (i.e., the smarter ones migrated north originally). The arguments clearly indicated that there was no genetic factor involved in racial differences in IQ, but rather that it was simply an environmental factor. In fact, when scores were compared even further it was found that New York City blacks scored higher than Alabama whites on the whole, a conclusion that definitely negates racist theories of intelligence that deny the influence of culture upon IQ scores.

One positive result of this approach to the problem of intelligence and race has been the realization that there can be no single standard for measuring intelligence. Rather, it is something that must be seen in its cultural context, for the only true measure of intelligence is one that measures the ability of the individual to act in a familiar environment. New testing patterns are being developed to get around

Burg-Wartenstein

Gerald D. Berreman (1930–) *has conducted fieldwork in the Aleutian Islands and India, and has studied social stratification in India and the United States. He has published numerous papers concerning the social responsibilities of anthropology and anthropologists, including "Is Anthropology Alive? Social Responsibility in Social Anthropology" (1968), "The Peace Corps: A Dream Betrayed" (1968), "Academic Colonialism" (1969), and "Bringing It All Back Home: Malaise in Anthropology" (1974). He has been active in the Ethics Committee of the American Anthropological Association, in an attempt to provide guidelines for the profession, particularly in light of the use of anthropologists by government agencies in counterinsurgency research in Southeast Asia and Latin America.*

some of the problems that plagued the old tests. How do you administer such tests to children who have not learned to read quickly or accurately, for example? Is the intelligence test to be a reading test, or should it be more? If it is to be more, then obviously it must not mark the pupil down on his score for poor reading ability. Likewise, language problems can come into play. If we write all tests in a standard white, middle-class vocabulary, surely we must recognize that this puts pupils at a disadvantage who have not learned that form of the English language.

Throughout this book we have pointed out that while society does place constraints upon the individual, it does not prevent him from acting out his individuality within certain limits. And we have also seen that the more diversified and heterogeneous a society becomes, the broader the limits of individuality. Thus, in our own society, with its constitutionally guaranteed freedom of expression, we would expect the greatest amount of individuality—and indeed we find this to be the case. Why, then, are we still plagued with the problem of the selective use and misuse of social science? Why do people disregard so much of the findings of social science in making their decisions about public policies? And why do social scientists, of all people, feel so constrained to keep quiet and watch their findings go unused, or worse yet, misused?

As Peter Berger has pointed out, society provides us with a warm, reasonably comfortable cave in which we can huddle with our fellows.[2] The study of society makes us better able to step out of that cave and act responsibly. An understanding of society is not an alibi for irresponsibility. Understanding racial problems is not an excuse for not doing anything about them—if anything, it is an excuse to do more. At the Nuremburg trials following World War II we held Nazi war criminals responsible for following orders without challenging them, for not speaking out against injustice. Should we not charge ourselves with the same responsibility to speak out? In opposing any of the evils that we see in our own society or anywhere else in the world, we are exercising our free will. Only when we refuse to use our free will are we in danger of losing it.

It is important to point out, in these days when students are rightly demanding relevance in their education, some examples of how social science has been made relevant in the past, and how it can continue

2. Peter L. Berger, *Invitation to Sociology.* Garden City: Anchor Books, 1963.

When the quality of education is truly equal for children of all races, the myth of racial inequality will disappear. (Jan Lukas, Rapho/Photo Researchers)

to be applied to present and future problems. It should also be emphasized that it does not take a Ph.D. to make a valid point, or to claim the right to apply an understanding of how society works to the solution of its problems. We have already demonstrated how with the proper approach to the understanding of racial differences and associated economic and environmental differences, social science has been able to prove the myth of racial inferiority totally false. The exploitation of this myth still continues, unfortunately, but at least it is becoming recognized for what it is, a totally unscientific and undocumented proposition based on fear rather than fact.

Social science has, in recent years, also dealt with deviance, ranging from such mundane things as divorce to more hotly contested issues such as homosexuality. The effect has been to show that deviance is not, as the moralist sees it, a vice among a handful of degenerates, but a fairly common phenomenon among all strata of the population. When Kinsey published his famous statement that 10 percent of all males in the United States had engaged in some type of homosexual activity sometime during their life, we were forced to take a more realistic view of homosexuality in our society. Despite the fact that such "deviant" behavior was apparently quite common, until Kinsey's report there was no attempt to seek legitimation from the rest of society on the part of homosexuals, for the prevailing attitudes in our country would not have allowed them to have their say. However, with the growing awareness of homosexuality has come a growing acceptance of it—slow, to be sure, but increasing nonetheless. Major changes in our legislation, for example, are a testimony to the changing attitudes of the American people toward homosexuality. And it is refreshing to note that anthropology has made important contributions to the growing understanding of deviant forms of behavior. Studies by anthropologists have pointed to some of the most bizarre practices known to us, and for many years these descriptions

The Tasaday, a "Stone-Age" tribe recently discovered in the Philippines. Will contact with western culture be their salvation, or their undoing? (John Nance, Panamin/ Magnum)

were valued more for their curiosity than for their scientific contribution to the understanding of human behavior. But as we become more aware of what is acceptable in different cultures around the world, we become more tolerant of what was formerly unacceptable in our own society. We become less demanding about the absolute validity of our own way of life and the exclusion of any other way that does not follow our moral code exactly.

In recent years social scientists have been able to demonstrate that many of the moral judgments that we, the people, make about our way of life are based not upon fact, but upon fiction. One of the clearest examples of this is in the argument over the value of capital punishment as a deterrent to crime. Study upon study has indicated that capital punishment does not in fact act as a deterrent to the crimes for which it can be enacted, yet the popular misconception continues. It has been argued over and over again that if a person knows that he faces death for committing murder, he will stop short of killing someone. Yet the facts do not bear out this argument. A recent article in *The New York Times* reported:

> The abolition of the death penalty in Canada on December 29, 1967, failed to bring any major increase in the number of murders, according to Government statistics. The figures instead show fairly even increases in years since 1961, in the years both before and after the death penalty was abolished.[3]

By bringing such evidence to public attention, social scientists may be able to turn the energies of the judicial system and the legislatures away from the argument over capital punishment, which in the long run is not productive, and toward the question of how to reform our courts and penal system so that they are more effective in dealing with crime.

These are but a few examples of the potential of social science in understanding current problems. I hope that in reading this book you have learned the value of the comparative approach that anthropology contributed to the social sciences. You have seen that behavior in your own society is just as conventional as anywhere else, and that in the eyes of a person from another culture it can be just as bizarre. It is right or wrong because we define it as such, but there are no absolute standards. All behavior exists in a cultural context.

3. *The New York Times*. January 21, 1973, p. 16.

Thus if we can learn to be tolerant of people in other cultures, we should also learn to be tolerant of different kinds of people in our own culture.

It is also the task of the social scientist to point out the causes of contemporary problems, and to set about solving them. From what you have learned about your own society and others, you are better able to identify the causes of these problems. But with that knowledge goes a responsibility to take action. It is not enough merely to identify a problem; it is a duty to do more. In the words of the late sociologist C. Wright Mills,

> If human reason is to play a larger and more explicit role in the making of history, social scientists must surely be among its major carriers. For in their work they represent the use of reason in the understanding of human affairs; that is what they are about.[4]

One final word. To my mind, the beauty of our society is that it allows freedom of expression. Dissent could not exist in a totalitarian state, and whether or not we agree with what a person says, we all believe in his right to say it. By that fact alone we must strive all the harder to identify and correct the sources of contemporary problems, even though the cause might lie in the very democratic institutions that form the backbone of our society. A phrase we often hear, or read on bumper stickers or bathroom walls, is "America—Love It Or Leave It." It is indeed a hollow phrase. It is like a child who has been caught misbehaving saying to his parent "If you love me you will not spank me." When did love ever preclude striving to make things better? Patriotism and acquiescence cannot possibly be equated today. In fact, silence or blind adherence are perversions of patriotism. The task of the social sciences in this sense becomes very clear. For it is as Edmund Burke said: "The only thing necessary for the triumph of evil is for good men to do nothing."

4. C. Wright Mills, *The Sociological Imagination.* New York: Oxford University Press, 1959, p. 179.

Suggestions for Additional Reading

Berger, Peter
1963 Invitation to Sociology: A Humanistic Perspective. Garden City, N.Y.: Doubleday & Company.

A sensitive and insightful look at sociology, and social science in general, from the point of view of how it can be meaningful in the context of modern social conditions.

Berreman, Gerald D.
1968 Is Anthropology Alive? In Morton Fried (editor), Readings in Anthropology, volume 2, pp. 845–857. New York: T.Y. Crowell.

The author raises some important questions about the role of anthropology and the anthropologist in the wider society.

Caudill, Harry
1963 Night Comes to the Cumberlands: A Biography of a Depressed Area. Boston: Little, Brown.

A tragic account of the destruction of traditional Appalachian culture brought about by the exploitation of the timber and coal industries in the region. The author speaks eloquently on behalf of the need for social planning and greater compassion for cultural differences.

Harris, Marvin
1975 Culture, People, Nature, Second Edition. New York: T. Y. Crowell.

This general anthropology textbook contains an excellent discussion of the debate over IQ and race.

Horowitz, Irving L. (editor)
1967 The Rise and Fall of Project Camelot: Studies in the Relationship Between Social Science and Practical Politics. Cambridge, Mass.: MIT Press.

A discussion of the attempt to involve anthropology and anthropologists in a program of counter-insurgency and anti-revolutionary activity in Third-World countries during the 1960s, and the problems this has created for the discipline.

Hymes, Dell (editor)
1972 Reinventing Anthropology. New York: Random House.

A stimulating and controversial collection of papers dealing with some of the most hotly debated issues in anthropology today.

Mills, C. Wright
1959 The Sociological Imagination. New York: Oxford University Press.

The author discusses the way in which the study of society prepares one to deal with the problems of society, and how a problem-solving mentality can be achieved and enacted.

Weaver, Thomas (editor)

1973 To See Ourselves: Anthropology and Modern Social Issues. Glenview, Ill.: Scott, Foresman.

A collection of articles dealing with the problems of anthropology in the modern world, especially the way the discipline relates to major social and political issues of the day.

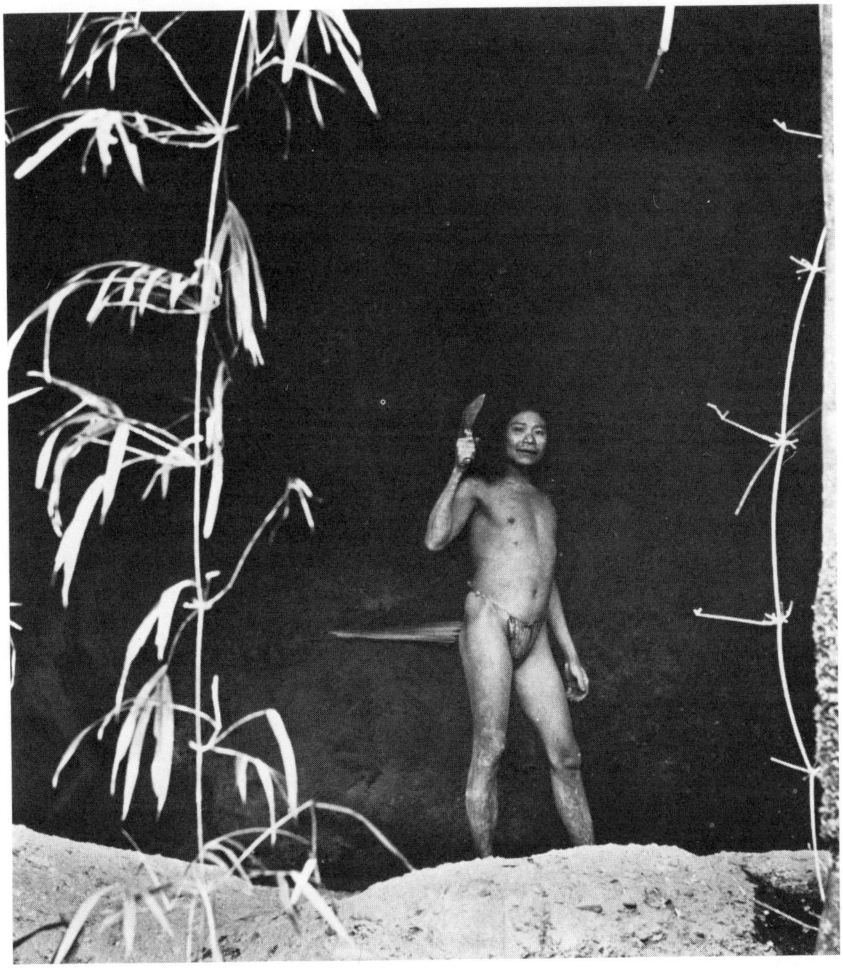

Index

Note: boldface numbers indicate location of terms in the glossaries.

78 79 80 81 . . . 3 4 5 6 7